D1093338

C333842827

John Gimlette

Elephant Complex

Travels in Sri Lanka

By John Gimlette

At the Tomb of the Inflatable Pig
Panther Soup
Wild Coast
Theatre of Fish

John Gimlette

Elephant Complex

TRAVELS IN SRI LANKA

Quercus

First published in Great Britain in 2015 by

Quercus Publishing Ltd
Carmelite House
50 Victoria Embankment
London EC4Y 0DZ

An Hachette UK company

A CIP catalogue record for this book is available
from the British Library

HB ISBN 978 1 78206 796 2
ExTP ISBN 978 1 78206 797 9
EBOOK ISBN 978 1 78429 105 1

10 9 8 7 6 5 4 3 2 1

Typeset by Jouve (UK), Milton Keynes

Printed and bound in Great Britain by Clays Ltd, St Ives plc

For my daughter, Lucy.

Contents

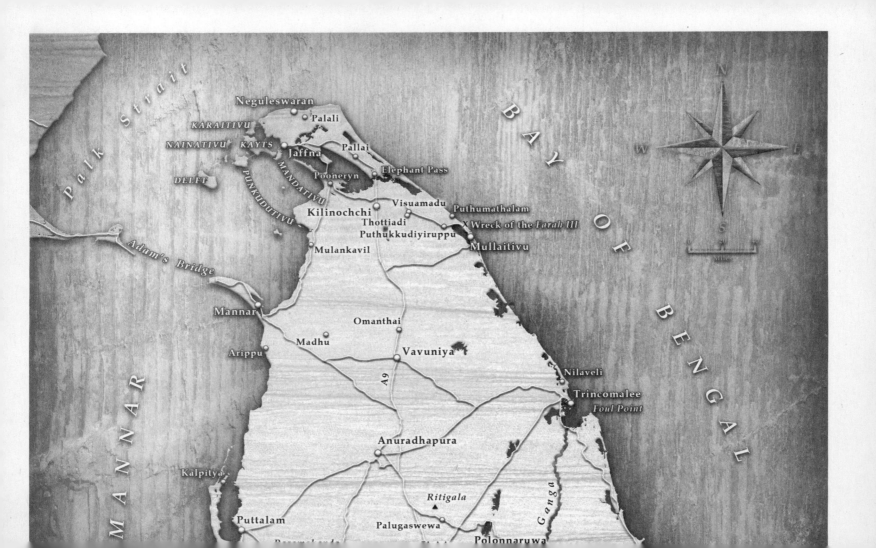

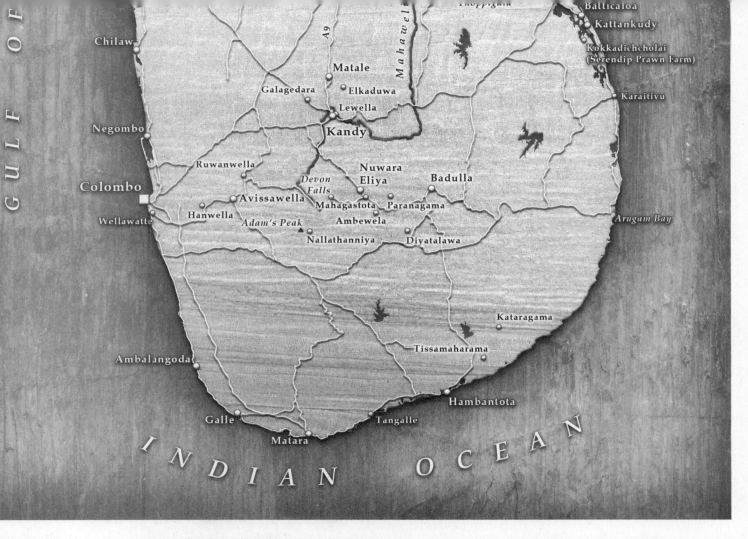

GULF OF

Chilaw

Mahaweli

A9

Thoppigala

Batticaloa

Kattankudy

Kokkadichcholai
(Serendip Prawn Farm)

Matale

Karaitivu

Galagedara

Elkaduwa

Lewella

Negombo

Kandy

Ruwanwella

Nuwara
Eliya

Colombo

*Devon
Falls*

Badulla

Avissawella

Mahagastota

Paranagama

Wellawatte

Hanwella

Adam's Peak

Ambewela

Arugam Bay

Nallathanniya

Diyatalawa

Kataragama

Tissamaharama

Ambalangoda

Hambantota

Galle

Tangalle

Matara

INDIAN OCEAN

Introduction

Ceylon was Oriental in the last measure of completeness – utterly Oriental; also utterly tropical; and indeed to one's unreasoning spiritual sense the two things belong together.

Mark Twain, *Following the Equator,* 1897

It may well be that each of Ceylon's attractions is surpassed somewhere on Earth; Cambodia may have more impressive ruins, Tahiti livelier beaches, Bali more beautiful landscapes (though I doubt it), Thailand more charming people (ditto). But I find it hard to believe that there is any country which scores so highly in all departments.

Arthur C. Clarke, 1970

This journey begins with a bus ride. A few minutes from my house in south-west London is a large and yet barely visible community of Sri Lankans, in Tooting. They're all Tamils, mostly refugees and mostly from a single town, Velvettithurai. Nobody knows exactly how many there are, although the usual figure is eight thousand. Whatever the number, there are now more Sri Lankans in Tooting than there were ever Britons in Ceylon (even in 1911, at the height of the empire, the British population numbered only six thousand). But Tooting, of course, is only part of the picture. Across the country, there are 110,000 Sri Lankan Tamils, with twenty-two temples in London alone.

For years, I've been intrigued by my Tamil neighbours. Perhaps it's their seclusion that's fascinated me. They demand little of the outside world; they have their own shops, their own after-school academies, their own charities, their own leaders and their own cafés (where lunch still costs four pounds). There are also Tamil newspapers and a special Tamil Yellow Pages, which offers a curious glimpse of another London: coy, jewelled and Asian.

The Tamils (or, strictly speaking, the Tamilians) even have their own internal crime wave, vicious gangs with names like 'The Jaffna Boys' or 'The Tamil Posse', who go at each other with knives, Tasers and samurai swords. In one year alone (2005), sixteen Tamils died at the hands of their own. London hardly seems to notice.

As Sri Lanka's civil war (1983–2009) drew to a close, I decided to explore this shy community further, and to begin with the temple. Tamil friends from elsewhere had plenty of advice about what I must do (I mustn't wear any leather, and I mustn't eat any beef for two days before), but none of them would come with me, and nor would they ever allow themselves to be named or quoted in anything I ever wrote. That, of course, made me more curious than ever.

I made several visits. From the outside, the Sri Muthumari Amman Temple still looked like a little department store. Its tiled art-deco façade – now cracked and grimy like old eggshell – had previously housed the Royal Arsenal Co-operative Society. But once over the threshold, a new world appeared, which I always assumed was Sri Lanka. My eyes would prickle with incense, and the air was greasy with the smoke of coconut lamps. Upstairs, there were twelve deities arranged around the old shop floor, and the walls (once a delicate Bakelite green) were darkened with soot. The gods, all made of silver and bronze, were tended by twelve priests, each half-naked with hair down to the waist. It would have been easy to forget where I was, except for the odd London bus, glimpsed through the vapours.

I was always the only white face amidst the crowds. The older men often offered me snippets of information, perhaps as a way of gauging my intentions. 'Our deities weigh six hundred and fifty kilograms each,' they'd say, or, 'Five hundred people worship here every day.'

From time to time, the most important deity, the goddess Mari Amman, would be ritually bathed in gallons of milk, rosewater and orange juice, before being dressed again in a fresh silk sari. Around her, the worshippers would prostrate themselves on the floor, and stuff her coffers with money. I'd never imagined such devotion in England, let alone a mile from home. On the notice board was a letter, asking every devotee to give the temple ten thousand pounds.

There was also a shrine to the Tamil Tigers. It looked like a four-poster bed, but with photographs and flowers. For many people around the world, the LTTE or 'Liberation Tigers of Tamil Eelam' has been the most heartless, cold-blooded terrorist organisation mankind has ever known. But not here. In this temple, the pictures staring back were of martyrs: a boy who'd died in a hunger strike; pretty girls in that distinctive tiger-striped camouflage. 'And these ones,' one of the worshippers told me, 'were poisoned, with nerve gas.'

The civil war in Sri Lanka may be over, but here, in Tooting, it's never quite gone away. You can still buy a LTTE calendar with a daily picture of either a martyr or some other figure inspiring to Tamils (an inexplicable mix that includes Marx, Churchill, Captain Cook and a Japanese kamikaze crew). More photographs of famous guerrillas hang in the shops, and – every November – the Tamils gather together for *Maaveerar Naal*, or 'Heroes' Day'. To the Sri Lankan press, Tooting is its Mogadishu. One newspaper, the *Asian Tribune*, even accused the temple of gunrunning – shipping out ball bearings and bomb kits in crates marked 'Tsunami Relief'.

Perhaps I shouldn't be surprised. This bit of London was once a hothouse of Tamil revolt. It was here, in 1975, that one of the earliest guerrilla groups was founded, called EROS (Eelam Revolutionary Organisation of Students), and it was from here that they set off to Syria for training. This borough was also once the home of the Tigers' political strategist, Anton Balasingham ('the brains behind the gun', as William Dalrymple once described him). Both Balasingham and the founder of EROS, Eliyathamby Ratnasabapathy ('a visionary,' according to *Tamil Week*, 'steeped in communist ideals') spent their lives fighting for a separate Tamil state within Sri Lanka, and then both of them returned here to die. It's said that, when, in December 2006, Balasingham's body was laid out at Alexandra Palace, sixty thousand people filed past to pay their respects.

The old warhorses may have gone, but there are still plenty of survivors of this struggle. Balasingham's wife, Adele (known to newspapers as 'The Australian Tiger'), was once head of the LTTE's women's wing, and now lives down the road in Mitcham. Meanwhile, in Tooting, you might come across the wife of another notorious rebel – Arul Pragasam – now working as a seamstress. Their daughter, Mathangi or 'Maya', would never forget the upheavals of her guerrilla childhood in Jaffna, and would become one of the most outspoken singers of her generation, better known as 'M.I.A.'

Then, of course, there's everyone else: witnesses to pogroms and death squads and area bombardment. 'Everybody has lost something,' they say. 'Everybody is traumatised.'

It's not difficult to see why people have fought over this island for thousands of years. Six centuries ago, a papal legate noted that 'from Seyllan to Paradise, according to native legend, is a distance of forty miles; so that, 'tis said, there may be heard the sound of the fountains of Paradise.' After months spent travelling the island, I now understand this completely. Although I'd visit areas that had been closed off for almost thirty years, and which had been devastated by war, it was still only Paradise Damaged. I don't suppose I shall ever again see such consistently lovely land-scapes: the gorgeous sprawl of lagoons and 'gobbs', the fantasy rivers and the hills so green they seem to glow with their own internal light. My work has taken me to all sorts of places, but none of them quite like this. Sri Lanka has to be the most beauti-ful country I've ever seen.

Everyone has wanted a piece of Paradise. The Tamils and Sin-halese have contested this island for so long that no one can truly say who got there first. To outsiders, the question may seem a dangerous irrelevance, but in Sri Lanka it's been sparking off wars for over two thousand years. Indeed, looking back over the last two millennia, it is hard to spot a century in which Taprobane or Ceylon (as it's been known) was neither occupied, invaded nor riven by catastrophic civil war.

It hasn't helped that it sits at the axis of the Indian Ocean, and that its neighbour is India, a land sixty times its size, and – now – with sixty times its population. Nor has it helped that there are always rich pickings for the predatory. As the mili-tary historian Geoffrey Powell, wrote: 'A country doesn't have to be rich to invite invasions, but Ceylon was always wealthy: a treasure house of spices and gems, elephants and rice.' When Marco Polo called by, he spotted gems 'the thickness of a man's arm', and to the Arabs, this was Jazirat al-Yakut, 'the Isle of Rubies'. It was a sure sign of trouble to come, and now – centuries later – the booty is everywhere. The British crown contains one of the island's four-hundred-carat blue sapphires, and its fattest jewel of all (the so-called 'Star of India') now reposes in the Museum of Natural History in New York.

But gems have not been the only temptation; you only need to look at a map to get a sense of this country's fecundity. It's all to do with the island's shape, like a planter's hat. Around the coast, there's a brim of brilliant green. But towards the centre, an enormous hummock of rock appears, about twice the size of Cornwall and over seven thousand feet tall. It's not hard to imagine the clouds rolling off the Indian Ocean, hitting this, and turning into torrents. Sri Lanka is completely wrinkled in rivers. They even wriggle through the so-called dry zones, feeding great blotches of blue.

All this explains the bewildering wildlife. Although Sri Lanka is only the size of Ireland, it's home to a startling array of creatures, from crocodiles and leopards to the 'ashy-headed laughing thrush'. Even more remarkable, not only does it host the biggest creature ever found on the planet (the blue whale), it's also home to the world's biggest land creature. Just one wild elephant would cause a stir, wandering about in the Irish Republic, and yet Sri Lanka has over 5,800.

Unsurprisingly, elephants have loomed large in the island's history.

For much of it, the *ali* has been seen as a symbol of power and authority, but also a pliable servant. The Sri Lankan elephant has always been mysteriously easy to train, and the export version even came to the attention of Alexander the Great. In medieval times, the Sinhalese kings made it a capital offence to kill an elephant, and they set them to work, building some of the biggest structures in the world. Then, in the Portuguese period, the elephants were gathered up again and sold, and, during the Dutch tenancy, they were set to work on the canals. Under the British, they cleared the jungles for tea, and only now are they no longer needed. A mere 140 remain in captivity.

Perhaps the wild elephants say more about the complexity of this island than anything else. It's said they follow the same paths all their lives, and from generation to generation. These paths are everywhere, and are often unknown to human beings. This means that Sri Lanka is densely criss-crossed with invisible corridors that have remained unchanged for hundreds, perhaps thousands of years. Sometimes an *alimankada*, or elephant path, won't be used for a while, and people will forget that it's there. But once the elephants are back on their path, there's little that will divert them. They'll break through fences and pickets, and have been known to sweep aside huts and little houses. Zoologists are uncertain whether to describe this as obstinate or determined, and perhaps it doesn't matter. All that's clear is that, in the collective elephantine mind, there is a great plan of this island.

Maybe the human mind works in the same way. Looking through Ceylonese or Sri Lankan history, it never feels quite circular. Rather, there are a recurring series of points of arrival and departure, with everything between lying disrupted and broken. Civilisations appear and flourish, and there's a great surge of progess before it all suddenly vanishes. No one is quite back where they started, and yet the same story will begin again, perhaps somewhere else. It's as if the island's history is a dense mesh of lines and pathways which – like the *alimankadas* – simply have to be followed. The issues and the protagonists have barely changed in thousands of years, and always there's that same sense of obstinacy and destination driving them along. Perhaps these pathways exist in some great and mysterious map, or perhaps it's just a state of mind, an elephant complex.

Intrigued by its strange history and by the neighbours I didn't really understand, I'd decided I wanted to see Sri Lanka for myself. I would take three months over it, and gave myself two years to prepare, making contacts and reading whatever I could. I had no idea of the task ahead. In London, I interviewed perhaps fifty people who knew the country well, and they all said such different things that I began to wonder if there were several Sri Lankas. Meanwhile, when I told the Sinhalese that I'd be writing about their island, they – like the Tamils – would almost invariably ask to remain anonymous. For some there was a fear there, which I never felt it proper to explore. Others just shuddered at the thought of their country portrayed.

The reading was almost as daunting. It was partly the sheer volume of material. Sri Lanka has one of the oldest documented histories in the world and, the further back you go, the more its story becomes tangled in scripture and myth. Even the literature of the modern age could be overwhelming. Under the British, Ceylon was always bookish, and impressively productive in English. Now, for a country of just over twenty million, it still produces each year a staggering tonnage of well-polished words.

In this great waterfall of ideas, Sri Lanka's story, I realised, was constantly changing. There was once a time when Buddhist scribes spent hundreds of years inking the great sagas on to *ola* leaves and then stitching them all together. From beginning to end, the stories never changed, and then – stacked up in the monastery libraries – they'd remain like that for centuries. Not anymore. These days, stories mutate and proliferate as they bounce around the world, before settling back in Sri Lanka once again. For some, there's a certain honour in obfuscation. 'A lie well told,' as the old Sinhalese adage goes, 'is worth a thousand facts.'

Everyone was at it. The Tamil Tigers maintained at least five websites during the war, each reinventing history. The tourist boards were just as bad, scouring their brochures of any mention of the war ('LAND OF SMALL MIRACLES', ran one strapline, at the height of the fighting). As Frances Harrison, a former BBC correspondent, put it, 'Denial has become a Sri Lankan habit.' The newspapers aren't always helpful either. Most are so full of trenchant and beautifully crafted opinion, it's sometimes hard to work out what's actually going on.

Outsiders can be sure of nothing anymore, and nor perhaps can Sri Lankans. Has the president, Rajapaksa, got just one little palace in London, or three? How many people are being kept in camps? What happened to the captured Tigers and their $200 million? These days, everyone is either feeding these stories, or fighting them with websites of their own. Almost nothing can be said without prompting blizzards of invective. The lone voice is seldom heard in this cacophony of stories. Even the Ministry of Defence has a website, churning out denials.

Perhaps portraying Sri Lanka has always been like this, with almost anything written becoming half wrong before the ink is dry. Certainly, countless outsiders – from Chekhov to Jan Morris – have written of the island's mystique. Leonard Woolf talked of a 'curious mixture of intense reality and unreality', but Britons have often taken the obliquity for granted. Perhaps Americans are more sensitive to it; certainly, they've tended to write about Sri Lanka as if it were a labyrinth. As author Mark Meadows put it, 'The circumstances are so complicated, detailed and delicate that no one individual can comprehend them.' For another American correspondent, exhausted by war, it was a maze all right, but a maze of deceit. 'Sri Lanka,' wrote William McGowan, 'was shot through with a psychology of avoidance

and denial, linked, in part, to the crucial process of saving face ...'
The mystique that was once quaint may now have become a
source of alarm.

None of this was encouraging. Perhaps, for a visiting writer,
the most troubling words of all come from a UN adviser, the
Australian, Gordon Weiss, writing at the end of the war: 'I was
warned before going to Sri Lanka that when I left I would know
the country less well than when I arrived, and in a sense this is
true.' For me, this was a daunting thought. What lay ahead was
not the search for comprehension but a battle with perplexity.

London, 2015

1

Colombo Jumbo

There is no place in the world where so many languages are spoken, or which contains such a mixture of nations.

Robert Percival, *An Account of the Island of Ceylon*, 1803

In Colombo, there is nothing to entertain [the tourists] apart from some swimming baths at the Galle Face Hotel.

Harry Williams, *Ceylon: Pearl of the East*, 1948

Every city should be judged by the courage of its thieves.

During my time in Colombo, I was only ever conned once, just after I arrived. I'd stopped a man in a suit, to ask the way. 'I'll show you,' he said. 'That's where I'm going.' As we walked, we talked about cricket (a mystery to me) and England (a mystery to him). 'I'm Jaiya,' he said, offering his hand.

A little further on, he mentioned an elephant.

'There's a ceremony here every morning, at seven.'

'Oh,' I said, 'that's about now.'

Jaiya frowned. 'Yes, we'll need a three-wheeler.'

And before I knew it, we were bobbing though the traffic like a big green bee.

'Where are we going?' I shouted.

'Our holiest temple, Gangarama!'

With Jaiya's mounting glee, I realised something was wrong.

But the elephant was real enough: a juvenile taking a bath.

'And these are all gifts to the temple!'

All around us – furry with dust – were stacks of offerings. Amongst them, I spotted cameras, clocks, an elephant's foot, a casket of Buddha's hair, a steam engine and a vintage Rolls-Royce. Just for a moment, I tried to forget that I was being gently robbed.

'Can we go back now, Jaiya?'

'Sure. To where?'

I tried to think where I'd seen policemen. 'Presidential secretariat.'

We drove in silence, everyone thoughtful.

'OK, what do I owe you?' I asked the driver when we stopped.

'Eight thousand, seven hundred rupees.' About fifty pounds.

I turned to Jaiya, who was blocking the door. 'Is that the right price?'

He hesitated, a little Rubicon before him. 'Yes, it's good.'

I managed a weary smile. 'So you work together?'

Jaiya blinked. 'Just give him seven thousand, no?'

I settled into the seat. 'I'd rather wait.'

They looked at each other. 'Wait for what?'

'For the right price.'

And so we waited, five stifling minutes, then ten. Outside, the sky was scribbled with kites, and I could feel the ocean pounding in my ears. Or was it my own blood? I hated this, pretending I felt in control. A squad of black-garbed, twig-limbed soldiers passed us. They wore long plastic coats emblazoned with 'THE PRESIDENT'S GUARD'.

'Perhaps the police know the price?' I suggested.

Jaiya pretended he hadn't heard. 'What you pay?'

I didn't know, but offered five hundred.

Suddenly, everything changed and Jaiya was wreathed in gratitude and praise. His ordeal was over, and he'd emerged with about two pounds and everything intact. From that moment on, I felt differently, too, about Colombo. Perhaps I could like this city after all.

If Alice had ever wanted another Wonderland, she could have come to Colombo.

In those first few weeks, I went everywhere. Sometimes, I'd walk for miles and feel I'd never left the place from which I'd started. The worst street for this was Galle Road. It plunges through almost thirty-seven miles of suburbs, the city changing only imperceptibly throughout its length. At one end, it's a canyon of billboards, glass and mildewed concrete, and it's the same at the other. It didn't help that I couldn't understand much, and that everything was written in dainty curls a bit like seashells. In some places, I was only able to find my way around by recognising the things on display. Amongst others, I remember Sari Town, Bra Street and Car-Wreck City.

But even with recognition, something still seemed odd. Eventually, it dawned on me that somehow the city had managed to turn itself inside out. The things that ought to have been on the inside – forts, parliament and embassies – were now scattered around the edges. Meanwhile, things that ought to have been safely out in the country would suddenly turn up in what should have been the centre: huge army camps, perhaps, or pelicans and a giant lake the colour of pea soup. Everyone, it seemed, was playing along with this little urban joke. It wasn't uncommon to find cows in the street, or men chopping logs. On *poya* or full moon days, the side streets would sometimes close altogether, and little games of cricket would erupt across the city. At times like this, the elephants had the place to themselves, riding round in trucks.

Of all the sudden, unexpected spaces, my favourite was Galle Face Green. It was slap next to the ocean, and was so long that the far end often vanished in the spray. Although never quite the hub of Colombo (nowhere is), it's always been thought of as the natural place to fly a kite, display an army, or walk off a dish of mulligatawny. In the evening, half the city would be here, crunching up roasted crabs, or tottering into the waves, saris hoiked up to the waist. Alice would have loved it. One of the gypsy's monkeys was always dressed as an Englishman, and, up by the lighthouse, all the anti-aircraft guns wore little quilted jackets.

But there was also a hint here of a city that didn't quite fit in, and was made up of everywhere else. From Galle Face Green, I could set off in any direction I wanted and always end up somewhere foreign. It might be a complex of Portuguese moats ('Fort'); or a huge Dutch camp for their African workers ('Slave Island'); or the solemn landscapes of the British. If Victoria's empire had been allowed to grow any further, much of our planet would now look like Glasgow. Colombo has all the usual details: kirks and clock towers, pillars, porticos and a touch of Gothic; a town hall on the scale of Capitol Hill, and the full range of department stores in various shades of claret and cream. In 1875, the British even walled off a square-mile of ocean to create a port that would be busier than Rangoon, Calcutta and Bombay combined.

With no obvious heart and such foreign fabric, it's taken Sri Lankans a while to appreciate that Colombo is theirs. Even now, a collective spirit is in short supply. There's no obvious pulling-together of a million people, no 'Big Apple' or 'Colombo United'. Although there's a Colombo Cricket Club, real loyalty is to be found elsewhere, in clubs like the Tamil Union or Sinhalese SC, all loosely based around race and class. Often, if I asked people where they were from, they'd come up with the village of their ancestors rather than the suburb they'd lived in all their life. As for their collective name, no one seemed sure. Are we Colombans? Colombites? Or even Colombeiros? For a lot of people, it wasn't a question they'd even thought about before.

Amidst such ambivalence, it's often been outsiders who've

made it their home. Colombo is lavishly foreign, even to those that live there. It's said that, once, this city babbled away in a hundred different tongues. Even now, the language can change from street to street – sometimes Tamil, sometimes Sinhala, and always with a smattering of something else. Elsewhere in Sri Lanka, Tamils and Muslims are scattered to the north and east, and make up a precarious minority. Not here. Almost a third of this city is Tamil, and a quarter Muslim. Meanwhile, there are all the others who've arrived in the wake of armies and empires. It was once wrongly assumed that all these people were merely passing through. 'Everybody makes their fortune and leaves,' wrote an English planter, in 1948. 'Afghans with usury; Chinese with silks; Indians coolies with rickshaws; Sinhalese make their money and go back to their village; the British work only to retire . . .'

Looking round, it seemed to me that no one had left, except the British. There were still Arab faces in the crowd, and Baluchis hammering pots in Pettah. Once, I had a Chinese tuk-tuk driver who said he was from Bambalapitya, where his father was the pastor. Another time, I met a guide who was blonde. 'No one can believe I'm from Colombo,' he told me, 'until I start to talk.'

All Wonderlands have their white rabbits, and this city has over a million.

They arrive every working day, a twitching mass of neurosis. Clinging to buses and trains, they're all already late, and a light panic settles over the city. For a few hours, its arteries are rammed solid and nothing moves. It's a curious moment to take a snapshot of Colombo; a city built by invaders and besieged by its commuters.

Then, as trading begins, something gives and the trucks start to flow again in torrents. This wasn't a time for me to be on foot. As an American writer put it, 'Merely crossing the road seemed like a strenuous karmic experience.'

Then, at dusk, the whole process is thrown into reverse. Once again, half the world is on the move, no longer rabbits, but a hot, angry reptile, snaking out of town. Tomorrow's papers will announce those who've died in this daily rout.

'*Tikak pissu*,' people say ('It's a little crazy').

Whilst Colombo may not have a centre, it's often felt that all roads meet at the Galle Face Hotel.

Almost without thinking, I booked in for a week. Outsiders have always been drawn to the Galle Face. This is partly because it's so obvious – a monumental slab of cream-of-ambrosial pink. With the sea to one side and the green stretching out front, there's always the sense that this is the place to watch the drama unfold. Occasionally, it's been part of the drama itself (a lock-up for Tamil MPs, or a roost for kings and queens). But mostly it's been a place to observe – duels, perhaps, or departing armies. Had I been out on the steps on 5 April 1942, I'd have seen eighty Japanese bombers arrive over Colombo. The city had little to celebrate that day. As the bombers departed, a lone Zero swooped over the green in flames, before pancaking into the sea.

I always enjoyed it here, even if I wasn't quite sure why. The doormen looked like Ruritania's Praetorian Guard; the brasswork flashed, the doors were theatrically huge, and everywhere there was an air of noble discomfort. At the end of the garden was an anti-aircraft battery, which was always manned, through tropical rains and midday sun. Out here, at the back, Colombo paused and the ambient sound changed from congestion to surf.

Each morning, breakfast would appear on the terrace like some magnificent durbar: vast silver tureens of kedgeree and porridge, and serried ranks of curry.

Jan Morris called this place an 'imperial caravanserai', but everyone seems to have enjoyed it. In the lobby was a long, marble list of memorable guests. I tried to imagine them all here together: Marshall Tito and Ursula Andress, Indira Gandhi, Noel Coward and Colonel Gadaffi with Bo Derek. I even found Prince Philip's tiny car parked on one of the upper landings, a 1935 Standard Nine. Once, when no one was looking, I jumped inside. The duke must've had a curious impression of Colombo, seen from knee height.

For Britons, of course, the Galle Face feels like home, except with more to moan about. My room looked slightly tired and chipped, and was so cold that, whenever I emerged into the steamy-bathroom heat of the city, my camera fogged up and wouldn't work for hours. Elsewhere, the rainwater was being collected in buckets, and, at teatime, the terrace was overrun with crows. This must be the only hotel in the world that employs a professional scarecrow, dressed in a bow tie and armed with a catapult.

Here, I also got my first glimpse of Sri Lanka at work.

The staff, it seems, were assiduous strikers, and upstairs there were framed pictures of butlers and waiters, unfurling their banners and blocking Galle Road. 'No one's ever been sacked,' said the barman cheerfully, and I soon came to realise he was probably right. Although the service was cheerful, it sometimes simply vanished. During my stay, it was the turn of the giftshop. Despite an enticing notice (*High quality items for the fastidious visitor*), it remained stubbornly closed. Some subtle administrative affront, it seemed, had left it unstaffed. One day, I met an old resident who explained how management works: 'Consult everyone. Hand out titles. Make every development seem like promotion. Think two moves ahead. Treat no one differently, and yet manage everyone as if only they matter.'

Employing people, it seemed, was like chess, except with hundreds of pawns.

In this rootless, polyglot city, it was inevitable I'd meet someone like Mohammed.

This wasn't entirely accidental. In London, I'd spent months assembling contacts, looking for guides through the maze ahead. It was harder than I'd thought. Whilst Tamils were anxious, so were the Sinhalese. No one wanted their opinion out there, roaming wild, even if they knew what it was. The people I met were always warm and generous, but also confusing. They affected nonchalance when they felt pride, and anger when they weren't really sure. I remember one woman standing in our kitchen, working herself into a state of bewildering rage. 'Don't quote me,' she said, and then spared no one in a slaughter of words. Beginning with every author who'd ever described her country, she finished with the Tamils. What, I wondered, have I let myself in for?

I did, however, get my list together, and – along the way – I learnt a few rules. The wobble of the head expressed ambiguity, and it was always bad manners to disagree. On the other hand, it was polite to be superficial (at least initially) and to avoid the big picture. The highest virtue, it seemed, was serenity, and being late was an expression of class. I also learnt that if people felt too junior to express a view – and most did – then they always knew someone who would. I was often being passed upwards, through the social structure. By the time I got to Colombo, my emails were lurking in ministerial inboxes, and I'd made tentative contact with generals, Test cricketers and a professor of elephants.

Not all of this worked out. From my huge, refrigerated room, I started making calls. Sometimes I'd hear Sinhala coming back and I'd try something from my phrasebook ('*Mama ingrishi rate*,' or 'I'm English'), only for the line to go dead. Once, I got through to the servants, but they weren't sure if the master was upstairs or in England. Another time, I was told the brigadier was on a pilgrimage, and was asked to call back in a month. Even when I did make contact, I was often deferred with intriguing excuses.

'Tomorrow's impossible. We're fasting.'

Or, 'Sorry, the Chinese are here.'

Or, 'I can't talk now. I'm in the sea.'

Things were always slightly easier with Mohammed Abidally, and we became good friends.

Usually, we'd meet at one of his clubs. The first time it was the Colombo Swimming Club. It was an odd place to find a man of such dubious buoyancy. Mohammed was like an Asian Mr Pickwick: genial, well formed and eerily English. He'd been at school in London, and still had a flat there. He also liked crisps and malt whisky, and never ate rice after six (always preferring 'cheesy toast' or fish and chips). But this Englishness was not something he took too seriously. Like the swimming pool, glowing in the dark, it was to be regarded as decorative only.

But Mohammed never struck me as particularly Sri Lankan either. Although he'd lived here all his life, and insisted it was the best place in the world, he had none of the anxieties of the Tamils or the Sinhalese. I discovered that he was always amassing fortunes – mostly in tea – and then giving them away, to other people's causes. Over the coming months, he'd introduce me to other philanthropists, Methodists out east, and Rotarians in Kandy. Mohammed was endlessly indulgent, and appalled by the intolerance of others. He explained that his ancestors were Indian Bohras from Kutch. 'They were always on the move,' he once told me. 'Our only country is our business.'

'You make them sound like jet-setting gypsies.'

There was a Pickwickian chuckle. 'Yes, we live out of briefcases.'

'And why have Bohras always kept moving?'

Mohammed frowned. 'Whenever there's trouble, we just up sticks.'

One day, I walked out to Pettah, a suburb of Mohammeds.

Although only a few were Bohras, most were Muslim. Here was Colombo at its most Brownian: a dense mass of moving objects, never quite colliding. I could hardly move for rickshaws, robes and tottering piles of Tupperware. In one sense, this was a compacted version of the rest of the city (some streets sold only cardboard packaging, and others only gold). In every other sense, it felt much older, like a little Aleppo or a steamy Damascus. I half expected to run into camels, or slavers, armed with jezails. *MULTI-NEEDS HARDWARE*, said the signs. *Blood Tested Here*. Even today, the people of Pettah are still known as 'the Moors'.

But if this made them sound like Othellos, they didn't seem to care. All that seemed to matter in Pettah was business and God. When I saw a trader with an orange beard asleep in a nest of boxes, I began to wonder if people here ever went home, and if the day ever ended.

No one can remember how it started, this riot of work. Some think Colombo was an emporium at the edge of the Arab world. Others say the Moors arrived as an army-for-hire. By 1344, there were already five hundred 'Abyssinians' in town, spoiling for a fight. Marco Polo, writing half a century earlier, explained it like this: 'The people of this island are by no means of a military habit, but on the contrary, are abject and timid, and when there is occasion to employ soldiers, they are procured from other countries, in the vicinity of the Mahometans.' If true, the Moors must, at some stage, have tired of the slaughter business, and moved into cardamon and cardboard.

At noon, everyone paused for prayer, and I followed the skullcaps, bobbling down to the mosque. Ducking through birdcages and turning left down Moor Street, we eventually came to a huge Battenberg cake of minarets and coloured bricks. The Jumi-Ul-Alfar-Jummah is a strangely bold building for a people who – for much of Sri Lanka's history – have tended to skulk in the footnotes. Even at those moments of bloody Shakespearean drama, they've only ever appeared in walk-on parts, as merchants and traders. Most of the time, they're happy not being noticed at all.

Except, of course, when they're selling jewellery or hi-fis or chests of tea.

Elsewhere, across town, Buddhism ruled.

It took me a while to appreciate this. Muslim Colombo was easily recognisable, and so were the Tamil gods, with their mountainous temples to Vishnu and Shiva. Of course, there were the *dagobas* and the occasional figure swaddled in orange, but

Buddhism seemed subtler, less architectural, and harder to discern in a person's appearance. It was only as I got to know the city, and the Sinhalese, that I realised that Buddhism was everywhere, perhaps the most insistent religion of all.

It was the detail I noticed first, before the bigger picture. There were the shrines in offices and homes, the purifying rituals, and the bus seats left empty for monks. Then my whole week would be transformed as a cluster of festivals appeared, and everything would shut. Nowhere has so many holy days as Sri Lanka, or the purity of intent. This was a city where kissing teenagers still needed to hide beneath umbrellas, and where *The Da Vinci Code* was banned. Even the idea of men and women shaking hands was faintly taboo.

In this regime of purity, sex was a difficult subject. It was seldom discussed, and there were no bodies in advertising, or public displays of female flesh. If a magazine ever ran one of those features, 'How to spice up your love life', it was usually recommending a new hairdo or a hostess trolley. Meanwhile, for outsiders, it's often been hard to reconcile the apparent contradictions: on the one hand, the horror of human exhibition, and, on the other, the *devala* statues with their sensuous bodily forms. 'Westerners,' an abbot once told me, 'can never understand that it's possible to be both sensuous and holy.'

But, as if the philosophical undergrowth wasn't hard enough, there was another thicket ahead: caste. Sri Lankans always find this hard to explain. Some people even told me it no longer existed. But I only needed to glance at the personal columns to see that caste was still out there, seeking jobs and shaping family life. Once, I went to tea with a novelist, who I'll call Elmo, and – over the debris of cups and crackers – he and his friends tried to explain.

'We don't have caste here like India—'

'No Brahmins, no untouchables—'

'All repudiated, by the good Lord Buddha . . .'

'But it survives?'

'For some things, yes. Like marriage . . .'

'If the ads say, "Caste immaterial," don't trust them, no?'

'Probably means they're desperate. Divorced, maybe—'

'Or bankrupt!'

'Or old! "Fifty, looks younger . . ."'

I asked where else caste appeared, and soon it was hard to see where it didn't. A person was who he was because of who his ancestors had been. This might make him forever a cinnamon peeler (*salagama*) or a beater of drums (*berawaya*). The long hand of the past had always guided politics along, and not even the Marxists had tackled the issue. In the sixty-five years since independence, all but one of the country's leaders had been chosen from amongst the landowners, or *goyigama* caste. Who you were, or, rather, who your people had been many centuries before, affected every aspect of your relationships with others. Even house visits, said Elmo, were once a matter of caste.

'In this household, *pariyahs* never made it past the gate—'

'The lower castes got to the veranda—'

'They'd address us from the garden—'

'One notch up, and they were up here on the terrace.'

'And only the highest castes got to see the apartments upstairs!'

Around the table, everyone laughed, and yet they knew. In this ancient, tight-fitting society, we all had our place, even foreigners. That afternoon, over tea, I was amongst jaggery boilers, water carriers and a maker of arrows.

Within these constraints, my new Sinhalese friends were still out having fun.

During those weeks in town, there were plenty of people to show me Colombo at play. Aside from Mohammed and Elmo the novelist, there were several architects, a lawyer, and an investigative journalist who always appeared dressed for tennis. I also met up with a few MPs, a surgeon who specialised in landmine injuries, a man who ran a chain of hotels with his sister, and a few people so rich that they had no idea what it was to work ('My family,' one told me, 'has spent the last three hundred years trying hard to do absolutely nothing at all'). Then there was a man who'd been with the special forces during the civil war, and who told me that, if we changed our breathing, we could lower our metabolism and survive on almost nothing.

All of these people enjoyed themselves, in their own Sri Lankan way. If they could afford it, they wore fancy jeans and drove around in four-wheel drives. A little eccentricity was always admired – perhaps a hat or an outlandish car (despite the crush and the corrugated roads, Colombo had already had its first outbreak of Lamborghinis). Exotic dogs, on the other hand, were not encouraged – for scriptural reasons – and nor was the ostentatious eating of meat. The more affluent spoke English to start with, only drifting into 'Singlish' as the evening went on. But everyone loved packing together, the sexes never quite in contact. An English doctor once noted that 'The Sinhalese are social people, great gossips, and when not occupied seriously, visiting and conversation are their principal amusements.' The only odd thing about this comment is that it was written in 1821, and that almost nothing has changed.

Life, it seemed, was as giddy as ever, and the gossip as vicious.

You only had to mention a name, and – with a great flourish – someone would whip out the proverbial knife to plant in their back. 'They can sue me if they want,' people would announce before exposing their neighbours, entrails and all. In these stories, the great and the mighty were always mauled. 'A good joke goes round the island in three days,' Elmo told me, 'but a political scandal takes only three hours.'

The days, it seemed, were full of distraction. Although gambling was banned and the racecourse had closed, there was always cricket, and Colombo was a city of parades. Some or other band was often tootling through the streets, accompanied by open trucks filled with choirs. For the crowds, these were mesmerising pageants, with their baby elephants clad in satin, and hundreds of children wearing false beards. Sometimes, amongst the spectators, I'd spot tourists looking slightly foxed.

For the 'Elite', as they were known, there were parties. These were often lavish and slightly shambolic, with something always running out, usually the drink. The women and children grouped up at one end, and the husbands at the other. For the men, it was acceptable – perhaps even posh – to get drunk (as long as it wasn't arrack or toddy). By midnight, there'd be nothing left of the children, except the faint glow of iPads, and their heads, face down, on the table. At one party I went to, given by some airforce officers, the food didn't arrive until two in the morning, and I remember the mess staff picking though the bodies, looking for diners. Amongst those asleep was my special-forces friend. 'Fear kills,' he said, as he nodded off. 'We only die because we make mistakes.'

No one much fancied the idea of night clubs.

'A lot of drugs, no? And people watching screens . . .'

A Spaniard, who'd been here years, told me few girls went clubbing.

'Which is why,' he added, 'boys tend to turn to boys.'

One evening, I met up with friends at the Cinnamon Grand. For those with money but no mansion, the big hotels (or 'five-stars') were the next best thing to a palace for the night. The Cinnamon Grand was the biggest and brashest of them all, so grand that the lampshades were thirty feet tall and the vases looked like grain silos finished off in lacquer. Every night, a crocodile of glossy black Pajeros formed at the lobby, trailing off down Galle Road.

I was early, and so I sat by a colossal fountain, erupting out of the marble. That night, the hotel was hosting two balls, a fashion show and a beauty pageant. Above the Niagaran roar of water, all I could hear was the clickety-click of expensive heels: beauty queens and debutantes in saris; the Wahabi women, curtained off in black; the mistresses like ponies and the carthorse wives. And who knows what else was happening amongst the well scented and the louche? A Colombo paper had recently suggested that there was even more to the five-stars than met the eye, and that a man could have whatever he wanted for ten thousand rupees.

When everyone arrived, we moved out to the pool, and the bodyguards settled in the shadows. It was still hot but the air was velvety now, and the darkness crackled with bats. We all ordered drinks, either gin or tea, and menus appeared. The man next to me was a stockbroker, called Romesh. 'Food is a hobby of mine,' he said, and ordered cream of vegetable soup.

At some point, I asked about the article in the *Sunday Leader*.

Around the table, there were huffs of outrage, but also fascination.

'Ten thousand bucks doesn't sound like much . . .'
'All Russians, I heard,' added Romesh.
'Here in Colombo, anything goes . . .'
'A massage in Bambalapitya was never just a massage.'
We'd all seen the small ads: 'Sexy, Energetic and Clean.'
It sounded like a new mantra for an imperfect age.

Foreign writers have never known quite what to make of Colombo life.

Some thought it hardly Oriental at all, whereas – to Mark Twain – it was Asia taken to extremes. Then there was Anton Chekhov, for whom it was a sensual place, replete with opportunity ('I had a dalliance with a dark-eyed Hindu,' he wrote. 'Where? In a chestnut grove on a moonlit night'). Pablo Naruda also found opportunities in 1929, although, the way he describes it, the encounters were fumbled and cold ('the coming together of man and a statue'). As the Chilean consul, he was often lonely, and he conjures a world that is 'lovely, and sly'. By contrast, another American, Mark Meadows, thought the city was a hag, and that – if it were human – it would be middle aged, 'mean, worldly and foul mouthed.'

More forgiving were some ancient Britons. Back home, Arthur C. Clarke is often seen as a paedophile, but not here. For many Sri Lankans he's the only writer who's ever truly understood them, and he's been feted with medals and fellowships and a grandiose grave. Meanwhile, there was less complicated affection from Sir Arthur Conan Doyle. In 1929, he announced his enthusiasm for life on Galle Road. Perhaps, in the era of bullock carts, the traffic jams were that much more exotic.

After weeks of parties, pageants, outsized furnishings and

elephants in clothes, none of these sentiments quite matched my mood. Perhaps my favourite comment was still that of Leonard Woolf, included in a letter home in 1904. 'I'm partially drunk,' he wrote, 'with the complete unreality of it all, and a very little whisky. I feel as if I were playing the buffoon in a vast comic opera . . .'

It wasn't just the rich, out enjoying this city. An English anthropologist, called Dr Widger, taught me that, even amongst the poor, life could be mysteriously jolly.

Tom Widger was an odd person to find charting the habits of the city. He was big, pale, gingery and conspicuously shy. Everywhere we went, he was a figure of inquiry and wonder, and I was never quite certain who was studying whom. The interest, it seemed, had always been mutual. 'I arrived as a teacher in the slums,' he told me, 'and now I've ended up studying my students.'

The more he knew about them, he said, the more there was to understand. 'The Sinhalese have one of the highest suicide rates in the world, and yet they're also the happiest. And the most generous. Despite the poverty, they give away more money here than almost anywhere else.'

As to their happiness, it is partly a matter of greenery. In this inverted city, there is still plenty of jungle, locked inside. These were the British Empire's gift to its packers and peelers: Havelock Park, Campbell Park and Cinnamon Gardens. Such clunky Victorian names may be a rarity in a country where things are often reborn as 'Socialist' or 'Resplendent', but the parks are special. For the poor, crammed into flats, these huge public spaces offer the only privacy there is. Every evening, the shadows fill with couples, urgently pawing each other between the patrols. The parks are a place of desire and love. For a long time, it was thought that the war memorial in Victoria Park was a fertility symbol, and there'd always be women there, praying for babies.

Even the slums are known as *wathtes,* or gardens.

'These places,' said Tom, 'are home to more than half of Colombo.'

He took me first to Maradana, the noisiest and densest of these human gardens. It was hardly herbaceous: a weft of silky black canals, and a sky full of aerials and greenish cement. A few of the blocks were of Marxist design, but – since the seventies – even poorer people had arrived and filled the spaces in between. We abandoned our three-wheeler and squeezed through on foot.

'I love this place,' said Tom, unexpectedly.

But perhaps the inhabitants did too. Every alley was sluiced and swept, and life was lived around the tap. Whole villages had been resurrected vertically, and, wherever the sun got through, there were bursts of marigolds and colour. At some point, we were spotted by the *gama niladhara*, or headman, who patted us into his home. It was a single concrete room, with his daughters curtained off, up one end. There were no possessions, and so the headman showed us his scars. He'd had no spleen since 1994 and was blind in one eye. 'It's lucky to survive a bomb,' he said, and didn't stop chuckling until the teapot arrived. With it came sticky rice, and an enormous ginger cat, called Booty, who was soon asleep in my lap. For one utterly ridiculous moment, it seemed that here was the happiest man I'd ever met.

After long goodbyes, we picked our way out, to the edge of the slum.

'Does anyone ever leave here?' I asked Tom.

'Difficult,' he said. 'Things don't work like that.'

Another trishaw wobbled into view, and Tom flagged it down.

'I want to show you a project, where they try to help.'

We set off across the old railway yards, towards the engine sheds on Tripoli Road. Everywhere, there were little homes, dug into embankments or perched in the trees. They were all illegal, or – in Tom's words – 'encroached'. In parts of Colombo, the encroachments were so bold you could almost lean out of the train and tap on the door. The people from the Warehouse Project were also squatters, unlawful and bold. It was a simple concept, explained Tom: plugging the poor back into the system. 'They feed them up for interview, and then point them at jobs.'

But we were already too late.

By the time we got to the old engine sheds, the roofs had gone and the army was in control. There were soldiers everywhere, and rows of khaki cots. Tom shrugged. Life could be complicated, and there were always obstacles ahead: money, pride, history and caste. The way he described it, I imagined that, however vigorously a man might climb the tendrils of his garden, there was usually a fortress above, or the rule of giants. In this Jack-and-the-Beanstalk world, it was often suicide playing the role of the axe.

'Killing yourself,' said Tom, 'is seldom a gesture of despair.'

Instead, it's a bid for contentment, where the limits have been reached.

A few weeks later, I discovered how this worked.

Up in Kandy, a young medical student had tried to kill herself, and I met some of her friends on a train. They were on their way to her funeral. But it wasn't the overdose that had killed her, they said. She was recovering from that when her boyfriend appeared, and gave her a glass of poisoned milk. He then got a syringe, filled it with insulin, and plunged it into himself. What puzzled her friends was why the boy felt that he needed to die. Hadn't he jilted her, and then killed her twice?

When I told Dr Widger this Jacobean tale, he wasn't particularly surprised. 'Suicidal behaviour,' he once wrote, 'provides a legitimate means by which inferiors can respond indirectly to wrongdoing by their superiors.' Suicide, it seemed, was the perfect revenge. Even the threat of dying could wipe out debts, bring lovers home, or blow away the constraints of caste. Every year, for over a hundred thousand Sri Lankans, an attempted suicide was an expression of outrage. It might be no more than frustration at the disappointments of adult life, a wife's imperfect cooking, perhaps, or her overbearing brothers. Meanwhile, some six thousand a year were dying (drinking weedkiller, mostly, or domestic bleach). To kill yourself was to kill someone else, at least in part. Once it was even a criminal offence to outlive an adversary, where he took his own life. 'By their law,' wrote an English officer in 1803, 'if any man causes the loss of another man's life, his own is forfeit.'

That must be a first for humankind: virtuous suicide and the crime of survival.

Colombo's giants needn't be ogres, as I discovered when a small army pulled up at my hotel. There were two SUVs in the cavalcade, all black paint and black glass, and out of one jumped four shaven-headed toughs. They all had guns under their shirts. It was only when I saw a young man amongst them, dressed in a tangerine T-shirt and embroidered jeans, that I realised they'd come for me. It was Vasantha Senanayake – a politician I'd met in London – and his personal protection.

'Jump in. We're going on a little tour.'

My jaw must have dropped. 'And all the cavalry too?'

Vasantha smiled shyly. 'It comes with the job.'

So it was that we set off, wailing, into the traffic. I shan't easily forget my first ever armoured tour. If ever the road ahead seized up, the lead vehicle would start blaring and the goons would wave huge lollipops out of the windows, forcing the cars aside. At night, the lollipops lit up, so that it looked as if we were flying along on tiny, angry wings. Vasantha hardly seemed to notice the swerves and the wails, and the genuflection of halted traffic. Greatness in Sri Lanka has often been a matter of entourage, and there's never been a time when the Senanayakes weren't great. Even the name means 'Leader of People'. For hundreds, perhaps thousands of years, they've led this country, often at the head of magnificent cavalcades. So, for Vasantha, being an MP was almost an entitlement, or a congenital condition.

On Galle Face Green, he paused at the foot of a huge statue.

'My great-grandfather,' he said, as if introducing him. 'D. S. Senanayake.'

From that moment on, Colombo felt suddenly smaller. Perhaps it was the sight of those great bronze feet. Or perhaps it was the feeling that, however big this city was, it was never quite greater than its greatest families: the Senanayakes, Jayawardenes, Bandaranaikes and now those cunning southerners, the Rajapaksas. Since independence, in 1948, just four families have provided nearly all the power. Vasantha's direct forebears have run Sri Lanka for eleven of those years, and he was indirectly related to almost all the other leaders. Meanwhile, the Senanayakes have produced two prime minsters, including perhaps the greatest of all, 'D. S.' or Don Stephen. Known as 'Jungle Jim', he was a huge boxer of a man, every bit as imposing as his statue. Even the British were diminished ('The village bully,' whined one official, with 'the language of the mud buffalo'). By 1948, he'd bullied Britain out, and the Senanayake clan had their first PM.

'And this is where he died, right here on the green . . .'

It wasn't a particularly Ceylonese death, even by the standards of 1952. One fine day – not unlike ours – he'd been out hacking, when he'd tumbled from his horse. Not even D. S. could survive the impact with municipal turf. Colombo had been deprived of a champion and was shrivelled with grief. A million people attended his funeral.

The rest of that day was a peculiar mixture of hired guns and great lives.

The bodyguards hurried us everywhere, caused a ripple of panic, and then hung back as if they weren't there. At one point, we stopped at a spa, filling its scented reception with incongruous muscle. Another time, we visited a gallery of Ceylonese post-impressionists. I don't know what the men made of the paintings – Bloomsbury with a touch of Buddhism, and a savage attack of tropical worm. Vasantha loved them, perhaps because they offered a bridge between his English education and the world he was expected to serve. It was a particular talent of his, creating links and joining up people.

Often that day, I thought I detected the beginning of greatness. With his stiff gait and gentle manners, Vasantha was like an elderly statesman of only forty. But he was also acutely sensitive to the mood around him, and every word he used seemed somehow polished and old. Even the government had recognised his great ability to soothe, and – some months earlier – had sent him to

London in search of friends. I have a terrible feeling that all he found was me. But maybe here too he was wise, recognising that – although Sri Lanka would often trouble me – eventually I'd come to love its landscapes, and perhaps its people too.

I once asked him if he'd ever want the top job.

Vasantha shook his head. 'My name is too big.'

'But that's good, isn't it?'

'Pedigree is an advantage with the people, not with other politicians.'

That day, as the goons sped us around, an unenviable pedigree emerged, often in pieces. 'I had a profligate grandmother who lost all our family papers. She'd go to Epsom and gamble away a few houses in an afternoon . . .'

As for his own experience, Vasantha described a lonely life amongst the patricians: distant estates, no siblings, a father who'd died when he was young, and always the overbearing sense of patronage and responsibility for others. In his grandfather's house, where he was brought up, there'd been over fifty servants. 'And that didn't include the *dhobis* – the launderers – who came in from outside, or the lower castes who came to empty to the latrines. After my grandfather died, the servants were reduced to thirty. They were retainers, easier to keep than to dismiss. There were gardeners for each garden, front and back, and a head chauffeur to direct the others. I don't know why . . .'

It was dusk, and we'd arrived at an ornamental lake.

Whilst the heavies fanned out amongst the food stalls, Vasantha went off, looking for *Bolo de Amor*. Across the water, on its own little jungly island, was the new parliament. It was said to have been a gift from Japan, and I could just make out long hipped roofs and a gigantic cylindrical bell. It all reminded me of something, but whether from history or childhood, I couldn't work out. Was this a space-age Camelot? Or the headquarters of *Thunderbirds*, circa 1340?

Vasantha returned, sat down and handed me a box. I didn't tell him what I'd been thinking. I suddenly had the feeling he'd just created the perfect tableau: a great Asian palace, a court of ancient knights, a renewed sense of duty, and a few hearty slabs of Portuguese cake.

There was, as I'd half suspected, more to parliament than met the eye. Far from being the work of warlords, I learnt that it was the brainchild of a chain-smoking ex-barrister who rode around in a Rolls-Royce, and who was extravagantly gay. The entire story of this island is written in the ancestry of Geoffrey Bawa; there are Scotsmen, Sinhalese, Germans, Tamils and Moors. All this makes parliament seem both less Asian and more Sri Lankan than anyone could ever have imagined.

There'd be many Bawas in the weeks ahead: hotels, universities and homes. Although he only became an architect at the age of thirty-eight, Bawa would leave a daunting legacy. Beginning in 1957, his version of modernism would startle the new Ceylon: democratic super-palaces, space stations on the beach and futuristic fortresses perched in the hills. To some, this was architects' architecture, theoretical and brutal. But to others, it was a life-affirming shot of confidence, proof that Ceylon was neither truly socialist nor truly feudal but somewhere in between.

I asked Vasantha if he knew any Bawa homes.

'Of course,' he said. 'Let's go and see Auntie Chloe.'

Sri Lankan homes are endlessly intriguing. I've never been quite sure whether our character is truly conveyed in our interiors but it often seems that our homes reveal the person we think we ought to be. In this, Colombo was no exception. For the Old Elite, home was sometimes the only confirmation of what they were, and so they lived in huge time capsules of tuneless pianos and ravaged chintz. One house I went to still had its stag heads around the walls, although they'd long since lost their ears.

But to others – if they had the money – home was still a place of evolving extravagance. Whilst there wasn't much they could do to the outside (lavished in barbed wire), the interiors would often be spectacular. Most houses I went to revealed impeccable taste, but there was no such thing as bad taste either. It sometimes seemed as if anything went: pink swimming pools, lights under the bed, or a courtyard of chrome-plated nymphs. Anywhere else, a hotel like Casa Colombo (once described in a guidebook as being like a 'whorehouse for departed Indian gurus') would be thought of as unmentionable but, here, it was a designer triumph.

Once, however, restraint was just as fashionable as funky.

Auntie Chloe's place was a case in point.

'A no-nonsense house,' promised Vasantha, 'for a no-nonsense lady.'

It was a strangely demure place for a designer so florid. I remember metal windows, rendered walls and a set of steep concrete stairs. But, on the first floor, I discovered that the garden had somehow travelled up with us, and seemed to fill the room. Emerging through all this light and greenery was the tall, slender-boned, no-nonsense auntie, Mrs de Soysa. Although reluctantly into her eighties, she seemed only to add yet more colour to this scene, with her flaming sari and mischievously ruby hair.

'Sit down, my dears!' she trilled, and, with a little bony clap, a maid appeared with china teacups, cucumber sandwiches and a Victoria sponge cake which we ate with silver forks.

It wasn't long before we got round to her friend, Geoffrey Bawa.

'I wanted glass, a place where the outside came in.'

'So Geoffrey was perfect?' said Vasantha.

'Exactly. I feel I live in the forest! And sometimes the birds fly in.'

Soon Auntie Chloe's stories were pouring free. Her family had owned over eighty estates and Ceylon's first car. Almost everyone in these tales went to Cambridge, including Bawa and her great-grandfather ('President of the union, no less!'). She also said that Geoffrey had designed the house in three days. It must have been a titanic encounter. Mrs de Soysa had once controlled twenty-four thousand acres of rubber, and was famously tenacious. Meanwhile, Bawa was six foot seven and equally unyielding.

'Did you remain friends?' I asked.

'Yes, we did. Good friends until he died in 2003.'

The last five years were the hardest. After a massive stroke, Bawa lost the power of speech, and all he could do was draw. There was now a renewed urgency about his work, as if he'd barely started the task he'd begun. More concepts appeared, sometimes half finished: hotels full of rock, jungle faculties and industrial chic. These may have seemed like mere baubles for the rich, but here was inspiration too: pure Sri Lankan genius. Such home-grown brilliance would give people courage and hope, commodities they'd desperately need in the difficult years ahead.

Not every Sri Lankan woman can measure her influence in acres.

A few days after the Bawa tea, I called in on my journalist friend. He was still in his tennis whites, and nothing about that visit went quite as I'd expected. There was a family of homeless people living in the stairwell and, from the apartment next door,

I could hear the sound of chanting and drums. Meanwhile, my friend was morose. 'I think I've gone too far,' he said and then sank into deep reflection. Unsure whether I should leave, I ended up talking to his wife.

I mentioned Auntie Chloe and her forest of rubber.

'She's the exception; a woman of power.'

'I thought Sri Lanka was a good place to be a woman?'

'Visitors always tell us that.'

'Two female prime ministers?' I tried. 'And a president?'

'Aristocrats! Dynasties, looking after their own.'

I probed a bit further, only somehow to flip a distant latch, releasing the fury.

'Listen, we still live in a very ancient society, no? And, John, you know what? Women are nothing here. We're empowered only if we're *born* to power! That's fine for the Elite, but, to the rest, it means nothing. Most women are worth no more than their dowry, and that's not much. Out in the countryside, we're just units of production. Cheap labour and baby-makers! The best thing a girl can do is head for the Middle East and get work as a domestic. Most have never even seen a microwave, let alone a set of company accounts! They'll be beaten, cheated and locked up, but they'll send home over a *billion* dollars. That keeps this country going! But do you think anyone cares? And as for all that stuff about respect, forget it! Out in the sticks, a woman is raped every ninety minutes. Do they sound like prime ministers and presidents?'

Beneath the jollity of Colombo, there was always a lingering tension.

At first, I'd hardly noticed it. There was barbarity on the roads, of course, but elsewhere the strain was more subtle. Everyone seemed to be working so hard to be normal, even seraphic. But it puzzled me, the intensity of the parties and the emphasis on pleasure. Why was reality always so rigorously denied? I also noticed how few people knew their country, because they'd never really seen it. Even wealthy people often told me that – during their childhood – going on holiday meant driving out just a few miles, to Wellawatte's beach. Then there were the roadblocks, and the sudden outbursts of rage. One day, I read a story about a man who, for decades, had put up with his neighbour tipping garbage over his wall, and then – suddenly – it was all too much, and he went round and battered her to death.

I imagined that all these things were somehow connected, and that this was how a city felt under siege. 'The last thirty years have been unimaginable,' Mohammed once told me, 'and only now are we beginning to recover.'

A city never forgets its greatest explosions. It's said that the sound reverberates for years, although only the victims still hear it. I remember once seeing some drunks who still had that noise in their heads. They were huddled round tables in a drinking den over on Slave Island. The Castle Hotel has been a lot of things in its time, including a printer's, but it was now a distillery and a flophouse, renting out rooms by the hour.

I only went there once, but it left a livid impression. The old façade had been painted an excruciating sunburnt orange, but the inside was chalky and blue. The manager was happy for me to look around, and so I climbed a huge, bifurcating staircase, slung with cables and cobwebs. The ceiling fans were petrified with rust, and time had obviously stopped here in about 1910. As

I climbed, I passed a print of Napoleon on his way into exile. It must have been a thoughtful image for those in the throes of lust. Upstairs, I wandered from bedroom to bedroom, now all quiet and rumpled after the efforts of the night. Debauchery – at least here – is a slightly queasy salmon-pink.

Back downstairs, the air was thickened with toddy and sweat. The drunks didn't even seem to notice me amongst them. Here were people drinking to forget why they were drinking. The manager said most of them had been coming here for years. It was noisy and yet no one seemed to be speaking. Everyone just sat there, numb. Perhaps things had looked just like this on 11 November 1995, the day the walls erupted dust and the room was engulfed in a blizzard of broken glass.

It was a tale constantly repeated across the city.

In some places, I could still see the scars: craters in the concrete or chunks of masonry missing. Even now, Dehiwala railway station was without its outer walls. Other places had managed better, swamping the memories with traffic or a heaving crowd of commuters. But it was the sheer scale of the bombing that was so hard to comprehend. Between 1983 and 2009, explosions became part of Colombo's routine, a sort of anti-landscape in which hundreds were killed. If I'd ever tried to walk from bomb site to bomb site, it would have taken me weeks, and now – just listing them – would fill several pages.

Nothing was spared, particularly where there were people. Some stations had only just been rebuilt when they were blown up all over again. Meanwhile, in October 1984, the main bus station experienced eight bombs in a single day. It's said that the crowd had run from one hail of shrapnel into another, only to be chunked and scorched as they fled for their lives. But if that was bad, there was worse to come. In January 1996, it was the turn of the Central Bank. It's not a pretty structure (a big concrete dovecote, sprouting skywards) but it never deserved what was coming. Twelve buildings were destroyed in the blast. The bomb was so huge that the man who planted it was left – quite literally – tattooed into the asphalt. Meanwhile, ninety-one people died and 1,400 were injured. I met a survivor of this atrocity, who'd been with those who'd died in the basement. She said she'd never quite been able to leave them behind.

'They suffocated,' she told me, 'and I see them every day.'

The bombers, on the other hand, were seldom seen. Huge explosions would bloom across Colombo, but there was hardly ever an enemy in sight. Throughout the entire civil war – Asia's longest – the city got only occasional glimpses of its attackers. Once, in July 2001, fourteen corpses appeared at the airport, but not before they'd destroyed twenty-six aircraft and a third of the national airline. Then there were the times when the bombers themselves turned up in tiny planes – not much more than crop dusters – trickling bombs on to the streets below. Whenever this happened, the government would turn off the power, and the anti-aircraft guns would light up the sky with tracer. It was like a giant all-night party, except no one knew whether to celebrate or cry.

But, of all these torments, easily the worst was the human grenade. Until Sri Lanka, the world had never seen the suicide bomb, but by the early nineties they were moving quietly through the Colombo crowds. This time, people did see the bomber – in the nanosecond before they died. Typically, the bomber was young, female and apparently pregnant. One of these attacks was caught on CCTV, and I remember watching it once, on YouTube. A dark, lissom girl in a sari stands before a desk, and is then suddenly catapulted backwards, out of shot, as the screen turns white. Was that courage I'd just seen, or a new strain of ignorance?

The city, I realised, had been transformed by this faceless onslaught. Everywhere, there was a light furze of razor wire, and the rich had retreated into forts. Each year, it's said, the walls had got higher and higher. The top brass still had dogs and sentry boxes, and at every main junction there was always a nest of guns. Civil war had become a habit – a long wait for an enemy who'd vanished. Perhaps, too, that's why the city was inside out, because the government had fled to the suburbs. Even the US embassy looked like a fortified henhouse, whilst the British were living in a bunker. It often surprised me how reluctant the land-scape was to return to normal.

One day, I went to the Vijitha Yapa store for a book on the conflict.

'I'm sorry,' said the salesman, 'but they're still being written.'

People often talked about the eerie war, fought on their doorstep.

Most of Vasantha's friends were too young to remember any-thing else. There was a TV presenter who wore huge pink ties, two cousins (also MPs) and a lovely, luminous girl called Indhi. They were all somehow linked to government, and, whenever Vasantha called one of his gatherings, they left their spouses behind. These dinner parties weren't like the other shindigs I'd known, but could be thoughtful and sober. Only one guest stood out as different. Professor Wijesinha was unmarried and middle aged, but I could tell he enjoyed the youthful rhetoric, and was always playfully testing his new ideas.

One night, we met up at a house the Senanayakes had built for their doctor.

In the opening salvoes, Indhi had said nothing.

'I hate politics,' she told me sweetly.

I wasn't quite ready for what came next.

'My father was a minister, and was killed by a bomb.'

Around the table there were murmurs of outrage.

'And war – I hate what it's done to us.'

Everyone weighed this for a moment, before deciding to agree.

'We never knew who'd be next,' said Vasantha, quietly.

'We were all scared . . .'

'My parents even travelled on separate buses . . .'

'It felt as if we'd lost control . . .'

'There were big robberies, no? Almost every day!'

Everyone had their tales of queues and funerals and blackened skies.

'And how did it all begin?' I asked.

Around the table, they looked at each other.

'That,' said Vasantha, 'is a difficult question . . .'

The professor had a theory, planting the blame amongst his rivals.

'OK, but is there a moment when it went wrong?'

There was no consensus on this, but, on one thing, they all agreed.

I needed to speak to the Bandaranaikes.

For much of the twentieth century, all roads have led to the Bandaranaikes, so it wasn't hard to find them. 'Give Sunethra a call,' people said, and so I did, and – a week later – she was driving me out to the family estate, at Horagolla. 'My ancestors have been there since the 1830s, thanks to the British . . .'

I must have sounded surprised.

She laughed. 'Yes, really! They paid us to keep an eye on the locals!'

We drove for an hour, picking our way through billboards and tuk-tuks.

'This was once the only way to Kandy, and it made us rich . . .'

Sunethra always talked like this. She was as spry and rebellious as everyone had promised. With her short bob and boyish figure, it wasn't hard to picture her as the person she'd been: the Oxford beauty, the wild child of the sixties, the natural Londoner, the columnist and always the rebel. No one, it seemed, had ever owned her, although one or two husbands had tried. She didn't even hold her forebears in awe; she loved them or loathed them, and owed them nothing. In her stories, they appear like the cast of some cruel masque: bejewelled landlords; a grandmother rendered chronically furious by the stupidity around her; an aunt, who ran away to England and took to the road (by the time her caravan was found, she'd already been dead for almost a week). 'Our family,' said Sunethra, with a sigh, 'is a mixture of genius and madness.'

Eventually the billboards thinned out and coconut palms appeared.

'This was all ours,' said Sunethra. 'A reward from the British . . .'

A few miles on, we turned into a drive. Up amidst the trees, there was a knobbly white mansion, and then, beyond it, Sunethra's house, an older building, cloistered and pantiled. Inside, our feet clattered on stone. This was the original Bandaranaike manor house – until grandfather Solomon had turned it into his stables. 'It was never grand enough for him, and so he built the new house and filled this one with horses. You can still see their names, up in the walls . . .'

48

Above us were neat, painted signs: *LADY DURHAM, WILD ROSE . . .*

'He also kept a zoo here, with tigers and other creatures.'

'And what was he like, your grandfather?'

'See for yourself,' said Sunethra.

Next to her desk, there was a portrait of Sir Solomon. In it, he was a whiskery, well-upholstered man, dressed in the manner of the Chief Native Interpreter, or *Maha Mudaliyar*, 1895. As well as a sash and braided tunic, he wore a sort of cassock and several large medals, the size of saucers. Sunethra studied the picture thoughtfully. 'Pompous and with a great sense of self-importance,' she said. 'He was always making trips to Buckingham Palace. It must have been difficult for the children . . . I'll show you his new house after lunch.'

We ate under the loggia: curry, and pineapple sprinkled with pepper.

Sunethra was still thinking about the tigers and the medals.

'He always dressed for dinner,' she giggled, 'in case the British dropped in!'

'And did they?'

'Actually, yes. The Prince of Wales ate here once, in about 1920 . . .'

After the maids had cleared the plates, we set off through the undergrowth to the new mansion below. Although it glowed a magnesial white, it didn't feel like a home. There were big, unusable chairs on the terrace, and everything was shuttered. Eventually, servants appeared, and, with a scrape of keys, we were in the gloom. Dustsheets were hauled away and the chandeliers came sleepily to life. There were four grand staircases, I noticed, but almost nowhere to sit. How Solomonesque, I thought, to be so big on grandeur and so light on content.

Sunethra must have read my thoughts.

'Sir Solomon liked everyone to stand in his presence . . .'

We climbed upwards through the plasterwork and gilt.

'Solomon. Aunt. Mother,' announced Sunethra, as we passed the portraits.

Then we came to a picture of a small boy, in 1904. He is only five, but already his eyes look sunken and sad, and he is wearing a ludicrous uniform with a feathery hat and sword. It was just the man I was looking for.

'This is my father,' said Sunethra. 'S. W. R. D. Bandaranaike.'

No one has changed Sri Lanka as much as S. W. R. D. Here at Horagolla were all the signs of eminence, and a few clues as to the catastrophe to come.

'My father was always lonely,' said Sunethra, 'especially as a child.'

The house can't have helped. With its overbearing dimensions, it must have been a daunting home. Apart from two sisters, there were no other children in his childhood. In the mythology of Horagolla, if local boys ever made it into the grounds, they were whipped and sent away. That left only a succession of sinister English tutors. One of them thought he'd toughen the boy up by killing a pig on the kitchen table. The only sport was shooting champagne bottles off the terrace with Sir Solomon's shotgun. All this seems only to have enraged the children's mother, and, in a fit of scorn, she fled back to her parents.

At the top of the stairs were photographs from Oxford in 1919.

Christchurch had done nothing to cure S. W. R. D. of his overwhelming sense of entitlement. In the group pictures of that time, he looks tweedy and owlish, and deceptively self-assured.

'My feeling towards Oxford', he later wrote, 'was more that of conqueror than a submissive and grateful son'. He'd decorated his digs with python skins and the pelts of Horagolla leopards, and – as a debater – he was fiery and dangerous. Even Evelyn Waugh noted his brilliance, although the admiration wasn't mutual. Waugh, noted S. W. R. D., was 'an undersized, red-faced, rather irresponsible youth.'

We climbed back down the stairs, past the feathery boy.

'I always think he looks so lost,' said Sunethra, touching the frame.

Many people would say he was, and that he spent his life being lost. After Oxford, he was both vaguely anti-British and yet also more British than the British themselves. He'd never regain his bearings, and in political life he was always torn in different directions. Even his full name – which he never used – was riddled with contradiction and opponents: Solomon (Jewish), West Ridgeway (a British governor), Dias (Portuguese), Bandaranaike (Sinhalese).

At the front door, Sunethra paused.

'This house was always difficult for my father. I think it explains him.'

I thought about this as we set off back along the drive. It was a pretty estate with its salad-green fields and its stooping clumps of coconut. Twice this driveway had been lined with people, in S. W. R. D.'s honour. The first time was in February 1925, on his return from Oxford. Sir Solomon laid on a three-mile procession of elephants and dancers, and then S. W. R. D. spoiled the day by announcing his intention to 'serve the people'. With that, he returned to Colombo and renounced all the trappings of his earlier life: fedoras, spats, Christianity, champagne and cutaway coats. From then on, he became a Gandhian figure, affecting the speech and the outfit of a Sinhalese sage. By the end, all that remained of his Britishness were his socks, a few hawthorn pipes and a greyhound called Billy Macawber.

The second procession was harder, without elephants and dancers.

'I remember it well,' said Sunethra. 'I was sixteen at the time.'

This time her father was carried back up the drive, bloodied and dead.

As we drove away, I remembered Sir Solomon's zoo.

'What became of your grandfather's animals?' I asked.

Sunethra smiled sadly. 'Ah, yes, the menagerie . . .'

No one was sure what had happened to the tigers, but the other animals had somehow muddled through the 1930s. It must have been a strange time for Sir Solomon, and perhaps his charges too. S. W. R. D. was no longer the puny sunken-eyed whelp, but a firebrand, never happier than before a crowd. He'd do anything to undermine the old order, even comparing Britain with the Nazis. But it had been hard to get any reaction. As one historian put it, Ceylon's home-grown bourgeoisie 'simply basked in the sunshine of Edwardian imperialism and complacently mimicked its masters.' The leisurely chatter about independence might have gone on for years, if it hadn't been for the war and Vasantha's bellowing great-grandfather. But, in February 1948, the British left.

It was too much for Sir Solomon, and, a few months later, he died.

'And, as for his animals, my father set them all free.'

Liberation, it seems, hadn't suited them. Sir Solomon's beasts no longer had the stomach – or the teeth – for freedom. It's said that, for a while, they'd hung around the estate but that, within a few weeks, most of them had perished.

There was still a lurking Britishness around Colombo.

To me, it was always most conspicuous in the schools; a dozen little Etons dotted through the city. There was St Thomas', Bishop's (established 1875) and St Joseph's, all churning out enthusiastic *faux*-Britons. Meanwhile, Royal College (motto: *Disce aut discede*, or 'Learn or Leave') looked as if it had been airlifted in from Berkshire, complete with all its turrets and quads. People never forgot these places, and Old Boys' matches would attract spectators by the thousand. The education might have been Victorian ('Cold showers, beatings, marmalade'), but it was also redolent of a less troubled era, if not quite a golden age.

Then, for those unable to take the big step from school to real life, there were the clubs. These were just like the schools, except with whisky. There were always games, and rules about socks, and a reassuring absence of women. Mohammed had already taken me to the Swimming Club (which had somehow managed to keep all 'non-whites' at bay until 1965), but there was also an Orient Club (which had kept out the whites), and a very stuffy Burgher Union. But holiest of all was the Royal Colombo Golf Club, which was like a beautiful slice of Surrey, lost in the middle of this clamorous city.

I remember once, at the Sinhalese Sports Club, gazing up at the portraits of past club presidents. I suddenly realised that these men, who'd done so much to entrench Britishness, were the same ones who'd cut this country free: D. S. Senanayake, J. R. Jayewardene, and Sir John Kotelawala. After years of denigrating Britain, they'd gone on to foster little Britains of their own. No wonder the communists had complained about independence: to them, it had merely allowed the ruling class to replace themselves with themselves. For years, nothing had changed; Union Jacks still flew, and – even into the fifties – a Buddhist criminal could still be sent off to the gallows with the words, 'And may God have mercy upon your soul.' As Sri Lanka's greatest historian, Kingsley de Silva, put it, 'The process of independence was so bland as to be almost imperceptible to those not directly involved.'

It's often infuriated American writers, this obstinate strain of Britishness. They despise the way a tiny clique still says 'cheerio' and fusses over royalty. Has no one noticed the Brits have left? And what's with Guildford Crescent and Torrington Square, and all those mansions with names like 'Prince Alfred Place' and 'Windsor Towers'? William McGowan thought the Elite were laying it on too thick, and that 'their capacity for mimicry was formidable'. But was it mimicry, or nurture? I once put this question to a Sri Lankan professor in London.

'Laying it on?' He laughed. 'No, we're Brown Brits!'

S. W. R. D. was also animated by the blandness of independence. In it, he saw an opportunity, the chance to become a champion, the father of something truly Sinhalese. The key to it would be language, and the revival of Sinhala. It was already a popular theme across the south. To a new generation of politicians, known as the 'Chauvinists', English was undignified; it was still the language of the courts and statutes and yet few people spoke it. It was also offensive, they said, to the island's religion. Once, a third of the world was Buddhist, and now this was a last redoubt. The Sinhalese were a chosen people, and the defence of their language was a matter of faith. To S. W. R. D., the romance of this rhetoric was irresistible. Ceylon, he claimed, had become 'an eastern out-post of the Vatican'. Buddhism had to be reasserted through the medium of Sinhala.

But, for all his elegant words, S. W. R. D. had never seen the danger. By making Sinhala the official language, the Tamils would become foreigners in their own land. That, of course, is just what the Chauvinists wanted. During the British era, Tamils had held two thirds of civil-service jobs, and yet they made up only fifteen per cent of the population. Now it would be the turn of the Sinhalese. S. W. R. D. did nothing to dampen their expec-tations, and so, by 1951, the issue had become a rallying point. In a matter of years, Ceylon would divide into 'them' and 'us'.

People still talk about the day when it all went wrong. It was an election rally in Polonnaruwa, in late 1955. S. W. R. D. had never been quite sure where the language issue was going, but he couldn't help blurting it out: 'SINHALA – IN TWENTY-FOUR HOURS!' Within months, he was in power, and his wild idea was out of control.

Back in Colombo, the Bandaranaikes had held court in a man-sion named – without any obvious irony – Tintagel.

It was a magnificent wedding-cake of a place, in a street of similar confections. But none of the other houses were quite as white and prim as Tintagel. Out at the front, there were iron gates and a cobbled courtyard, and beyond were the well-iced layers of balconies and balustrades. The whole spectacle was then gar-nished with lanterns and tiny potted shrubs. It was all said to have been commissioned by a gynaecologist in the thirties, and I can only imagine that such nuptial splendour was good for trade. The only other use for such a celebratory creation would have been as a boutique hotel, which – as it happens – is what it's become. Naturally, I booked in.

I don't suppose I did much to raise the tone. A few weeks later, Tintagel would play home to Prince Charles and his entourage. Meanwhile, my own baggage train was hardly impressive: a tuk-tuk full of books and laundry, and half a kilo of Bandaranaike speeches. Under the portico, I caught a glimpse of myself in the gingery marble, looking upside down and slightly overawed.

Glass doors swung open, and there was a whiff of polish, and then more Palladian splendour. But, as I stumbled into the cool, I had a sudden feeling I'd long since missed the boat. It was all far too exotic for S. W. R. D.: deep reds, chunky silverware, plump Spanish upholstery, carpets from Kathmandu and – from Germany – huge mossy spheres that loomed overhead like mysterious, unweeded planets. At some point, I was relieved of my foul luggage, and, a few hours later, the shirts reappeared in my room, perfumed and rejuvenated, and wearing cardboard bow ties. None of this was easy to square with the great reformer, the educationalist and the ascetic. Whatever else had inspired the brilliant Paddy Lands Act, it wasn't moss balls.

But there were still a few vestiges of the Bandaranaike era. Much of the acanthus had survived, along with the panelling up the stairs. In the woodwork, I could see all the scars of family life: scooter marks, perhaps; prams, claws or an airborne toy (as well as Sunethra, there'd been two other children and Billy Macawber). Then I discovered that the hotel still didn't have a liquor license, and that all those coloured bottles in the bar contained only water. The ghost of a great teetotaller, it seemed, was still hard at work.

Sunethra could never be persuaded to linger at Tintagel, although she still owned it. One day, she called by with some books, and I asked her about her father and this house. She hesitated, staring up into the plasterwork, as if it had trapped his booming voice. 'He wasn't a child's man,' she said. 'He'd be tired and shouting, and, most of the time, I think I was terrified.'

The forecourt beneath my room played an unhappy role in the bloodbath to come.

The language issue had proved a spectacular punt. Despite his genius for reform, S. W. R. D.'s short reign will always be remembered for its cracked heads and burning shops. As a gamble, the legislation he'd promised – making Sinhala the only language – wasn't so much poker as Sri Lankan roulette. By depriving the Tamils of their language and their livelihood, S. W. R. D. had stuffed a bullet in the gun and set the cylinder spinning. It was anybody's guess who the first shot would hit.

For three years, Tintagel rang with the sound of indecision and panic. The first draft of the new law, in 1956, prompted a Sinhalese hunger strike, and a toughened-up version brought the Tamils out in revolt. The following year, S. W. R. D. was forced to make a pact with the Tamil leader, and, within days, hundreds of angry *bhikkhus*, or monks, were camped out on Tintagel's forecourt, which was then a lawn. In the photographs of that time, the house is wreathed in barbed wire, and S. W. R. D. looks no longer owlish, but stringy and scared.

'I remember the day he went out on to the lawn . . .' said Sunethra.

It wasn't S. W. R. D.'s greatest moment, tearing up a pact.

'He told the crowd: "Whatever happens, it will be your fault . . ."'

S. W. R. D. never recovered from the riots that followed. The old confidence was gone, and he began to dabble in horoscopes and the occult. It's said that, as trouble fanned out through the slums, he could be found in the Orient Club, lost in a world of snooker.

In the end, like Caesar, he was killed by his friends.

It was typical of S. W. R. D. to die in a blaze of irony. His death was ordered by a man of peace: Colombo's most senior monk. It was motivated not by some affront to the faith but by lubricious scandal (the monk had been having an affair with the minister of health, and blamed the government for his exposure). The revolver used was British, and the man sent to fire it was a monk. S. W. R. D., who'd converted from Anglicanism to Buddhism, would be killed by a Buddhist who, afterwards, would convert to Christianity.

For most Sri Lankans, 26 September 1959 is still a difficult day. That morning, the monk stuffed the revolver under his robes and went round to Tintagel. There, he queued up with well-wishers beneath the portico with the gingery floor. As S. W. R. D. turned, the huge bullets spiralled through him, shredding his pancreas, colon, liver and spleen. The relics of that day – the gun, the misshapen slugs, and the bloodied shawls – are still revered, and now have a museum of their own. I remember noticing that the prime minister's watch had been smashed to bits at exactly twenty past ten.

At that moment, the actors in this gory scene had dispersed. S. W. R. D. was rushed to hospital in a Cadillac, where he dictated one last speech – as elegant as any – before he died. His last journey would be back to Horagolla, as a *bodhisattva*, or enlightened being. Meanwhile, the high priest and his mistress were hauled off to jail, whilst the monk went to the gallows. In a sure sign of the senselessness to come, he expressed surprise at his fate, and fell through the trap spouting the Gospels.

On my second day at Tintagel, the early monsoon found its way through my ceiling. Outside, great prisms of water exploded on the balcony and, inside, the cornicing began to weep. Before long, I had my own small and not-very-ornamental pond, and, naturally, this caused a flurry of black-clad flunkies. Eventually, order was restored with mops and buckets, and a hefty salver of chocolate brownies.

But, for some reason, I didn't sleep well that night. Perhaps it was the last droplets thudding on the plaster. Or perhaps there was just too much historical turbulence, at least in my head. I got up, made some tea, and nibbled another brownie. Sunethra had said that this was once the room of her sister, Chandrika. I don't suppose they'd have recognised much: not the flat-screen, the duck-feather duvet nor the decoration, all reassuringly vanilla. For those that knew Chandrika (including twenty-one million Sri Lankans) boutique wasn't really her style.

Just before dawn, I went downstairs and wandered through the empty Bandaranaike rooms. The murder under the portico ought to have been the end of their era, and yet, in some ways, it was only the beginning. Two women in this household would go on to become heads of state. One was S. W. R. D.'s widow, Sirimavo, who'd step into his role and become the world's first female prime minister. The other was his daughter, Chandrika, who, in 1994, became prime minister and then, a few months later, president. Between them, they'd run this country for almost twenty-three years.

Outside, I could hear sweeping, the signature sound of a new Sri Lankan day. Perhaps yesterdays had never meant much at Tintagel, and I suddenly realised that, throughout the house, there wasn't a single reference to the Bandaranaikes: no books, no plaque and no pictures. That was surprising considering no building in the world has provided so many elected heads of state. Maybe princes don't like to be reminded of the frailty of life? Whatever the reason, Colombo's White House was, once again, just a house that happened to be white.

'I hate what politics has done to this family,' Sunethra once told me.

They'd all paid a high price. S. W. R. D. had ended up responsible for the carnage a generation on, and – even amongst his own – he was revered but not much loved. His widow, Sirimavo, would serve two terms, beginning in 1960 and 1971. During her time, the youth rose in revolt, the economy collapsed, and Ceylon was transformed into, first, *Sri Lanka* ('The Resplendent Isle'), and then a 'Democratic Socialist Republic' (always a sure sign of liberty in trouble). Only once everything had been nationalised – including tea – was Sirimavo defeated and stripped of her civic rights. Her daughter, Chandrika, would fare better in office but, for her, politics was endlessly cruel. It had left her not only fatherless at the age of fifteen, but also widowed (her husband was gunned down in front of her and the children), and then – during her presidency – she was vilified, betrayed, bombed and half blinded. Only now, after a life spent clambering out of the wreckage, had she acquired a certain poise. She was always in the papers, mildly rebellious. It worried her sister that, one day, Chandrika might once again run for office.

'We don't want to lose any more,' said Sunethra. 'Enough have died.'

'And what would Chandrika say,' I asked, 'about your father?'

Sunethra smiled. 'That,' she said, 'is something you must ask her yourself.'

Chandrika still lived nearby, in what appeared to be a huge box of jungle. It was just what I'd imagined of a president's home: high walls and steel gates, with an eyeball pressed up against the slot. Inside the compound, there were gunmen milling around and rows of black SUVs. That afternoon, a steady stream of visitors was ushered in and out. When I booked my appointment, I was told I'd be allotted half an hour. Madame Kumaratunga-Bandaranaike would see me between lunch and a visit from the Indian High Commission.

The house was more surprising, if only because it was slightly forgettable. It was a mansion, of course, but, in my memory, it's completely drained of colour. Inside, I was placed in a large drawing room, where nothing quite seemed to match. There was an old Dutch dresser, some bamboo seats, a splashy modern painting of a Sinhalese dancer, and few different pots of ferns. I had a feeling that, for my host, home was just a place where you happened to live, a repository for heirlooms and family gifts. I suspect that Tintagel was like this before the designers moved in.

'She'll see you now,' said her PA, and showed me to a dining room.

The furnishing was equally incidental and sparse. When I heard the sound of cutlery coming from upstairs, I realised that this wasn't really a dining room at all, but an outer anteroom in the Bandaranaike court. I wondered how many diplomatic hours had been wasted in here, and what great hands had drummed on this table. Madame K-B was always famously late.

After twenty minutes, there was a swish of silk.

'Mr Gimlette,' she said. 'How kind of you to come . . .'

She wasn't quite what I'd expected. Somehow, I must have built up a genetic picture, based on her prime-minister parents: a stringy father, and Sirimavo, who could look pugnacious and clumpy. But Madame Chandrika was none of these things, and nor was there any hint of the violence in her life. She was handsome and stately, in a silk blouse and with a carapace of glossy black hair. This surprised me, how youthful she seemed. It was now nearly eight years since she'd relinquished the presidency, at sixty.

'I understand you're from London?' she said.

In the pleasantries that followed, we discovered that, for part of the year, we were near-neighbours, and that we both hated driving. 'I'm blind in one eye,' she said, 'so I don't have the courage for driving in London.'

'And I'm all eyes, and don't have the courage for Colombo.'

The formality slipped a little but was always there. It was, however, impossible not to like Madame Chandrika, or feel slightly in awe. I liked her just as I had Sunethra, although it was hard to believe they were sisters. Whilst Sunethra was gamine and seditious, Chandrika always seemed to find the balance between grandeur and conspiracy. We soon established that she didn't like the new Tintagel. 'I find it a bit garish,' she added (unnecessarily).

But there was no further glimpse into the Bandaranaike soul. Unlike Sunethra's description of their parents, hers was polished and political; there was a recurring theme of sacrifice and duty; S. W. R. D. was an affectionate man, acutely sensitive to those around him; meanwhile Sirimavo was a seasoned politician ('the grand dame of politics, the Iron Lady'). Listening to all this, I couldn't help but be touched by Chandrika's loyalty, but I also kept wondering: if she's right, how could it all have gone so wrong? I turned the conversation to the Tamil issue.

'Do you think your father let the genie out of the bottle?'

Chandrika paused. Outside, I could hear her next visitors arriving.

'Yes, he did, although he had no idea where it would lead.'

In Colombo, however bad things have become, they've never spoilt a good game of cricket.

I'd never known a game exert such power. It wasn't just that it was played in the street, and on every scrap of gristly earth. It also filled news-stands, TV schedules and hoardings, and was plastered over buses. Almost nothing was sold without some gurning endorsement from a wicketkeeper or Mr Sangakkara, the captain of the national team. Cricket faces were everywhere – all thriving, it seemed, on lager, candy and Milo malted milk. People often told me that cricket was what they wanted for their boys, a quick way upwards through the layers of caste and class. And it was true; cricketers could sometimes find themselves running the country. Vasantha once introduced me to the exquisitely coiffed Thilanga Sumathipala. Not only had he been president of the cricket board, he was also king of the bookies and a government MP.

'Cricket,' he purred, 'is a religion here.'

For a while, this worried me. To get a sense of Sri Lanka, did I really need to understand cricket? It was a daunting thought. For me, the allure of cricket has always been a mystery, and I've never been able to watch it without feeling fidgety and distracted. It's like a battle that never quite gets under way, or ballet without rhythm. How are children ever encouraged to find it engaging? And why don't adults ever seem to grow out of it?

I had a lot to learn, and so I started reading. Cricket was introduced by the British army in 1832. All the big names – like

W. G. Grace and Don Bradman – called by on their way to Australia. The Sri Lankans were always good enough for Test cricket but, until 1982, they never had the premises. In 1996, they won the World Cup. When the Indian fans realised that they'd been beaten by their pipsqueak neighbour, they set fire to the seats. Cricket is the only game everyone loves, and yet basketball is the national sport. A cricket pitch is twenty-two paces long, which is the same length as a meditation walk in the Buddhist tradition.

I was still mystified. 'What is it everyone likes?'

My friends said different things: the rituals, the pace, the outdoors.

It was almost as if, in cricket, they'd found a truly Buddhist afternoon.

'Nah,' said Elmo the novelist. 'It's all about fate.'

I was intrigued. 'What? Doomed to play cricket?'

'No; doomed generally. You see, Sri Lankans are fascinated by the idea that we live on the brink of non-existence. One minute we're here, and then we're nothing! Bang – *gone*! Cricket's like that. In any other sport, you can recover from your mistakes, and you have the rest of the game in which to rally. Not cricket, *men*. Your champion goes out there and he's brilliant until – *wham* – he's a goner! Out of the game! Sri Lankans love that: the idea that your fate's postponed but never thwarted! It doesn't matter how good we are, we'll all get whacked, and we'll never know when . . .'

Another question troubled me.

Has cricket brought Sri Lankans together, or divided them?

To answer this, I enlisted the help of two great names. The first was Sidath Wettimuny, one of the country's first Test cricketers, who'd opened the batting from 1982 to 1987. He was so silvery and charming that it was hard to envisage him slogging sixes. One afternoon, we sat on his terrace, drinking tea to the deafening tweet of bulbuls and babblers. Sidath told me he was from a cricket-ing family and that he went to a cricketing school, long before the time of cricketing money. These days, he is in the garment busi-ness, working with M&S, and turning out hosiery by the ton.

'Cricket is more democratic now,' he said kindly. 'More poor kids.'

The other person I met up with was Aravinda de Silva. Though not poor exactly, he'd been part of the new democratic elite, and the self-made team of 1996. People still consider 'Mad Max' (as he was known) the finest batsman the country's ever had. Now a car dealer, he had an office near Tintagel, and I met him there early one Sunday morning. He was stocky and ruffled, and, in his shorts and T-shirt, looked like a muscular, if slightly sleepy, sparrow. It was easier to imagine him in a dust-up, and yet he turned out to be uncannily courteous. He also loved the new democracy.

'Most players now are from the outstations. They're tougher too . . .'

'And are all the races included?'

'Always were! Muralitharan's a Tamil, Dilshan a Muslim . . .'

Like Sidath, he saw the country united in cricket. As long as a hero was dressed in whites, he could be anything from Moor to Malay. Aravinda even thought the LTTE had been fans, and that – during Test matches – the civil war had come to a halt. It was a tempting image, and for a while I came to believe that, in this absurd game, the Sri Lankans were at their most serene and indulgent.

Sadly, the cricket idyll wouldn't survive these travels.

A few weeks later, I was in Jaffna, and asked the Tamils the same questions. They were horrified at the idea of being lulled by cricket. 'We like the game,' people said, 'but we hate the national side.' A teacher I met put it like this: 'They wear that lion on their shirts. It was the same symbol on the barricades, and on the soldiers, and on the planes that bombed us. I can't wear that symbol, or carry the flag. We sometimes used to cheer for whoever was playing against Sri Lanka, and this caused the soldiers to fire into the air . . .'

It wasn't even true that there were ceasefires induced by cricket. On 29 April 2007, the Tigers launched an air raid on Colombo, during the Barbados World Cup, and once again the sky lit up. But, this time, cricket fans had no idea they were under attack, and simply thought they'd won.

So, after all those weeks, I learnt what I'd already known: that cricket's for others, that it's a potent distraction, and that it's only a game.

Life, for the Tamils, has seldom been a game of cricket.

In England, it's easy to spot those who arrived with the 'first wave'.

Most of them are elderly now, although their speech is still curly and rich. They're like a lost generation of dons with their flannel and tweed, and the vocabulary of Trollope. It appals them how badly Englishmen speak English. They're always professionals – engineers, surveyors and doctors – anyone who could afford the ticket out. Often they came via West Africa, where they'd been replacing British officials at the end of the empire. The parents of George Alagiah, the journalist, ended up in Ghana in 1961, and never quite recovered from the shock of migration. 'They were timid travellers,' he later wrote, 'driven more by the need to escape than the desire to arrive.'

In Britain, the early Tamils usually ended up in the jobs that no one else wanted: in Scunthorpe, Stoke and Widnes. The doctors found that their patients couldn't unravel the tangle of consonants, and so they'd shorten their names, and the Parajasinghams became the Dr Singhams, and the Chandrakumars, the Dr Chandras. You could say their whole lives have been pared down. Once, as a junior lawyer, I visited one of these truncated doctors at his surgery near Blackpool. His few possessions, I noticed, were still stacked up in boxes, as if at any moment he might load up the car and head off, back to Colombo. 'I still have a house there, somewhere,' he told me, 'although I haven't seen it for forty years.'

The children of the first arrivals became the next generation of professionals, more confident than their parents, but always Tamil. They'd even inherited their parents' fear of being forgotten. A friend of mine, who was a journalist on the *Independent*, once told me that being a Tamil was like living in a bell jar. 'Everyone can see you, and can hear you shouting,' she said, 'but they can't hear what you're trying to say.'

But, for the next wave of Tamils, there'd be no possessions, and even less tweed.

The Tamils who arrived in the eighties weren't always professionals in search of a future. Most were glad just to get out alive. The violence, when it came, was sudden and unexpected. For years, the Tamils had found themselves being quietly marginalised, eased out of mainstream life, excluded from universities and the civil service, and dumped by the army. This process might have continued unnoticed but for the four thousand charred and battered corpses of July 1983.

No one has forgotten how the war began, or where.

'Get a bus to Borella,' I was told, 'and head for the cemetery.'

In Colombo, anyone who's anyone ends up at Kanatte.

Jungly and endless, it's like the city itself, except shoulder high. There are long, leafy avenues and crossroads, and – just like its living, breathing sibling – dead Colombo is divided into districts. I found a sportsmen's section, a cluster of defunct poets and singers, a sprawl of judges, a Japanese quarter and a small, cluttered suburb for the middle-ranking dead. Meanwhile, the Senanayakes had their own mini Highgate, and so did the Bandaranayakes, complete with outsized angels, now mildewed and green. Then there was a British enclave, looking splendidly austere and Gothic. Amongst the residents, I spotted Sir Robert Peel – scion of the English political dynasty – who'd been so badly burnt in the raid of 1942 that he'd ended up buried alongside another sailor, with whom he'd fused.

Of all these long-dead districts, easily the biggest was that of the Buddhists. Even here, there was no one around, except the egrets, looking cranky and prim in their ragged white cassocks. Some of the tombs were carved with elephants and lumpy skeletons, or had inscriptions in English ('May he achieve Nirvana'). I was surprised to find that Sir Arthur C. Clarke had somehow slipped in amongst the faithful ('He never grew up,' read his epitaph, 'but he never stopped growing'), but it wasn't him I was looking for. Actually, I wasn't sure what I was looking for. In all the heat and weeds, it suddenly seemed that my curiosity had got the better of me and that this was a prowl too far.

Just then, a bony figure popped up from amongst the tombs. I assumed he was a gravedigger, but he was so naked and thin that he might easily have been one of the occupants. All he wore was a loin-rag, and his body was like a diagram, except with tufts of dusty hair and a hot, thready pulse. It was obvious he wanted to show me around, and so, for a few rupees, I had my own Yorick.

'Soldiers?' I tried, and made a sign for thirteen.

'*Ow, ow,*' he said. Yes, yes.

With that, we set off through the trees. As he walked, I could hear the gravedigger's lungs rattle, and every now and then he'd stop to hack up another parcel of yolky phlegm. Not long, I thought, before he's rubbing shoulders with his clients. 'Soldiers, soldiers,' he kept muttering, and then, near the main avenue, we found ourselves in amongst them. It was the heroes' quarter, a few dozen tombs for the braided and the brave. Everyone here had died a percussive death: shot, shelled, killed by an exploding human, or caught in a car bomb and blasted through the chassis. One admiral is remembered with a concrete peaked-cap, but one of the brigadiers had an entire soldier mounted on his tomb, cradling a T-56. The expression on the figure's face seemed honest to me: not heroism but utter disbelief.

Almost exactly thirty years earlier, on 25 July 1983, a febrile mob had gathered here.

They'd come for a mass funeral: thirteen soldiers ready for the soil. What remained of the dead men had been flown in from the north wrapped in polythene. They'd all been members of 'Four Four Bravo', an army patrol. Three days earlier, they'd been sent out to Thirunelveli; one moment they were contemplating the brittle Jaffna landscape and the next they were caught in a deafening maelstrom of white-hot metal. There was no time to explore the stickiness where eyes had been, or the loss of arms and legs. Gunmen appeared and killed them in the smoke. As armed conflict goes, it was a peculiarly unheroic moment. The first thirteen soldiers to be killed in the civil war hadn't even known who it was they were fighting.

Great leadership might have saved the situation but the

government seemed only to stand aside. In Jaffna, the army was left to its own devices, and killed forty-one civilians. Meanwhile, in Colombo, the *goondas* (or 'thugs') assembled, armed with electoral rolls. The lists they brought to the cemetery contained the names and addresses of all the city's Tamils. As the writer Shiva Naipaul recalled in *Unfinished Journey*, 'Before the axes could be wielded, before the petrol bombs could be thrown, before the pillaging could begin, a little paperwork had to be done.'

With their lists and cudgels, the men surged out, into Borella. '*Rata jathiya bera ganna,*' they urged, '*petrol thel tikkak dhenna!*'

(To save the race and people, give a little petrol and oil!)

These days, Borella wears this tragedy lightly.

The shops have all been rebuilt, and even the Tamils are back. *REAL MEN'S TAILORING*, say the signs. *No Limit Fashion*. Behind the shopfronts is a labyrinth of lanes. They are perhaps more canyon-like now, with higher walls and vast steel gates. It's still an area popular with politicians. This was where my friend, Vasantha, held his political dinners, deep inside a cube of forest. Except for the razor wire, you'd never think anything was wrong.

But the mental scars have proved harder to heal. For most Sinhalese, 'Black July' is still a moment of shame. Even to the most obstinate of Chauvinists, it's a *Kristallnacht*. Beginning in Borella, the thuggery spread out across the island, destroying over eighteen thousand Tamil properties, including cinemas and factories. All that people argue about is how many died. Was it ten thousand, or two, or somewhere in between? No one knows.

But if, in this blaze of amnesia, the figures have been lost, there are always the photographs. It still surprises me how gleeful the *goondas* look as they lay out the Tamils. There's the happiness of looting neighbours, and the ecstasy of fire. A naked man is battered to death, to the obvious contentment of the crowd. For how many centuries must you detest each other, for *that*? Then there is the burnt-out minibus. It's said that the thugs jammed the doors before setting it on fire, and then watched as the passengers screamed themselves to death.

There's no easy way to describe those few days, or to make sense of what happened. Shiva Naipaul wrote of a young boy, dragged from a bus and hacked 'to limbless death'. Others were killed with bottles, strung up, or slung with tyres and set on fire. Naipaul also recalled a girl so enthusiastically raped by the mob that, in the end, there was nothing left to violate, and no more volunteers. Even in London, the Tamils who survived still find it hard to articulate their terror. One woman, who was only seven at the time, told me that all she could remember were her trembling hands. She could still feel them, she said, scrabbling at her earrings as the *goondas* stood over her, demanding everything she had.

Amongst ordinary Sinhalese, there were many small acts of mercy.

'Our home became a refuge,' said Sunethra, 'for weeks.'

It was the same at Vasantha's house. 'We were all afraid . . .'

By now, the mob was moving street to street, looking for prey.

'If they saw a *pottu* on your forehead, you were dead . . .'

'And they tested everyone, making them say difficult Sinhalese words . . .'

As the death toll mounted, the government fell conspicuously silent. The president, Junius Jayewardene, lived in Borella, and must have known of the horror on his doorstep, and yet the police were nowhere to be seen, and neither was the army. Eventually, after four days, he went on air. There was no condemnation of the killers. He described what happened as 'a mass movement of the generality of the Sinhalese people'. They'd simply reacted to the violence of the terrorists. There was no sympathy expressed towards the Tamils, merely a promise to safeguard the rights of the Sinhalese.

For many Tamils, it was a point of no return.

'We knew,' they say, 'that no government would ever protect us.'

This, then, was the start of an exodus and a quarter of a century of war. Already, the mobs had displaced over 300,000 Tamils. Although the government tried to close down the ferries, over half of them fled, mostly to India. It was the beginning of yet another race in exile, nowadays almost a million strong. Meanwhile, of those that stayed, some drifted back to their Colombo homes, and to an uncertain future. A few even changed their names to become less Tamil. Then there were others who headed north, to Jaffna, seeking safety in numbers. Some would join the separatists, looking for guns and a chance of revenge.

Their moment would come, later in this journey.

Back in Borella, a weird normality returned. Although there was outrage overseas (across India the graffiti read, 'INVADE LANKA. SEND ARMY NOW'), Jayewardene didn't care. He banned all talk of separatism and had the Tamils expelled from parliament. 'I'm not worried,' he said, 'about the opinion of the Jaffna people now.' Four weeks later, the Ministry of Tourism announced, 'The sun is shining, the people are smiling again!'

But what followed wasn't really normality. No one has ever been punished for *Kalu Juliya*, or Black July, and so it's always there, unresolved. If there was ever innocence in Colombo, it was lost that month, and all that survives is an obstinate sprig of denial. Even now, people would sometimes talk to me about the war and its causes as if they still didn't understand. 'Why us?' they'd say. 'Why did it happen to us?' But really they knew.

Before leaving Colombo, I thought I caught a glimpse of the future.

Vasantha had asked me to come with him to Parliament.

'Everyone will be there,' he said, as we set off, in convoy.

From the outside, the great hall looked ominous and martial, but, on the inside, it was like the afterlife itself. Huge copper doors led us deeper and deeper, into the marble. Natural light appeared only in slots, and everyone was dressed in white. Even the stewards looked fleetingly celestial, except for the trays of cake and tea. The first person we met was Moses, or was it good king Duṭugämuṇu? He had a long white beard and robes down to the floor. It would've been easy to imagine him dispensing tablets of law. But that, I'd been told, was now the president's job. Here, in South-East Asia's oldest democracy, the role of parliament had become eerily serene.

Vasantha was obviously popular with the other MPs, and everywhere we went, he was ruffled and cuffed. We shared a lift with the government's chief whip, who was also the minister of water. When he spoke, he let out a rumble of laughter, which was swiftly echoed by those in his wake. Somehow we got into conversation, and he asked me what I hoped to find in the Interior. As I couldn't think of a one-storey answer, I said, 'Elephants.'

'You'll find plenty of those around here,' he replied, and the entire lift shuddered with mirth.

Upstairs, the atmosphere was more expectant, as if something might happen. I spotted a bundle of monks from the Heritage

Party, and the serjeant-at-arms, looking flustered and magnificent in a colourful sash. One of the committee rooms was so full of people that all I could see was linen, squashed up against the glass.

'A Chinese delegation has arrived,' explained Vasantha.

Only the president was missing. I could tell by the absence of aura. On television, Mahinda Rajapaksa was always whiter than everybody else's white, and somehow looked not just elected but anointed. Amongst the faithful, he was known as *Vishva keerthi sri thri sinhaladheeshwara*, or the Universally Glorious Overlord of the Sinhalese. It had been a remarkable journey for an actor, who'd dabbled in movies. Even his family were amongst the chosen. That day, there were three brothers in the House; two were ministers, and one was the Speaker. Each wore his *kurakkan*, the spotless shawls of an improbable peasantry. This, after all, was the age of robes, and holy MPs, and gunboats named after saints.

Perhaps, I thought, that's how destiny looks: a bit like the past, only perfect.

But was there ever a golden age?

'Yes,' people said. 'You'll find it in your search for elephants.'

It would be buried under nine centuries of heat and thorn.

The road to the Interior would be strewn with doubts.

Colombo was aware of the rest of the island but was never quite sure where it was. People knew their ancestral villages, of course, but often that was all. They'd swear they lived in the most beautiful country in the world, but few had ever seen it. I never met anyone who'd been to the far north, the extreme east or all the way up the west coast. There'd been the occasional pilgrimage to Kandy, but Mullaitivu, Pooneryn and Batti were just names from the war. Jaffna was considered exotic (if a little unspeakable) and as for the rest, it was just a large blur, known as the 'Outstation'. 'Be warned,' I was once told, 'this is a country of two halves: Colombo and beyond.'

Even the rich had their doubts about the countryside. Often, they still had estates out there but it was not a place to live. It wasn't just the insects; there was also the matter of caste, loneliness and the surfeit of silence. This is hard to believe until you've heard teenagers phoning home, begging for Colombo. Sometimes, the very thought of the Interior would bring on a rash of acquisition: nets, cool boxes, portable toilets and four-wheel drives. Even a long weekend could sometimes seem like a trans-Amazonian expedition.

I was given lots of advice on what I might need, or how I'd die. Out in the bush, there'd be scorpions, landmines, rabies, marauding elephants and – of course – the serpents. If there is one thing they love telling you in Colombo it's that, out there, more people die of snakebite than anywhere else in the world.

With hundreds of miles ahead, none of this was particularly encouraging.

2

All Quiet Among the Reservoir Giants

The people worship idols and are independent of every other state . . . their food is milk, rice and flesh, and they drink the wine drawn from trees.

Marco Polo

The Ceylonese . . . are particularly fond of bathing, and often plunge into the water several times a day. In this gratification, however, they are often interrupted by alligators.

Robert Percival, *An Account of the Island of Ceylon*, 1803

On my map, there was no trace of a golden age.

In the area I'd expected to find sumptuous kingdoms, there was nothing but a bald expanse of greeny-brown. *Dry Zone*, said the key, when what it really meant was 'scrub'. Although it was dimpled in blue, there was little sign of human life, and the roads were suspiciously straight, as if desperate to get out. I could also see a railway, wandering around, looking for towns. The area didn't even have a proper name, just a statement of location: 'North Central Province'.

Such sparsity would have surprised the Ancient Greeks. By 300 BC, Alexander the Great knew all about the fabulous wealth to be found here, in 'Taprobane'. His ambassador in India, Megasthenes, was sending back reports of tortoises so big that you could build a house within their shell. Meanwhile, Alexander's general, Onesicritus, noted that this was the place for war-elephants, more ferocious here than anywhere else.

All this made intriguing reading, and yet Taprobane remained obstinately brown. Weren't there supposed to have been millions of people living here once, in this vast dystopia of weeds? Looking back, I don't suppose I ever fully came to terms with the ancient kingdoms. I'd make several visits during those months in Sri Lanka, but easily the most memorable was with a driver called

Prinithy Hewage. Like my map, he never quite gave me the full picture. Although he spoke a lot of English, he'd learnt only the nouns.

This took a little getting used to, as we extracted ourselves from Colombo.

'Traffic-traffic. Fastman. Badbugger. Incident.'

Prinithy's driving was always like this, a vigorous test of vocabulary and nerves.

I noticed that he only ever looked forward, and never to the sides. People had often told me this was the knack to Sri Lankan driving, ignoring everything else and filling up the space ahead. Whether true or not, the drive north was rich in incident, and weak on verbs. At first, nothing seemed to happen at all, except showrooms and soot. But then a large bridge appeared, and way below I could see swimmers and a stick-man digging for sand. After that, the objects came faster and faster, all lavishly announced by Prinithy Hewage: pickle shop, beauty girl, monkey, cashew, petrol shed.

At one point, we were even stopped by the police for an accident that hadn't happened. Two great bellies appeared at the window, trussed up in khaki and silver buttons. The constables clearly had no use for verbs, but they did ask for money. We opted for the police station at Mundel, where I explained my perplexity to Inspector Manawdu. He smiled beatifically, and wished us well amongst the elephants ahead.

Prinithy drove faster after that, so as not to be stopped. Within a few hours, the trucks and rickshaws had fallen away, and we found ourselves in a huge, sparkling seascape of lawns and coconut groves. The palms were a coppery green, and, beyond them, the ocean looked like a long thin ribbon of amethyst. I wondered what the first humans had thought when they saw all this, and whether it had stirred feelings of deliverance or greed.

The Sinhalese know. Here is the story of how it all began:

Prince Vijaya is a cruel and callous lout, from somewhere in northern India. Strictly speaking, he's not a human being because his grandfather – who the family have now killed – was a lion. But the prince is lucky enough to have seven hundred friends who are as obnoxious as he is. Sensing danger in such unbridled youth, Vijaya's father has their heads shaved, and then crams them on to a ship and pushes them out to sea.

The unruly complement of hooligans then sails south, until it reaches this bejewelled coast in 543 BC. Noting the rich colour of the trees, Vijaya calls the place 'Tambapani', or 'Copper Palms'. But he's also surprised to find that there's no one here except *yaksas* and *nagas*, or devils and snakes. There's not much he can do about the serpents, but he and his friends soon set about the imps. The demon-queen, however, is smarter than they'd thought, and, when she turns herself into a winsome teenager, Vijaya can't resist her. Once she's started producing babies, however, the prince abandons her for a Pandyan girl. The great she-devil dies of disappointment, although her babies survive and set up home in the forest.

It's not an edifying tale, but, from all this bestiality and betrayal, a new race will emerge: the People of the Lion.

After Chilaw, we turned inland, and things looked slightly less bejewelled.

To begin with, it was hard to get used to the flatness and dust.

The road ahead was like a tunnel through the brush, ending in a shimmer. *Beware of elephants*, said the signs, and, in places, the undergrowth looked knotted and smashed. For a while, we saw no one except a lone figure struggling along under an enormous fish. Then we came across peacocks, and a carnival of birds. Everything here seemed to be celebrating something, probably survival. Even the names sounded jubilant – chats, shrikes, warblers, babblers and whistling-ducks – and I noticed that all the herons had turned a deep luxurious purple. Only the buzzards seemed to have misjudged the mood. We'd see them by the roadside, snipping off shreds of snake, their eyes the colour of sulphur and their feet like garden shears.

By now, we were amongst the *wewas*, or giant ponds. These were the dimples on the map. Some were hard to spot, like distant slivers of the sky. Others were nearer and bigger, sprouting huge silky-skinned kumbuk trees, or leaking off into the woods. A few were huge, with their own little fleets of boats. At Paramakanda, we got a chance to see just how pocked this landscape was. A vast saddle of rock had appeared out of the forest, and so we stopped the car and climbed to the top. At the summit were a small *vihara*, or temple, and a ball of stone about four storeys high. I couldn't imagine how the ball had got there or why it didn't roll away, but it gave the place an air of wisdom and balance. We sat down in its shadow, to contemplate the ponds.

Below us, little silvery *wewas* set out in all directions. I could also make out channels and brilliant bouquets of salad-green. Suddenly, the dry zone no longer looked like a desert but an enormous table, laid for lunch. It was once thought that these great collections of water were natural, but now we know that they're a feat of genius.

* * *

What happened here is probably unrivalled in the history of lakes. Three thousand years ago, there was almost nothing here, except perhaps the buzzards. But then a tribe of technocrats arrived, with a remarkable vision. Little is known about them, other than their brilliance at physics. Soon, they were channelling water in from the highlands, 150 miles to the south. Their calculations were so precise that these *ellas*, or channels – some up to forty feet wide – dropped no more than an inch a mile. None of this was achieved overnight but, by the early thirteenth century, the hydraulic kings had built over five thousand *ellas*, changing not only the landscape but also the flora, the fauna and the climate.

There was more ingenuity once the water had arrived. Although the land was flat, there were natural basins almost imperceptible to the naked eye. The ancient topographers had found them, although no one knows how; their instrumentation hasn't survived. Their engineering, however, has. With a remarkable understanding of the area's geology, they'd stopped up the basins with earthen bunds. This was complex engineering, but they'd also discovered the science of spill stones, silt traps and underground conduits, and could build colossal pressure valves, or *bizokotuwas*, the size of a house. Some of the bunds were assembled with stones weighing up to ten tons each, and at least one of the inland seas they created is over twenty miles in circumference, and contains some four thousand acres of water. But it wasn't just one. During the age of hydrology, 18,387 'tanks' or reservoirs took shape, each one, on average, 350 times the size of a modern-day Olympic pool.

Naturally, this spawned a society of irrigators. A man's status depended on the water he used, and everyone grew rich and sleek. It wasn't necessarily a beautiful kingdom, and nor did it influence the world beyond. One early Chinese trader had said the ground was 'damp', the rice 'dear', and the natives 'boorish'. But by 250 BC, the reservoir kings had the confidence to embrace a set of new and sophisticated ideas, based on the teachings of Siddhartha Gautama, better known as Buddha. When, forty years later, an army of Cholas appeared from India, the engineers sent them packing.

That evening, we stopped at Tonigala, by a tank full of lilies.

I've never seen a pool so squeaky and pink. It was a popular spot for bathers; men up one end (in loincloths), and women (fully robed) up the other. According to an inscription, carved in the granite, they'd been coming here for at least 2,249 years. If the *Gazetteer of the Puttalam District* for 1908 is anything to go by, these are the oldest words in Ceylon. They explain that this tank was built by the greatest of the reservoir kings, Duṭugämuṇu himself. Swimming here is the Sri Lankan equivalent of bathing with King Arthur.

All life had gathered here in a blaze of feathers. There were cormorants and ibises, and those little blue sparks of static, the kingfishers. But it was the bathers I envied. Every Sri Lankan believes the day should end like this, in water as cool as stone. I now realise they hate showers and the absence of ritual. Bathing is a contemplative, outdoor experience, like a baptism at the beginning and end of every day. I remember thinking how digni-fied it looked, and had a sudden urge to join them. But this didn't work out as planned. When they saw me coming, all the frogs took fright and rose to the surface as one, before bouncing off across the lilies.

During my time amongst the ancient tanks, I stayed at the Mud-house. Although everything was made of clay and sticks, it was curiously chic. My room was a giant mud pie, furnished with bright orange rugs and paraffin lamps. Every night, exquisite curries appeared, flavoured with the forest. The chef, who looked like Abraham Lincoln, aged twenty-seven, knew all the herbs, and had cures for everything from hairiness to cancer.

At dusk, the staff all pedalled off into the bush, and so I went to bed. The frogs were obviously braver here, and gathered in my cistern where they sang themselves to sleep. Out in the woods, I could hear the *pop*, *pop*, *pop* of gunfire. It was the locals, I was told, making sport with the wild pigs.

People here haven't always been so modest in their dwellings.

Half an hour away was a city that was once one of the biggest and most ostentatious in the world. These days, not many out-siders have heard of Anuradhapura, but in Roman times it was so huge that it would have taken an entire day to walk across. It's reputed to have had over fifty miles of ramparts and a population of two million, or about the same as Paris today. For over 1,400 years, this was the island's capital, and it's been the seat of 113 kings and queens. Few cities on our planet have been continu-ously occupied for so long, even if – at times – it has almost vanished in the thorn.

Prinithy Hewage loved it, and was soon scrambling his words.

Even without him, it would have been hard to unravel Anu-radhapura. The new areas of the city were forgettable enough, but the old parts were gloriously obscure. I spent the day clambering over ruins and roots, but, by the end, it all still felt obstinately abstract. How, I wondered, did a forest of 1,600 ten-foot stone columns ever function as a building? Why all the suburbs with their giant, empty plinths? I suppose it's the highest compliment a city can pay itself, to create things no one else understands.

At one point, I found myself under some enormous stone eaves with several thousand fruit bats, who gave a collective squeal of disgust. At other times, the guards made me take off my shoes or my hat, so as better to feel the sun burning upwards through my feet or like red-hot filaments on my scalp. Perhaps that's why I never really made sense of things. Where had everyone lived? Of all the structures that have survived, almost none seemed to have doors or windows, or even discernible interiors. This was odd given that the *Mahavamsa*, a contemporary chronicle, described a magnificently functional city. There'd been different sections for physicians, scavengers, heretics, foreigners and wandering ascetics. The king had also provided land for widows, and bullock-carts to ferry the cripples around. Here too were some of mankind's first hospitals, and even the city's animals had their own doctors.

More mysterious still were the *dagobas*. All around, they rose up out of the jungle like great white handbells, fresh from outer space. One of them, the Jetavanarama Dagoba, seemed to fill up the sky with its stupendous parabola. With a base almost twice the size of Trafalgar Square, it was built just as the Roman Empire was falling apart. For a long time, it was the biggest brick building in the world, and – during the British period – it was calculated that it had absorbed over ninety-three million bricks, enough to build the city of Northampton. What act of provenance had inspired civil engineering on that scale?

Even more perplexing was the Ruwanweliseya Dagoba. Although slightly smaller, it was another creation of that great hydrologist, Duṭugämuṇu, and – unsurprisingly, perhaps – it was inspired by the shape of a bubble on water. By the time of his death in 137 BC, it was almost finished, a building of dizzying geometry, and surpassed in size only by the pyramids of Cheops and Khafre, at Giza. Perhaps it was the heat, but it suddenly struck me how half-hearted and tawdry the present has become compared to the golden age. Duṭugämuṇu's city would enjoy not only three vast reservoirs, but an entire new caste of sanitation workers, its every member born into a life of drains.

My day would have been much easier if only trees could talk.

At the heart of Anuradhapura is a bo tree (or *ficus religiosa*), thought to have been an offshoot of the tree known to Buddha. It's now been here for twenty-three centuries, which makes it not only the oldest tree known to man but also one of the oldest living things. Its long, knobbly limbs were now supported on thick calipers of brass but, otherwise, it had borne the centuries well. Sometimes it's been at the heart of the story, being attacked with axes, or – on one occasion – blown up by a bomb. But it would also remember the kings, the countless invaders, the monastery city, and perhaps even the odd Roman.

The coins of Imperial Rome were always turning up in the city's litter. I remember seeing trays of them at the National Museum, and I enjoy the idea that these two great powers had some awareness of each other, richly fuelled with myth. Ovid knew all about Taprobane, although he thought it was the 'last outpost of the world'. Pliny too was busily gathering up tales of an improbable empire which survived without slaves or litigation, and where everyone lived to a hundred.

Meanwhile, this bo tree had probably provided a moment's shade for the island's first European, in 45 A D. Annius Plocamus was a Roman tax collector whose visit was entirely accidental.

He'd been diligently harvesting the ports of the Red Sea when his ship was blown off course. Landing in Taprobane, he'd enjoyed six months of giant bells, elephants, Chinese curiosities and a top-knotted king, before returning home. It must have taken some explaining to the boss.

The bo tree would have seen all this, and more. It would have known too how the golden age ended, and that, wherever there's gold, trouble soon follows. Ahead lay four hundred years of casual regicide and ingenious horror. It began in 477 AD with the murder of King Dhatusena. He'd just finished another stupendous reservoir, with a three-mile wall of granite, when he was captured by his son, Kasyapa, and entombed – still alive – in his favourite wall.

Kasyapa then fled down the old Anuradhapura Road, and so, naturally – fifteen centuries later – we set off in pursuit.

All down the Anuradhapura Road, there were huddles of oily, black crows.

Prinithy Hewage would often steer the car at them, although I don't think he ever intended any harm. It was enough just to enrage them, and to send them flapping around like a squall of angry lawyers. Crows have an ambiguous role in the Sinhalese order. To be a *kaputu* in Sri Lanka is to be both publicly despised and secretly admired. They are vile and diseased, and yet without them there'd be no sacred trees, whose seeds only germinate in the corvine gut. They're scavengers too and yet also a scourge. In the artwork of the temples, it's from crows that the sinners beg for mercy as their flesh is pecked away. Nobody forgets a bird like that. Although, by law, it's forbidden to keep them as pets, everyone likes to earn a little of their favour. Prinithy was always saving rice from lunch, and then sneaking off to feed it to the crows.

Further south, the banyan trees grew thicker and bolder, closing over the road. They looked like great candelabra, dripping huge cascades of molten wax. It's hard to think of them as stranglers, murdering their neighbours. When Kasyapa had passed this way, he was right to be worried. He knew that the rightful heir, his brother, Moggallana, would soon come after him, intent on revenge. But he was also troubled by his own irredeemable sin. In the Sri Lankan tradition, there's always been a far worse punishment than death (which is merely a temporary phase). It is, of course, to return to this world as a crow.

There was more ambiguity ahead, amongst the work-gangs of beautiful women.

I never got used to this sight: supermodels in saris, breaking up roads, crusted in dust. Sometimes, this work was done by soldiers or teams of Chinese, but usually it was women. I didn't know whether to feel admiration or horror, and outsiders have often felt like this. Paid labour, wrote Leonard Woolf, in 1906, 'is repulsive to the national character . . . almost slavery'. Another English traveller made a similar remark in 1681: 'To work for hire is reckoned for great shame; and few are found that will work so.' When presented with low-paid work, Sinhalese men often find an excuse, or at least a wife to send out instead. For the women, it's different. Manual labour is something they do when everything else has failed.

Prinithy hardly noticed the women, so diminished was their status.

'What do they earn?' I insisted.

'Good money,' he said. A thousand rupees, or five pounds, a day.

But it wasn't about money. The concept of work itself was much admired; it was just the business of working that seemed so unnatural. There was once a time when this entire society had been marshalled into action, slopping out channels and carving plinths. But, as the reservoir-states had failed, so too had the *rajakariya*, or feudal system, together with the structure of work. For a long time, everyone had become a little king, and the idea of toiling for somebody else seemed vaguely disgusting. Even now, Sri Lankans struggle with the concept of dignified labour. That, I suppose, is why these women were here, shovelling their way across the plains.

Eventually, the road began to rise, and a huge plug of magma appeared.

It was King Kasyapa's outrageous last resort: Sigiriya.

Sigiriya has to be the most beautiful battlefield ever built.

It probably hadn't changed much since the day the slaughter began. The centrepiece was still a towering, tectonic freak: the solidified innards of a volcano, left behind after the rest had washed away. From a distance, its orange sides looked smooth and unassailable, rising fifty storeys out of the jungle. Around the base were terraces, each big enough to be a farm in itself, and then – beyond them – the massive outer ramparts, disappearing off into the forest. According to the *Culavamsa* chronicles, Kasyapa spent eighteen years preparing for his brother's arrival. Everything dates from that period, 477–495 AD: the palatial water courses, the corbelled pools and the giant vegetable plots. With its own internal nurseries, the fortress could've survived a siege forever.

I hired a guide, called Vin, who was paralysed down one side.

'Wild elephant.' He grinned. 'They're very dangerous here . . .'

We hobbled our way upwards through the outer layers of Kasyapa's scheme. It was now prickly hot, and the air felt like flames on my face. I was surprised by the things that grew here in the rock: pretty halmilla, the yellow-flowered mi, and that dainty parasol, the mora tree. Vin told me the evil king had worked hard to expiate his sin. Here were the outlines of hospitals, public pools and even houses for the poor. It's funny how sweet guilt can look. Kasyapa had also undertaken an *aposaka*, or a vow of asceticism. Clearly, he'd no intention of coming back as a crow.

This made it all the more surprising to find his collection of girls. By now, we'd reached the column and were climbing upwards along a groove in the rock. The steps were narrow, cut for tiny medieval feet. At times, the path turned into rust and ladders, but – about a hundred feet up – we found ourselves in a cavern, and amongst a dozen fifth-century beauties. Each one was life sized and half naked, and painted on to the rock with such delicacy and expertise that it almost felt as if we'd slipped unnoticed into the royal harem.

Or maybe this was just the king's stash, a pornographic den for a disintegrating tyrant? True, the maidens were suspiciously taut and pneumatic, but here was something far grander than porn. It's now thought these images had once covered the whole out-crop, from top to bottom. It may even have been the biggest mural ever painted: five hundred girls, covering an area the size of two soccer pitches. Far from being a peep show, this was an exclamation, across an entire landscape. Eye-popping though they may have looked, these were no dolly birds, but *apsaras*, or celestial nymphs. In the battle to come, these astonishing girls would provide the magic or – like the road-gangs – perhaps even the muscle.

Higher up were some of Kasyapa's less spiritual defences. There was only one way to the summit: along the groove, through a fifty-ton pair of paws and then up a spindly metal staircase pinned to the cliff. Cut into the rock face were tiny ledges for sentries, so designed that, if they ever nodded off, they'd tumble hundreds of feet into the gardens below. We also spotted an anti-siege engine, still sprung and ready for use after 1,500 years. It was a truck-sized slab of rock, held in place by two small nodules of granite. A few taps and it would be off, smashing its way through people and forest.

We found nothing on the summit, except Kasyapa's throne and some of his plumbing. The palace had long gone, leaving only a moonscape and central Sri Lanka spreading out beneath us. The stone seat had a sign on it, saying, *DO NOT SIT ON THE THRONE*, but it was too great a temptation. Whilst we sat, Vin chatted away about the disparate strands that made up his life. His daughter was a chambermaid in Dubai. They used to pray every night at the temple. A fortune-teller once told him he'd have a car. It had been dark, and so he never saw the animal that broke his back.

'But I have a good life, ah?' he said. 'I think I am blessed.'

Kasyapa probably also thought he was blessed, the day his brother arrived.

It's hard to imagine why else he left the fortress he'd so carefully prepared. Mounting his war-elephant, he rode out to meet Moggallana on the plains below. But his elephant tripped, and, thinking the worst, his army panicked and fled. Realising all was lost, Kasyapa tilted his head back and plunged a dagger down his gullet. With this, Moggallana had to vent his rage elsewhere. A thousand of Kasyapa's followers were thoughtfully slashed to bits, and his fortress was abandoned to the monks.

It was the end of royal Sigiriya but not the end of royal murder. The next chapter of the golden age has a Quentin Tarantino feel. Twenty-eight monarchs were murdered, mostly by their heirs (including fourteen between 523 and 648 AD). Another four kings killed themselves, thirteen were slain in battle and eleven simply vanished. During the chaos, thousands of Sinhalese fled, back to north India, where their ancestors' journey had started.

Next to me, on the huge throne, Vin suddenly stirred.

'Let's go, ah?' he said. 'We don't want to be around once the sun sets.'

The elephants came that night, although – like Vin – I never saw them.

As the sun cooled and dunked itself in the forest, the sounds changed. The squeals of the day turned into the whirring of the night. Just occasionally, everything would pause, as if listening, but then it would all burst into life again with industrial fervour: bandsaws, bug-powered lathes, sirens and even a creature like a factory hooter. But then came another sound, of crackling branches and saplings uprooted. I could also hear the ponderous shuffling of enormous feet.

This was the signal for the evening's battle to commence. By now, I was in a bungalow a few miles from the rock, and the staff said it was always like this. Soon, I'd hear them, sounding the alarm with saucepans and skillets. I could see nothing through my shutters, but there were voices out in the undergrowth. Then came the fireworks and a light barrage of crackers. For a while, there was more shouting and metalwork, but eventually the crunch of trees became more distant. Then I heard the waiters padding back to the lodge, and life returned to an insecty whirr.

'Nothing new,' said the cook. 'We've been doing that for centuries.'

This little, timeless war even had its own name: the human–elephant conflict.

I'd often read about it, and the fallout was always colourfully reported in the papers. The previous day, 150 beasts had descended on Siyambalwewa, destroying as many trees, and pillaging three villages. Meanwhile, every week, there were pictures of elephants with their feet in the air, or farmers squashed in the rice. Vin was obviously lucky to have survived. My friend, the surgeon, had told me that few of his patients had survived the tussle, and that usually all he could do was tidy them up, ready for the coffin. Every year, he said, about eighty farmers died like this, along with 250 elephants.

But, as the cook said, there was nothing new about all this. Or, at least, it was a battle as old as the reservoirs themselves. Until the age of the hydraulic kings, there were few elephants on the island. They were small, timid creatures – quite unlike the African version – living mostly in the forests of the central highlands. But when the kings transformed the dry zone, it was too much. Mankind had turned the land into a giant elephant salad, and soon they were in amongst it, and their numbers went mad. The kings didn't mind; the elephants were biddable, and easily sold. They became the tractor of their time, as well as the warhorse, the limousine and the executioner. Even in the seventeenth century, it was common for criminals to be torn apart by an elephant, or for a wild herd to be billeted on their land.

But, despite their usefulness, there was always a fear of elephants. Giant stone plinths were all very well in the city, but, out on the road, an army was needed. Travel amongst the reservoirs held particular terrors, even long after the golden age. In 1679, an Englishman travelled this way, and found people living in tree houses. Against elephants, resistance was impossible, he warned. 'The best defence is to flee.'

During the British period, this old struggle took on a new dimension. Suddenly, elephants were regarded as pests, like greenfly or moths, and the shooting began. The population fell to three thousand from fifteen. This is probably the aspect of British rule that the Sri Lankans hate most of all. Several sportsmen would claim up to a thousand kills. During its Edwardian heyday, the big name around here was T. C. Wiggins. He already had hundreds of trophies to his credit when he decided to go after the 'Yakkure Rogue'. This ought to have been popular with the locals, given that it had just 'smashed a boy to pulp'. But that was to misunderstand how things work here, with elephants. The bull took nine bullets before it found the strength for a final charge. Wiggins caught the full force of it, and was flattened out against a tree.

When I told this story to the cook, he wasn't surprised.

'Clever bugger, the elephant. Knows when a man is bad.'

Across the plain was a tiny abandoned city, nestled high in the rock.

Of all the creations of the golden age, Ritigala was the most extreme. It was the wildest, the most enigmatic and the most devout. For a while, Prinithy Hewage tried to persuade me against going. 'Too high,' he said. 'Too many elephants.' Eventually, we agreed he could stay in the car, and with that we set off through the straw.

After an hour, we left the paddy and were enveloped in forest.

It was dark in here, with only flickering tongues of sunlight. The road began to climb and, a few miles on, an enormous stone staircase appeared. At the bottom was a clearing and a watchman, barefoot, pink-eyed and weeping arrack. 'Three thousand,' he slushed. But when I asked to see the tickets, he simply snarled and wobbled back, into the shade. Ahead, I could see the staircase rippling off up the mountain, and so I began to climb.

At first there was nothing but the steps. They reminded me of children's bricks, they were so chunky and so perfectly slotted together. But then I found myself on the rim of a gorge full of jungle. The steps now spread out, along the rim and all the way down to the bottom. I then noticed that both the rim and the steps continued around the back of the trees, enclosing a hole about the size of an athletics track. But, whilst it looked like a stadium, this was the Banda Pokuna, one of the most ambitious tanks of all. Until the day it burst, it had contained over two million gallons of water, mysteriously suspended in the flank of the mountain.

There was more childlike brilliance above. The staircase brought me to a hospital, with vast stone jars, and a series of pools so elaborate they even had their own islands, all heavily moulded and corniced. But this was no ordinary reservoir city. It was built by the 'Ragged Ones', or *Pamsukulitha*, a community of ascetics who thrived in the seventh-century chaos. Rejecting earthly wealth, they dressed only in clothes that others had thrown away or which they'd gathered from the dead. They despised the other cities, and, amongst the masonry, I found a urinal in the shape of Anuradhapura. The Ragged Ones even rejected the idea of housing. Instead they lived in caves, which is why their city was just a staircase.

* * *

This threadbare world had fared badly in the torpor to come.

After the chaos came a period of lethargy. By the ninth century, there were no new works in the reservoir cities. Arab traders described a dissolute kingdom whose people had enthusiasm for nothing but cockfighting, 'waging even the tips of their fingers, to be chopped off then and there if they lost.' Up north, the Cholas had sensed weakness, and were always sending invasions, along with the Pandyans and the Pallavas. In 993, Ritigala was sacked, followed, a few years later, by Anuradhapura itself. As places of greatness, it was the end for both, and, for the next nine centuries, the weeds were in control.

After that, there was only one last, great spasm of life amongst the tanks.

Prinithy Hewage's final task was to take me out there, to Polonnaruwa. In doing so, he made no secret of his sense of doom. It wasn't just the elephants but the thought of unemployment. Although I told him I simply had to get back, he was always offering me new reservoirs or ever more lost cities. I think he hoped we'd drive around forever (or at least until a transfer of wealth was complete). He'd even found a way of filling out the silences with English. By twiddling the dials on the radio, he'd got the easy-listening station. 'Across the Emerald Isle,' cooed the DJs. 'Music to set your soul free . . .' This uncomplicated prattle would've been easy enough to shut out except that Prinithy was ready with the volume. By the end, we were soaring through the paddy like a jet, emitting dangerous blasts of Dolly Parton.

'Polonnaruwa!' he yelled, as we entered a town full of soldiers.

Then, suddenly, the road ended, and a miniature ocean began. I hadn't seen waves for ages, and now here they were, happily lapping the trees. I even spotted a fish eagle, looking ruffled and cruel, with a face like a Monday morning. Prinithy turned everything off, and we just sat and stared. Between us and the horizon was one of the greatest and wettest of the ancient schemes. Here, parked at the edge of the city, were 5,600 acres of water, all held in place with a ten-mile berm. It was the work of a man whose grandfather had fled the ruins of Anuradhapura, and who'd become known as Parakrama the Great. Between 1153 and 1186, not only did he take the fight to India (and Burma), he built another 1,470 reservoirs, including this, one of the largest of all.

The eagle rose lazily, and flapped off down the berm.

'OK, time for the big city,' I said.

Prinithy looked puzzled, but followed. Along the lakeshore were the well-nibbled ruins of Polonnaruwa. From the air, it must have looked like a box of biscuits, scattered through the scrub: huge, crumbly discs, shortbread columns, and even the odd gingery figure. But, on the ground, it was obvious that here was another burst of genius. Everywhere we went, the stone seemed alive; the elephants had a real heftiness about them, and the dancers would wriggle. Even the concept of sleepiness was dreamily rendered in a carving of Buddha, the length of a bus. Then there was a lotus pool, with its attenuating tiers of petals. Such a geometrical complexity would have been hard enough to draw, let alone hack out of granite.

'Three million people once lived here,' said Prinithy, without much conviction. 'And the city wall was eighty miles long.' People were always coming out with figures like this. But it was hard to envisage such quantities, even here amongst the enormous crumbs. I like to think that, although Polonnaruwa never had the dimensions of Anuradhapura, it made up for it in detail. I was once shown some of the objects that had tumbled out of its soil:

Chinese porcelain, a hydraulic toilet and some surgical scissors. It was like glancing backwards, and finding the present.

Time, however, was the one asset Polonnaruwa had lacked.

It may have been the most sophisticated of the reservoir cities, but it was also the shortest lived. With Parakrama's death, things were soon on the slide. The reclining Buddhas would be the last great public works, and they left the city exhausted. There was another flurry of murders, and then, in 1293, the invaders returned. A mere 223 years after its establishment, Polonnaruwa was battered to bits, and with it went the golden age. By the time Marco Polo arrived, later that year, there was no mention of great cities, just people who ate rice, drank 'tree-wine' and wore sarongs. Thirty decades on, Friar Odoric of Pordenone would remember almost nothing at all, except a bird with two heads. Perhaps it was all that tree-wine.

These days, the elephants have the reservoirs mostly to themselves, and – once again – men are living in trees.

On our way back, we stopped at Minneriya. There, we hired a local guide with a truck, and set off through a tangle of hard, knobbly undergrowth. I'd never seen thorn so dense, and we were soon burrowing into the dark. But then suddenly the day reappeared, and with it a vast, diaphanous slash of blue. This reservoir, according to the guide, was built 1,800 years ago, and – although abandoned – it had always survived the annual drought. No doubt that's why everything still hung around. Along the shore there were hornbills, peacocks, more fish eagles and then whole chorus lines of feathery white, in an advanced state of ballet.

At first, we didn't see many elephants, just the odd bull. But then, as the shadows lengthened and the green intensified, the thorn came to life and was soon pouring elephants. They came in couples, family groups, troupes, circuses and armies. It felt like all the elephants in the world were here, in a ritual so regular and massive it's known as 'The Gathering'. Some paused to pick clumps of grass, whilst others gambolled off into the water. It's ridiculous to describe animals as looking happy or sad, but these beasts were overjoyed. Huge herds, fifty strong, danced around, flapping their ears and waving their trunks. This is as near as elephants get to holding a shindig.

There'd be no such beach party for the survivors of the reservoir cities.

If anarchy didn't drive them out, the mosquitoes would. In this province alone, over 1,600 tanks were left dangerously dere-lict. Malaria finished the work of the Cholas, and the kingdom imploded. From then on, the island became a mosaic of mini-kingdoms, and wouldn't come together again until 1815 (some would say it still hasn't). Meanwhile, South-East Asia's greatest rice fields reverted to what they'd always been: *talawas*, or wild plains.

As for the ruins, they were soon forgotten. The Portuguese would plunder parts of the masonry but they could never make sense of the whole. To them, the statuary spoke of a revolting, sex-mad society, more bejewelled than clothed. After that, the thorn took over, and the roots, prising everything apart. Polon-naruwa wasn't rediscovered until 1820, and Anuradhapura until 1823. By then, visibility was down to twenty yards, and it would take almost a century to clear away the undergrowth. As for Sigiriya, the first outsider to see it was Major Jonathan Forbes, in

1831. The nymphettes, however, he missed altogether (because there was a leopard living in their cave).

To begin with, the excitement of rediscovery was mostly British. To people reared on the study of Rome and other defunct civilisations, it was thrilling to find yet another. The archaeologists were soon on their way. But what they'd unearth would affect the Sinhalese in a way no one had predicted. The Chauvinists saw the reservoir cities as evidence of Sinhalese greatness, and of the foreignness of others. Even S. W. R. D. Bandaranaike could be rendered strangely sentimental at the mention of Anuradhapura. For him and his supporters, it would become their spiritual Jerusalem or Shangri-La.

Even now, these ideas were appealing, perhaps more so than ever. They explained the robes and the proto-medieval parliament, and the overbearing sense of entitlement. For many, to suggest that this island be anything but Sinhalese was an affront to the ancient order. It didn't matter that the cities had been overlooked for over five hundred years, or that their kings had often been Tamil, and so had their armies. Geneticists aren't even sure there's a distinct Sinhalese stock, or that the people who think they're Sinhalese aren't a glorious mix of everyone else. But, whatever the truth, the mythology was still flourishing amongst the old reservoirs, just like the elephants.

Beyond Minneriya, there were plenty of latecomers.

Along the A11, we came across a tusker, a few cows and a pair of juveniles, stripping down a tree. This wasn't particularly surprising; only a third of Sri Lanka's elephants live in national parks and the rest run wild. The cows had a new calf with them, who looked quizzical and fluffy, like an outsized chick. If she survives the traffic and the farmers, she could be tramping this road into the 2080s. Elephants like their regular paths, and her ancestors may well have been taking the same route since the fall of Rome. They won't have come far. Elephants here don't migrate, and have a range of only around twenty square miles. But, within that, they're always on the move. When your body needs 550 lb of foliage a day, along with twenty-two gallons of water, life is a constant meal.

As the light failed, we found ourselves back in the rice. It was a tempting prize for a hungry, three-ton Hoover. From time to time, we spotted little fires in the trees. It was the farmers preparing for the skirmishes ahead. Prinithy Hewage shuddered and, with the car aimed at Colombo and easy listening howling from speakers at an elephantine fifty watts per channel, we plunged into the night.

It was hard to dispel this image of men and elephants slogging it out in the trees, and so, a few weeks later, I returned to the lakes. What was it like, I wondered, to share your farm with a pest the size of an armoured car, and to live in the treetops?

This time, I went by train.

The railways were a stubbornly antique feature of Sri Lankan life. Despite new German engines and Chinese carriages, the whole system still had a clunky Victorian feel. I got on at Fort, in Colombo, which has been belching out trains since 1867. I don't suppose much had changed; there were still Ladies' Waiting Rooms and large station clocks made in Ludgate Circus. With its iron bridges linking the platforms, it reminded me of Chester or Newcastle, except that everything was layered in rust. Perhaps painting was impossible amidst the crush. It's said that, every year, these railways carry over eighty million passengers, and that their journeys – if stretched out end to end – would go round the world seventy-seven thousand times. Whilst there have been brave attempts at modernisation, the old ways usually triumph. I discovered that, although I could order tickets online, I'd still have to queue to pick them up.

Time was beautifully distorted that day. After a Victorian start, the centuries were soon tumbling away. At first, there were the slums, and the huge mechanical signals, and third class, packed with fishermen and farmers. Pedlars would appear with baskets of pastries, and sliced pineapple powdered with chilli. Then we'd be in jungle, dipping in and out of the dark. We passed Ragama, the rocky outcrops of Kurunegala and eventually Maho, where a man with no legs somehow grappled aboard. Then, suddenly, the landscape shrivelled and receded, and we were back in the dry zone. The tiny hovels, which had begun this journey as trackside slums, were now perched in the trees.

Things could hardly have looked more sparse and Jurassic when my station appeared: Palugaswewa.

I was soon amongst familiar faces: Maulie and Mahathun.

I'd met them both on my earlier visit. Maulie de Saram ran a small lodge on the shore of a ten-acre tank. It was an unusual place, built entirely of scrap. My room was made of tree trunks and aluminium ducting, and there were no external walls. From a distance, the Galkadawala Forest Lodge looked like a Jacobean theatre that had been shorn of its auditorium and turned inside out. The jungle was easily drawn into this structure, and so – at sunrise – I could lie in bed, drinking tea, surrounded by monkeys. There was always a column of ants somewhere, or a duet of frogs behind the mirror, and occasionally the polecats called by, raiding the eaves for eggs. Naturally, I loved it, and would have happily stayed for weeks.

I was also fond of Maulie, although, unlike her house, she never revealed much of her inner self. She mentioned a life in sales and a father who'd been an academic, but otherwise her past was shut away, and, like so many Sinhalese, her smile seemed to radiate sadness. But, to those around her, she was flawlessly generous, and I often wondered how such a forgiving person had ended up in such an unforgiving place. She told me once that she'd arrived during the war, with jets screaming overhead. That only made Maulie seem more opaque than ever.

'What to do, ah?' she'd say. 'It's out of our hands.'

Mahathun was her neighbour, a farmer. He didn't look like a farmer but was knobbly and professorial, and rode everywhere on a bicycle so ancient it sang. He had ten cows which he treated like children. They all had their names, and their own rice paddy, and every day he'd give them each a bath. They'd never be butchered, and when they died, they'd be buried as if they were family. 'All animals,' he'd say, 'should be treated with the utmost love, even wild ones.' If he could help it, nothing would ever be killed. That's why, whenever he burnt off the old grass, he'd say a prayer for those about to die.

Every day, we all set off into the surrounding scrub. Sometimes, I swam in the reservoir, paddling amongst the lilies and huge bleached trunks of mara and kumbuk. These old wrecks were often haunted by cormorants, who'd huddle together in the upper limbs like some sinister synod. Mahathun was no great swimmer, although he'd usually splash around the edge, with an enormous cake of soap. But Maulie never came in. At first, I thought it had something to do with temperature.

'No,' she said, 'too many crocodiles for me.'

But if the lake was slightly imponderable, the bush was a maze. The blocks of thorn were laid out in streets, or like the vesicles of some enormous vegetable brain. Some of these passages we followed for miles, zigzagging deeper and deeper into the growth. Mahathun called these 'elephant paths', or *alimankadas*, which did nothing to ease my anxiety. Yet, somehow, he'd know when it was safe to be out. The other farmers didn't. Once, we almost ran into some cowherds, wide-eyed with horror and slung with shotguns. Mahathun hated guns and fireworks and the poachers' snares. These snares were just big enough to blow off a foot. 'They're everywhere,' he said. 'Never leave the path.'

Every now and then, the track would widen and a meadow would appear. Mahathun was proud of this grass: *iluk* for roofing, and *lewu* for the cows. The elephants liked it too. We'd find mudbaths, damba trees worn smooth by itchy hides, and teak saplings utterly ransacked. Although it looked like the work of teenagers, Mahathun was always respectful, and never referred to the bigger beasts by name. The elephant was 'Big Bull', the leopard was 'Grandmother', and the sloth bear was 'The Optician' because it always went for your eyes.

Beyond these clearings, we'd be back in the thorn. It didn't seem to have an end, just a series of sunlit pauses. I now realise that this morass of prickles extends hundreds of miles northwards, to the old kingdom of Jaffna. After the collapse of the reservoir-cities, a belt of vicious flora divided the island in two: Tamils to the north, Sinhalese to the south. For the next five centuries, Ceylon owed its peace to this: a giant hedge.

Only two thoughts ever troubled me during those unforgettable days at Galkadawala: how soon till lunch? And, when was dinner? It wasn't hunger that brought this on, but an unfamiliar sense of longing. As a child, I'd been sent to a school where the food was so bland and over-boiled that everything since has been a treat. But it's also meant that, for me, food has a low status, and has never recovered from being sludge and slop. In Sri Lanka, however, even I had recognised that eating was different, and not the function I'd always known. Amongst the Sinhalese, food was delicate and ritualistic – even slightly obsessive – and nowhere was this more true than here at Maulie's.

She had two cooks, called Weerasinghe and Somasiri. I often went to watch them, perhaps in the hope that this would hurry things on. Their apparatus was mostly made of clay and bamboo, but, once it was all steaming and boiling, they looked like alchemists at work. Not even the ingredients were familiar; they looked more like cures foraged in the bush. Maulie once said that Sri Lanka was a land covered in food, and that old Weerasinghe found most of our lunch whilst out on his walk. He and Somasiri would then set to work on their roots and leaves: grating, paring, subliming and titrating, or whatever was needed to produce their edible magic.

Some of the dishes had English names – like jackfruit curry – but most I'd never seen before. There were huge architectural crisps, rich beetroot broths, columns of rice, sweet ratatouilles of garlic and roots, hoppers, string hoppers, mini curries of lemongrass and okra, rotis stuffed with fennel and buttery chickpeas, pancakes baked as thin and fine as millinery, and the exquisite *karapincha*, which looked like a leaf and yet tasted of peppery lime. But it was the chemistry of all this that was so beguiling, and the sensation of colour and landcape and the perfect kiss. I hope one day I'll know that taste again, but I fear it's unique to the enchanted hedge.

My last night, I slept in the treetops.

Mahathun had been happy to find me a *massa*, or watch-hut. That evening, we'd walked out through the rice fields until we came to a lone *palu*, with a tree house about thirty feet up. It was about the size of a double bed, and had a thatched roof and a long ladder wriggling down the trunk. Mahathun had said that, although he couldn't stay, I was welcome. Climbing up to the platform, he'd lit a small fire to flush out any snakes and I'd laid out my mat. It would take me a while to get used to the swaying, but, for Mahathun, this was home. He'd usually spend six months of the year up here, defending his rice.

As the day drained away, he explained how tree-life worked. It's about persuasion, and letting the Big Bulls know what's yours. You can't relocate them, because they just die. Electric fences work, but they're too expensive. So you have to let the *ali* know you're here, and worry them a little. Some people use crackers, but the Big Bulls get used to them, and then you need guns. So the old ways are best; the *massa*.

'But what do you do when the elephants turn up?'

'Ah, that's when you sing, no?'

A strange evening had suddenly turned slightly surreal. Mahathun had an entire repertoire of elephant-scaring songs, and was soon working through them. These were nerve-tingling warbles, somewhere between fado and a muezzin's call to prayer. Even more surprising, they drew a response from some distant trees, and soon the whole paddy was singing along. At that point, the fireflies appeared, filling the tree house with their twinkly light. It was like being in the cockpit of a tiny, thatched jet.

At midnight, Mahathun left, to be with his cows. For a while, I lay wondering what to sing if the elephants turned up. Perhaps the Bee Gees would show them who's boss, if only I could hit the notes. It was exhilarating to be up there, basking in stars. I had hoped for a disjointed night, so that I wouldn't miss a thing. If there weren't elephants, there'd surely be wild boar and porcupines. But, in the end, the rocking was too much and, the next thing I knew, it was dawn, and I was plastered in straw. Below me, and all around, the rice was already pale blue and squeaking with peacocks.

Then a jackal appeared, picking its way across the paddy.

There goes obstinacy: 2,400 years of cities and he's still not a pooch.

The jackal must have heard my thoughts. It looked up, saw me, and – with a doggy sneer – veered off into the ancient scrub.

On the way back to the coast, my bus had to stop for a gang of elephants. They were necklaced in steel chains and carried concrete pipes. All that stood between them and their native forest was a mahout. He was a wreck of a man, with white tennis-ball hair and a hollow, leathery face, tented over bones. He carried a pole tipped with a tiny spike and, from time to time, he'd snarl at the elephants and they'd shrink away.

It puzzled me, their compliance. If they'd had jackal minds, they'd have long ago hammered him into the verge. So why didn't they?

I once took this question to the professor in Colombo, who'd made elephants his life. In his answer, there was science, of course, but also an unruly streak of affection. He said elephants were often misunderstood. They don't remember people, and they have no concept of revenge. They can't read or plan, and understand only fifteen words of command. But they are sensitive to mood, and recognise confidence, domination, love, weakness and fear. And they adapt too. They have to, being so big and so few in number. That's why, if they're captured, they'll accept that their situation's changed, and that – to get the food they need – they'll have to adapt to work and chains. It's about survival. For that reason, a Sri Lankan elephant can be trained at any age, even in its thirties. The training is cruel and brutal, but by the end you have an animal that's ostensibly tame. Of course, they're not *truly* tame, just opportunistically compliant. There's still a lot we don't understand.

And what about the mahouts?

This time, everyone had a view.

Prinithy Hewage had thought they were all drunks.

'You have to be,' said Elmo the novelist, 'to live with the risks.'

Others thought it was the drink that got them killed.

'The Big Bull,' said Mahathun, 'always knows when you're not in control . . .'

'Just one lapse,' said the professor, 'and the mahout's dead.'

And that, I thought, explained the human wreck, with the tennis-ball hair.

This bus journey finally ended in about 1480, amongst the Gobbs of Serendib.

Along the north-west coast, great drenches of sand were laid out, one after another. In places, the sand arced out into the sea, enfolding islands and reefs, and filling the shallows – or

gobbs – with silt. One of these islands, a long, gnarly slab of lime-
stone called Mannar, is Sri Lanka's largest. On the map, it's about
the size and shape of Manhattan but looks stretched and taut, as
if one end's been nailed down whilst the other's been dragged off
towards India. There's also something else that's odd: a line of
'stepping stones', or shoals, trickling from one country to the
other, across twenty-four miles of water. Even the name sounds
improbably alien: Adam's Bridge.

One of the first things I did on Mannar was to head for these
shoals. At the far end of the island was a pier head almost a
quarter of a mile long, but abandoned now and psoriatic with
droppings and salt. Underneath it was a small navy base. The
sailors told me they were there to stop the Indian fishermen
scraping the ocean bare. They now held twenty-one trawlers
under arrest. But when they weren't rounding up fishermen, they
were renting out their boats, and so I hired a launch and two ratings, and we set off into the shallows. *SRI LANKA NAVY*, said
their T-shirts. *Dance among the Angel Isles.*

The boys were happy to be out, and so was I. The sky was king-
fisher blue, and the shoals the colour of silver. We always kept the
sandbanks to our left – sometimes no more than dollops; often
great hummocks of seabed. There were supposed to be sixteen
islets – half of them Sri Lankan – although they were always
shifting about. After an hour, they seemed to peter out altogether,
and I could make out faint wisps of India off in the haze. We were
almost at the midpoint of the Palk Strait.

'Do ships ever come through here?' I asked.

The boys squealed with laughter, and the driver cut the engine.

'*Tchah*! OK, India wants a channel here . . . but look!'

And, with that, he jumped overboard, vanishing up to his
knees.

We all waded back, on to one of the sandbanks. It was larger than I'd imagined, spreading out as far as the eye could see. The emptiness of it all was unnerving, like a planet in draft. When the boys found an old whisky bottle, it brought on a bout of cartwheels. We didn't find much else: some minute purple flowers, a parrot fish with massive dentures, and a whorl of plastic bottles. Perhaps these are the new seashells, disgorged by the tide, undigested. But even India's garbage could make little impression on the nothingness of it all. This is what it must be like to take a stroll on the ocean floor.

Once, it was possible to follow these dunes all the way to the Indian city of Rameswaram. Hindus believe that's how Rama arrived in Sri Lanka, with his army of monkeys. For the Moors, it was Adam who came plodding over the Bridge. But, whoever it was, this was no longer a walkway from India to Mannar. In around 1480, a huge hurricane came bowling through the straits, severing the long drool of sand, and leaving the island much as it is today.

Since then, Mannar has never cared much for change.

I got a bus from the pier back down the island to Mannar town. It was obvious that the novelties of modern life had seldom thrived. Not only had the pier failed, but so had the lighthouse, a passenger terminus and a bold, Edwardian railway. The track was now just a streak of cinders again and the stations were wearily dismantling themselves, flapping off their roofs and reverting to rocks. Meanwhile, out in the scrub, I could see dogs hunting in packs and old carriages becalmed in the sand. There were soldiers too, living amongst the ruins and the rust. War could always be relied on to turn the clocks back.

The man next to me said the Indians wanted to revive the ferry. 'And the train! But why would *anyone* want to come here?'

The town had fared better, if only because it was cheerfully medieval. From here, a long, thready causeway led back, across the gobb, to the mainland. It was a fragile link to the present. At this end, the intercity buses stopped, along with huge swathes of time. When I first arrived, I stepped down on to a sandy street and was immediately swamped with donkeys. Then traders appeared, in robes and long beards, with trays of lychees and hair restorer. At some point, I also came across a gargantuan baobab tree, planted by Arab merchants in 1477. It wasn't a pretty sight, with its mountainous folds of puckered grey flesh. I had a feeling it might be the most obese tree in the world, or at the very least an ogre from *The Arabian Nights*.

It was hard not to be enchanted. For all its woes, Mannar was determinedly perky. In Pilawoos Hotel, all the waiters had dyed-orange beards and would lob the food around as if they were curling. *NO BUSINESS HERE*, said the signs, an impossible injunction in a town where no one did anything else. When an electioneer turned up, he suddenly found he had an entourage of donkeys. No sooner were his posters pasted up than the donkeys peeled them off and ate them. I decided I had to stay, so I found a room in a large, mint-green villa, just off Post Office Street. The owner was an old pharmacist, who was gradually working his way through the wreckage of an *Encyclopaedia Britannica*.

'Mannar,' he'd say, 'was a great emporium, known to the ancients . . .'

I often thought about this as I wandered around.

I'd half hoped to find great chunks of geometry, or perhaps a giant plinth. There's a theory that it's all there somewhere, just waiting to be found. It's not an easy idea, but it was once explained to me by the wizardly Dr Roland de Silva, in Colombo. A genial scholar, he was living in a house built without glass or paint, in the manner of the reservoir kings. He described how Mannar was at the centre of ancient commerce; how ships were forced out of the Palk Strait and through Mannar's lagoon; how, at the narrowest point in its channel, an entrepôt formed and began scooping in the wealth. Everyone called by: the Chinese, the Romans and the Arabs. In time, Mannar became so rich that it began building cities of its own, including Anuradhapura.

It's an intriguing theory, lacking only stones.

Meanwhile, until the masonry appears, Mannar can be certain only of the Arabs. Not only did they give it the baobab tree, but also a religion, the robes, the beards, Adam and the donkeys. With the demise of Polonnaruwa, this coast had been theirs. By the time the Arab world's own Marco Polo, Ibn Battutah, had arrived in 1344, the island was so familiar, it even had an Arab name: *Serendib*. It was also rich, so rich that the Sultan of Puttalam was handing out fistfuls of pearls. To Ibn Battutah (who'd just survived eighteen years in the Maldives with three wives), it was all thrillingly excessive and – climbing into a sumptuous palanquin – he set off down the coast, with thirty-one attendants. He'd have loved Mannar, particularly the fatboy trees and the iconoclastic donkeys.

Apart from Mannar, not much remains of Serendib, except the word.

It began with a fairy tale that took four hundred years to creep round the world. It appeared first in Persia, in 1302. Then it showed up again in Venice in 1557, by which time it was known as

Peregrinaggio di tre giovani figliuoli del re di Serendippo. From there, it went north, briefly attracting the attention of Voltaire before arriving in England. Here, it was seized upon by Horace Walpole, who was impressed by its silliness and had it adapted into English as *The Three Princes of Serendip.* These days, no one remembers much about the story, but they do understand a recurring concept: the faculty of making fortunate discoveries by accident, or – as we now say – serendipity.

Down on the waterfront, there was a permanent shadow. Its source was a ruin so big that it shut off the shoreline and towered over the channel. Mannar had always despised its fort, and now seemed to shrivel away in its presence. It was a brutal stump of grey, and conspicuously foreign. For much of the civil war, this was the army's last foothold on the island, and it had been regularly taunted and spattered with missiles. Although the ramparts rose like escarpments, they were still spewing scree into the moat.

I'd often walked this way, but the fort was always locked up. Then, on my last day, I found the gates open and slipped inside. At first, I just stood and gaped. A small, tightly encircled town had been utterly blasted away. In places, there was nothing left but gravel and splinters of china. It took me a moment to reassemble things in my mind, and what appeared was Europe. Here were things that had never been seen before in Taprobane and Serendib: heraldry, latrines, gunpowder stores, tombstones, belfries and bathtubs. Welcome, I thought, to the next five hundred years.

There was no one around except soldiers, shovelling rubble. When they saw me, they stopped work and came over to stare. Their corporal was a lumpen man, of imperceptible intent. It was his leer that troubled me. Was it avarice? Or lust? Or perhaps even trauma? Or maybe it was just surprise at the sight of a *suddha* (or white man) again, inside his fort.

That night, I mentioned all this to my landlord, the pharmacist.

'The fort was started in 1560 . . .' he began.

He'd never been inside but he'd often studied it, from the safety of books.

And what did he think about the people who'd built it?

'Bastards,' he said. 'Drunken bloody louts . . .'

It was the Portuguese, settling in, along the wild west coast.

3

The Cinnamon Forts

The country around this place is particularly wild; and perhaps there is no road in the island more dangerous to travel, from the multitude of wild beasts with which it is infested.

Robert Percival, *An Account
of the Island of Ceylon*, 1803

The Portuguese as conquerors were the most unpleasant race, probably, who have ever discovered the secret of power.

Harry Williams, *Ceylon: Pearl of the East*, 1948

Of all this island's invaders, none has fought like the Portuguese, or ended up so hated.

The anger, it seemed, was everywhere: in paintings, plays, sculptures and soaps. Even in religious art, the Portuguese would always turn up in ironwear, trailing gore. Everyone had their favourite stories, of prisoners on spikes and barbecued babies. Often, on the weekends, one of the newspapers would rekindle some ancient atrocity. These were popular articles. It was always reassuring to know that life today was less cruel than it had been, and, in this, the Portuguese were a gratifying source of outrage. Several times, I turned up at a temple, only to find that I was four hundred years too late, and that they'd rolled it off the cliff or reduced it to pebbles.

But I still found the hatred puzzling. After all, the Portuguese hadn't simply plundered the place and vanished. They'd left so much of themselves behind. It wasn't just cakes, lace making and a dainty new dance (the *bailá*), there was also a new god, new saints and even a new name: *Ceilão*. But, above all these, Portugal's most insistent legacy was to be found in the phone book: pages and pages of Salgados, Rodrigos, Fernandos, de Silvas and de Soysas. It was almost as if the conquistadors had never quite left.

The language too has become deeply infested. These days, you can't paint a *pintura*, eat *paan*, or sail your *batel* without breaking out into Portuguese. It is everywhere, from the wardrobe (*almariya*) to the veranda (*estopo*) and in every room (*camaraya*). Even the Sinhalese 'thank you', *bohoma istutiy*, sounds suspiciously Latin. Then there is all the Portuguese technology, which entered the language after 1507. Amongst this newfangled gadgetry, there's the *camisa*, *butoma* and *oroloso*, or shirt, button and clock.

Only the infrastructure has gone. The Portuguese forts were mostly destroyed and remodelled, or have disappeared under town halls and concrete. According to Raven-Hart, only a handful of their inscriptions remain, other than tombs. Gone too are the palaces, the slave-yards and the barracks. So where would I find the Portuguese, if only in spirit?

The answer was here, where they'd started, in the badlands of the west.

Heading down the coast, I was joined by a man who knew the road well, and who'd fought in its dirtiest war.

Ravi Weerapperuma had always regretted leaving the navy and was curious to revisit his past. But he was also an unusual person to find in a war story. Although he was tall and powerfully built, with noble, Romanesque features, he had about him something of the mystic. He once told me that, if only we could stop interacting with nature, and could stop the vibrations, we'd be able to make ourselves completely disappear. I'd been introduced to him in Colombo (he was the special-forces adviser) and, whilst I didn't always understand his karmic vision of conflict, we became good friends, and have remained so ever since. When

I told him where I was going, he said I'd need a four-wheel drive, and the next thing I knew, we were meeting up in Mannar.

Our trip soon had the makings of an expedition. Ravi had brought not only a small, copper-coloured juggernaut, but also his son. Although Tejala was only twelve, he had all of his father's steely reserve, and even a touch of miniaturised mystique. As we drove along, he'd sit somewhere high up in the luggage, coolly plotting the route. He'd never heard his father's story before, but now absorbed it all as if it made perfect sense.

'We never talk about the war,' said Ravi. 'I have no photographs of myself from that time, and I don't wear the medals. I loved the navy but not the killing. No one wants to kill someone. The object of war is anyway to use minimum force. I served for twenty-two years and saw terrible things. *Terrible*. That's why I want to teach people how to survive. No one needs to die. To die is to err. Survival is a state of mind.'

South of Mannar, the tarmac came to a crumbling end, and the sand began.

The woodland was now stunted, and the air hot and brittle with salt. In places, everything had been scorched away, and pools of crimson had formed in the hollows. The thorn tresses looked as if they'd been added later in ink, they were so spare and black. It was a beautiful place, in its own dessicated way. I was surprised at the creatures that lived here: we saw small deer, ibises and a mongoose, fussing around in its feathery, poacher's coat. Once, a brahminy kite swooped in low to assess our nutritional value. It had burnt-orange wings and, beneath the rump, a sprig of meathooks, neatly stashed.

All the place names here were Tamil: Vankalai, Kankanku-lam, Puvarasankandal. But sometimes the places themselves had gone, leaving only lintels or slabs of cement. The woodland too had been slow to recover, and was often stripped back hundreds of yards from the road. 'That was us,' said Ravi. 'We had to cut everything down. We never saw the enemy, but they set claymores on the trees. A terrible weapon, ah? When it blows off, it sends out hundreds of little steel balls. We lost a lot of men along here.'

Only a few farmers had returned. We could see their huts out in the thorn. They were flimsy structures, overawed by the landscape's natural poverty. Ravi said there were two types of roof: corrugated iron or cadjan. It wasn't much of a choice: roast alive or get eaten by ants.

Lesser mortals might've been deterred by Sri Lanka's wilder parts, but not the Portuguese.

In Lisbon, the fifteenth century had unleashed an unstoppable wanderlust. Part of it was about acquiring wealth on a truly Venetian scale. But the Portuguese were also inspired by Marco Polo, and soon their navigators were setting out in all directions. By the end of the century, they were in Brazil and the Cape of Good Hope, and, in 1497, Vasco da Gama had stumbled on India. Eight years later, they made their first landing in *Ceilão*.

At first, the Sinhalese welcomed the new arrivals. Only later did they realise how vicious their visitors could be. Here's a description of the first Portuguese, taken from the *Rajavaliya*: 'They wear jackets of iron, hats of iron; they rest not a minute in one place; they walk here and there; they eat hunks of stone [bread] and drink blood [wine]; and they give two or three pieces of gold and silver for one fish or one lime; the report of their cannon is louder than thunder . . . Their cannon balls fly for miles and shatter fortresses of granite'.

By contrast, the Portuguese were rather less impressed with their hosts. According to the diarist, Ribeiro, the Sinhalese were 'well made, almost white skinned, most of them big bellied . . . they do not understand nor possess arms . . . They do not kill each other much, because they are cowardly fellows . . .'

With natives like that, the pickings would be easy.

The Portuguese began here on the west coast, with pearls.

Just beyond Arippu, we found ourselves deep in the spoil.

Oyster shells were heaped up as high as houses and all along the shore. Huge, clinking hills bulged out of the beach and rolled off into the woods. The shells were piled so deep that we could drive in amongst the drifts. No one knows when people first started diving here, but Ibn Battutah knew about the pearls and so did the ancient Chinese. At the height of the industry, in 1905, divers were bringing in eighty million molluscs a year.

We got out and waded over the heaps. On the seaward side was a small village made of branches, and scattered with fishbones, plastic and ragged scraps of shark. The pearl fishery had long gone, and, with it, the divers. Once, over five thousand of them had descended on this shore, mostly from the Persian Gulf. For a few months each year, it would be transformed into a city of twigs, complete with showmen, hawkers, conjurers, jewellers and drillers. It was a scene, noted Percival, in 1803, 'that exceeds in novelty and variety almost anything I have ever witnessed'. It must also have been one of the smelliest, with its rotting mountains of mollusc and the attendant miasma of flies. So insalubrious was it that soldiers were never posted here more than four months.

As we edged through the fish litter, I asked Ravi about the pearl banks.

'They're about twenty miles out, at around six fathoms.'

'Anything left?' I asked.

'Not much. It all ended suddenly, around 1925.'

Until then, the entire city would float out there, every day. Some divers did up to fifty descents a shift, weighed down with rocks and wrecking their health. The horrors were so lurid they were even made into opera: *The Pearl Fishers*, by Bizet. Many died, not that anyone cared. The divers had their magic and their charms, and the colony got its tax. Even Leonard Woolf, who'd once officiated here, was unable to muster much more than mild distaste.

Back on shore, it was pure fate whether a man made his fortune. The oysters were sold off, unopened, for a few pence each. Sometimes the buyer got lucky, but not often. There were only three to four pearls in every three tons of oysters. For the many millions of empties, death was in vain and they were merely spoil. They'd serve no purpose except as hills and food for the flies. It may not look much now, but this was once the world's greatest lucky dip.

On the edge of the midden heaps was a mini stately home, built by Sir Frederick North, later the Earl of Guildford.

It was a bold little mansion for such a pearly knight. The Doric was once described as 'the most beautiful house in Ceylon'. But the wind had long since gnawed away the upper floor, and His Lordship's glorious bedroom. Now the grand staircase simply stepped out into the storms. The sea too was getting its revenge on vanity. Since 1804, it had sucked away almost half a mile of sand and shell, finally reaching the foundations. The front had already been whipped off and now lay, face down, on the beach below.

Ravi studied the erosion with interest.

'Funny, ah? Sri Lanka is gradually moving east.'

Back in Arippu, the Portuguese had spent their loot more wisely on a blockhouse.

The oblongs of brick were still there, mounted with gables. These days, it's a shelter for cattle, and long waxy roots were probing their way through the walls. The doors had sunk into the grit, but, in places, cow-sized holes had appeared in the walls, and so we crept inside. It was more a strongroom than a fort. During the early years of Portuguese *Ceilão*, that was all that was needed. The Sinhalese kings had been overawed by the sight of modern warships. Under the treaties of 1505 and 1517, the visitors were encouraged to help themselves to the booty, in return for a little protection.

In the darkness and stink, it wasn't hard to imagine the rookie soldiers, or *reynols*. As one historian put it, 'the rank and file were the sweepings and off-scourings of the slums of Portugal'. As the empire had grown, so had the demand for manpower, and soon criminals were being thrown in the mix. To be banished to the Eastern colonies was the worst punishment a man could suffer. It's said that, as they rounded the Cape, they all threw their spoons overboard, knowing that, for the rest of their lives, they'd be eating with their fingers. Only half would survive the voyage, and even they had no guarantee of work. Soldiers weren't paid when they weren't on campaign, and so, in Colombo, most spent their time pilfering and surviving on whatever they could.

Once in Arippu, they were little better off than the cattle. It was a degrading existence in the heat and thorn. They were only half clothed and half fed, and the army only paid them twice a year, at Christmas and on the Festa de São João. The rest of the time, they were expected to work as *chetties*, or hawkers. It's hardly surprising that the common soldier became so fatalistic and brutal. Nor is it much surprise that they were soon heaving themselves on to the locals, muddying the gene pool. Women, like pearls and feathers and elephants' teeth, were merely part of the booty.

But all these things were fripperies compared to the big prize, deep in the forest. It was a small tree but it would change everyone's lives: the *kurundu*, or cinnamon.

The jungle soon thickened, and more and more lunches appeared.

At first, we headed south along a wide orange scar. It looked as though some great extraterrestrial craft had plunged in through the trees, hurling everything aside. But this wasn't the work of aliens but the government, which, after months bulldozing, had long since given up the ghost. After that, the trees swelled up around us, and the earth smelt steamy and sweet. The road now shrunk to a path as it twisted around in this tangle of outrageous flora. Ravi knew all the names: *palu*, the axe-breaker with a soul of steel; *puswela*, the huge vines that spiral out of the canopy like giant bedsprings; and *machang*, with its trunk of tarnished silver, and fruits as pert as plums and a horrible laboratory yellow. These little treats, according to Ravi, were irresistible to bears, who'd gorge on them and then stagger around for days, blearily psychotic.

Our own lunches were almost as surprising. There were lots of them that day. Ravi had fought all the way up this coast and he still knew all the old naval outposts. By ringing ahead, he'd ensured that, everywhere we went, a welcome was waiting. We began our journey with chicken served on linen tablecloths at Silavathurai, and ended it with liveried china on the banks of the Kala Oya. Another time, a sailor stepped smartly out of the forest with a box for us, full of string hoppers. His mouth dropped at the sight of his old wartime leader, Commander Weerapperuma, back in the scrub. Word soon got round. For a while, we had two motorcycle outriders in spotty green suits, T-56s slung across their backs. When it was time to part, Ravi watched them peel away and vanish into the trees.

'Our mistake,' he said, 'was to misunderstand our enemy's fear.'

At some stage, we passed into 'Ten Lakes' or Wilpattu, and the national park. It was all brutally magnificent, just the sort of Sri Lanka I'd come to love. Being on the western edge of the old reservoir states, the *villus* here were like the other tanks except wilder, more remote and expressed in Tamil. The crocodiles looked bigger too. Every pond and every swamp of silty gloop seemed to have its own armoured thug. Although known as 'muggers', this didn't do justice to their villainy. They were like tree trunks with a four-foot mantrap grin. In 1797, a vast, twenty-foot specimen was brought back to Colombo, slung between two carts. Percival describes how, when the beast was cut open, it was found to contain a local man in an advanced state of digestion.

When I told Ravi about this, he winced.

'They're still big killers, especially amongst women, washing clothes.'

For centuries, it seems, the creatures here have been working on their reputation for ferocity. In the seventeenth century, it took pilgrims six months to make their way up the west coast from Colombo, running a gauntlet of 'elephantes, wild buffaloes, tygers, and other beastes'. Leopards, in particular, developed a taste for the tenderised traveller, particularly in times of cholera. The home-grown explorer, R. L. Spittel, tells of a man who woke in the night to find a leopard in his tent, devouring his companion. Percival, on the other hand, thought the most dangerous of all the beasts was the buffalo – particularly to Europeans, 'to whose dress or complexion they have the greatest antipathy. The scarlet coat is the chief object of their resentment . . .'

Whilst we never encountered killer leopards or bigoted buffaloes, the elephants were discernably edgy. Once, we ran into a nursery group, bathing in a *villu*. Although we were quarter of a mile away, our presence clearly spooked them, and – with a flurry of trumpets – they rumbled off into the forest, bawling and bellowing and spouting fountains of dust. Even the Portuguese had been impressed by such displays of might, and were soon rounding up the export models at the rate of about forty a year. The first one arrived back in Europe in 1507. Poor 'Annone', as she was called, ended up in Rome, where she was stuffed with bread and cakes, died of dyspepsia and was buried in the Vatican Gardens. No wonder today's west-coast elephants looked so wary.

But it wasn't just elephants diving for cover. Everything scattered before us, slithering, bounding, slinking and lolloping off, into the dark. For the last thirty years, this had been bandit country, where anything momentarily stationary was felled and picked clean. Nihal de Silva, the author of *The Road From Elephant Pass*, said that, during the civil war, Wilpattu was 'a neutral zone where the army and rebels were present but did not really confront each other.' This was to say nothing of the poachers, bandits, illegal loggers and deserters. Most of the park staff were murdered, and secret ammunition dumps still turn up from time to time. The area was so dangerous that, when de Silva's novel was made into a film, it had to be shot in Malaysia. Not even the novelist himself survived this anarchy, and, in 2006, he was touring the park when his vehicle went over a pressure mine. The remains of that day, the deformed stumps of reddening metal, were still visible out in the long grass.

Nothing has enjoyed these magnificent badlands quite like cinnamon. It thrives on want. In healthy soil, it's said that the trees take seven years to reach maturity, but give them poor, sandy grit, and they're ready in five. This makes western Sri Lanka one of the most productive places in the world, at least in terms of this pungent bark.

Only occasionally did we spot cinnamon growing wild. It's an unassuming shrub, even slightly suburban. To begin with, those who lived on the coast hadn't recognised it as the source of cinnamon, and were solely reliant on the magic logs that floated downstream. Word of the bark's miraculous properties soon spread as far as China and Rome. Arab traders quickly discovered that, with a bit of mythology, they could charge more. Even Herodotus was persuaded that cinnamon sticks were daringly harvested from the nests of the phoenix.

But it was the Portuguese who transformed cinnamon from a curiosity into a commodity. It began as a protection racket; the Sinhalese would pay 250,000 lb of cinnamon a year in return for support against the Tamils. But, before long, the arrangement turned into full-blown extortion. In the first half of the sixteenth century, the Sinhalese would be so beautifully robbed they'd hardly notice. By 1551, the kingdom had split into two and, in this enfeebled state, a tame heir was produced. His effigy was shipped back to Lisbon to be crowned 'Dom João Dharmapala'.

Despite occasional attacks from the breakaway kingdom, the Portuguese were now free to plunder the forest. It still hadn't occurred to anyone that the cinnamon could be cultivated, and so the foraging was done on an industrial scale. The wildlife didn't, of course, make it easy. For every four hundred peelers sent looking for cinnamon, there had to be twenty-five soldiers, who went ahead, banging drums and discharging muskets.

The profits, however, were stupendous. The English thought that the trade was worth more to its colonial masters than Potosí's silver mines had been worth to the Spanish. Even in 1803, by which time other colonies were producing cinnamon, it was still bringing in the equivalent of thirty million pounds a year.

Not surprisingly, such wealth worried the Portuguese. 'The odour of cinnamon,' wrote one general, 'will bring others to Ceylon.' With too few men to saturate this land, a string of forts was needed, set at intervals, no more than a day's march apart.

'And the next one's Kalpitya,' said Ravi.

There, we'd stay with his old school friend, surely the last of the conquistadors.

Deputy Minister Perera was a splendidly Falstaffian character: full bellied, genial, strong in arm and loud in reproof. In a well-domed polo shirt and baggy shorts, it was easy to picture him in doublet and hose. He had a barrelling walk, as if barging his way through a dense clutter of inconvenience. I found it hard to think of him as a friend of Ravi's; the one, subtle and intriguing, and the other, magnificent in quarrel and belch. The minister was always roaring at people, and pausing for laughter. With his lighter, ruddier complexion, he made all those who fluttered around him seem shadowy and insubstantial. Most of the time, this was his huge retinue of gunmen – enough black-clad guards to fill two SUVs. 'People were always trying to kill us,' he scoffed. 'But life has to go on . . .'

The Pereras had an estate on the scraggy neck of the Kalpitya peninsula. It didn't look much at first: a bleak expanse of saltpans and a long, spindly forest of palms. As for the ancestral home, only the gates were grand. The rest was a complex of cement and corrugated iron. Inside, the rooms were hot and musty, and so we all sat outside amongst the house plants, which were also refugees. The Pereras' planters' chairs forced us to loll backwards, in positions of unnatural apathy, and, every now and then, a maid would appear with a plate of cream crackers. It took a while to appreciate that this was a hub of commerce. All night the trucks ground through the sand, hauling away coconuts and salt. 'The best coconuts in the world,' boasted the minister, 'making the best toddy, the best arrack and the best charcoal for gas masks.' I also learnt that a snake would never cross a coconut mat, and that you could never be poisoned, eating with a coconut spoon.

But most surprising of all was Madame Perera, or Chrysantha. An opulent figure, she was always exquisitely jewelled and caparisoned in satin, as if in denial of all the salt and husks. Sometimes the whole world would stop as she rustled into view, resplendent in pea-green or a shimmering vision of lemon. She told me that, in Colombo, she spent her days with a personal trainer but, out here, she went to funerals. 'Every day! You'd never guess the people who are dying!'

Between funerals, she'd sit amongst a bank of twinkling phones. As her children refused to visit the estate, she was forced to track them round the world. She told me she could be up all night, texting ('Hardly slept at all!'), and she always had about her the insistent ping of dependants.

Had she ever thought of visiting them, I asked.

She thought about this for a moment (*ping*).

'Sheffield, maybe – but not the USA. *Eugh!* Too far!'

Her husband, Niyomal, shared his wife's distaste for Americans.

'Why are they so *incompetent*?' he blasted. 'Messing every-thing up!'

I must have looked puzzled, but he had a list of examples, from Bay of Pigs to Abu Ghraib. Had he not been such a courtly host, the British would have got a broadside too (as a government minister, there was always a spasm of anti-Britishness, just below the surface). Instead, he rounded on Sri Lanka's cricketers, accusing the national side of everything from complacency to sloth. But all of this was a distraction from the main source of his spleen: the Anglo-Saxon West. It was a theme that so excited him that he almost overlooked where his children were, and no longer seemed to hear their relentless pings.

That evening, the minister had a party to go to, and insisted we join him.

'Boys only,' sneered Chrysantha resentfully.

Leaving her with her phones, we set off in cavalcade. The party was being held in a tree house at the local air base. For one of the senior officers, this was as high off the ground as he ever got, and he told me he was appalled by the idea of flying. Another officer produced a set of night-vision goggles, so we could watch the deer grazing greenly in the murk ('Good scopes, no?' he said. 'Great for shooting terrorists!'). Everyone settled down amongst the branches, and we drank Johnnie Walker, with slices of spicy wild boar. 'My constituents always find me a nice fat pig,' said the minister proudly.

All night, he held court. Most of his thoughts emerged in Sin-halese, although – for my benefit – there were magnanimous moments of English. It was a demanding performance, and I lost count of the platters of boar we ate and the bottles of whisky that sluiced it all away. No one else said much, and the local doctor was so silent that I wondered if he was mute. By one thirty, the political agents – two robed figures from Chilaw – were nuzzled together, fast asleep. By two, the minister had announced his intention to give chickens to all the fishermen and turn them into farmers. By three, he was finished. It had been a great display of Perera power, little changed, I imagined, in the last five hundred years.

A few weeks later, I travelled to the end of the Kalpitya peninsula, and to the outer edge of Portugal's defences.

At times, it was hard to remember what was being defended.

The peninsula was seabed-flat and bleached the colour of bone. There'd been no rain for months and the palm trees looked salt-burnt and crisp. The goats, if they hadn't been wearing huge A-shaped collars, would've eaten the entire landscape in a week. For the people that lived here, it was a difficult, windswept life. From the bus, I could peer down into homes made of branches and leaves. There was a girl drawing water from a well, a cupful at a time, and a pedlar nursing a basket of whiskery catfish. Everything was scribbled in barbed wire. Most of the locals were refugees from the war, deposited here on this briny drool of sand and shell, where no one would mind.

Perhaps it wasn't as inert as it seemed. Sri Lankans always insist that the people of 'Calpetty' are happy with their sky and their sand, and their freedom from possessions. The Ministry of Tourism says that, one day, fresh water will appear, and with it gardens and golf, and this will become the new Bali. No doubt the fishermen can't wait. Meanwhile, they have their beautiful brutality, and maybe that's what old Kalpitya is all about. Just as cinnamon needs cruelty, so the coconuts need their salt.

The road ended in a slum of fishing boats, with a view over Portugal Bay. An old carpenter, with Giacometti limbs and a huge crinkly head, was sawing the prow off a skiff. Most of the boats looked as if they'd been sawn up, or crushed, or dragged through a storm. It was surprising, the people and dogs still living in this wreckage. Occasionally, little rafts appeared, bobbing through the ooze. Known as *theppamas*, they were made of tree trunks stapled together with copper. None of this had changed much since Portuguese times, and nor had the stink. Kalpitya had been drying fish for centuries, and the air was as acrid as ever.

I was too late, however, for the Portuguese fort. The Dutch had pulled it all down and replaced it with something even more gruesome. Although it was still a naval base, the commandant was – thanks to one of Ravi's letters – happy to let me inside. As only the radio operator spoke English, he was assigned to show me around. In the first courtyard, we came across the skeleton of a blue whale, laid out like an air crash. Beyond it were Holland's formidable embrasures, gnawed away by the wind. There was little sign left of the Portuguese, except for a tiny Jesuit chapel – more like a consecrated bunker – and some deep tunnels leading under the ramparts. I was about to explore these further when I noticed that what lay ahead was not so much darkness as the hotly pulsing velvet of bats. For the gunners who'd lived here, it must have been a bewildering assignment, like a posting to the end of the Earth.

Portuguese Kalpitya may have lost its form, but its spirit lingers.

Across the peninsula, the Lusitanian god still holds sway, with all its miracles and angels and earthly visions. Few places in Sri Lanka have such a high concentration of Roman Catholics. It's said that the Portuguese found easy converts amongst the wretches fishing this coast. Under Buddhism, fishermen had always been reviled as killers, and were consigned to the most contemptible caste. They hadn't even been allowed to participate in the temple ceremonies. And so when, in 1543, the Franciscans appeared, offering processions, pilgrimages, holy water, feasts, fasts and prayers for the dead, the fishermen were converted in numbers.

I soon discovered that, at the heart of this, the fishiest outpost of the Catholic world, was Tallaivillu. There'd always been an aura of miracles about this place, if only because the grass all around glows an improbable green. This cool glade of colour and juicy shoots soon turns into casuarinas, and then vanishes into the sand. All it's ever needed is a visit from heaven, which, in the early 1600s, is what it got.

The arrival of St Anne cannot have come at a better time. The Portuguese conversion of Ceilão was not going well. The natives were proving reluctant neophytes; the puppet king, Dom João Dharmapala (1541–97), would be not only their first Catholic sovereign but also their last. After that, the Portuguese became more insistent, banning all other religions, an edict that soon turned to slaughter. Then came another order from Lisbon: 'In my kingdom, there is to be no pagoda, or if there is to be any, it is to be destroyed.' Every idol was to be shattered and all the pieces scattered. St Anne, it was hoped, would lend a more delicate touch.

The great stone cross, set up on the spot where she appeared, was still there, beneath the casuarinas. It was still a repository of hope, crowded with candles, and festooned with the clothes of the sick and the dying. Beyond it was a tiny uninhabited city of dormitories and wells, set out on streets of scalding sand. Twice a year, a sea of buses appears, the firepits are kindled and fifty thousand pilgrims fill up the cells. Some stay for days, hoping for a miracle. One family had decided to make it a fortnight, and were still camped under the trees.

'Even the sand is holy,' they told me, scooping it into pots.

'And do you always take a little home?'

'Of course,' they said. 'It protects us from scorpions.'

Amidst the dormitories, a little basilica appeared. Inside, all I could hear were the flies and the whisper of feet. Everything was stupendous and gilded, tumbling with angels and acanthus. It was a display of grandeur as much as piety, with more than a hint of overweening power. Even the scriptures were more coercive here, the paintings bloodier and the statues more muscular. Here was Rome at its most persuasive.

The focus of adoration was St Anne herself, now encased in glass. Some approached her on their bellies, others on their knees, singing as they crawled. According to a notice, the statue was 425 years old, which placed it somewhere between the Spanish Armada and the fall of the puppet king. But, it seemed, there was no end to the miracles she still performed. Women prayed for their children, or laid out pictures on the marble, with supplications for the dead, the diseased and the broken-hearted. Not everyone was Catholic. Buddhists, I discovered, also came here to pray for babies, as did the Tamils and Moors. The Portuguese would have liked that, the idea of their subjects, willing at last, happy to borrow a bit of the magic.

Back at the Pereras', Madame Chrysantha was off on a holy journey.

She told me she often travelled huge distances, out of devotion to God or her husband's parliamentary seat. Several times, she'd crossed the country, searching out Kalpitya's fishermen and bringing them home. Every year, she said, they set off during the monsoon and sailed round the island to fish the calmer waters of Trincomalee. It was a round trip of about a thousand miles. For Chrysantha, this was only ever a problem in election years. 'They're all gone, and my husband needs their vote, no? *Aiyo!* What are we to do? So I set out to fetch them. I take forty buses with me, and I bring them all back! That's democracy, no? I even went during the war. My children begged me not to, but I went all the same. Not even my husband would go. Ha! He was too *scared . . .*'

That afternoon, she was planning a more modest trip: a pilgrimage into the badlands. It was a five-hour drive, she said, through the bush to Madhu. 'Every month, I go and come. But Madhu is a very holy place, our own little Lourdes, no? The Blessed Virgin is four hundred years old, and she protects us from the wild animals. During the war, the terrorists tried to steal her, but the Holy Father took her and hid her in the forest. He is in direct communication with God, and lays on hands. Before you've even met him, he knows your telephone number and where you live! It is a miraculous thing, the Kingdom of God.'

After Kalpitya, the Cinnamon Road (as I'd come to think of it) ran sweeter and greener. The rice reappeared and, with it, the sensation of salad.

As far as Ravi was concerned, these were no longer his old battlefields, and I could feel his mood flatten. He was not like any war veteran I'd ever met before. I'd known some American

World War Two veterans, and they told me that the war had been the best time of their life but also the worst, often both at once. For Ravi, it was neither. War had simply filled his life, or at least twenty-two years of it, and he seemed to regard it with feelings that weren't readily identifiable as either pain or pleasure. Instead, it was a sort of normality, and this meant I could never be quite sure whether Ravi was untouchable or merely damaged. Later in this journey, I'd understand his war a little better, but, for the moment, it was enough to realise that, given the opportunity, he'd fight it all over again, with more maturity perhaps, with more humanity and more disobedience, but with the same determination.

As we re-entered the outer limits of everyday life, I sensed Ravi becoming uncharacteristically ordinary. He took a fatherly interest in the rice and the oxen, and the town that made nothing but knives. Although, in the weeks to come, I'd see plenty more of him and his son, Ravi never seemed quite the same again. Whereas once he'd hoped that the navy would need him again, as much as he needed it, now he was merely wistful. Perhaps, with the end of our trip, he'd finally come to terms with the foreignness of the past, and the difficult journey back.

At Negombo, there were goodbyes, and we went our separate ways.

Ravi knew I'd hate it here: a sickly city, of momentary pleasures.

Every sea-girt country has its watery Gomorrah, and Sri Lanka has Negombo.

Initially, I surprised myself by thinking it wasn't so bad. The beach was wide and demure, and, offshore, there was usually a regatta of skiffs, all billowing sails of liver-brown. Meanwhile, the fishermen were leery and lustrous and swaggered around like martinets, and, during the day, small glass cabinets were wheeled on to the sands, filled with prawns and patties, fried crabs, fish buns and other creatures up to their whiskers in batter. These snacks were always sold with a dash of faith. *MASH ALLAH*, read the signs, or *Power of Jesas Hot Hot Spacial Wada*. Here were the locals at their happiest, with a mouthful of fish, sweeping the sky with a flashy new kite.

But, in the midst of this community, there was a town that didn't really belong here at all. Everything seemed foreign: the cowboy bars, the neon, the fortified five-stars, the quad hire, the smoothies and the full-body massage. Some shops even had names like 'Tesco' and 'Asda', although they sold the same old trinkets, aged in urine or held together with pins. It was hard to imagine anyone savouring any of this. Many people come here merely to function – to marshal old flesh, to fill up and discharge. Negombo is one of the few places in the world where – they say – a European grandmother can feel so at ease hiring a young buck for the night (according to one NGO, there are five thousand beach boys around the island, serving women alone). Here, you can always tell the old hands, the ones who've been before. They look hooded and unsatisfied, and unwittingly cruel.

For reasons I can't remember, I'd booked into the St Lachlan Hotel. It included a baronial hall lined with faux panelling and hung with plastic antlers. This chilly Caledonian theme was clearly lost on the Negombo regulars, and so, for most of the time, I had it all to myself.

Negombo has a long and unhealthy tradition of depravity. In the ancient world, there was always a suggestion of *nagas*, or snakes. Then it was discovered that its thin, infertile soil was perfect for cinnamon, and that it grew better here than anywhere else. With that, foreigners settled on the place like a rash: first the Moors and then the Portuguese. It was hardly auspicious.

I've often wondered if Negombo wasn't the beginning of the end for the conquistadors. By the early 1600s, cinnamon money had rendered the colony eerily degenerate. The army was now recruiting nine-year-olds, and everyone else had a nest to feather. Almost nothing was sacred. In his extravagantly grim memoir, *Fatalidade Histórica da Ilha de Ceilão*, Ribeiro would note that 'the King's treasury is like an owl, from which all the birds pluck feathers . . .' Any ideals had long since withered. Back in 1514, the Pope had despatched the Portuguese to gather up souls. A century on, their expeditions were about nothing more godly than the pursuit of loot. In his secret report, the governor, Jerónimo de Azevedo, described a morally degraded world in the throes of collapse. 'We Portuguese', he wrote, 'are very bad Christians, without the fear of God . . .'

In their personal lives, too, the colonists were coming apart. The only women sent by Portugal were criminals and doxies, and sex was maddening society. A French visitor, Pyrard de Laval, noticed that wherever there were lots of Portuguese – like Negombo – all restraint was lost. 'Venereal disease is very prevalent,' he warned. 'As for the pox, it's no mark of shame here. They even boast of it . . .'

The sickly soil and insatiable vice – it all made me think.

Perhaps Negombo had never recovered from its past?

These days, it's no real secret what happens in Negombo, but as soon as you ask who's doing what, the industry vanishes in a puff of denial.

This wasn't always the case. There was once a time when people openly flaunted their abuse of children. Hadn't Prince Vijaya's crew deflowered a boy as soon as they'd landed? Westerners, too, have been surpringly careless in their pursuit of boys. Whilst Arthur C. Clarke's conduct may still be contentious, other visitors have been spectacularly indiscreet. The explorer, Raven-Hart, was a renowned homosexual quester, who canoed everywhere naked and always had boys at his side. Even Victorian generals could be surprisingly careless. In 1902, the commander of the British forces in Ceylon, Sir Hector 'Fighting Mac' MacDonald – hero of the Second Afghan War, the First Boer and Omdurman – was found cavorting in a railway carriage with four Sinhalese boys. As his biographer put it, 'Ceylon furnished MacDonald with a lethal combination of a military command that was inactive and uninteresting, and a community of boys who were interesting and very active.' Although he survived the scandal in Colombo, back in Europe he was publicly shamed and, in a Paris hotel, he took up a pistol and blew out his brains. In the long history of Ceylonese paedophilia, it was a rare act of regret.

But all that was before the crimes against children took an industrial turn.

In Colombo, I'd been to see a child protection charity, called PEACE. Its director, Mohammed Muhuruf, had been investigating abuse all his life. Although now Father Christmassy and affable, he'd never lost his fight. It was a constant battle to keep the abuse in the public eye. There was a chance I could help him, and so he agreed to sit me down and talk me through the facts. Yes, he said, I could go to Negombo, spend a few days and find out what I could. He might even find me a contact, but, before I went, there were things I needed to know.

'This is a beautiful country,' he began, 'but also poor. Poverty, you understand, explains most of this abuse. Maybe ninety per cent of Negombo's child prostitutes are from the squatter families, living round the edge. They're literally *broken* by poverty. But, you know, there are lots of reasons children get involved. Drugs. Alcohol. Maybe the mother is in the Middle East, working, and their *appa* is drinking all her wages. Or perhaps the child was raped, and is then ostracised by the community. So that's how it all starts. But it's a big problem, right? The government says there are only a thousand child prostitutes, but we don't think that's right. Most of the NGOs put it at about fifteen thousand. But one of them thinks even that's an underestimate, and that there're thirty-five thousand boys and five thousand girls. And that's just the children. If you count the over-eighteens, you may have another fifty thousand. Imagine that. It's an *industry*, no?'

'And is the problem getting worse?'

Mohammed nodded. 'Undoubtedly. The whole thing's maybe ten times bigger than it was in the eighties. It's partly the end of the war. We now see far more children from the north. But, you know, it's really about the internet. Sri Lankan children are all over it, particularly boys. They're now known for being easy and cheap, and a lot of European websites make no secret of what's to be had. Germany's bad, but also Britain and Sweden. And they've created hotspots of abuse, like Negombo or Mount Lavinia, Unawatuna and Matara ... It's like plague that we just can't see.

'And, make no mistake, the damage is incalculable. We can often help the girls – but not the boys. Maybe only five per cent of them ever recover. What's happened is too deeply embedded in their memory. Some, of course, die of AIDS (we get about sixty cases a year), but the rest become isolated, and they often miss out on school and turn to drugs and crime. You could say they're taking their revenge on society. But, to me, they live a nightmare. And do you think the paedophiles care? These are pretty sick people. To access the sort of websites that brought them here, they've often had to prove they can be trusted. And you know what that means? *Showing and telling.* Posting pictures of themselves with children. That's how desperate they are. You're going to need to be careful. You sure you still want to go?'

Not much, I thought, and yet here I was – three weeks later – in the huge boudoir of a fortified house. Next to me was a young Sinhalese, dressed only in shorts and a topknot, murmuring throatily and urging me on to the mattress.

The last few days had not gone well.

To begin with I'd thought it would be easy to track down the paedophiles, and that this was a trade still much on display. At that stage, I'd still harboured the heroic notion that, as a writer, I might make a difference, and that I'd soon be in amongst the pimps, drawing them in. But I had no idea how much had changed in recent times, and since the days of 'Fighting Mac' and Raven-Hart. But then nor had anyone else. These days, Sri Lanka can no longer find its paedophiles, and – even when it does – it doesn't know what to do. Each year, only a handful of offenders are ever brought to book, and the Westerners are usually deported. They are seldom charged. Negombo's most notorious paedophile, Victor Baumann, was allowed home in 1996, despite fifteen years of abuse (although, back in Switzerland, he was soon clapped in irons). At least, after that, Sri Lanka upgraded its punishments. Until then, the maximum fine for violating a child would barely have paid for a decent breakfast.

I'd spent hours trudging around in search of the trade. Beginning on the beaches, I walked for miles, but was never offered anything except seashells and cricket. I then turned to the hotels. Some people say they're all involved, hustling children up the service stairs. I limited myself to those I'd found in the press reports, but it was a forlorn venture. There were giant clams, boutique colours and towels sculpted into necking swans, but never anything else. The staff were always endearingly camp, but exuded innocence. I even told them that I was alone, unmarried, here to stay, and looking for a long-term let, but it brought not a flicker of vice. Not even trishaw drivers would be drawn. 'Where's the action?' I'd say. 'I want something different.' But there was nothing. A great and vile industry, it seemed, had utterly vanished.

At that point, my contact had appeared at the St Lachlan. Lalith – as I'll call him – had been hunting paedophiles for fifteen years. I never knew what his official job was, but he had a long green coat and a ratcatcher's bag. He said nothing when I told him about my efforts, but his yellow eyes smiled. 'You won't find them out there. No one's selling openly anymore, or not like they did. Right now, it's about networks: mobiles, SMS, internet groups, guest houses working together, private houses, membership only. The whole thing's disappeared, into the ether . . .'

'And where are the police in all this?'

'They often try and threaten me.'

'*You?* Why?'

'Say I'm bringing Sri Lanka into disrepute.'

'But this is a big political issue, isn't it?'

'Should be. But, you know, politics and this stuff get very mixed up. Around the country, there's at least fifty politicians accused of abuse. Yes, *fifty*. As for the rest, they just don't seem to see the problem. Look, let me show you something . . .'

From his bag, Lalith produced a thick, battered album.

'We took this off a Swedish guy, a few months back . . .'

I flicked through the pages: child after child, bewildered and naked.

'Bloody hell, Lalith, this is toxic stuff . . .'

'It's OK; it's OK. It's a very important book, part of the politics. How else do I make people understand what's going on? Last week, I took it to a seminar of MPs. "Look," I said, "the man who made this also made 290 hours of films. You want to know what's happening in your country?" Then I made them look at the pictures and a bit of the film, and one of the women was sick. Yes, this is a toxic business, if only people knew . . .'

'The private houses. Where are they?'

'We know a few. Big steel gates, and lots of security.'

'Any chance of a visit?'

Lalith hesitated, and then scrawled an address.

And that's how I found myself, a little later, with the boy with the topknot.

'I'm looking for a friend,' I'd said. 'I think he lives in this house.'

My heart had sunk; it was so easy, getting in through the gates. Perhaps the police were right, that there was nothing to these stories, or it was all a game of the mind? The house was airy and bland, and Topknot seemed like any other houseboy, chirpily eager. I guessed he was about eighteen, and he had great long thumbnails, like scoops. 'Come and have a look,' he'd said, as if we'd somehow find my fictional friend inside. I followed, breezily answering all his questions with lies. Yes, I was unmarried and alone.

Inside, we paused amongst the books and works of modern art. Topknot explained that the master was away, back in Europe. There were often people staying, from Germany and England. Did I want to see the bedrooms?

'Why not?' I said, and so we set off into the dark.

At that point, Topknot was suddenly transformed. Perhaps it was the sight of a huge empty bed. It was like watching Ariel morph into Caliban: one moment the dippy domestic and the next a hoary old pro. 'Feel my balls,' he gurgled, 'I want to suck you . . .'

It took a moment to get away. Unable to stem the torrent of concupiscence, I had to break for the path. But I'd seen enough, and heard too much. Even as I wriggled out through the gates, I was showered with offers, now squeaky and desperate. None of this proved much, but at least I'd satisfied myself of one thing: the worst things they say about Negombo are probably true. Although the touts may be virtual now, ancient vices still pollute this coast, as corrosive as ever.

After that, I gave up on my search and just wandered the beach. Once away from the neon, the sand widened and emptied, and I could feel my mind clearing and the Topknots and Calibans draining away. A few miles on, the air turned rich and pungent, and I found myself amongst cackling fishwives and the morning's catch. All sorts of sea monsters were laid out amongst the nets and, suddenly, this seemed normal, and I felt my happiness restored.

Beyond the fish, a set of vast ramparts rose up out of the sand. It was the old Portuguese fort, now a prison. I remember thinking how symmetrical that was: a building that had spent several hundred years keeping the Sinhalese out, and then the next few hundred keeping them in. Outside, there was a queue of girlfriends and babies, so at least that hadn't changed. I bought a slice of fried fish from the jailers' canteen and climbed up on the outer rampart to eat it. Amidst the clank of stone and metal, it wasn't hard to imagine the earlier incumbents.

From here, the Portuguese had sent out their last and most preposterous expeditions. They were preposterous for the sheer certainty of failure. It was one thing to send in raiding parties, in search of cinnamon. It was quite another, despatching armies to bring the highlands to heel. Several times the Portuguese would march on the breakaway kingdom. But it was always the same story, whether in 1594, 1630 or 1638. The Kandyans or Sitavakans would let them in, and then the invaders would wander the gorges, decimated by disease and showered with rocks from above. Weakened and demoralised, they'd then try to find their way out, and at that point the highlanders would descend in their thousands and cut them all up. In the last of these encounters, at Gannoruwa, only thirty-three men survived, out of six thousand.

The Portuguese had never been able to bear such losses. The army was already bulked out with criminals and children. For a while, it tried to fill its ranks with African slaves, and, to begin with, the *kaffres* (as they were called) were a daunting prospect and had the Asians cowering in terror.

But not even its slaves could save the colony. In the last decades of their rule, the Portuguese resorted to the only weapon left to them (and the one that everyone remembers), and that, of course, was terror. These are unedifying stories, of lopped hands and butchered infants. Even Jerónimo de Azevedo – who'd proclaimed the ungodliness of the Portuguese – was given to moments of cruelty. Babies, he discovered, conveyed a powerful message, and would often end up wriggling around on the end of his lance. 'Hark,' he'd say. 'How the young cocks crow!'

In all these tales, a theme emerges: a once-proud empire had run its course.

By 1656, a new enemy had reached Colombo.

For years, people have avoided Fort. Once, it was the heart and soul of this city, and became known as 'Colombo 1'. In its day, it had also been a hub of Asian trade. Ibn Battutah called by, and Ptolemy marked it on his map. Here, too, had been the biggest and strongest of the *fortalezas*, although all trace of the Portuguese has long since gone, leaving nothing but a name.

In time, this district would become my favourite part of Colombo, but when I first walked through it, I didn't know whether to be charmed or dismayed. The art deco was flaking away, the banks were sprouting trees and the great candy-striped department store, Cargills (*Est 1906*), was open but almost empty. Once, settlers had been able to buy anything here, from Christmas crackers to caviar, but now there were ghostly rectangles where the cabinets had been. It wasn't just a case of faded grandeur, Fort was showing all the signs of lifelessness.

On my return from Negombo, I stayed on York Street. My hotel, the Grand Oriental, was two thirds abandoned, its austere hospitality crammed up one end. Once, this was *the* place to stay. Chekhov was here for six days in 1890, on his way back from a penal colony on the island of Sakhalin, in Siberia. It must've been like a transfer to heaven from hell, and he'd settled down to a little philandering and a new story, 'Gusev'. A few years later, Mark Twain called by, but, being too late for a room, had to content himself with dinner. In fact, Bella Woolf once wrote that, if you hung around the lobby long enough, you'd meet everyone eventually. These days, I doubt she'd have wanted to linger. The waiters were wearing slightly comical sailor suits, and Tchaikovsky rumbled out of the gloom. The Grand Oriental Hotel's only redeeming feature was the view from the restaurant: a truly Victorian scene of ships and steam, and fleets of Chinese trawlers.

So what happened? How did this pearl of the Orient become its Havana? 'Terrorists,' people explained, 'and twenty-six years of civil war.' The bombs that crackled round the city had found a focus in Fort. On a single day in 1984, five devices exploded here. After that, no one could park and the district began to choke on its checkpoints. Business left first, followed by the government, and Fort began to die. The only people who'd stayed were the dealers in grog and old coins, and those too poor to move.

After the initial shock, I became more attuned to the signs of life slowly returning. Most of the checkpoints had been rolled away and gradually the colour was seeping back. Every day, the pavements were being torn up and new ones laid, and even a few swanky new bars had opened. Most surprising of all was an old military hospital, built in 1681. Once a mouldy police station, it had suddenly become the Covent Garden of the city, complete with bands and outdoor cafés. The surgeon's old quarters were now a spa and, where there was once cholera and dropsy, there was now a 'Ministry of Crab'.

I loved all this, but not everyone was happy. Some liked Fort just as it was, sleepily inert. Conservationists feared the arrival of render and plastic cannons, and film-makers would miss the dust and decay (even Duran Duran had once made a video here, in some decomposing tea-rooms). As for the drunks, they'd miss the oldest and sleaziest bars in Colombo, where – with arrack at twenty-five cents a shot – you can forget everything you've ever known, and perhaps a few things you didn't.

But, whatever happens here, I suspect the details won't change:

the gypsy with a cobra; the street cricket; the little khaki tuk-tuks marked *SL ARMY*. In this remarkable city of surprises, Fort will always be at the heart of the drama.

During the first half of 1656, Fort hosted an unforgettable contest.

On the inside were the Portuguese. Their entire city was compacted within the walls, including children, governors, elephants and Moors. Amidst the crush was the historian, João Ribeiro, then a captain in the army. He'd describe how, in the months to come, the besieged would eat not only all the elephants, but also their shoes. Most of the colony had already fallen, and it must have been obvious *Ceilão* was finished. For the Portuguese, there was nothing left to fight for but pride. They gave it everything they'd got.

Beyond the ramparts was the new enemy: the Dutch. They were a formidable foe, and seemed unstoppable as they spread like wildfire through the old Portuguese possessions. Holland had been a colony itself until 1580, and now it had possessions from South America to Java. The Dutch had even formed a company to gather up the booty, the *Verenigde Oostindische Compagnie*, or VOC. It would create the world's first private empire. During its first year of business, 1602, the company had set its sights on cinnamon, and – a generation on – VOC troops were at the gates of Fort.

The siege lasted seven months. It infuriated the Dutch that such a deadbeat nation could put up such a fight. But, eventually, on 12 May 1656, the Portuguese gave in. As Ribeiro put it, the survivors marched out of Fort, 'looking like dead people'. There were only seventy-three left, all scabby and fleshless.

It must have been puzzling for the Kandyans, the sight of

Europeans at each other's throats. King Rajasinha II had agreed to help the Dutch with their siege, in return for some forts on the coast. It was immediately apparent that the VOC had no intention of honouring the deal. Furious, the king set fire to the surrounding countryside and returned to Kandy. He may have got rid of one enemy, but he'd now acquired another, this time pale, mercantile, black clad and Protestant.

After reading that, I was always on the lookout for the last traces of the Portuguese. All I ever found was a belfry, called Caiman's Gate. It was barely more than a stump of stone, and had an unlovable history. For centuries, its bell had sounded every night as a signal for the drinking to end and the taverns to close. It wasn't much of a legacy. Sri Lanka's most trenchant historian, P. E. Peiris, always claimed that the Portuguese left behind nothing of any public utility, and only a 'veneer' of religion.

It was surprising how completely they'd disappeared. You'd have expected more in a city of de Silvas.

4

A State of Perpetual Vacation

And always it is the same; the slender palm trees lean-
ing over the white sand, the warm sun sparkling on
the waves as they break on the inshore reef, the outrigger fishing boats drawn up high on the beach. This
alone is real; the rest is but a dream from which I shall
presently awake.

> Arthur C. Clarke, *The Treasure*
> *of the Great Reef*, 1964

The chief trait of the original Dutch character, which
those in Ceylon retain, is their fondness of gin and
tobacco.

> Robert Percival, *An Account*
> *of the Island of Ceylon*, 1803

The way the Sinhalese describe their world, it has no heart, just a pulse around the edge. Nowhere is this pulse felt more strongly than along the south coast.

Much of the island's population lives down here and, looked at on Google Earth, it's like a long, thin town, stretching over a hundred miles. For Buddhists, this is also their 'Bible Belt', and the only part of the country that's never been conquered by Tamils. Further east, even English can sound rare and exotic. Perhaps all this is what makes the Sinhalese here different, an exaggerated version of themselves: richer, poorer, more impetuous and ebullient. Whatever they think elsewhere, they believe it here even more.

Then there are the tourists. Ever since the sixties, this has been an earthly paradise for Europeans: a long streak of sand and hotels. Nowadays, almost a million people are packing themselves in, year after year. It might be a matter of physics. Arthur C. Clarke used to insist that the Earth's gravitational pull was stronger here than anywhere else.

Being paradise, it's easy to forget the world beyond. Contentment seems to seep amongst the tourists like gas. Even the war, only a few hundred miles to the north, was happily overlooked. A friend once told me that this had been the most relaxing holiday he'd ever taken, 'although we did hear a bomb whilst sitting by the pool.' Not even the lotus-eaters were so becalmed. Meanwhile, at the height of the fighting, in 2007, the World Travel Awards nominated Sri Lanka as 'Asia's leading destination'. Such is the south coast and its siren-like charm.

Several times, I found myself back here. Once, I took the new Chinese motorway that swept emptily out through the hills. At four pounds a go, this was too luxurious for most Sri Lankans and so they'd battle it out on the coast road, and – usually – I'd join them. Here, sand and tarmac ran endlessly in parallel, and squashed between them was a rich filling of tower blocks and villas and hot little towns. Somehow, I never found all this quite as calming as everyone else.

Far better was the day I took the train. I decided to leapfrog most of paradise and head straight for Ambalangoda.

The train wobbled out of Colombo and was soon amongst sawmills. Pencil-scented breezes gushed in through the windows and at last the carriage began to cool. The Marxists had worked through the woodwork, and covered everything in stickers. The man next to me was a healer, with a briefcase of unguents and stones. He'd said nothing until a man appeared out in the sawdust, beating a dog.

'An unfortunate sight, no? But our dogs here are dirty.'

'Can't they be culled?'

The healer winced. 'Killed? That would be against our beliefs.'

I changed the subject. 'Tell me about your cures.'

Over the next hundred miles, a curious picture emerged of life in the south. Ginger is the best cure for colds, and wild lily for baldness. Everything has its place, and so do people. A man must never appear before his superior with his hair down, or with his sarong drawn up. There are omens everywhere. If you hear a gecko croak, you shouldn't leave home. Nor should you swim at twilight. Those who become possessed need to make offerings of *puttu*, or fried food, and rooster's blood. The people of Colombo are horrified by the magicians down here, but wouldn't use anyone else.

I decided on Ambalangoda because I'd read about the masks. In Sri Lanka, nothing reveals a man's thoughts quite like his mask.

I was barely out of the station before I was enveloped in masquerade. Colourful, gurning faces were piled up on stalls and in showrooms, and dangled over the street. Tourists tend to think of this as kitsch, but Ambalangoda has always been a place to stock up on charms or a brace of puppets. These caricatures are not merely part of a drama but intrude on reality, reshaping the present. Some of them I recognised: the Kandyan soldier, his face all bloody and slashed; the frog-eyed village clerk (a notorious pervert); and then all the Punches and Judys of everyday life. Deceit is a common theme of the tales that accompany these masks, and the violence is bouncy and the lust catastrophic. Punch, here, isn't just a drunk and a wife-beater but a despoiler of youth, and to own him or watch him is to have your revenge.

One of these places described itself as a museum, and – for a few rupees – I was given a tour of the demons. The woman who showed me around was skinny and watchful and affected detachment. 'Some people still believe in magic,' she said tentatively, and then we were in amongst the masks of *sanni*. She told me there are eighteen devils in all, representing every condition from joint pain to madness. They were foul, snaggle-toothed imps, tufted with oily-black hair and resplendent with disease. At an exorcism ceremony – or *sanni yakuma* – the relevant devil would be summoned, and a person wearing his mask would be soothed and berated, and finally evicted. If I wanted a mask, said my guide, there was a shop at the end.

Somehow, this amused me, the prospect of tourists taking Miss Smallpox home, or perhaps her colleague, *Deva Sanniya*, the Spirit of Cholera.

Back on the train, it was midday and my carriage was full of foreigners. It was hard to tell who was on holiday and who'd settled. In the weeks to come, I'd realise that even those who'd lived here for years still looked like tourists. They were the lotus-eaters who'd forgotten to go home, and whose lives were now moving along at holiday pace.

Amongst the settlers, there was never much work. Some were retired and had sunk their pensions in a plot of sand. Others painted, or dabbled in hotels. A few of them wrote or maintained websites, but their prose was so insistently happy that I began to wonder if, amidst the pleasure, there wasn't a hint of anxiety. Perhaps it was only safe to be happy here, and in a state of perpetual vacation.

The English had a peculiar way of surviving all this, reverting to type. Never good at blending in, they'd created their own Little England, criss-crossed with social divides. At one end, around Hikkaduwa and Bentota, there was the old regime, the free spirits who'd never moved on. Things got posher to the east, they said, amongst the 'arts and crafts' clique. What they meant, of course, was Galle, and it was true – the English there were in a constant state of either partying or poetry. Meanwhile, the smart money was further on still, in Tangalle, snapping up headlands or a pad with a beach. I once met one of the new locals, with an accent as fruity and fresh as the Fourth of June. 'Half of Gloucestershire's here,' he told me. 'Haven't you noticed all the black Labs?'

Quite what the Sinhalese made of all this was anyone's guess. The original word for foreigners was *parangi*, a Persian term, suggestive of disfigurement and syphilis. Even now, it was rumoured that some Sinhalese would wipe down the chairs after a white man's visit, and clear away the cutlery in gloves. But was that really likely? *Suddahs* (or 'whites') and the Sinhalese had been on unhygienic terms for centuries. In the early 1800s, it was the proud boast of Sinhalese ladies to claim that their daughter had lain with a white man. 'Even women of the highest rank,' wrote Percival, 'do not think themselves degraded by having connexion with Europeans.'

Since then, of course, much has changed. Sri Lankans have come to realise that the *suddah* has often brought industry to their island but seldom wealth. These days, he's only a figure of economic salvation amongst the beach boys and the chronically desperate. To an old goat like the writer Raven-Hart, this came as something of a shock. During his last months in Ceylon, in 1963, he concluded that, to the Sinhalese, the white man's presence was now a matter of complete indifference, and that they hardly ever gave him a thought. I wonder about that. Although people didn't often ask me questions, here are a few:

'What kind of snakes do you have in England?'

'Does snow hurt?'

'Is it true you always choose your own wife?'

'Do the palms of your hands ever go dark in the sun?'

After a while, the never-ending village that ran alongside the track began to fall apart. Some of the houses had been merely stripped of woodwork and wiring, and left gaping at the sea. Others had undergone a more fundamental change, with enormous pressure having been applied to the walls and their entire contents sucked out through the holes. A few had been torn away altogether, leaving only a concrete outline and a few stubs of plumbing. Everyone remembers the moment this happened: 9:33 a.m. on 26 December 2004.

Although it had been nine years since the tsunami, long stretches of the foreshore still looked crushed and scattered, and rinsed of life. In places, whole villages had gone, only to be replaced by a sprawl of graves. Occasionally, I spotted boats, way inland, shipwrecked in the paddy. People would describe how, just before the wave hit, the ocean seemed to empty and a great wet desert appeared. Then, very soon, the water returned, now like a ridge across the horizon. Until this moment, it had been travelling at over 600 mph, but as it reached the shallows it rose and strengthened, gathering up seabed, beaches, foreshore, roads, villages and rice. From above, it must have seemed as if the coconut palms were fleeing, as they filed out to sea, whilst the coastline withered away.

Even up here on the tracks, the great slab of water had smashed its way through, now the length of the country and as high as a house. Entombed within it were cars, tuk-tuks, buffaloes, houses, the young, the old, pieces of fishing boat, toilets, jagged sheets of iron and whole restaurants complete with all their customers, sitting down to breakfast. If the water hadn't killed people, the flotsam would. Some of it, like the boats, was hurled up to two miles inland. It was a day of superlatives, but with nothing to celebrate. One of our planet's greatest earthquakes, centred just off Sumatra, had unleashed energy 550 million times greater than the Hiroshima bomb. The planet itself had vibrated by a centimetre, and, within ninety minutes, the shock waves had hit Sri Lanka, leaving it with the deadliest day in its history. Some thirty-five thousand had died in areas under government control, together with another nineteen thousand in the rebel-held north.

The jungle, I realised, had long since recovered, and was, once again, bunching up against the track. The human labyrinth would take longer to recover. On the coast ahead, I'd get used to the sight of hollowed-out towns and gaping homes. It wasn't uncommon – particularly on the east coast – to see people still living under tarpaulins, or in shacks made of wreckage. In places, long tracts of shoreline could seem utterly abandoned, as if everything had been scraped away. Over half a million people had been displaced, hundreds of wells had been contaminated with salt and thousands of acres of paddy would lie sterile for years.

Nothing had been spared, not even the train. On that day, it had been 'The Queen of the Seas' chuntering up the coast. At Seenigama, the great scarp of seawater had punched its way through the trees and the helpless train was whisked around like a long steel whip. On board, there were 1,700 passengers, and most of them had survived this insult. They climbed on the roof, or took shelter on the landward side. But then, half an hour later, came a second wave, bigger than the first. It smashed the train against the trees, crushing those behind it, and then the water roared in through the windows. The doors couldn't be opened and people drowned on the ceiling and under the seats. For a long time, no one would know what had become of the train, and it took the rescuers hours to locate it. When they did, they found only a few dozen survivors, and only nine hundred bodies were ever officially recovered. The rest had been carted away by their relatives, or washed out to sea.

I asked the guard what had become of the train.

'Well, we got it all going again. It might even be this one.'

A week later, I took a taxi back to Seenigama to see a man called Kushil Gunasekera.

It had always fascinated me, his variant of grief. I'd already got used to the idea that, for many Sri Lankans, the tsunami was far too big to mourn. People would tell me that they'd lost a spouse, or perhaps their children, but it was always done with a sense of detachment, as if there'd been one life before the tsunami but now there was this one, quite different. The dead were 'lost' and had gone to the 'Land of the Sands', and that was that. Of course, there'd been a bereavement process, but it was a concentrated matter: fifty days of gruelling despair, and then the curious calm. Only the Europeans made their sadness so publicly protracted. It was said that, in Galle, there was only one annual gathering to commemorate the dead, and that was the Gloucestershire lot. Amidst such serenity, it must have looked like a meeting of the hunt.

For Kushil, too, the old world had been lost, and yet he'd somehow replaced it with one of holy design. From it all, he'd emerged with his own tiny philanthropic empire, known as the Foundation of Goodness. We'd been introduced in Colombo through my cricketing contacts, and one day I'd been to see him in his office, which was dominated by a little Buddha twinkling with coloured lights. Kushil was never quite what I'd expected; he had flawless skin, fluffy white hair and a certain boyish vulnerability of expression that was wholly misleading. For a while, we'd chatted happily about the cricket memorabilia in which he was nested.

In an earlier life, he'd been an agent, managing – amongst others – the great Muralitharan.

Kushil always seemed unsurprised at the way things had turned out. In 1999, he'd abandoned cricket and had returned to Seenigama and the family estate to look after his people. Not even the tsunami had surprised him particularly, nor the destruction of everything he'd owned. There was no memorial to that day, I noticed, except a line near the roof, showing the height of the water. Grief hadn't featured in the task ahead. Kushil's foundation had rebuilt over a thousand homes, with celebrities and cricket clubs picking up the bills. Bryan Adams had contributed a swimming pool, and the MCC a computer centre. Surrey had even built a cricket club just like itself, which was now busily converting orphans into stars. 'So you see,' said Kushil, 'we have turned this setback into a blessing . . .'

It still puzzled me, the air of detachment. I even began to wonder if Kushil had been here at all when the big wave struck. But then, as I got to know him better, he told me exactly how it was.

'At 9:33, people came running inland to say the sea is coming. I didn't know what they meant, but we ran up through the back roads, picking up kids as we went. Then – *aiyo!* – we came to a barbed-wire fence and were caught by the wave. Afterwards, the village was covered in bodies. Everywhere. Over seven thousand people died on this little bit of coast, including a hundred and twenty-five in this village. We try not to dwell on that day, but it's not easy. There were tough choices to be made. When everything's going crazy, who do you save: the mother or the child?'

Further up the track, Galle had been restored. Almost everything was back where it should be; the clutter of smashed-up buses had been cleared away and the station rebuilt. Even the cricket pitch had been pampered back to life, and was now glossy and smooth like pea-green satin. Only the fort had survived the water intact, high on its promontory, overlooking the sea. Elsewhere, across the town, seven thousand had died.

Beyond the cricket pitch, the ramparts rose up like cliffs, and I found a little archway, with a passage leading inside. This wasn't like any of the other forts I'd seen – odourless and defeated. Galle was a muscular structure, big enough to deflect a tsunami, and encompassing eighty-nine acres of smells and sounds, and its own little town. I soon discovered that the best time to walk the walls was at dawn, when the shadows were still cool and damp, and the sea was the colour of knives. Whenever the townspeople clambered up on to their walls, they'd stare out over the ocean, as if they'd never seen it before. But, most mornings, there was hardly anyone around except soldiers – or perhaps the occasional newly-weds, trailing a cortege of hairdressers and photographers, and clutched together in improbable embraces.

The fort-dwellers loved telling stories about their walls. It was widely believed that there was still enough gunpowder hidden away to send the whole thing sizzling off into space. One of the tour guides also told me that the great coral blocks had been cut by Mozambican slaves so fierce they'd had to be muzzled to stop them eating their masters. She said that their descendants had survived until 1990, living like cavemen in the western ramparts. But, however tall these stories sounded, Captain Ribeiro's were always better. He'd reported that, in 1640, the Portuguese had fought so hard to retain the fort that, afterwards, it had taken the Africans three days to heave all their bodies into pits. Even then, it was all in vain. By the time the smoke had cleared, the fort was Dutch.

That, then, is why every morning felt like Holland. If I was quick, I could manage all fourteen bastions before breakfast. Most of them still had clunky, Teutonic names – like Zwart, Clippenberg and Akersloot – and above the archway was the VOC's coat of arms, dated 1697. It was obvious that, whatever had stood here before, the Dutch had smothered it in breastworks and the latest contraptions. There were iron runners for guns, giant pepperpots where the sentries had stood and gunpowder stores like huge strongboxes, chipped out of stone. I even found a siege-proof sewer, which – twice a day – was flushed by the tide.

The Dutch worked hard to make all this theirs.

It hadn't been easy. To begin with, they tried to win over the Kandyans with gifts. In 1602, they presented the king with a few baubles and two musicians. It may not seem like much, but the king was charmed. In contemporary portraits, Vimala Dharma Suriya is seen in a goatee beard, puffed breeches and a lace ruff. The Portuguese had already tried to baptise him and had given him the title 'Dom Juan de Austria' (although he had no idea what Austria was). The Dutch, however, were more to his liking, and the king gave their ambassador an umbrella, and promised to rename the island 'New Flanders'.

A second meeting was arranged with rather less success. This time the parties met in Batticaloa. Unfortunately, the Dutch representative, Vice-Admiral Sebalt de Weert, got a little tipsy during this encounter and made a joke about the king's wife. It may not have been his best quip but it was certainly his last. 'Bind that dog!' ('*Bandapan me balla!*') roared the king. With that, Kandyan swords slashed the admiral apart, and – just for good measure – his forty-seven companions were butchered too. Only one man was spared (although a few escaped), and the king sent him back to his ship with a note, in faltering Portuguese: *WHO*

DRINKS WINE IS NOT GOOD. GOD DOES JUSTICE. IF YOU WANT PEACE, PEACE. IF YOU WANT WAR, WAR.

The Dutch wisely overlooked the incident.

After that, however, they were slightly less reliant on charm and flexed a little muscle. The Kandyans recognised a massacre-in-the-making and agreed a truce. But the VOC had no intention of sharing its conquests, and so, in 1656, King Rajasinha set fire to the coast and returned to Kandy. The Dutch, however, couldn't afford another war, and so they resorted to gifts. It's surprising the things that will buy off trouble. One list of presents includes 'Two or three fine Persian horses and Persian goods, some tea, porcelain, and Indian preserves'. It was also noted that the king liked 'pictures, paintings, portraits, representations of battle scenes, and snuff'.

But the Dutch knew that chutney alone wouldn't save the empire. Forts were needed – just in case. And that, of course, explains the magnificence of Galle.

There was still a tiny Dutch town within the ramparts.

Everything was there, just as it had been, on a grid of shaded streets. It was almost as if a little period of history – the *Hollandse Tijul* – had been cut out and lovingly preserved. The old hospital may have been crumbling away, but the *kerk* (church) was still lofty and polished and proclaiming reform. Inside were the great and the good, remembered in extravagant tableaux of skulls and bones: proctors, treasurers, *schippersen*, the master of the orphanage, the *kerkmeester* and the *kolonel*. Their homes too – the big, lumpy cottages of pantiles and pillars – would have been just as they remembered them, except now with a stranger asleep on the *stoep*.

Not even the VOC's warehouses had changed much since 1669. They were still the huge red barns they'd always been, yawning in the heat. For a few rupees, I could wander in amongst the contents: bits of shipwreck, huge swords like industrial skewers, tobacco boxes, Bellarmine jars and brass spittoons (the Dutch, it's said, were keen on expectoration, and every house had deployed 'spitting pots for the women'). I remember thinking how functional it all looked, as if it wasn't finesse that mattered, only wealth.

Most of these things could still be bought, somewhere round the fort. The hawkers, who were mostly Muslim, always had the odd *antiek* up their sleeve, and perhaps a box of *compagnie* coins. Meanwhile, in the shops, you could buy anything you wanted, as long as it was Georgian. Usually, it was a matter of snuffers or rusty green spoons, but occasionally more impressive bits of the past would loom up out of the dust, like a palanquin, perhaps, complete with several centuries of worm. It was funny to think of all that furniture, finally returning to Europe. Until the arrival of the Dutch, the Sinhalese had never known chairs like this, upright and bony and totally alien to their idea of repose. Not even the British had liked this stuff ('heavy and clumsy', grumbled a new arrival in 1803), and now here were the tourists, ready to take it home.

Elswhere, people still enjoyed their little Dutch ways. Up on the ramparts, ladies were making lace, and, over in the courts, there wcre lawyers, blasting away with Roman law. A few treats, too, had survived. Until recently, the old *bakkerij* on Pedlar Street had been popping out over a thousand loaves a day from its Napoleonic oven. Even now, I could have sunk my face into a plate of sugary *poffertjesen* (fritters) or *breudher* (a cake of heart-stopping butteriness that's served with a slab of Edam). These days, such feats of ancient gluttony lack only wenches and grog. The Sinhalese had never kept pace with Dutch drinking. 'Wine,' they'd say, 'is as natural to white men as milk to children.' As for the wenches, there was once a time when there were three hundred *soldaten* stationed in Galle, and 'no dearth of places of ill repute'. All that had gone, and now – even at its most lively – the fort was sleepily Islamic.

During that first visit, I stayed in the old officers' mess, dating from the 1680s. It was now the Amangalla Hotel, although I still had a soldiery number daubed on my door. Downstairs was a picture of a European lady in a chaise, being lowered over the side of a ship into a lighter below. At dusk, I'd sit in an enormous arched dining room, which – with its polished hardwood floors and towering candelabras – felt like a scene from a Rembrandt. Sipping gin and lime, it was tempting to imagine that evenings had been just like this for the *officieren*, three hundred years before. A little corner of Old Holland had been perfectly recreated, and now all that was missing was the Dutch themselves.

Although I never found the Dutch in Galle, elsewhere I'd often meet their descendants.

Wherever they were, they were known as the 'Burghers'. Some I met in England; white migrants, but with Asia coursing through their veins. Although there were those who still thought of Ceylon as their homeland, they'd never admit it. Public displays of nostalgia were now frowned on, even if their families had lived there hundreds of years. In this new, diminished role, they were left with nothing but powdery photographs and an ever-shrinking reservoir of stories. One man – now living in Fulham – told me how his mother had given his milk tooth to a squirrel (so that the others would grow strong and even), and how she'd held a party when he had his first shave. The Sinhalese had called them the *natumarayo*, because they were always dancing. But, amongst Burghers, what had really mattered was how Dutch you were. The highlight of the year was always Queen Juliana's birthday, when they'd all rush off to the union for a hearty rendition of '*Het Lieve Vaderland*', and a feast of cake and curry.

'It all seems a long time ago,' said the Fulham Burgher.

'Do you still feel foreign?' I asked. 'Even here?'

'We're always foreign, wherever we go.'

Other Burghers I met in Sri Lanka. One was a tour guide, although everyone assumed he was a missionary. Another worked for a human-rights NGO and was always ducking the political shrapnel. Then there was a hotelier from Kalpitya, whose brother had once stolen a helicopter and set off on a one-man mission against the Tamil Tigers and was never seen again.

Burgher history, I realised, was full of people like this. There were the De Heers, the Loos, the Brohiers, who were descended from Norman Huguenots, and Willy Gratiae, who collected snakes. In the arts, Lionel Wendt's films often fell eccentrically silent, and Carl Muller's novels explored new levels of depravity. Then there was Lyn Ludowyck, who sang obscure pieces from operas that no one had ever heard of, and Jessica Cantley, whose love life was unnecessarily complicated and who was once blasted with a shotgun during a game of croquet. Meanwhile, of all the drunks, the most famous was an Ondaatje, whose rages were exquisitely – and often painfully – portrayed by his son, Michael, in a memoir, *Running in the Family*. Perhaps Burghers were always in the wrong place at the wrong time, victims of geography and impulse. In another memorable incident, Wilfred Batholomeusz was shot whilst out hunting. It seems his friends had mistaken him for a wild boar.

The Burghers had always liked Galle. It was a town in their own image, neither truly Asian nor truly European. The British had never known what to make of them. Burghers were too white to be natives, and yet too native to be whites. Even into the 1870s, they were considered half-breeds and excluded from the clubs. Seventy years earlier, Captain Percival had written of his disgust at the sight of these Dutchmen, weirdly mutated by their time out east. The men wore robes and were always unwashed and half-cut. As for the women, they'd spent too much time amongst their slaves and had become cruel and coarse. The British had never seen such gin or so many rats, and it would take their terriers weeks to flush out the towns.

But now, like the rats, the Burghers were mostly gone. Modern times hadn't suited them, especially the socialism and the bodies in the forest. But it was the riots that really horrified them, and the thought that they would be next. Unlike the Boers out in the veldt, however, they had no retreat. Most fled to Australia, although a few went west. For many, it's been a restless existence. Some, like Sir Christopher Ondaatje, Michael's brother, have never quite settled. He keeps making his fortune and then moving on. Maybe the man from Fulham was right, and that it's now the Dutchman's lot to be forever foreign.

If you were to design a child's perfect holiday, it would involve beaches, a castle, a little magic, something gruesome and a few monsters – and, of course, that, broadly speaking, describes Galle.

Of all my visits, easily the best was with my family. My wife and daughter, Lucy, had flown out to join me, and, for a few days, we'd settled in the fort. Having a child there gave the place a startling new quality of make-believe. As I rushed around trying to show her everything, I suddenly realised how improbable it all was: the musical bread vans; the George VI pillar boxes draped in monkeys; a hearse wearing a white satin skirt; the rain trees, which shrivelled at night and then opened in the morning with their own tiny burst of wintry weather. It was hard to know what Lucy made of it, aged eight. Perhaps, to the Willy-Wonka-ed imagination, all this was normal, but I like to think the signs of enchantment were there.

We stayed in a Dutch mansion, which had once been the printer's. It had sloping floors and a crooked staircase, and the front door could only be opened with a giant, three-pound key. Every morning the macaques came pattering over the roof, and, in the lanes, pedlars appeared. Our landlord said there were more than a hundred of them, and each day they'd come wheeling through the fort, selling everything from underpants to milk. Everyone had his own squawk: *'Kiri! Malu!'* ('Milk! Fish!') Some of the bicycles were festooned with goods, but others were mounted with entire glass cabinets, stacked with samosas and cakes. The fishman, meanwhile, had an enormous pair of scales welded to his bike, so that, whenever he appeared, he looked like Justice on wheels.

After that, things would settle down again, like the town in 'Sleeping Beauty'. For a while, we tried to work out how far we'd travelled back in time, and eventually – on the basis of the cars – decided on 1948. It was surprising the things you could find in the heat, with no one around. I particularly remember a heap of tuk-tuks, now fossilised with rust and riddled with bullets. In such an imponderable place, it would have been slightly less surprising to find a literary festival. Galle had often had them, and, although they'd stalled recently, they'd always been rich in celebrity and incident. Gore Vidal had been memorably testy, especially when all his luggage was lost and didn't turn up for a week. It wasn't much better for Vikram Seth, who'd been mistaken for a Tamil and arrested for sketching a crow.

At teatime, the spell would ease and Galle would come squawking back to life. An ancient bus appeared and took away all the day's convicts, each with a little picnic of rice. Then there'd be howls of rage from under the mara tree as three interlocking games of cricket battled for its shade. At that point, everything would turn a dusty, antique yellow. The English had their parties, and the Moors had their prayers. It was time to head for the walls.

By sunset, everyone was up here: monks, clerics, hawkers, Labradors, and the newly-weds, still looking magnificently dangerous in their sequinned doublets and daggers. It was like a curtain call, bringing a long, hot pantomime to an eerie end. Later, the exorcists would get to work, but for now it was enough to trail a kite or just watch the sun as it slithered deliciously into the sea. For a few rupees, the boys on Flag Rock could be persuaded to plunge off the rampart. I wondered if – just for a moment – they imagined they were birds, until the Indian Ocean rose up and smacked them in the face. Everyone in this scene seemed to be nursing some sort of fantasy. Once, one of the spectators told me that, during the tsunami, the sea had rolled back and a Grand Canyon appeared.

And had he seen that himself, I asked.

'No,' he conceded, with a wobbly smile. 'I live in Toronto now.'

Our last day, we hired a boatman and set off up the Kepu Ela.

It would have been a quaint day on the river, but for the monsters. Like Ratty and Mole, we set off with sandwiches and flasks, and without any idea of where we were going or who might eat us. For a while, it all looked reassuringly familiar, even to Lucy; the reeds, the doves, the herons in their tatty frockcoats, and the kingfishers shimmering past like darts. But then we turned up a side-channel and Asia reappeared in a glorious blaze of rice. Suddenly, there was a huge obsidian eye on the gunwale, and the sound of rapid grunty breath. We all jumped, and the boatman giggled. 'Buffalo!' he grinned, and we flopped back into our seats. After that, the real monsters didn't seem so bad, even though they were draped about our heads. Every old tree had its dragons, some as long as Lucy. But, despite their weaponry – wire-cutter jaws, chain mail and a handful of daggers – these *kabaragoyas*, or water monitors, were unnervingly harmless. After millions of years of looking like dinosaurs, they'd now settled down to a life-long siesta.

For hours, we bobbed through the rice. Once, we came to a small wooden farm, and half a dozen children came slithering down the mudbank to proclaim their surprise. We were now in cinnamon country, said the boatman. The channels turned into more channels, and soon we were pleasantly lost. On the map, this watery network covers the coast like plaid, and it was all begun by the Dutch. Out there was an entire system that had once gushed spices and wealth. Land like this had made Rotterdam exorbitantly rich. Investors could have expected a forty-per-cent return on their stake, and – even by 1670 – the VOC was the richest company in the world. It owned two hundred ships and a private army of over thirty thousand men, and would cover its land in canals. Sri Lankans often told me Holland had left them with nothing (except cake and law). But the truth was perhaps too big to see. Here on the littoral, this was the gift of the Dutch: the landscape.

Miraculously, at dusk, we tumbled out where we'd started, in

Galle. It was the end of an interlude. Lucy and Jayne flew home happy, or at least bewitched.

Meanwhile, to the east, Sri Lanka's story had taken an ugly turn.

Returning to my own travels, I went next to Matara. I'd been hoping to find a giant elephant house but ended up with a revolt against the modern age, and its prophet, martyred on the golf links.

The elephant idea was always slightly half-baked. For this, I blame Philippus Baldaeus, a contemporary of Vermeer, from Delft. In 1655, he'd turned up in Jaffna as a missionary. The Tamils weren't much impressed with his Calvinism (they already had their hands full with a million gods, and the Virgin Mary), but he did keep a journal. It was published in English as *A True and Exact Description of the Moft Celebrated Eaft-India Coafts of Malabar & Coromandel and also the Isle of Ceylon*, and it makes grisly reading, a sort of X-rated guide to the island's atrocities. But Baldaeus also describes a great round-up of elephants, here on the coast. First they were maddened with thirst, and then they were driven – up to a hundred at a time – into pens. But then, even better, they were brought to Matara and sent to school.

I had an idea that this college of elephants was now the government guest house. It was one of the few buildings left within the ramparts, a vast bungalow built out of plaster and rocks. A waiter let me wander through the rooms and out to the laundry. Although it all looked slightly bulldozed, it was far too pokey for ninety-five elephants. I decided to try reception. The receptionist listened carefully as I explained about the hunt and the Dutch, the thirst, the stables, the massive walls and the exports to India. When I'd finished, he looked at me sadly and smiled.

'No, sir, I am sorry. We don't keep elephants here.'

The revolt is harder to explain, having once been so vivid.

There'd been two uprisings here in Matara, and spreading out along the coast. During the first, in 1971, the bodies had turned up everywhere: by the roadside, in the trees, or out on the beach. They were seldom buried, although sometimes they'd be burnt. The human bonfire became a common sight. Everyone knew who the rebels were. Most were local Sinhalese boys, who'd run away to join the People's Liberation Front (*Janatha Vimukthi Peramuna*) or JVP. Angry and unemployed, they'd resorted to Marx. Their revolt was based on the concept of excision; they were constantly obstructed by the Elite and only bloodshed would cut them free. *IT'S BETTER TO DIE THAN TO KNEEL!* ran their slogans. Their first bombs had been made out of condensed-milk tins, but soon a more assertive massacre was under way. By April, whole areas had fallen under their control, at least by night. At that stage, it was politicians dangling in the trees.

During that first uprising, Colombo had panicked and sent its soldiers out into the forests. The army hadn't seen service since World War Two, and was dangerously jumpy. In the round-up that followed, it had scooped up anyone unruly: rebels and troublemakers, and perhaps the odd junkie and pimp. At the same time, an old Victorian sanitation law, allowing the police to cremate bodies before an inquest, had been revived. Under government licence, anybody could now disappear – and between ten and fifteen thousand people had done so, mostly boys in their teens.

Whilst this may not have been the Massacre of the Innocents,

Sri Lanka has never been the same from that moment on. It was the beginning of the great amnesia, a time when whole sections of society could vanish without a single memorial, prosecution or inquiry. These days, the uprising is hardly even mentioned. I tried to look for it once, amongst some history books for children, but there was nothing. A whole chunk of Sri Lanka's story had almost vanished.

The JVP, on the other hand, were still around. I'd once been to one of their rallies. They weren't so much Marxists as a cult. Around the stadium, everyone had worn Che Guevara T-shirts, and most of the men were sporting berets and wispy beards. I'd met a doctor, a cook and a customs officer, who'd all called me 'Comrade' and described their vision of a Sri Lankan Cuba. I wasn't sure what they made of me, but at least I wasn't a spy. That day, the spies were dressed as groundsmen, about fifty of them, clustered in the shadows. 'Special forces,' whispered the doctor, 'just waiting for trouble.'

I asked what it would be like, the new Cuba.

'We'd root out imperialism . . .'

'Get rid of all Western ideas . . .'

'Close down the tea plantations . . .'

'Bring back self-sufficiency . . .'

'Have education like Cuba's . . .'

'And free housing . . .'

'Free health care . . .'

'And firing squads?'

The doctor frowned. 'No, maybe not that . . .'

'But you'd use violence?'

'Last time we had no choice.'

'And if people aren't ready for your revolution?'

It was the cook who answered this:

'Sometimes, Comrade, you need to root out evil.'

Once, such ideas were common currency in Matara. Now, looking round, it seemed like any other great Sri Lankan town, a whirl of words and peel and gnashing metal. It's hard to think of a place less like Havana, and yet, by 1987, it was ready for its second revolution. It had even had its own Che Guevara, who'd copied the original in almost every whisker. There was only one difference: his name. It would evoke the local kingdom of Ruhuna, a place synonymous with Sinhalese resistance and the crushing of the Tamils. He was Rohana Wijeweera.

Although none of this had sounded very Cuban, Matara was hooked. The idea of Sinhalese destiny had never lost its appeal, and Wijeweera promised a return to the golden age. Tea would be replaced with pre-colonial crops; every building over two storeys high would be pulled down; Sri Lanka would return to a life of ascetic simplicity, centred on 'tank, temple and paddy'. Even the communists were outraged, and warned of a return to 'the bullock-cart age'. But no one was listening. Wijeweera had a thrilling message for the young, the malnourished, the discontented and the unemployed. By November 1987, almost half the south was behind the JVP. The rich were now hated, and so were employers. Even foreign charities like Save the Children were targeted as 'neo-colonial'. A particular sore was the presence of an Indian peace-keeping force, up north. *FIGHT THE INDIANS*, ran the graffiti. *FIGHT THE MONKEYS!*

A frenzied, animal excitement had settled over the coast.

'*Pavathina kramaya varadity!*' people chanted. 'Everything is wrong.'

* * *

It's what happened next that's so hard to understand. In Colombo, those who remember 1987 still think of it as the most terrifying time of their life.

'Even the war,' said Vasantha, 'was never that bad.'

'Bodies everywhere,' said Elmo. 'In the road; nailed in the trees . . .'

It wasn't like the killing in 1971. This time, there was no escalation; the JVP simply began with an overwhelming wave of horror. It was like a pogrom that came by night. The killers were never seen, and always melted away like ghosts. Every day began like a battlefield, scattered with the dead. At first, it was the politicians, but then it was teachers, bus drivers and anyone breaking the strikes. Tradition has it that, here in Matara, the first victim was bundled into an oven and cooked alive. In his last roasted moments, he murmured the names of anyone he could, and they were all spirited away, into the forest, and shot.

But the slaughter didn't stop in Matara, and was soon fanning outwards, into the country.

After five years of civil war in the north, there was no shortage of deserters, ready to train the guerrillas. On average, twenty-five people were assassinated every night, and, on the worst day – 21 December 1988 – two hundred people died along this coast. In all, over eight thousand civilians would be liquidated, along with one hundred and six politicians and sixty-two academics. At the University of Kandy, twelve severed heads appeared, neatly arranged around the campus pond.

Amongst the dead was Madame Chandrika's husband, Vijaya.

'He was shot,' she told me, 'in front of our children.'

In parts of the south, order collapsed. The JVP called these 'liberated zones', and, like the Khmer Rouge, they declared that the world had started all over again. Taxes were abolished, the prisons were opened and the hotels closed. The rubber factories were burnt down and everyone was forced out on strike. Doctors were made to work for nothing, and it became illegal to read a government newspaper, on pain of death. The new commissars even stipulated how the dead were to be disposed of, how many mourners and how many monks, and the height of the graves.

Only in one respect was it like 1971: the government's response, ponderous and brutal. The president, Junius Jayewardene, said he had no truck with the kids who'd gone mad in the south. 'We cannot treat them as humans,' he said.

So began the *Beeshana Kalaya*, or Time of Great Fear. Like the JVP, the army's hit squads always worked at night. Sometimes, they'd display the corpses of those they'd killed, like the university lecturer in Tangalle. The idea was to render the concept of resistance psychologically unsustainable. *EYE FOR EYE*, ran one of their posters. Another depicted a jumble of corpses under the caption *TWELVE OF YOURS FOR ONE OF US*. The soldiers always knew where to find the guerrillas, because this was their home too. By July 1989, the counter-killings were claiming up to a thousand lives a day. In the highlands, or hill country, many of the dead ended up floating down the Mahaveli. I once met a man who'd lived by the river. 'We couldn't swim in it anymore,' he told me, 'and we no longer ate the fish.'

I'd often ask people how many were killed.

As before, no one knew. 'Thirty thousand? Sixty?'

It still horrified them to think of the state as a contract killer.

To my journalist friend, this was the start of sinister habits.

'If we could do that to our children, what would we do to *others*?'

Meanwhile, Wijeweera, the chief of the Che Guevaras, had yet to be caught. He was a master of disguise, and was always popping up and then vanishing again. Once, he'd been briefly detained and was coldly defiant. 'You may win a medal for arresting me,' he'd told the officer, 'but all your family will die.' A few days later, he disappeared. He wasn't finally captured until November 1989. This time, he was found on a tea estate, trying to shave off the beard. After a fleeting appearance on television, announcing the end of the revolution, he was killed. He was shot, of all places, at the eighth hole of the Royal Colombo Golf Club, 'attempting to escape'.

The mopping up went on for months, and has never really ended. By 1990, seven thousand suspects had been hauled away. Perhaps the most famous was Richard de Zoysa. Several of my friends had known him, in Colombo. He'd had long flowing hair and a motorbike, and had campaigned noisily on harmless issues like homosexual rights. One night, a white van appeared at his home and he was bundled inside. He reappeared a few days later on the beach at Mount Lavinia. The pathologist said his body had been so traumatised that it might have been dropped from a plane.

'And was no one ever brought to account?' I asked.

People would look at me as if I'd understood nothing.

'The white vans are still out there,' they'd say, and there the subject ended.

Before leaving Matara, I paid a visit to the very end of the Sinhalese world.

A few miles outside town was a promontory of dense jungle that suddenly tumbled away in a gorgeous haze of salt and spume. The sea was a bubbling midnight-blue, and all down the coast the great breakers growled. Here was the Indian Ocean at its most frothy and furious. It was hardly surprising the beaches looked so white and pristine, after a scrubbing like this. To the east was the journey ahead, a long pale-blue wisp of sand. Up here, on the rocks, the whole of Sri Lanka seemed to be behind me, which, in a sense, it was. This was the most southerly spot on the island. It would have been the perfect place to contemplate the frailty of fate, and that's exactly what the ancient kings of Ruhuna had done. Ibn Battutah reports that they'd even installed a life-sized Buddha, cast in gold. There'd been a temple too – somewhere – until the Portuguese had rolled it over the edge. Now all that remained was a lighthouse.

For a little fee, the keeper let me in. It was like climbing through a ship that had been turned on its end. Up on the prow, I had a gull's-eye view of the ocean, swinging around below. The keeper appeared at my elbow.

'What's out there?' I asked him.

'Nothing, sah; this is the end.'

It was true, of course: nothing but brine.

Until Antarctica, that is, and the frozen columns of the West Ice Shelf.

East of Matara, there was no more railway, and little sense of a Promised Land.

The safe, self-assured string of towns and temples had ended. Once again, the wilderness had closed in, and even the main road felt foreign and vulnerable as it crept through the scrub. From now on, I'd be reliant on buses or whatever lifts I could find. Everyone here seemed to be a coachman-in-the-making, willing to think up a price. They'd find me however deep the forest, however remote, and off we'd go in some ancient van. It was like travelling around in a one-seater bus – except without the band. (The big red government coaches were always deeply infested with minstrels. They'd squeak away and bash their instruments until everyone paid up. Michael Ondaatje once said that Sinhalese music sounds like a scorpion in a test tube, or a frog singing at Carnegie Hall. In the confines of a bus, it becomes a form of auditory extortion.)

Water, too, would become more scarce. For a while after Matara, I could see the curve of the Earth defined in rice. For hours, it seemed, we bounced along through this ocean of green. Distant coconut palms wobbled in the heat, and then melted away. There were still a few ponds too, and, on one, a man was floating around on an old inner tube, picking lilies. But then the landscape changed as the moisture failed. The paddy turned a crispy yellow, tufted with thorn and straw and outcrops of hard, knobbly trees. Gradually, this thickened into a sprawl of crackly undergrowth that rattled in the breeze. It's said that thirst is what finally killed off the ancient Kingdom of Ruhuna, one day in 1780. A huge downpour had swept away its berms, obliterating all the reservoirs, and so – when the dry season returned – the kingdom simply shrivelled up and died.

There were towns along the way, but they too felt shrunken now. Even the Dutch had built their forts out here only gingerly. All that remained of the one in Tangalle was a doorstep, carved 1773. Meanwhile, the town's dogs howled as if they were still jackals, and the cows had invaded the cricket pitch, hungrily licking up the stubble. I did, however, find a small clock tower. The British had always measured civilisation in clock towers. It would be the last one until Batticaloa, a few hundred miles up the east coast. 'The country that lies between these two places,' noted an early, Georgian colonist, 'presents the wildest appearance. Few of

It's thought that the Wanniyala-Aetto, or 'Veddas', have been in Sri Lanka for over 18,000 years, and they may be its original inhabitants. In 1911, there were 5,342 Veddas whereas now there are barely 500. With hunting banned, men like Waruge Sudubanda (*above*) are reduced to peddling souvenirs.

Many Sri Lankans hark back to a golden age. In 250 BC, Buddhism arrived on the island and would flourish among the great new cities. Polonnaruwa (*above*) and Anuradhapura would also be home to some of the world's largest structures and the hub of a hydrological network of over 18,000 reservoirs.

The island's Buddhism not only took on the icons of Hinduism (*left*), it also permitted the continuation of caste. Groups like the Rodiyas were considered untouchable, even into the 1960s. Only in Victorian times did they find a role, as photographers' subjects (*above*).

Although Sri Lanka is only the size of Ireland, it's home to over 5,800 wild elephants. Here too is the largest animal in the world (the blue whale), not to mention a startling array of creatures from crocodiles and leopards to the ashy-headed laughing thrush.

An Execution by an Eliphant.

DON'T GO BEYOND
THIS AREA.
මෙම සීමාවෙන් ඉදිරියට
යන්න එපා.

Elephants have played an unforgettable role in Sri Lankan society: its warhorse, its limousine and its executioner (*left*). These days an uneasy truce exists between them and the farmers, although each year hundreds of elephants die in the inevitable clashes.

One Impaled on a Stake

Europeans transformed Sri Lanka. First came the Portuguese (1505-1658), bringing God, gunpowder, surnames and shoes. Holed up in forts like Kalpitya (*left*), they encouraged the idea of rule by terror (*right*).

Next came the Dutch (1658-1796), who rebuilt the coast in the image of home, with forts like Galle (*above*) and a system of immaculate canals. It's often said that the Hollanders gave the island nothing but it isn't true; they left it a landscape.

For three centuries, Kandy resisted the Europeans. No one knew it better than English merchant Robert Knox (*left*), a hostage of the king for twenty years (1659–79). He described a court that was, by turns, ascetic and sex-mad. But it was the last king, Sri Vikrama Rajasinha (*right*) who created today's city (*below*) – at vast expense. Eventually, in 1815, his courtiers rebelled and let the British in.

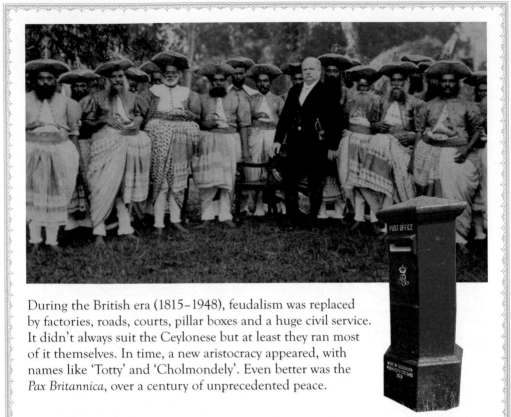

During the British era (1815–1948), feudalism was replaced by factories, roads, courts, pillar boxes and a huge civil service. It didn't always suit the Ceylonese but at least they ran most of it themselves. In time, a new aristocracy appeared, with names like 'Totty' and 'Cholmondely'. Even better was the *Pax Britannica*, over a century of unprecedented peace.

In 1942, shortly after its raid on Pearl Harbour, Japan's vast carrier fleet descended on Ceylon. At the Naval Dockyard in Trincomalee, the wreckage of that day can still be seen (*above*). The *Sagaing* (*in the foreground*) had been carrying whisky and ammunition and burned for a week.

S. W. R. D. Bandaranaike (*inset*) is often blamed for the island's racial tension. Although an Anglican, educated at Oxford, he formulated a dangerous variant of Sinhalese pride. In 1959, he was assassinated by a monk at the family home, Tintagel (*above*). Colombo is still a product of those times, a city that's pious, ebullient, ceremonial and watchful.

Racial tensions would lead to the longest civil war in Asian history (1983–2009), fought with drones, 'shit bombs', mines and home-made tanks. No one knows how many died, but the toll included over 27,000 guerrillas. Meanwhile, 800,000 people were displaced and Sri Lanka's army became one of the biggest in the world. Yet, somehow, the tourists still came, and the economy grew by five per cent a year.

the Cingalese have the intrepidity to inhabit these parts, where they are in constant danger of being attacked by the numerous wild beasts . . .'

Mindful of this, I settled for a few days near Rekawa. The beasts that live here are amongst the wildest on the planet, certainly in spirit. By day, their vast beach made a hollow, booming sound, and the sea was mountainous and turquoise. But, by night, the sand was pallid and ghostly, and waves would merely whisper round my feet. This is when the turtles appeared. They looked like upturned boats, dragging themselves out of the surf. For the last year, they'd been travelling the oceans, no one knows where. But the task of egg laying is so primordial and urgent, they ignore human beings. With their ungainly paddles, they rowed past me – painfully slowly – up the beach. On a good evening, the sand would look as if it had been ploughed by Sherman tanks.

Further up, a villager was guarding a cluster of craters.

'Every nests,' he told me, 'have maybe two hundred egg.'

One of the great hulls was still at work, paddling sand over the hole.

'How long will you need to guard it?' I asked.

In the sand, the eggs looked like ping-pong balls, glossy with mucous.

'Until they hatches. Sixty days . . .'

'They must be valuable?'

'Taste good, yes. Every egg, twenty rupee!'

A clutch of behemoths, I thought, worth a night at McDonalds.

I thanked the guard. 'Have you always done this?'

'No, sah. Before, I was one of the thiefs.'

In such a wilderness, it was surprising to find a Chinese city, almost new.

The first sign of it was a change in the road. It had suddenly grown crash barriers and slip roads and another four lanes. The landscape, on the other hand, had hardly altered at all. If anything, it was drier and harder, and more desperate than ever. Some people think that the hinterlands of Hambantota were hit by a meteorite in prehistoric times, which is why little grows here, and why the earth is a brilliant red. This obviously wasn't much encouragement to traffic, and so the highway had remained obstinately empty. Across the lanes were huge dollops of elephant dung. At least some things don't change, I thought: wild beasts asserting their ancient right to terrorise the roads.

But, up ahead, more chinoiserie appeared. First, it was a ten-storey hospital nosing up from the margosa trees. Then there was a construction camp, run by 'China Harbour'. It was like an ants' nest of labourers, all dressed in blue and pouring out into trucks. Local people said they were convicts, sent here to suffer. Opposite, on a ridge of orange rocks and tree stumps, was one of their early works: a vast, shapeless conference centre, the biggest in South-East Asia. Although it still wasn't finished, it already looked brutally obsolete. Cranes were now lifting mature trees into place, as if to excuse it.

Not that anyone was fooled. The government was always parading its plans for Hambantota. President Rajapaksa had declared that the whole town would eventually move up here, on to the ridge; that it would be 'The Wonder of Asia' and that – one day – it would be the capital city. He didn't seem to worry that there was no water or work, or that the population lived 148 miles to the west. It helped, of course, that this was his constituency.

The presidential portrait was now pasted up all along the highway, his face a picture of saintly glee.

Bits of his Chinese city, meanwhile, were now popping up everywhere, out in the scrub. After a few days in the old village, I found a driver, called Sam, to take me off on a Chinese tour. I'm still not sure whether what I saw that day was a work of genius or a ghost town in the making. For a while, we saw nothing at all, except the dense mesh of thorn and wood apple, and long silvery stands of teak. From out of the thicket, a woman in a sari appeared, her arms as thin and dark as whipcord. She had a pot of water on her head, and set off across six lanes of nothing. It was hard to imagine all this as the Wonder of Asia, covered in godowns and pagodas, and happy factory workers astride their Flying Pigeons. Perhaps I'd got it all wrong, a victim of Chinese whispers.

But then, suddenly, a stadium bubbled up out of the woods. It was a handsome piece of concrete, like an arrangement of gigantic pots. No one was around, so we went inside. From the highest seats, we could gaze down into a tiny bowl of wickets, or out across the wilderness towards the mountains at the centre of the island. The Chinese had brought everything with them, from the sockets to the scoreboard to a peg for the umpire's hat. I wondered what they'd made of cricket. Did they have a word for 'a googly', or 'leg spin', or 'silly mid-off'? Perhaps it didn't matter. At a cost of $8 million, they'd built a cricket ground with thirty-five thousand seats. Now all it needed was thirty-five thousand backsides to fill them. Judging by the debris in the press box, there'd been no major tournament here for a year, and – out on the pitch – the turf was now discernibly feral. I was later told that not even the locals called by anymore. They'd only be tempted inside if the tickets were free.

'A funny place for cricket,' I said absently.

'Well,' said Sam, 'at least it never rains.'

A few miles away was an even more remarkable work of emptiness. It was another Chinese creation in the president's name: the Mattala Rajapaksa International Airport. This had cost $210 million, and, like all ambitious airports, it had a car park the size of Monaco, and a mausoleum's appetite for marble. Everything gleamed and squeaked, and – as the main doors slid open – there was a perceptible hiss as the atmosphere cooled. Mattala even had the longest runway in the country, and a huge army of check-in girls in baby-blue jackets and pillbox hats. But what it made up for in livery, it lacked in planes. There was nothing on the apron, and nothing on the indicator boards. No, said the girls, I couldn't fly to Colombo, and, no, there weren't any flights today. It turned out that there were only ever fourteen flights a week, and nothing from abroad. Some days, the only visitors were coach parties, who came to gaze at the carousels whirring emptily around, and to marvel at such a beautiful place so busily doing nothing.

'One day, this will be a hub of the Indian Ocean,' said Sam blandly.

Maybe, I thought, or a little treat for the archaeologists.

Like the airport, my hotel had been built for the hordes that had yet to arrive. It was called the Peacock Beach, and seemed to have spent most of its existence closing down. The shops in the basement had long since seized up with dust, and its double-decker bus hadn't moved for months. I usually had the pool to myself, except for the kingfishers and a persistent crow, who'd paddle like a puppy. Every morning, I was woken by the sound of monkeys, rattling the teacups out in the corridor. There was then a huge and courageous display of breakfast – curries, fish, eggs and porridge – which all went solemnly cold, and was eventually hauled away, uneaten. For some reason, I found all this enchanting, which left even the manager slightly surprised.

I also began to appreciate what it was the Chinese wanted.

From my room, I had a view of the horizon and an endless trickle of ships. Some of them looked like islands, huge hulks of mauve, sliding imperceptibly along. By night there was a whole archipelago of lights, constantly changing shape and colour. I now realise that almost everything sailing to or from the Far East has to slide this way. On the world map, all the shipping lines seem to converge at this point as they round the Indian subcontinent. From my bed, it was only eight miles into the middle of this watery superhighway, used by thirty-six thousand ships a year. My last night, I lay there, thinking about this. I'd been told that, by dawn, over 150 bulk carriers would have slithered by. How many Barbie dolls was that? And how many tons of Zambian copper? I must have nodded off, trying to work it out, and fell into a deep industrial sleep.

Next morning, I was up with the monkeys, and so were the ships. Most of them, I discovered, were from China. The Chinese have always considered that this is the gateway to the Western World, or perhaps its throat. Their first concerted attempt to control 'Seylan' was in 1410, when the Muslim admiral, Ching Ho (or Zhenge He) appeared with a fleet of fifty-six ships. Although Ching liked what he saw, he didn't stay. Instead, he plundered what he could and sailed home. Amongst his more exotic booty was a very indignant Sinhalese king.

Now, at last, the Chinese had a port of their own.

That last day, I asked Sam if he'd take me down there.

I'd already spotted the harbour from up on the highway. From that distance, the ships looked like tower blocks edging through the scrub. I'd also seen the dumper trucks at work. They reminded me of scarabs with their beetle backs and thick black ooze. There were millions of tons of mud to be moved. Nothing about this harbour was natural. Hambantota's lagoon had been barely deeper than a garden pond, and yet the new bulk carriers would draw water up to five storeys deep. The Chinese were now digging a hole big enough for thirty such ships, together with a credible chunk of the People's navy. They'd pay a high price for their toehold – $1 billion a year in soft loans, weaponry and holes – but it was something they'd wanted for centuries. Now here they were, at the heart of the Indian Ocean, straddling the traffic.

More puzzling was what Sri Lanka got from its Chinese city.

Sam turned off the highway and down the harbour road. All the signs were now in Mandarin, and at the end of the road was a large basin, the size of a London park. It was the first to be finished, and – back in Colombo – it was being roundly mocked. 'It has a rock in the entrance!' people howled. 'Which they didn't even notice!' But, rock or no rock, that day there was a single Japanese carrier tied up to the quay. It was disgorging three thousand second-hand cars, and was the ugliest ship I'd ever seen: white, windowless and the shape of a bread van.

'Why here?' I asked Sam. 'Why build a terminal here?'

'Don't ask me.' He shrugged. 'Let's speak to the site manager.'

At the development office, all the girls giggled and fled to their desks.

'I'll give you two minutes,' said the manager from behind an acre of teak.

'Why here?' I began.

'We're right on the shipping lanes. We're a service port.'

'Isn't that a bit medieval?'

'What?'

'The idea of ships stopping for water and food.'

'Not at all! And we're taking deliveries too. Look at the cars . . .'

'But it's still another eight hours' drive to Colombo . . .'

The manager tapped his watch. 'I think that's two minutes.'

'What about the rock? Is it true?'

'Just politics. People play funny games.'

Back on the road, I felt as confused as ever.

'Who'd want to come out here to pick up a car?'

'Actually, a lot of people,' said Sam, 'thanks to Kataragama.'

'What, the temple?'

'Yes, they like to take their new car, and get it blessed.'

The journey to Kataragama is supposed to be painful.

To get there burnt, battered and blistered is to understand what it offers. By arriving in a van, I'd already placed myself way beyond the realms of comprehension. Many of the people I saw had travelled there on foot. Some had walked the length of the island, a journey of perhaps eighty days. Every year, a few perish in the jungle, and that week there was talk of a woman killed by a leopard. Even those who'd made it looked broken and starved. Their *pada yatra*, or foot pilgrimage, had left them utterly listless. Swaddled and exhausted, they lay around in rows, like the figures in a Henry Moore. In places, there were thousands of them, spread through the woods. I still find it hard to compute, this landscape of pain and hope. But, since 137 BC, Kataragama has known almost nothing else, and now it gets over a million pilgrims a year, on the promise of atonement.

Not everyone walked, although they'd all somehow suffer. On the day I travelled out to Kataragama, it was holding its last procession of the *Maha Devalaya*. Over 150,000 pilgrims would be heading to the complex. Some had driven all through the night on rice-cultivators, or had ridden down from the hill country, clinging to tractors. Buses were packed so tight that you couldn't see daylight through the bodies. The traffic jam crept through the scrub like some lumbering polyphonic reptile. Everything hooted or sang, and most of the vehicles had been decorated with greenery, the mark of pilgrimage. At Tissamaharama, this great honking hedge came to a halt, allowing everyone to get off and plunge into the tank. It may have undone a little precious suffering, but at least the gods would be spared the stink. As the pilgrims immersed themselves amongst the lilies, there was a collective coo of pleasure.

I abandoned my bags at a guest house and went the rest of the way by trishaw. The driver, who was called Saman, had decorated the interior with pictures of straggly girls in thick black bikinis. I had hoped for something a bit more penitential to get me through the roadblocks. But I needn't have worried. All around me, the pain had been temporarily suspended, to be replaced with an infectious holiday spirit. Stalls had appeared at the roadside, selling watermelons, bananas and bundles of firewood. Further on, they sold plastic machine-guns and nuts. Cows now grazed amidst the traffic, and the singing got louder. Two incense sellers were fighting on the verge. A huge fish appeared in the door, demanding a buyer. *AVOID ENTERING DRUNK*, said the signs, but it was a hopeless request in a place so spiritually tipsy. In 1642, the Portuguese had got this far, only to be driven back when their guides went stark raving mad.

Then Kataragama appeared in a blaze of bulbs. It was as if the night sky had been dragged down to earth, and was being run off the mains. Perhaps paradise will look like this, if they can afford the bills. I was hardly out of the trishaw before I was swept along in a surge of faith. This was always an important moment in Sri Lanka's spiritual cycle. Suddenly, its two great religions were united in a single focus of devotion. Although they'd never readily shared their island, they would share a deity. To the Buddhists, he was a guardian figure, the Kataragama Deviyo, whilst to Hindus, he was a son of Shiva, Lord Murugan. But that's not all. Ironically, the Tamils also knew him as Skanda, the implacable, multi-limbed god of war. It was to him that the pilgrims offered their pain. Kataragama's god, it seemed, was not so much loved as feared. From amongst the multitude, the hallelujahs rose like groans: '*Harō-harā! Harō-harā!*'

I was now being carried away in the crush. Fortunately, I could just make out Saman, bobbing along behind. The human torrent swept us out through more toy stalls, confectionary tents, an emporium of coloured string, and up over a bridge across the Menik Oya, or Green River. Below, I could see a bath of biblical dimensions, and hundreds of pilgrims shampooing their hair. Then we were in the temple complex itself, and the crowd swelled with elephants and mahouts. I don't remember voices, just a smothering mumble of prayer. Eventually, Saman managed to swim through the tangle of arms and drag me off into the trees.

'Short cut, boss. This way . . .'

Out of the light, I couldn't see anything, and had the unpleasant sensation of stumbling on limbs. I could also feel cold bony fingers clutching at my shirt. As my eyes got used to the dark, I realised why nobody else was cutting through these woods. They were the haunt of those for whom atonement had failed: the maimed, the mad and the mendicant. Most of them were asleep in the leaf litter. One had elephantiasis, and feet like huge rotten fruits. Another, an old woman with a face like a sparrow, let her tunic drop open as we passed, revealing puckered skin, her breasts all raked away. Saman hardly seemed to notice this mutilated community. Kataragama had always made a spectacle of pain and the mortification of flesh. Last week, he said, I'd have seen men dangling from hooks, or with skewers through their arms. 'They very holy. Skanda protects them . . .'

I wondered if things ever went too far.

Saman frowned. 'Dead persons, you mean?'

'Well, yes, I suppose so . . .'

'Every year. Someone make little hole and – *chee!* – he cuts his throat!'

I was relieved to be back amongst the lightbulbs. We'd ended up at the heart of the procession, and I could hear whips fizzing and cracking overhead. Drummers came thrashing through the crowds, followed by elephants, blundering along, half blind beneath their enormous burqas of silk. Acrobats swooped in amongst them, a whirr of peacock feathers and silver armour. Then came the dancers, girls in puffed sleeves and pantaloons. For some of them, the heat and the bulbs were too much, and they were scooped up and carried away over the heads of the crowd.

Beyond the spectators, the weary slept. It was like a human jigsaw puzzle: Tamils and Sinhalese slotted together so tightly that nothing could move. Tiny fires smouldered amongst them, and the heat that rose off this pile of sleep was pleasantly scented with camphor and woodsmoke. Tomorrow they'd all go home, sore, perhaps, but, arguably, atoned. They'd also return to their separate lives, whether Buddhist or Hindu. Neighbours they might be, but between them there'd always be a gulf of ideas. Only once a year did their lives truly interlock. Kataragama may have been strange – extreme, even – but it was also Sri Lanka at its most complete.

Beyond Tissamaharama, the road came to an end. The jungle melted away into shallow, green lagoons of brine. The next town was another fifty miles on, the other side of a semi-arid zone, known as the Yala. Officially, there was no way through and, although it was a national park, most of the region was out of bounds. It still had its temples, of course, usually perched high up on knobs of rock, but no one was sure who'd built them or when. During the civil war, the Yala had become so empty and forgotten that the rebels moved in, and had remained undetected for years. The Sinhalese still regarded it with awe, and only the pilgrims ever tried to get through. I had little choice, it seemed, but to turn back and retrace my steps. It was a fitting end to my travels in the south. At the beginning of this journey, humankind had filled the surrounding space with exuberance and rage, and now it shrank to the edges.

I didn't leave immediately, but lingered on the fringe. I found someone who arranged camping in the park, and who had a few tents on the banks of the Menik. These were unforgettable days, spent dipping in the river and pottering around in jeeps. The *pelessa*, or grassland, looked dried-up and dead at first, but then there would be brilliant flashes of life: a cloud of Common Jezebels or a sudden chorus line of storks, or even a long family of mongooses, like a rivulet of fur. Once, a dozen peacocks burst out of the thicket, fabulously feathery and shrill. Naturalists must have a word for an apparition like that. A pea-mob, perhaps.

The manager of the camp was an ex-artillery major of exquisite subtlety and manners. Having compacted so much noise into the first half of his life, he was now spending the second gathering up the silence. Most of the time he blended into the shadows, but, at dusk, he'd usher to the table an outlandish dinner – soup, roasts, puddings, coleslaw, a cheeseboard and cakes. All this I'd contemplate alone, beneath a canopy of monkeys, whilst the major hovered nearby under the kumbuk trees. Although he was solicitous and thoughtful, I think he dreaded being noticed. He once told me his favourite creature was the Malabar pied hornbill, which makes a hole in a tree, climbs in and then stops up the door with cement. But there was nothing he couldn't name, and he loved the things that simply survived: acacia, ironwood, *milla*, *agil*, the salt-resistant bushes, *maleeta*, and that old desperado, the toothbrush tree.

Best of all were the leopard moments. The major said there were more here, in this little area, than anywhere else in the world. They were easy to find; you followed the screams and the trail of hysterical langurs. I always enjoyed these encounters and the thought of something so big and luxurious perched in a tree. Once, we caught one heading home, a sort of sticky-pawed walk straight up the trunk. Altogether, we spotted five, lolling in the branches. Their expression was familiar, and seemed somehow to mirror my own feelings for the journey I'd done: that curious mix of perplexity and pleasure.

5

The Garden in the Sky

The interior of the Island abounds with steep and lofty mountains, covered with thick forests, and full of almost impenetrable jungles. The woods and mountains completely surround the dominions of the King of Candy, and seem destined by nature to defend him.

Robert Percival, *An Account of the Island of Ceylon*, 1803

The Great road . . . the route which embassies took, and by which armies set out in splendour and straggled back in rout.

Raven-Hart, *Ceylon: History in Stone*, 1964

In Colombo, mention of the highlands always stirred up a hint of ambivalence.

People were often telling me about its noble culture and how grand it was. Every Sri Lankan child knows that the old Kandyan kingdom is a natural citadel; that its animals are bigger and hairier than anything found in the lowlands, and its people broader and paler; that it's the source of all the mightiest rivers; that it held out against the Europeans for almost three hundred years, and that its aristocracy are purer and more difficult than anywhere else. All of this was impressive, if not entirely endearing. I was even told that you needed Kandyan ancestry to get on in politics. If you can't manage a grandfather, then at least find a Kandyan wife.

Physically, too, the old kingdom could be imposing. Most lowlanders have to live with the sight of it towering overhead: *Kanda Uda Pas Rata*, or the Five Lands above the Mountains. Nowhere in Sri Lanka is more than seventy kilometres from the sea, and so – heading inland – it's never long before a crown of purple appears. Close up, this great wall of granite looks impenetrable, and most coastlanders can only imagine what happens on the top. This makes the central highlands seem detached and alien, like some enormous garden up in the clouds.

It was never an easy ascent. Until 1820, it took four weeks to scramble from Colombo to Kandy. The only way up was a woodland path, guarded by watchmen and blocked with huge gates knitted from thorn. The Kandyans called this muddy track 'The Great Road' – a joke considered so good, the name has stuck. To prevent major incursions, their kings made it illegal to widen the path, build bridges or even cut back the trees. All intercourse between 'Cinglese and Candians', noted Percival, had been 'completely cut off'.

Even now, the Kandyans who make it to Colombo are seen as rarefied and different. Few have Portuguese names, and almost none are Catholic. But everyone agrees it's more than this. The Kandyans affect airs and graces, perfuming the language with their flowery words. Even I learnt to spot them after a while. They were always anxious to disown the coast and all its doings. They preferred to establish themselves deep in the past, with a family history of fighting prowess. At every opportunity, there'd be displays of flummery and pomp, particularly at weddings. Only the Kandyans wore national costume: cream turban, pearly waistcoat, pointed slippers, silver breastplates and a massive girth of silk. Lowlanders were never quite sure what to make of it – although, if they'd had enough whisky, it made them laugh.

To understand all this, I decided, I had to find the Great Road.

It was soon obvious I'd set myself a preposterous task. I was looking for a muddy track, barely the width of an elephant and abandoned over two centuries earlier. There was nothing on the government's maps and nothing in the *A to Z*. A few friends had heard of the Great Road, but not since school. Even when it was the only path to Kandy, its route had been a closely guarded secret and was constantly changing. Kandyans themselves had needed permission to travel it, and little passports of clay. As far as anyone knew, they'd never made a map.

'The path's gone,' people told me, 'a victim of weeds.'

It was true I didn't have much to go on. But I did have Baldaeus and friends, or at least copies of their charts. After months on the road, this huge sandwich of notes was now pungent and curly, but I could still read the maps. To begin with, it was hard to find what I wanted. Baldaeus' contribution (1672) was covered in dotted lines, but none of them led to Kandy. The Dutch historian Valentijn's drawing (1724) was better, particularly on watch-houses, but his mountains were all over the place and looked like little dog shits. The worst of all was Percival's map (1803), which showed the Great Road wheeling off into the hills as if it were an autobahn.

I was about to give up, when I reread a chunk of Dr Davy. Born into the famous Davy family – his brother was Sir Humphrey, inventor of the miners' lamp – John was a man of exacting habits and inconspicuous humour. His travelogue offers the first microscopic view of Ceylon, an exploration of soil and snakebite and why things die. He also describes climbing the Great Road in 1817, just three years before it closed. It was a ludicrous expedition. Although the Kandyans had been only recently – and temporarily – pacified, the British governor thought he needed a holiday. He took with him his wife, three elephants, Dr Davy and a troop of pretty dragoons. The Europeans were carried up in *tomjohns*, or palanquins, which must have been like climbing a mountain whilst still in bed. Naturally, a revolt soon welled up around them, and it was another fifteen months before they all got home. Fortunately, however, Dr Davy had noted every step of the way. All I had to do was find the places, plot them on a map, and join up the dots.

Working backwards from Kandy, I soon had a handsome zig-zag tumbling out of the hills. But things got more difficult in the lowlands. Colombo had clearly expanded outwards to meet the hills, covering everything in a thick deposit of industry and asphalt. No *tomjohn* would find its way through that lot, even in single file. I decided to skip a section, and begin again at Fort.

It ought to have been easy to find the way in. The Dutch had built eight enormous bastions – with names like Leyden, Haarlem and Hoorn – and these were linked together with moats, ramparts and three great gates. Surely something had survived? But Fort was no longer a fort, and so, for a while, I had nothing. Then someone told me about Delft. The main gate had somehow survived, pinned down under a couple of banks. If the Great Road had a beginning, it was surely here, at Fort's front door?

I hurried down to the banking district. Although now a dazzling dental white and sprouting skyscrapers, it was Delft all right. I could even make out the place where the sentries had stood. I unzipped a camera.

'You can't do that, sah!'

Three baggy old toughs had appeared, in black suits and walkie-talkies.

'I don't understand . . .' I said.

'No photos, sah. By order of the Ministry of Defence.'

I was even more puzzled. 'But this was built in 1658 . . .'

It didn't matter. I was led away to the security room.

'We need to call the ministry . . .'

There were several minutes of mumbling, and then the suits rang off.

'You can take one photograph, and then you must go.'

All three of them glowered at me as I took my picture. I was thrilled. It seemed I'd touched an ancient nerve, and was there-fore clearly making progress.

Holland's governors had often pondered the Great Road, and what went on up the other end.

Their old residence was, I discovered, round the back of the Grand Oriental. Used until 1680, it was a graceless building, not so much a palace as a warehouse of fine ideas. Huge, shapeless columns held up the roof, and the rooms inside were lofty and bland. The men who built this place were businessmen, their hearts turned to God and their eyes on the bottom line. In their portraits, the governors always look busy and pinched, and every-thing's black, from their Guy Fawkes hats down to the bows on the shoes. This building may have kept them cool, but elegance would have to wait.

It took several visits before I got inside. These days, the *residen-tie* is an Anglican church, and, most of the time, it's shuttered tight against the heat. But, one morning, the door was open and I wandered in. There was no one around except a tiny figure, stripped to his shorts. He was straddling the lectern and buffing the eagle with polish and rags. It was a curiously violent sight, and when he'd finished, he went off to scuffle with the pulpit.

The Dutch, meanwhile, had left little of themselves, except per-haps a sense of woe. Around the walls, the perils of colonial life were remembered in marble. Particularly unlucky were the Perthshires, who'd lost forty-three soldiers during their tour of duty, without a war to be seen.

It worried the governors, not where the road led, but what it might bring. Who were the Kandyans and what were they up to?

How many were there? And how were they armed? A military expedition was out of the question (the Portuguese had made that mistake). Besides, by 1658, the Dutch were happily settled around the coast, and there they'd stay. It never troubled them that *Zeilan* was only ever a colony around the edges.

But it did worry them that, in their midst, there was still a savage, heathen king. Things had not gone well with Rajasinha II. He was still furious at having been cheated out of a port, and every now and then he'd raid the coast, pinning a few Dutchmen up in the trees. The VOC sent him ever more lavish gifts, but he wasn't appeased. Once, the French even tried to outdo them, sending a consignment of 'Persian horses, tigers, civet cats, parrots and cockatoos in gilded cages'. The king, however, was unimpressed. He had Louis XIV's representative seized and enslaved, forcing him to become Keeper of the Golden Armour.

Rajasinha himself remained something of a mystery. In his portraits, he was bald, bearded and pot-bellied. It was known that he loved animals, that he was a good swimmer and a fine horseman, that his wife was a Malabar, or Tamil, that his people referred to him as a deity and that even his dirty washing was revered. It was also rumoured that he was the only Kandyan allowed to wear stockings and shoes, or to sit in a chair with a back. But, beyond that, he and his kingdom remained dangerously obscure.

This was partly because the Great Road was so unusable, and partly because anyone entering the kingdom could never leave. The king had become an assiduous collector of Europeans. They were hostages, of course, but also curios. As with the French ambassador, Rajasinha liked to have them around at court, supervising his linen or managing his china. By 1672, he had between five hundred and one thousand specimens in his human menagerie, including fugitives, lost hunters, Portuguese priests, the entire crew of *The Persia Merchant* (washed ashore at Kalpitya) and half a dozen Dutch diplomats who'd scrambled up the path in the hope of a truce. But captivity wasn't always irksome. Some of the captives made arrack, and some ran taverns. One of the Dutch diplomats married a Sinhalese girl and became Chief Blacksmith. Meanwhile, Messrs Plessey and Bloom looked after the king's horse (although they were banished to the mountains when it died of old age), and a drunk called Richard Varnham was put in charge of nine hundred soldiers. Few of the captives, however, ever made it home.

Back at the residence, all this was making life difficult. For a long time, the governors had no idea how secure their colony was, or what the Kandyans were doing. Then, on 2 November 1679, a curious character appeared here, amongst the shapeless columns. He was filthy and scratched, and had a beard down to his waist. Although he was barefoot and dressed in the manner of the 'Cingualays', he was clearly a Londoner. He said he'd been a captive of the Kandyans for almost twenty years, and that he'd just escaped. The Dutch couldn't believe their luck. Here was everything they'd ever need to know about life the other end of the Great Road. His name was Robert Knox, a merchant of Wimbledon. Here is his story.

Robert and his father, old Captain Knox, had been sailing the coast of India when, on 19 November 1659, their merchantman was damaged in a storm. Making for the coast of 'Zelone', they and fourteen members of the crew were captured by the Kandyans. They were then marched away up a narrow jungle path, the equivalent of the Great Road on the eastern side. For the captives, it was a hard walk in seaboots and frock coats. Eventually, after five days, they reached the inner kingdom.

There, the king had his latest specimens dispersed and billeted on villages. Escape seemed impossible. The kingdom twittered with spies, the Great Road was viciously gated and constantly watched, and anyone caught running away could expect an imaginative death – picked apart with pincers, perhaps, or trampled by elephants. Most of the Englishmen accepted their fate, and some even married. But not Robert Knox. Being of Puritan upbringing, he was appalled at the thought of coupling with heathen women and a life of pleasure. He was also an ugly man and, in matters of the human heart, he could be tetchy and dour. As old Captain Knox lay dying of malaria in February 1661, Robert swore he'd 'avoid strong drink and lewd conduct and try to get back home'.

It was another eighteen years before he saw his chance and ran for the coast. In the meantime, his beard grew and his clothes all rotted away. Eventually, he adopted the manner of a Kandyan gent, eating off banana leaves, cooking spicy 'carees', wearing a sarong and telling the time by the four o'clock flower. His captors were constantly moving him around, but, wherever he went, he built a new farm and started trading all over again. He even taught himself to knit and began a hat business, kitting out the villagers in Puritanical beanies.

It was never an easy relationship between him and his captors. Each regarded the other with unalloyed contempt. To the Kandyans, Knox was a foreigner and therefore belonged to the scavenger caste. To Knox, the 'Chingulays' were 'crafty and treacherous', born liars, cruel and sex mad. Men were always lending out their wives and daughters, and young women were encouraged to brag about their conquests. Only prostitution was taboo. Convicted whores would have all their hair hacked off, together with their ears.

But, despite his disdain, Knox never forgot his time in the highlands, and years later would look back on it with something like regret. When he got back to London, he transferred to paper the book in his head, and it was published in 1681. As a chronicle of the lives and habits of the Sinhalese, *An Historical Relation of the Island Ceylon* has never been surpassed, and it still informs our understanding of Kandy. Knox's contemporaries enjoyed it too, and it was translated into German, Dutch and French. It also caught the eye of another writer, Daniel Defoe. Although his castaway, Robinson Crusoe, would end up alone, on the other side of the world, in tone and guile he is unmistakably Robert Knox.

History doesn't relate what our hero made of his fictional self. He died a year after Defoe's book was published, in 1720, and is buried, back where he began, at Wimbledon's church.

Knox's chance of escape finally came in September 1679. By then, he was a respected hatter and travelling salesman, and knew the country well. He and his assistant, Stephen Rutland, soon realised that the only way out was up through the dry zone. Loading their backpacks with garlic and combs, they set out on the sales trip of their lives, and wandered out of the kingdom.

Even today, this would be an imprudent walk. Knox and Rutland spent a month over it, starting out in slippers and ending up barefoot. First, they crossed the area of 'human–elephant conflict', where – like me – they found people living in trees and the rivers 'exceedingly full of alligators'. Then, skirting some 'ruins' at 'Anurodgburro', or Anuradhapura, they entered the badlands, their skin now lashed by thorn and 'all of a gore'. Finally, on

18 October 1679, they emerged at Arippu, at the VOC stronghold. It was the same little building I'd visited, now a cowshed. The fugitives had, however, made a more memorable appearance. The Dutch had never seen anything so disgusting and hairy, and bundled them on to a ship, bound for Colombo.

For Knox, it was the end of his captivity, after nineteen years and six months. But the Merchant of Wimbledon wasn't home yet. Ahead lay a fifty-two-day voyage to Jakarta (then known as Batavia), followed by another of seven months to Erith in Kent. And before all that, of course, he'd have his long meeting with the governor, here at the residence.

Whenever I stayed in Fort, I'd begin the day with a walk through the naval base. I liked it in here because the traffic never made it past the roadblocks, and the sounds of the city simply petered out. I was also fascinated by the sight of a navy waking up, sending out enormous columns of runners with an ambulance trailing behind. And what were the sabres for, and the sparkling cavalry boots? I was never quite sure if I was meant to see all this, but everyone greeted me with a stentorian 'Good Morning!' and there was even a café that sold navy breakfasts and blue silk ties.

Around the back of the base was a large, white, windowless bunker. Like the ratings, it looked as though it'd been freshly laundered and starched. If the VOC had ever had jump jets, this is where they'd have kept them. It was a hangar of a place, with high-vaulted ceilings, blast-proof walls and stone-flagged floors. These days, it is supposed to be a maritime museum, although, for a long time, the two jowly old janitors wouldn't let me in. They were like bulldogs, wobbling with rage when anyone drew near.

This was almost more exciting than the exhibits, although I did find a handy device for lifting elephants up on to ships.

The old Dutch barracks – as they were – had never had a happy history.

Thanks to Knox, the Dutch had, for a long time, avoided confrontation. They were only stirred into action when, in 1761, the Kandyans swept down on to the coast, smashing everything to bits. Three years later, a little army marched out through the hangar doors, intent on teaching them a lesson. It wasn't a well-planned enterprise. No sooner were they up the Great Road than the Kandyans sent them packing under a blizzard of boulders and arrows.

The following year, a more impressive force gathered on the flags. It was a corps of *Jagers* – six hundred crack troops, mostly German or Swiss – under a spiffy new commander, Baron van Eck. Instead of bayonets, the soldiers carried machetes, and they wore natty sailcloth uniforms with protective caps. They were also supplemented by 1,200 Malays, recruited for their astonishing ferocity. The impact of such a formidable force was only slightly marred by the fact that the Malays insisted on travelling with their wives and fighting cocks. The Kandyans must have wondered what was happening to them when they saw this army come squawking through the hills. They let it get all the way to Kandy before moving in for the kill. Years earlier, Knox had warned the Dutch that – at a moment's notice – the Kandyan king could rustle up over thirty thousand warriors. It seems his advice had been overlooked.

Eight months after leaving, van Eck's *Jagers* were back at the barracks, bloodied and diseased. Almost half of them had perished. Never again would the Dutch venture up the Great Road.

My own ascent now needed a driver. At this point, a Kandyan joined my journey, filling it with volume and bulk. Although Sanath had been recommended by an agency, my heart sank when I saw him – the thick neck, massive forearms, tiny stubbly head and the big, meaty grin. He was also wearing children's clothes, stretched sausage-tight across his Popeye frame. Everything about him, it seemed, was ready to burst.

He was soon bellowing and roaring at the traffic. It took a while to unscramble his rage and work out who he was. I didn't think I'd ever met anyone so loud and conspicuous, and yet Sanath saw himself as a secret agent. During the war, he'd been with the army, doing plain-clothes work at the airport. It wasn't hard to imagine him prowling through the passengers, listening to everything and understanding nothing. The mirrored glasses and the earpiece had, I suppose, become a habit. Perhaps it explained his driving too. We were always squealing round corners and riding the kerbs, as if we had SMERSH or the Tigers hot on our heels. I began to wish the Great Road was over before we'd begun.

'Out of the way!' he'd snarl, as we lurched out through Pettah.

Muslims were particular irritants, and so were the Chinese.

'*Chee!* Dirty buggers, always eat some dogs . . .'

Women, too, had him straining out of the window. I was never sure if this was for their benefit or mine. Sanath knew he was an oddity – unmarried and forty-two – and was always making excuses. There was supposed to be a girlfriend in Anuradhapura, but she never sounded very real. Then there was an older woman who he often spoke to on the phone, and who'd leave him hissing with rage. 'These people,' he'd say, 'are like frogs in a well!' By this, I assumed he blamed womankind in general for failing to appreciate his muscular charm.

But, like all Popeyes, there was a small boy within. During our weeks together, he often cried, and every morning there were new ailments – little coughs and aches – all demanding pity. He also resented our differing roles, and having to sleep in the drivers' quarters. But it was no good asking him in. Whenever he sat at a dining-room table, he'd pick his teeth and belch, and lord it over the staff. He was only himself again once we were out, speeding through the paddy. At these moments, he'd make a great display of stopping and pissing in the rice. 'The whole world,' he'd roar, 'is a toilet for men!'

This was typical of Sanath. During those first few days, I couldn't decide whether to dislike him or loathe him. But at least he seemed vaguely familiar, and might easily have tumbled from the pages of Knox.

Before leaving Colombo, we stopped in the Vale of Wolves, or Wolfendahl. Jackals had once gathered up here, and, from the top of the hill, the city still looked rich in pickings. But the jackals had long gone, and all that was left from their era was a large Doric church. Across its iron gates were three enormous letters: *VOC*. I asked Sanath to stop, and we parked amongst a little cluster of *predikants* and governors, now safely tucked up in their giant stone beds. Sanath regarded it all with candid distaste. To him, few things were more absurd than Christianity, with its lambs and its Virgin, and the big guy who was tortured to death.

He wasn't even soothed by the interior. It was like walking around in the mind of Vermeer. There was the same sense of palatial perspective, and of whitewash and jewels. Rich, creamy light splayed across the walls. The air smelt of stone and was suspended with vast clusters of candles and brass. I found the governor's pew, still with a peg for his hat. There were also pews for the slaves, built so high that the wretches inside couldn't be seen. This building had caught the world at a peculiar moment. When construction began in 1749, Dutch Ceylon was at the zenith of its pleasure. By the time work was finished, eight years later, it was on the brink of collapse.

The verger appeared, beetle-like and quick.

'We've changed nothing, no?' he trilled. 'It's all as it was!'

He showed me the vast contraptions around the doors – locks, apparently.

'It keep the prisoners in, during services!'

Out in the vestry, there were portraits of the governors.

'And this is the last one, Johan van Angelbeck . . .'

It was an odd image: an effete young blade, bewigged and frock-coated, staring dreamily into the distance, blissfully unaware of what was about to happen.

In the end, Colombo was lost for a piece of cheese.

The British had wanted it for years. It wasn't cinnamon they were after but a place to park their fleet. Eastern India had no suitable harbours; Madras was woefully exposed and Calcutta was a hundred miles up the Hooghli. But Ceylon had Trincomalee, and all that was needed was an excuse to invade. That came when Holland supported the American rebels. In 1795, a full-scale landing was launched. By the following February, the island was in British hands, all except Colombo.

Its capture was contrived by a professor at St Andrews University. Whilst on holiday, Professor Cleghorn had met the Compte de Meuron. The count's brother, as it happened, was the commander of the VOC's Swiss garrison in Colombo. Cleghorn and the count agreed that, for £4,000, the mercenaries would change sides, and all that was needed was to get a message to the brother. Somehow, it had to be smuggled through the city's outer defences, and that's how a hollowed-out cheese enters this tale.

It worked. The Swiss took the cash, and poor van Angelbeck was jolted into surrender. The British captured three hundred cannons and a huge amount of booty. 'Ceylon,' announced their prime minister, William Pitt the Younger, 'is the most valuable colonial possession on the globe.' Meanwhile, van Angelbeck never recovered, and the following year he died. He's now bricked up under the floor of Wolfendahl Church, in his daughter's grave.

So began a new chapter in Sri Lanka's story. The British had made the change look easy, with their bribery and cheese. They'd replace van Angelbeck with Sir Frederick North (the man who'd built his mansion up amongst the oyster shells). A classics scholar, aged only thirty-two, he'd have plenty of time to make his mistakes. His first task was to deal with the Kandyan kingdom. He decided on a great peace pageant, at Sitavaka. It would be like the Field of the Cloth of Gold.

Except, of course, halfway up the Great Road.

Sticking to the backroads, our journey was soon pleasingly medieval. Colombo had eventually shrivelled away, and we were enveloped in greenery and hills. This was well-muscled countryside. Everyone was out, wrestling the mud. One farmer was hacking back old lilies with an axe, a heroic figure the colour of clay. If ever we stopped, all we'd hear was the squeal of the forest and the suck and plop of buffaloes, ploughing the water. Occasionally, we'd come across an *ambalama*, one of the small, stone dosshouses built in the thirteenth century for travellers. They were still communities of sleepers, places for men to chew beetel and snooze amongst their friends. Travel, on the other hand, now seemed to puzzle them, and as we passed, they stared out, blearily amazed. In one village, they'd closed off the road altogether, and were using it as a track to race their carts.

Near Hanwella, we stopped amongst a large group of Kuravars, or gypsies, camped on the banks of the Kelani Ganga. Their encampment was a sort of anti-village made up of all the things nobody wanted: branches, dust, stringy dogs and shreds of black plastic. It's said that the first Kuravars came from India, and that they only speak Telagu, a mix of Tamil and Hindi. They've always been outcastes and trespassers, wherever they go. R. L. Spittel described them in 1922, hunting rats and iguanas, and boiling up frogs in old kerosene tins. Perhaps little had changed. They were still born on the verge and that's where they were buried. In every sense of the word, they inhabited the road.

No one was much interested in us. The women were sorting out a heap of rags, and the men were in hammocks. Eventually, Sanath found two who spoke Sinhalese. They said they made their living telling fortunes and showing off their pythons. They could also sell me a *nagatharana*, a magic stone for sucking out the venom. Soon, they said, they'd be leaving, heading up country.

'They never stay long,' explained Sanath, 'because of the worms.'

'*Worms?*'

'Yes, the ground is infested. It's their curse. For mistreating the snakes.'

Sri Lanka has a long tradition of road-dwellers and outcastes.

Everyone of a certain age remembers the Rodiyas. It's hard to imagine a people more accursed. As a caste, they emerged over two thousand years ago to be punished in perpetuity. Their crime was to have sold human flesh to the king, pretending it was venison. Forty generations on, they were still being abused and spurned. Rodiyas weren't allowed into villages and temples, and couldn't use ferries or public wells. Their very touch was enough to pollute the flesh. Knox reports that the worst punishment for a Kandyan noblewoman was to be sent to the Rodiyas to be ritually raped. Many chose the alternative: to be drowned in the river.

Unsurprisingly, the Rodiyas became the island's rat-catchers, and lived as creatures of the road. For a long time, killing one wasn't a criminal offence. Even in Dr Davy's time, they were still 'the vilest of the vile'. Like the gypsies, they lived on carrion and made their money training monkeys and snakes. Because they couldn't be apprehended, they had to be shot at a distance. All this only changed in Victorian times, as the focus moved to the women. They were considered wild, noble and unrestrained. They became popular photographic subjects. The Rodiyas would enter the modern age pouting and squirming and, of course, almost naked.

This ancient punishment only ended in the 1960s. By then, there were around eight thousand Rodiyas left, and – despite the riots – they were readmitted to society. For the first time in two millennia, they could live where they wanted and send their children to school. Most changed their names and vanished in the crowd. Few remembered them, except men like Sanath. Even as a child, he'd absorbed their alchemy, and the sexual magic. 'They had powers,' he thrilled, 'to make a girl love you.'

That first day, we got no further than Hanwella, and the outer rim of forts. For centuries, this was the front line between Kandy and everywhere else. All the great powers built fortresses here, most of them to be battered or burnt to the ground. Although Hanwella was only the size of a football pitch, it dangled over the river, and was an obvious place to fight. Few places have known so many battles or seen so many armies curled up in the soil. This human mulch had clearly suited the Kandyan flora, and the ramparts now formed deep crevasses of discouraging jungle.

The British, it seemed, had never cared for the fort, and had scraped it away and built a resthouse. I wondered if they'd also planned a cricket pitch, or just the pavilion. Edward VII had once stayed here, and had left behind a large stone bench. It was all too much for Sanath, who set off on a twelve-hour mission to wash the car. After that, I had the place to myself, except for a glorious tournament of birds. In the dining room, there were large gold bows on all the chairs, and I sat in there like a wedding-for-one. There was only one thing on the menu, and that was 'Chopsey'. It turned out to be a nursery version of curry, tasting mostly of ketchup. The waiter hovered over me whilst I ate it, and when I'd finished he asked if I could get him a job in England (and lend him fifty pounds).

Back in March 1800, Lord North's delegation had, of course, been making rather more impressive progress.

At the head of the column marched Major General Hay MacDowall, a shaggy-looking warrior with a huge dimpled chin. He'd been told to provide a procession 'as splendid as possible ... to make an impression on the minds of the Candians'. His superiors would not be disappointed. The general had brought with him 1,164 soldiers, a troop of Bengali artillery, two howitzers and four four-pounders. There were then thirty-two cases of gifts for the Kandyan king, including rosewater, sugar, muslins, gold and silver cloth, a complete six-horse stagecoach and a betel dish that had once belonged to Tipu Sultan, the Tiger of Mysore.

It had taken eight days to shift this lot the thirty-odd miles from Colombo. So far, they'd only lost two men. One had died of 'coup de soleil', unsurprising with temperatures up in the nineties. The other had been seized by a crocodile whilst rinsing his breeches in the Kelani. More worrying was the fact that this was supposed to be the flat bit, and that the Great Road hadn't even started to rise.

These days, there'd be no room for a pageant at Sitavaka. The forest had closed in again, the town had vanished and the fort was more an overgrown quarry than a last redoubt. Once a capital city, bigger than Kandy itself, now it wasn't even marked on the map. Sanath took a while to find it, plunging down country lanes and ducking through the rubber. When we finally got there, we were both disappointed; Sanath couldn't believe that the Dutch had got away with a fort so big, and I couldn't believe it had become so small. There was nowhere to park two great armies, and no field for a Cloth of Gold.

For a while, we scrambled around on the bastions. A mongoose rippled through the blocks and vanished through a crumbling embrasure. Everywhere, the masonry was being prised apart by the slow dentistry of roots. At its height, in 1675, this place had included a warehouse of 'brandi' and a massive armoury full of 'powder, grenadoes and bells'. It was the Khe Sanh of its time, a firebase deep in enemy territory. To go beyond it was an act of war.

From up in the canopy came a wicked cackle: a magpie-robin. The Sinhalese believe it's a reliable portent of doom, and I could see Sanath, his head cocked to one side. 'Listen!' He grinned. '*Listen* to that! It's Sinhala . . .'

I listened but heard only the cackle.

'What's it saying?'

Sanath howled with glee. 'Dead! Dead! *Dead!*'

If only General MacDowall had taken the advice of a magpie.

To begin with, things seemed to go well. On 19 March 1800, his enormous fancy entourage tottered out of the jungle and set up their tents below the fort. Amongst them was the diarist, Captain Percival, who noted that, although Sitavaka was already almost in ruins, it 'presented as beautiful and romantic an appearance as any spot in Ceylon'. The next day, with the thermometer at almost a hundred, the general's embassy scrambled down the hill with its gifts for the king.

Across the river, the Kandyans watched in astonishment. They'd never seen anything quite as strange as the British. It wasn't just their dressy uniforms and watches and their drawings, there was also the stagecoach. What was it for? Across their entire kingdom, there was only one road wide enough to take it, and that was Kandy's high street. Slightly more alarming was the 'heavy metal'. Artillery in this quantity had never made it up the Great Road before. Wisely, the king kept the bulk of his welcoming party – some seven thousand soldiers – out of sight, just in case.

Meanwhile, he penned his response to the British flirtation. A messenger carried the letter as if it was a sacred object, wrapped in white cloth and held over his head. It invited the visitors to proceed further into the kingdom.

The Great Road – as I now know – is as vicious as ever. Origin- ally, I thought I'd walk great sections of it, and had visions of myself cheerily clambering over boulders and climbing steadily into the Kandyan kingdom. Of course, I knew it would be difficult, but, if General MacDowall had managed it with cannons – parbuckling them from tree to tree – then surely so could I? Perhaps I'd find old waymarkers, or the odd *ambalama*. I might even meet the descendants of those who'd pelted the Dutch with chunks of pre-Cambrian Ceylon. In the history of country walks, mine would be a triumph.

That, however, is not how things worked out. For a start, I was still struggling to find a piece of the path. The lowlands were now a tangle of lanes and tracks, jungle trails and buffalo drives. Which one was the Great Road? It might have been all of them. Knox had warned that, for security reasons, 'The ways shift and alter . . . new ways are often made and old ones stopped up.' This was to say nothing of the vegetation, which – left to itself – would gobble up a road in weeks.

Then I remembered that, according to Dr Davy, the road between Avissawella and Ruwanwella had run along the banks of the Kelani Ganga. There we are, I thought, a good ten-mile stretch of ancient path. On the map, there was a road bridge between the two towns, and that was where we'd start.

Or, at least, that was where I'd start. Sanath took one look at the jungle and declared that he'd brought the wrong shoes. Alone, and feeling slightly haughty, I stepped off on to the Great Road. It was easy at first – widely spaced palms, boulders and spiny grass – and the water beside me looked inviting and drowsy. After about fifty yards, I reached a small promontory. From here, I could see how the thick jungle poured down the hills and over the banks. But, way upstream, I could see a clearing, a path and fishermen or dhobis. With my ambitious plans now shrivelling by the minute, I decided that this was my objective. I edged my way into the gloomy undergrowth, and almost immediately slid headlong into a gully, ending up in a stream at the bottom. A pair of kukuls rose into the canopy, hooting with delight. I unstuck myself from the gully floor and returned to the bridge.

There, I'd remembered seeing a local man, sitting at a stall. He was naked except for a loincloth, and was stuffing pillows with wild kapok. I asked about a path, and, before I knew it, he was waddling off into the jungle, beckoning me to follow. This time, we negotiated the gully with more dignity, only to be lost in the elephant grass beyond. For half an hour, we wandered round and round in circles, wading through darkness and termites and great, soft stumps of rotting wood. Eventually, we ended up in the same gully, knee-deep in slime. By then, I was a sodden, sticky mass of insects and scratches. The pillow-maker, too, looked spent, and so I gave him a few rupees and we padded back to the road, feeling defeated and foolish. After weeks of research, I'd managed 150 yards of the Great Road.

MacDowall, on the other hand, had covered this path at a bewildering four miles a day.

I wondered if by this stage he had already been planning his next fiasco. The problem with the jamboree of 1800 was not that it was a catastrophe but that no one realised how catastrophic it could have been. Even without the arrows and rocks, jungle travel was perilous enough. Percival describes a little Georgian army infested with ticks and leeches. 'If a soldier were, through drunkenness or fatigue, to fall asleep on the ground, he must have perished by bleeding to death.' Then there was 'hill fever', which the British attributed to cold 'damps', the 'hot and sultry vapours of the day', and the 'thickness of the forest'. For them, the only antidote was plenty of tobacco and arrack. But even the sepoys suffered, particularly with 'Cochin legs', 'Berry Berry', 'fluxes, dysenteries and fevers'. The cure was to 'rub the patient in cow dung, oil, chinam, and limejuice . . . and then bury him up to the chin in hot sand.'

Remarkably, this smelly, chain-smoking army of drunks did reach Kandy. After four weeks, they arrived at the miniature city, only to be told they couldn't come in. Even MacDowall was only admitted in the dark, and had to be out by dawn. Not a single woman was seen, and the villages emptied whenever the British approached. There followed two insufferable weeks of flummery and talks, and then the foreigners left, wobbling back down the Great Road. It would be another three years before the unwise MacDowall returned, this time without gifts.

After Ruwanwella, the landscape took a sharp, vertical turn. Until then, we'd been pottering around at only thirty metres above sea level. There was once a time when anyone, with four days to spare, could have dragged a barge upstream. MacDowall had sent those with dysentery down from here, hurtling them back to Colombo in less than eight hours.

'A nice place,' leered Sanath. 'Lots of garment factories . . .'

'What do you mean?'

'All those *Juki girls*! On the machines . . .'

'Maybe you should live here?' I suggested.

'Nah. Too much trouble, too much work.'

Higher up, the heat and clutter of the littoral seemed to fall away. I'd asked Sanath to take the backroads, and most of the time we were in the forest, spiralling upwards through the rocks. We passed a tree full of flying foxes, huge dollops of black draped in the branches like a Jesuit laundry. The villages were never big – more a scattering of huts arranged up some stairs. In one, they were holding a greasy pole competition, a rare sight in the iPod age. Sanath laughed when he saw it, and blew his horn, scattering the crowd. More than ever, I wished I was walking.

Then, at the very top of the escarpment, I had an idea. In one direction, I could see Colombo, now so pale it was almost sky. We'd arrived at Balane, which was known to the Portuguese as 'One Way Pass'. Their armies were always marching through, and then never coming back. Of the 1594 expedition, only fifty men survived. They were sent back down the road, castrated, ears clipped and with one eye for every five men. The Kandyans were serious about their independence.

In the other direction, I could see the kingdom's natural ramparts buckling away to the south. The peaks looked like lions' heads, books ('Bible Rock') and ogres. But there was also something out there I'd almost forgotten: a path, as old as the Great Road, and still walked by thousands of people every year. Although it went nowhere but up, it too was narrow and steep and infested by leeches. It was also a veritable boulevard of ancient celebrities. Everyone had been this way at some stage or other, including Marco Polo, Parakrama the Great, Ibn Batuttah, Babu Khuzi (a holy wanderer, who'd had the life sucked out of him by leeches) and the Royal Eunuch to Queen Candace of Ethiopia. And that's not all. According to the fourteenth-century *Voiage and Travaile of Sir John Maundevile*, Adam and Eve had also called by 'whan thei weren driven out of Paradys'. These were footsteps I simply had to follow.

Sanath, however, hated the idea of all that effort. '*Chee*, a foot-path. Eugh!'

'Good. Then that's settled. We're off to Adam's Peak.'

I began climbing just after two in the morning. Ahead, a distant helix of lights curled upwards into the sky. The elderly had already set out, keen to reach the summit by dawn. Most of my fellow mountaineers were old ladies, bearing gifts of vases and statues for Lord Buddha. Many were barefoot, and some were being carried by their families. They'd remember this as *Svargarohanam*, or the Climb to Heaven, and before them were over 8,500 steps. They thought I was wildly exotic, climbing a mountain without any obvious spiritual purpose. Lots of people asked to take my photograph, and then set off singing '*Sadhu! Sadhu!*' ('Hallelujah! Hallelujah!'). At 2,243 metres, Adam's Peak may not be the tallest mountain on the island, but it's certainly the most Kandyan.

I was relieved that Sanath wasn't with me. His excuse was a plump Australian called Betsy, whom he'd spotted at our guest house. Despite the conspicuous presence of her parents, Sanath thought he was in with a chance, and that wooing a teenager was a manly excuse for shirking the climb. I'd therefore hired a guide in Nallathanniya, the nearby village. I'd expected a local man, but Timmy was a student from Colombo, and alarmingly fat. But he was also a gentle and thoughtful boy, and had turned up with a backpack full of cakes, cheese, milky tea, crackers and four litres of water. I begged him to leave it all behind, but he wouldn't have it. I was his first client, and it was obviously a matter of honour to provide me with breakfast every hundred paces. Before long, he was gasping for rest, and, a short way into our climb, we lost contact altogether.

I was soon being spirited upwards on a surge of faith. By three, there were hundreds of pilgrims crawling up the steps. Crammed together, shoulder to shoulder, I was surprised how pleasant they smelt – of sandalwood and smoke. It felt as if we were all going on holiday together, helping each other into the stars. On the mountain itself, there was a *te kade*, or tea shop, almost every step of the way. These were cheery places where we could fill up on jaggery, flat bread, boiled cobs, chickpeas and pancakes. Only the monks held back, bound, as they were, to beg. One, I noticed, had a few coins in his bowl, and a Ferrero Rocher after-dinner chocolate.

Occasionally, everyone would stop to listen to a sermon. These were beautifully half-lit moments; hundreds of upturned faces gathered round a single bulb. For a few minutes, I'd have the great staircase to myself, and all around me I could hear crickets and fighting cats and the frogs sawing up the night. Ibn Batuttah had said there were two paths to the summit: this one, *Mama*, and a more difficult one called *Baba*. He'd gone up Daddy's and down Mummy's, which – without the steps – had taken three days. He'd also found the wildlife more trying. There were bearded 'wanderoo monkeys', which were always attacking people and 'ravishing' the women. Even worse, there was a sort of super-charged leech which 'when anyone draws near, springs on them.' Happily, I remained unmolested and uneaten, probably because there was more fragrant fare on offer.

After a few hours, the summit appeared, and the urgency mounted. The bushes now smelt sour and human, and long, quavering mantras crackled out of the dark. Some of the pilgrims fell to their knees, chanting the last few hundred feet. At Esala Post, the old ladies made a vow not to participate in impure acts, and so I offered a hasty mumble of my own. Then we were on the peak, hundreds of us, squashed on to a podium the size of a tennis court. At first, I felt awkward and out of place without robes or a gift, but no one seemed to notice. The pilgrims were now either prostrating themselves before a shrine, or they'd slithered to the floor and were fast asleep. A policeman in pink woollen gloves moved amongst them, swiping at hats and poking at shoes.

At dawn, a perfect isosceles triangle – brooding and ghostly – appeared in the clouds to the west. It was our shadow, cast in the first chill rays of light. When they saw this, the pilgrims rushed over to the balustrade with a collective murmur of awe. Perhaps it confirmed what they'd always believed, that Sri Lanka had been somehow singled out. I also wondered if Marco Polo had seen it, and whether this is what had prompted his bold (if slightly premature) assessment that here was 'the prettiest island in the world'.

But, amongst the faithful, there was something far holier than the miasmic triangle: a footprint. It was now protected by the shrine, like a twelfth-century pillbox. We were allowed to visit just long enough to shower it with coins. The great religions have never agreed who it was who'd planted their tarsals here. Finding a perfect fit was the great Cinderella-quest of the late Middle Ages. The Muslims claimed it was the impress of Adam; the Christians, St Thomas; the Brahmins, Shiva; and the Chinese, Pan Gu, the world's first man. Only the pilgrims knew the truth; this is *Sri Pada* (the Holy Foot): proof – if proof were needed – that the Lord Buddha stepped into the heart of the island and made it his spiritual base. 'I don't care what people say,' one of the pilgrims told me. 'This is our country, and everyone should know that.'

I thought a lot about this as I clambered down: the holy redoubt, the painful road and the Kandyans, as tenacious as ever.

It was light now, and I could make out the village, three miles below. A monk in Diesel sandals tied an orange ribbon around my wrist and told me I'd be lucky for the next three months. The loudspeakers were broadcasting long, swashbuckling tracts of the *Mahavamsa*, and, way off, down the valley, I could see a new white *dagoba*, nosing prettily out of the forest. Yet another mysterious concept, I mused, blissfully untainted by the last few thousand years.

About halfway down, I came across Timmy, who greeted me with my seventh breakfast. He was still horrified by the sudden, uphill course his career had taken. I could tell that – that afternoon – he'd be on the bus, back to the coast. With the help of four other guides, we helped him down to the village.

'I'm not an upcountry type,' he said sweetly. 'I think it's the air.'

I also found Sanath, back at the hotel, asleep on a couch. He'd never got to meet the girl. She and her parents had also set out the night before. '*Chee*,' he sneered, 'too much walking.'

We re-entered the old kingdom, not through Balane but a more sinister pass. Skirting round to the north-east, we came up the gorge at Galagedara. There were no fruit stalls here, or views of lions and bibles. It was dark and itchy, and the jungle closed over the road. At its narrowest point, we came upon a figure like Hercules, half naked and with a mane of wild steel hair. He also had a heavy club, and was lashing out at the cars. Sanath accelerated, weaving skilfully around the blows. Oddly, he said nothing, as if the encounter was perfectly normal.

Above us, through the canopy, I could just make out Galagedara Hill.

'Any chance we can get up there?' I asked.

Sanath thought about this, and nodded. 'We'll try.'

I knew he'd enjoy the challenge, or the prospect of a mission. Although he may have been uncomfortable in company or on his feet, Sanath loved throwing his car down holes or bursting through the jungle. Before long, he'd found a forest trail and we were corkscrewing upwards through the boulders. It was quiet up here, off the road. For a long time we saw no one, and then some rubber-tappers appeared, washing in a waterfall. They all stopped and stared, as if we were a herd of dragons or a passing spaceship. Further up, there were more farmers, perched in the crook of a jackfruit tree. They were smoking *beenis* and chewing betel, their chops watery and red. Captain Percival had noted that, amongst Kandyans, it was no shame to have rotten teeth, 'for they look on white teeth as fit only for dogs, and a disgrace to the human species.' As we passed the tree party, their mouths fell open, a trio of gummy wet *O*s.

After the rubber trees, the forest became even steeper and the track petered out. We completed the last few hundred feet on foot, shinning upwards through the long grass and granite. Two small boys appeared and wanted to show us their heifers, a television mast and a large cairn of purple rocks. We then all crept out to the lip of the escarpment, and peered over the edge. Below us, it seemed, lay much of Sri Lanka: mountains wrinkling off into the haze, silvery wires of water, and the rice like splinters of mirror. The boys said that sometimes they could make out the sea, although they'd never been down there themselves.

Their uncle appeared, and invited us home. Whilst the house was modern, there was no furniture except a plastic table and a plate of rice cakes. A huge family appeared, to watch me eat. They said they didn't know much about the world below, but of one thing they were sure: the last king of Kandy had set his banners up here, mounted in the purple cairn.

It wasn't long before General MacDowall was back, pounding up the Great Road. Since the pageant, he'd spent three years assembling a large force of over 1,900 men. It included Bengalis, Malays, 'coolies', lascars (or native auxiliaries), the 51st Regiment of Foot (Yorkshiremen, but mostly 'old men and boys'), parts of the 19th and a few veteran Grenadiers. It wasn't the cream of the British army, but the mood was musical enough. At the end of January 1803, the soldiers set out from Colombo, playing their pipes and thrashing their drums, 'full cheerfulness and joy'. So confident were the officers of victory, they even brought the column to a halt outside 'The Coca-nut Club' and sat down to a magnificent dinner.

If MacDowall had learnt anything from his earlier jamboree, it was to avoid Balane. This time, he'd go for Galagedara and march up the pass. In every other respect, his invasion of Kandy was just like all the others in the preceding two hundred years: the highlanders would pour down enthusiastic but ineffective fire from above, and then disappear. This time, it was left to the 51st to pursue them over Galagedara Hill.

It's not hard to picture the old Yorkshiremen, panting up through the forest: red woollen tunics, canvas knapsacks, heavy felt shakos pulled over the eyes, and hair scraped back and plaited with tar. So far, the experience of Ceylon had left them alternately roasted and drenched, and then bloody with leeches. But they were experienced infantrymen and, on 19 February 1803, they made it to the ridge in remarkable time. But the Kandyans had long since gone, leaving nothing but the purple cairn. They were already heading back to their capital, and preparing to burn it down.

At the top of the escarpment, a beautiful world seemed to well up before us. The sky was full of greenery and forests and great cataracts of water, and beyond were the mountains, drifting away like smoke. The lower slopes were delicately contoured in rice, but the rest was just as nature had left it: terraced, ornamental, wooded and turfed. I'd never seen a place so fortuitously landscaped, or so accidentally designed. 'It is undoubtedly the finest country in the world,' wrote one of the Englishmen of 1803, 'and deserves the name of Paradise.'

It was also cooler up here, and more serene. We passed a village of potters and a field of tiny red cows. Even Sanath seemed calmer now, back in the home he could hardly believe. I remember seeing a man in a stream, washing his elephant, as if it were the family saloon.

We skirted Kandy, which lay in a loop of river. On the far side, the Mahaveli Ganga had carved a wide, sandy furrow through the hills. The water was low now, but still whipping around like a snake. Trees and weeds had crept down the banks, and were gingerly spreading over the empty silt. Come the rains, they'd all be swept away and a great river restored. The ancient Kandyans had always believed this was a highway to the afterlife. The ashes of their dead kings would be brought here by a masked boatman whose job it was to paddle them off into eternity, and never to return.

We stopped on the bridge, at Lewella. Below us, the river

writhed around amongst the dunes of silt. Cormorants darted in and out of the currents, and two fishermen had nested down in the driftwood with a can of toddy. Several skinny dogs had assembled on the bridge, as if something was about to happen. Sanath loved this place, and said that, when he was a student, he'd always come down here to bathe. I asked him about the name, Lewella. The last part meant 'sand', but what about the rest?

'Blood.' He grinned. 'These are the Sands of Blood.'

Once, there was a man here who knew all about Lewella, and how it got its name.

Adam Davie was one of life's well-rehearsed failures, and had arrived in Kandy with MacDowall's expedition. Poor Major Davie had only one skill, and that was in disguising his inadequacies until the very moment leadership was needed. Until now, he'd gone happily unnoticed, but then, on 20 February 1803, the expedition had reached the city to find it in flames and everyone gone. Only the pariah dogs remained, and there was no loot, no prize money and nowhere to stay. Davie was one of the first to wander in amongst the blackened stumps and the curious complex of palaces and temples. In one courtyard, they found the charred remains of the stagecoach. MacDowall installed a new king, a hapless man called Muttasamy.

Then fate began to close in on Davie, as nature took its course. Dysentery and beriberi were soon amongst the British troops, reducing men to ulcers. The Kandyans had only to wait. Quietly, they mustered in the hills, picking up stragglers and slicing off noses and limbs. Eventually, a mere three months after his triumphant arrival, MacDowall decided to pull out. Blundering back down the Great Road, he left behind only a few hundred soldiers, with Davie in charge.

It was the moment Adam had always dreaded, and he reacted with hysteria. Howling and weeping, he begged to be relieved of his command, but his request was refused. 'God only knows,' he wrote, 'what will become of us here.' He was right to be scared. There were now up to fifty thousand Kandyans surrounding the city, and only twenty Britons capable of loading a three-pound gun.

Davie can't be blamed for the chicanery that followed. The Kandyan *adigar*, or chief minister, was also spying for the British, and so it wasn't unreasonable to trust him. He promised that, if Davie's men gave up their positions, he'd look after their sick. But this was never the deal it seemed. No sooner had the able-bodied contingent left than the Kandyans stormed the palace, which was being used as a hospital. There, they battered the patients to death, 148 in all. Only one escaped, a tough German gunner, called Sergeant Theon.

Meanwhile, unaware of what had happened in Kandy, the survivors assembled at Lewella. Unable to cross the river, Davie surrendered Muttasamy first and then all his guns. The puppet king was immediately beheaded, and his servants shorn of their noses and ears. The true king, Sri Vikrama Rajasinha, then ordered that the Europeans be killed. Only Davie and two other officers were spared. The other thirty-three were led off in pairs and pounded into the mud. Only one got away, an old trooper called Barnsley. He reappeared some days later, at a British fort, with an unforgettable message: 'The troops in Candy are all dished, your honour.'

Davie was added to the king's human zoo. Whilst his companions either died or escaped, he never left Kandy and may even have lived until 1812. It's said that he spent much of his last few years out here, on the Sands of Blood. He must have cut a forlorn figure: barefoot, stooped, distracted, and wearing a magnificent outfit of rags. His letters, smuggled out in quills and lumps of jaggery, speak of a man slowly losing his mind. To begin with, he urges another invasion, but no one comes. His sentences begin to fall apart, and he begs for laudanum. By the end, only opium will soothe his demons, and the rest of his letters make no sense at all.

6

Kandy

Afternoons in Kandy have a ghostly quality whilst the evenings are luminous.

Leonard Woolf, c.1904

I seem to have spent much of my time in Kandy in such excursions, in getting away from it in fact; it is a thoroughly unattractive town.

Raven-Hart, *Ceylon: History in Stone*, 1964

Kandy always claimed it had the biggest tree in the world. One of the first things I did when I arrived was to pay it a visit.

It was supposed to have been out in the botanical gardens, a giant Java fig. I'd seen one of these monumental vegetables before. Just stepping under the branches was like entering a theatre, or a vast auditorium of leaves. Kandyans said their tree was more voluminous than anyone else's. It ought to have been easy to find, but I seemed to spend ages running around in the rain. The only person I saw was a farmer, wearing just a loincloth. He was also running, but the cows he was chasing were in no mood to be caught. They were raiding the most beautiful larder they'd ever seen: a succulent spread of orchids and borders and weird, unearthly fruits.

Eventually, I found the place where the fig should have been, and stopped in horror. All that was left was an enormous stump and some bright red dunes of sawdust. As I sifted through the debris, a very old man appeared, like a genie in the drizzle. He studied me thoughtfully, and smiled. 'You're very unlucky,' he said kindly.

I nodded. 'But not as unlucky as the tree?'

'No, but it's been here for many generations, and you missed it by a day.'

233

For a moment, this worried me, the idea that I'd arrived in Kandy just too late for anything that had ever mattered. It was now home to almost two million people, and in every valley there was a thick sediment of buildings and streets. A railway had wriggled into the hills, and there were now aerials and tunnels and a tiny pink cap of pollution. At last, it had become the place that the Kandyans always said it was: *Mahu Navara*, or the Great City. It was hard to relate any of this to the mythical place that Major Davie had known: scorched, abandoned and haunted by dogs.

And was Kandy still a mountain redoubt in anything but height? For centuries, this was the last resort of the Sinhalese kings. They'd first holed up here in 1592, and, for the next 222 years, they'd kept the Europeans at bay. There was no need for complex breastworks. Usually a hedge was enough, and the mountains would do the rest, or the mighty Mahaveli River. Although shallower and less unruly now, it still wraps itself jealously around the city. Few places have been so fiercely defended by geography. Even in the Second World War, Kandy was seen as a natural citadel, the obvious home for South-East Asia Command. I once visited the old Hotel Suisse, where all the admirals and generals had stayed. Not an antimacassar had moved, and the cane furniture was exactly as they'd left it, as if the whole thing might start all over again.

I soon realised that Kandy held on to everything tenaciously, especially the past. At heart, it was still a town of monasteries and palaces. Sometimes, it felt as if the lawyers and tailors had their own little quarter, and the monks the rest. The focus of all this holiness was a tiny fragment of human tissue, considered to be a last remnant of Buddha and over two and a half thousand years old. Encased deep in a complex of temples, strongrooms and caskets, it was a single tooth. Kandyans often told me that, whoever holds this Tooth, holds the island in their power.

In front of this complex was not a piazza but a huge royal pond. From here, the valleys radiated outwards like a series of interconnecting rooms. But everything always came back to the lake, which held the city spellbound. I occasionally walked the two miles around the shore. There was a place for the queens to bathe, and a royal boathouse but no boats. No one ever touched the water or ventured in. People said they were afraid of it, and that, out in the depths, there was an older Kandy that had drowned. Sanath believed this too.

'The lake is hungry,' he said.

With so much hungry water, the town had been forced upwards, into the walls of the valley. Beyond a rim of temples and monasteries, it rose in ever more secular tiers: seminaries and courts to start with, then the mansions of the great and good, a few noble hotels, and then everyone else, vanishing off into the jungle. Only the wildlife ignored this hierarchy, and was always pouring over the city. Each evening, millions of crows would appear in the rain trees round the lake, and everyone would flee. During the night, it was the turn of the leopards, who'd come down and drink from the hotel pools, and eat all the dogs. Then, at dawn, the daily battle would commence, as the Kandyans took on the wildfowl and the fruitbats, in a vigorous exchange of droppings and rockets.

Everyone, it seemed, was drawn to Kandy, not just the wildlife and monks. Or perhaps it was simply that it never let anyone go. Knox would have recognised all the big family names, and – given the right occasion – they'd all have dressed up, just as they had in 1679. Some even had the same titles, like 'The Keeper of the Tooth', and the world around them was much as it had been then:

gilded, reverent, manicured and royal. For me, that would always be the real joy of Kandy, the illusion that, at least in spirit, this was still a great kingdom, and that all it lacked was a king.

Back in his own town, Sanath had become slyly aristocratic. He was furious when I booked into the Queen's Hotel because he particularly hated its drivers' quarters. After this, he'd always be half an hour late, blaming the mosquitoes.

But even if I'd put him in a suite, he'd still have been unhappy. He despised the Queen's and everything about it. To proud Kandyans, it was still an alien creature, squatting on the lake. It hadn't even been built here, but had arrived from Victorian England in the form of a kit. You could still see the girders, under layers of acanthus and gold. There was also a gold lift, myriad gilt mirrors – all more foxed than reflective – and a few of acres of Burmese teak flooring, now uneven and bouncy, a bit like the sea. In my room, I found a menu, urging me to 'Experience the Colonial Flavour' (onion rings, apparently, and chicken nuggets). I suppose it was all grand once, in the days of ballrooms and punkah wallahs, and the visit of Empress Eugénie. But, over the years, atrophy had set in, and parts of the hotel were already closing down. The monks had now reclaimed the car park and were trying to shut down the bars. For Kandyans, the place was all wrong: the wrong sentiment, the wrong style and the wrong queen.

For a while, I tried to avoid Sanath. This was easy during the day but harder at night. The Kandyans just disappeared and I could never work out where they went to play. There were no night clubs or drinking dens, and the lakeside was still under avian attack. Meanwhile, the streets simply emptied and the parks were all locked up on the grounds of decency and order. Then I heard about some dancing, across the lake. The Kandyans were famous for their piety and pageants, and this one didn't disappoint. I don't suppose it had changed in centuries: a blur of trumpets and conchs; acrobats in silver armour; cartwheeling drummers and gorgeous girls, dancing as softly as moths. At times, it looked like warfare set to music, or a deadly circus. The evening ended with the jugglers swigging at the kerosene and then spewing up magnificent gouts of flame. As I left, all I could hear was the sound of tourists, swooning in terror.

For Kandyans, this of course was merely a foretaste of the *perahera* to come. Every year, the entire city rises up in a spectacle of flaming torches, jingling armour and elephants. For ten days, the great beasts would press through the crowds, until – at the moment of ecstasy – the greatest tusker of all would appear, fabulously caparisoned, and there, on his back, would be the Tooth. This, for hundreds of years, has been the high point of millions of lives. But not everyone's appreciated it. The first Englishman to see it thought it 'something from the bowels of Pagan Hell . . . hallucination of voodoo intensity'. The *perahera* also brought out the worst in D. H. Lawrence. 'I don't like the silly dark people,' he wrote, 'or their swarming billions or their hideous little temples . . . nor anything'.

I like to think I'd have enjoyed it. The problem was it was several months away, and that was more onion rings than I could face.

I eventually relented, and called Sanath. The next thing I knew we were in the hotel bar, throwing back the beers. Sanath was now ebulliently happy, and, just for a moment, I felt a flutter of pity. The beers didn't make him any less brutal, but they did make him grander. That evening, he talked about the last king of Kandy as if he'd known him, and as if the last two hundred years hadn't really happened.

'A very strong man,' Senath insisted. 'Always lots of girls . . .'

'But didn't they come with the job?'

There was a snort of contempt. 'No, he was *potent*.'

I must've looked doubtful: Sri Vikrama Rajasinha was famously fat.

'You'll see,' said Sanath. 'Tomorrow, we'll go to his harem.'

By the morning, Sanath was less sure of the king's prowess, and didn't raise the subject again. But we still set off for the *palle vahala*, or harem, which was up behind the Temple of the Tooth. To my surprise, it was now described as the National Museum.

I'd never been to a harem before, but this, I suppose, would have been a pleasant place to store one's women: a single-storey mansion, built around a series of courtyards, with a pantiled roof. Although there were few clues as to the function of the building – or the performance of its master – it was obvious he'd lived in exuberant times. In one of his portraits, the neatly bearded king was wearing a bold chintzy blouse, red striped pantaloons and an enormous golden hat. Englishmen who met him were always puzzled by these outfits, and often found themselves comparing him to both Henry VIII and Elizabeth I. Like them, Sri Vikrama Rajasinha had been determined to make an impression. Coming to the throne as a nonentity in 1797, he'd spent the next seventeen years courting greatness, beginning with colour and jewels.

Some of these costumes had survived, and I now found myself staring into the needlework, wondering about the man who'd worn them. Tiny flakes of pearl were held in place with stitches of silver, and together the whole ensemble shimmered. Had the Europeans known how exquisite the Kandyans could be, they might have treated them with more respect. Despite centuries of isolation, Kandy had produced objects of utter perfection, some of which had ended up here, in this menagerie of women. There were vast pots, flawlessly patterned and glazed; palanquins made with Chippendale precision; arrowheads like jewellery and halberds like cutlery. Then there were the king's daggers, all lavishly filigreed and etched. To have been killed by one would have been an honour, like being battered to death with a Fabergé club.

Only the medical charts seemed out of place. The eighteenth-century Kandyan had no idea about himself or what went on inside. The human corpse was an object of dread, and so its anatomy went unexplored. As far as anyone knew, the lungs looked like a pair of runner beans and the heart was a blob.

I'd have given anything to see all this come back to life. The court of Sri Vikrama Rajasinha would've made unforgettable theatre.

Centre stage would've been the king himself. According to Percival, he considered himself 'the greatest prince in the whole world'. Everywhere he went, he was preceded by pipers and drummers, and men cracking whips and letting off guns. Only the *adigar* was allowed to stand in his presence, and everyone else had to crawl. Even then, they were expected to keep up a chorus of flattery, endlessly 'repeating a long string of His Majesty's titles', or praising the fragrance of his feet. Whether they were chiefs or professional musicians, to them the king was *dewo*, or god.

The courtiers had been given curious roles. They're described by Dr Davy in superbly purple detail. Amongst others, there was the keeper of the king's betel nuts, a chamberlain responsible for his knife and fork (the *batwadene nilami*), and the master of the royal toilet. The latter was responsible for combing His Majesty's hair and, on his staff, he had twenty petty chiefs and a cast of more than five hundred extras. Only the best families, however, could wash the king's feet.

Floating around this fairy-tale court, there were then all the minor players: acrobats, coroners, poets, conjurers, crown-appointed tricksters and the royal swordsmen (employed to fence, as bloodily as possible). Busiest of all were the lawyers. Justice could be painfully retributive. A cuckolded husband was entitled to hack off his rival's ears, and a creditor could enslave his debtor. Across the kingdom, there were about three thousand slaves.

As to what went on here, in the harem, it was hard to tell. Although the king had a favourite consort, Rangamma, there was no limit to the wives he could've had. Kandyan queens were usually Tamil, carefully selected in India. At a royal wedding, both the king and his new wife would be entirely shorn of their hair, and would then spend the day squirting each other with scented water. After that, the guests were served lemonade, along with an enormous three-hundred-helping curry. Whatever else this sounds like, it was hardly the orgy that Sanath had imagined.

From the harem, I picked my way back across the temple complex to the Royal Palace. I arrived just as the guards were seeing off the monkeys with a fusillade of rockets. The crackle of explosions made everyone jumpy, and a cluster of anxious faces appeared in a gun port. The building was just like the harem, except bigger and mounted on a colossal plinth to keep the elephants out. Inside, I could feel myself breathing stone, and the coolness seeped upwards out of the flags. The curator wasn't pleased, being woken from his arrack, and regarded me with rheumy distaste. Perhaps he thought I'd steal the king's bath, or a couple of tons of sculpture. We moved awkwardly from room to room, him always at my shoulder. One of the biggest chambers was scattered with cannonballs and housed an enormous loo.

I gazed up into the friezes, catching the courtiers in a moment of dance. It was somewhere here, amonst these rooms, that the British patients had been clubbed to death. That, surprisingly, was the beginning of a short but very brilliant age for royal Kandy. Her soldiers had surged out across the island. Suddenly, poets and acrobats were everywhere, climbing into forts and burning whatever they could. The British response was desperate, and even the governor, Lord North, was forced to sign up as a private. But, eventually, order was restored and the Kandyans decided they'd made their point and headed for home. Ahead lay an unprecedented ten years of peace. In that time, Sri Vikrama Rajasinha would remodel his city, creating the place it is today, lavished in parapets and golden finials, water, light and the dancing figures.

Even now, Kandy's courtiers could be intriguingly theatrical. In the months before arriving, I'd built up a long list of contacts, which would supposedly land me amongst the great and good. But, as in Colombo, these connections were soon falling apart. People were busy, or having operations, or out on their estates. One man told me he was trying not to eat anything that month, and another that he'd been bitten by a spider.

Even when I did meet people, it wasn't always a comfortable experience. I often felt more foreign up in Kandy, and slightly less wanted. On one occasion, I visited a local politician who introduced me to his two great slathering mastiffs. 'That one's OK,' he said nonchalantly, 'but that one, you can never quite tell.'

Another time, I was taken to lunch at the Kandy Club. Once much despised ('a centre and symbol of British imperialism', according to Leonard Woolf), the club now looked tired and grey. My host was a financier and a vegetarian, and a distant cousin of the Keeper of the Tooth. The only thing the stewards could find him to eat was a plate of lettuce and chips. This did nothing for his mood. He spent lunch dissecting the world, in a search for his country's critics. 'The great powers like to denigrate us,' he told me, 'to keep us in our place.'

I had more luck with Dr Amal Karunaratna. He was an academic, with a long, bearded face, furrowed in thought. But the frown soon lifted away at the prospect of a guest. One morning, he showed me round the family mansion, which was just above the lake. He said his forebears had always been communists, and yet the house was more like a temple. As he moved from room to room, opening the curtains, huge Buddhas would loom up out of the dark. Eventually we got to the dining room, and a long table, carved out of tamarind. 'That's where Mountbatten sat,' he told me, 'and this is Lady Churchill's chair.'

Of all these courtiers, there was one who was like a masque all of her own. She was known locally as 'Cruella de Vil', thanks to a pair of Dalmatians and her ice-queen couture. But it was a vicious name for someone so manifestly genteel, and whose life had tottered along from one tragedy to another. Besides, her real name was far more expressive and replete with drama. She was Madame Helga de Silva Blow Perera.

One afternoon, I climbed the hill to pay her a visit. The house her father had built was on the edge of the jungle, high above the lake. It was now a hotel and at the bottom of the drive was a sign: *HELGA'S FOLLY. THE MOST EXTRAORDINARY HOTEL IN THE WORLD*. At first, the extraordinariness wasn't very obvious, except for the blasts of colour: a large interwar villa painted red, a hallway in bubble-gum pink, and the reception a bright, throbbing green. Across the walls, there were huge cartoon bats, Kandyan weapons and giant Christmas baubles. Journalists were always beating a path up here to snigger at the strangeness of it all. Madame Helga would tell them it was her 'anti-hotel', but this was often wasted on them, and so it would re-emerge as 'Fawlty Towers'.

I explained to the receptionist who I was, and he made a call.

'Madame Helga will see you at six,' he said.

I waited in the drawing room, a long, lemony room, beautifully cluttered with heirlooms and oddities. I somehow found myself sitting on a book the size of an armchair, and out of the candelabras poured great waterfalls of wax (for Kandyans this is the oddest feature of Helga's Folly. 'Why use candles, when you can flick on the lights?'). But the room was also like a family memory bank, disgorged in three dimensions. Great de Silvas and Blows were everywhere, in portraits and posters and clippings from *Tatler*. There were ambassadors, composers, editors, Colombo MPs, barristers, fashionistas and dilettantes. I even spotted a Yugoslavian princess, and Le Corbusier coiled around Aunt Minette (with whom he'd had a short but outrageous affair). Helga was everywhere too: Helga the schoolgirl, circa 1950, Helga in London, modelling Dior, and then Helga the teenager, running away with the ill-fated Mr Blow.

'This was all my father's idea. "Stick your life to the walls," he'd said . . .'

I turned, and there was the full-blown Madame Helga, gazing up at her past. She'd arrived so lightly that, at first, I wondered if she really needed the floor. But it was only the silk that had relieved her of sound – a long Chinese tunic, cream blouse and a length of pink around her waist. She also carried a cane that was topped with a large silver skull, and I now noticed that it was with this that she delicately levered herself around. Pulling herself away from the cuttings, she offered me a hand. It was almost weightless.

'Yes, "The pain must come out," he said. "Get it up on the walls . . ."'

She wafted me on to a large green silk cushion and goblets appeared, their rims crusted with salt. We drank, and she talked. Sometimes, I wasn't sure if she knew I was really there. I never saw her eyes; all evening she wore her sunglasses, which filled her face like a pair of televisions, inertly brown. For a while, she talked about the people who'd been here – Nehru, Olivier, Vivien Leigh and Gregory Peck – and then the rest of her life appeared. Mostly it emerged in fragments, which, I suppose, is much how it'd seemed at the time.

As she talked, more guests arrived and we went through to dinner.

No one ate much. Two of the girls were vegan and just looked at the food.

'And I don't eat much, either,' said the man next to me. He was an artist but was dressed in the robes of a wandering sage. He'd come with his daughter, who was also a painter, and they nuzzled each other as if they were deeply in love. I was beginning to find it hard to compute the emotions at work.

We listened to Madame Helga's stories. They were never cheerless exactly, and yet somehow she'd lost almost everyone she'd ever loved, usually by their hand. By the end, I began to wonder if even Helga understood her own life and what it had become. Perhaps that's why her father had suggested putting it all on the wall, to make a map, so she could find her way through it. Or perhaps she'd learnt to avoid too much reality, to build a great set and to treat it all as a play.

In the end, it was the courtiers themselves who'd killed off the kingdom.

To properly appreciate the last of royal Kandy, I got up one morning at four and set off across the city. The traffic had yet to stir, and the light was still soft and bluish. The rain trees were dripping caterpillars and, in the canopy, thick clusters of fruit bats were slowly unbuckling themselves and flopping away across the forest. There was no one around except guards, and the bhikkus now pattering down from the monasteries with their black umbrellas and their bundles of scripture. Just for a moment, it seemed that Kandy was once again the last resort of its most magnificent king. In 1804, with the flight of the British, Sri Vikrama Rajasinha had begun his greatest works, flooding this valley and creating a city of warrior-priests.

My walk took me first along the edge of his lake, its frilly parapet wall like a trimming of lace. Along the way, I paused at the great bathing house he'd built for his queens, its watery halls now echoing and cool. Then I was in the complex of temples and making my way through the *ambarāva*, a tunnel through the walls. Towering overhead was an eight-sided pagoda, the *Pattiripuva*, its pantiled roof now turning pink in the rising sun. Not only had the last king created the lake and the lacy ramparts, he'd also built all this: the tunnel, the Octagon and much of the palace beyond.

It was exactly as he'd imagined it, his fortress of thought. I wandered great stone corridors and through doors big enough for elephants and howdahs. Every detail was designed to impress, or overawe. A vast staircase led upstairs and, at the top, I found myself in the king's library, which was stacked to the ceiling with scriptures. Amongst them, I spotted a book an inch tall, containing 'over five hundred stories'. How odd that, in Kandy, I'd come across the biggest book I'd ever seen, and now the smallest – and not much in between.

At dawn, hundreds of pilgrims appeared, along with their seers and sages, and I followed them into a much older building, a great wooden structure encased within the complex. This was the *digge*, or the housing for the Tooth. Inside, it felt like a galleon, its giant limbs of timber magnificently jointed together. This, however, was no vessel but a destination in itself, the node to which nearly thirteen million Sri Lankan Buddhists are inexorably and joyously drawn.

Slowly, we approached the Tooth. Some of the pilgrims were now on their bellies, or crawling along on their knees. But none of us would ever see the object of our quest. These days, the Buddhist world's greatest relic wears half a dozen caskets and a coat of steel. Once, travellers had been able to peer through these onion-like layers of security, but they'd never agreed what they'd seen. Dr Davy describes a 'dog's canine', Bella Woolf said it was three inches long, whilst the great historian, Tennent, always thought it 'more crocodile than man'. But, whatever it looks like, everyone has wanted it. The Chinese even sent two military expeditions to retrieve it, in 1284 and 1407. When the British eventually got their hands on it – four centuries later – the first thing they did was wrap it up in a few more layers of iron.

* * *

Back outside, the sun was up and the long open space between the temple and the outer shrines – the *Deva Sanghinda* – was a brilliant grassy green. Vendors now shuffled around in the shadows, selling water hyacinths and incense, and, from time to time, a commando of monkeys would gambol down the stone-work and rob them of flowers. No one seemed to bother. It was already too warm to care.

It was here, on this walled plain, that the dreams of Sri Vikrama Rajasinha all went wrong. By the time he'd finished building his city, Kandy was spent. Without his wealth, he no longer seemed divine. A few of the courtiers rose in revolt and the king responded with all he had left, and that was terror. The year 1814 began with forty-seven rebels impaled on sharpened stakes. But when the king couldn't find their leader – an impetuous courtier, called Ehelepola – he ordered that the family be found and brought here to the plaza. As the king watched from the Octagon, first the children were decapitated and then their mother was made to pound their heads in a mortar. She was then taken to the lake, draped in stones and ritually drowned. Even Kandy was shocked, and contracted in grief. For a week, no fires were lit and nothing was cooked.

On the coast, the British watched and waited. With Napoleon yet to be defeated, the governor was under orders to leave Kandy alone. But this all changed when Ehelepola appeared at his door, begging for an army. For the next six months, delicate plans were laid. This time, there'd be no battling up the Great Road; the invasion would come from within. A vast slush fund was assembled for securing Kandyan friends, and by the time the British set out, in January 1815, the war was almost won. Not a single soldier would die. 'The leeches,' ran one account, 'shed more blood than the Kandyans.'

Within a month, 2,762 troops were closing in on Kandy. The unravelled king now found himself abandoned, and – this time – it was his courtiers who let the enemy in.

After all that had gone on before, what happened next feels like Gilbert and Sullivan. In this scene, there are spies and archers, feathery generals, acrobats, priests, nobles in pearly doublets, and a little mechanical clock that makes everyone laugh.

The scenery was still there, known nowadays as the Audience Hall. Only the players were missing. But even without them it was hard to take it all in: a long, palace roof, suspended on a hundred stalks. Close up, I could see these columns were intricately fluted and carved, and getting in amongst them was like being in a forest of table legs. But otherwise the stage was now empty. Back in 1814, it was here that the courtiers had signed away their monarchy, and 2,357 years of independence. For the first time in its history, the island would come under a single ruler, and the Kandyans – after 167 sovereigns – would become curiously kingless.

In the temple next door, I found some paintings of this final scene. In one, I could see the governor, Sir Robert Brownrigg, in his plumed bonnet, and Ehelepola, now sitting on a horse. Ehelepola had been disappointed not to be crowned, and his new title ('Friend of the British') had left him less than impressed. Next to him was a pale and slightly sinister character. John D'Oyly had been the grand spymaster, and his face was eloquently blank. He's said to have spoken seven languages and to have had ears in every home. It was he who'd planned this war and who'd drafted the Kandyan Convention. The clock, too, was his idea, a gift for the Keeper of the Tooth. Once set in motion, it caused peals of delight, and everyone forgot what a momentous day this was.

Only one person was missing from these pictures, and that was the king. He'd fled into the hills and had been hiding in a cave. Later, he'd be found by his nobles, who stripped him of finery and bound him in creepers. He was only saved by D'Oyly, who appeared out of nowhere and bundled him off to Colombo. Then, in February 1816, the king sailed out of this story on a magnificent man-of-war, HMS *Cornwallis*. The crew would remember him as a jolly, if slightly imperious, passenger. On one occasion, he smashed up his bed with an axe because a servant had slept on it, and at least once he had to be asked not to beat his wives. Eventually, however, after four weeks at sea, the ship reached Madras. From here, the king was taken to Vellore, where he'd spend the next seventeen years in gilded captivity. He'd never return to Ceylon, but would eat and eat until finally the dropsy claimed him, at the age of fifty-two.

Whilst researching this picaresque tale, I happened to meet one of the governor's descendants. Ceylon had never entirely let go of the Brownriggs, and Henry was now a dealer in Asian art in London. Hesitant and thoughtful, he was always modest about his ancestor's role. 'Really,' he said, 'the person of interest is D'Oyly . . .'

I wondered if Sir Robert had talked like that. In his portrait, he looks discomfited by the artist's gaze, as if he'd rather be anywhere else. When he arrived in Colombo, in 1812, he was already well into middle age, and wasn't looking for a war. He and Lady Sophia liked touring the countryside, and – like the current Brownrigg – were always gathering up bits of art. Presumably, there'd been lots of royal booty, and I asked Henry what had become of it.

'It's now everywhere,' he said. 'Most of it came back to London . . .'

It took us a while to piece it all together. The king's jewellery had gone to auctioneers in Covent Garden, and was sold off in clumps. His royal standard ended up at the Chelsea Hospital, where it hung in the chapel. It was still there in 1915, when it was spotted by two early champions of independence and promptly adopted as the new nation's flag. Meanwhile, the royal seat – once the only chair in Kandy – still had some travelling to do. First, it went back to England with the Brownriggs, who then presented it to the British Crown. For a long time, it sat in Windsor Castle, where it was part of royal rituals until 1934, when the Duke of Gloucester sent it home. 'You should find it in Colombo,' said Henry. 'Have a look in the National Museum . . .'

I did as I was told, and there it was: a tiny kingdom's enormous silver throne.

I spent ages searching Kandy for some sign of the British. There wasn't much; the Queen's Hotel, a few pillar boxes and an absurdly English church, which had somehow landed amongst the *deva-las*. Elsewhere, any lingering hint of Britishness had been artfully excised; the street signs were now all in Sinhalese, the roofs were hipped and frilled, and the dancers all wore armour. None of this should have surprised me. Dr Davy had always warned that the British would make little impression on Kandy. 'We have pulled down much,' he noted, 'and built little.' By 1818, Britain's only noticeable contribution was a jail.

The Bogambara Prison was still there, much enlarged and rebuilt. I'd pass it whenever I climbed Ehelepola Road. With its slatted windows and dumpy, crenellated bastions, it didn't seem very British, and was said to have been modelled on La Bastille. From the top of the hill, it looked like a huge basin of criminal salad. There were fruit trees and stupas and hundreds of convicts. They always seemed to be out, brushing their teeth and scrubbing their shorts, but, whenever they saw me, they looked up and waved. Kandyans had once considered imprisonment an unspeakable punishment, far worse than hacking off limbs. So much did they dread confinement, they wouldn't even allow themselves to be shut inside a carriage. This building was proof of how savage and unfeeling the British could be.

It hadn't taken the courtiers long to tire of their guests. The British had turned out to be nothing if not oafish. Only D'Oyly knew how to eat with his fingers and deliver a poem. The rest had no understanding of caste or religion, no concept of holiness and only a hazy idea of hygiene. They'd also set up a military post in the Octagon, and were always tramping through the temple in their boots.

Worse, they didn't seem interested in pageantry, and had turned government from a spectacle into a dull, bureaucratic slog. Even old allies, like Ehelepola, had become unhappy. But it was his brother-in-law who rose in revolt. Keppetipola was one of the kingdom's *dissavas* (or ministers), a huge man of extravagant dress. The British, he declared, must be chased back to the coast.

History was soon repeating itself. Across the old kingdom, British heads began to appear on stakes, and sixteen thousand warriors descended from the hills. They hanged the Moors as traitors and seeded the forests with spring-guns and snares. Then they closed the roads, and the farms began to fail. In the year from October 1817, no crops were grown, and up to ten thousand people would starve. As usual, Kandy emptied and the garrison fell sick. Like all the others, the Third Kandyan War was more a struggle with disease than a clash of blades. Only forty-four

British soldiers died in combat and yet, across the island, one in five Europeans would perish.

To his credit, Brownrigg – now barnacled in sores – stayed in Kandy and took charge of its defence. Each morning, he had to be lifted from his bed to issue his orders. But there wasn't much he could do with so few troops. He tried to keep order, but the fighting soon became spiteful and desperate. Small detachments of soldiers set out in all directions, burning houses and scouring the landscape of any dissent. Dr Davy called it 'partisan warfare' – a year of his life so bleak he refused to describe it. He must have wondered if it would ever end, or if this beautiful country would be emptied of life.

Then news came through that one of the raiding parties was trapped. Major MacDonald had been holding a tiny hill at Paranagama, and Keppetipola was closing in, with seven thousand men.

A few weeks later, Sanath and I were over in Uva province, and caught up with the revolt. It was a bad-tempered journey. Sanath was now tired of driving and tired of my nineteenth-century directions, and I'd had enough of his moods. In silence, he threw his car over the mountains and into the long Uva–Paranagama valley. From the ridge, we began coiling down through pine trees, and it was hard not feel a surge of pleasure. It was also intriguing, the things we passed at almost three thousand feet: Friesian cows, a man wearing only his underpants and then – half a mile on – a tree full of clothes. But Sanath didn't seem to register any of this, and only perked up when we came to a bus lying upside down on the verge. 'See?' he snorted. '*English* roads.'

Eventually, we reached the valley floor, and there was the

hillock, swelling out of the rice. I recognised it from a watercolour I'd seen: *Paranagama, c.1818*. It had been bald then, but was now covered with a tiny mop of forest. Sanath followed a track through the paddy field, and then we got out and clambered up the mound. Near the top, there was a small temple, from which an elderly monk emerged. For a long time, he and Sanath stood talking together.

'What did he say?' I asked.

'That, in the British period, they called this Fort MacDonald.'

'And did he know what happened here, during the revolt?'

'Very bad things. They tied people up in that tamarind tree.'

I was puzzled. 'But the tree wasn't here . . . ?'

Sanath shrugged. 'That's what the venerable *bhikkhu* says.'

'But he wasn't here either . . .'

It was no good. Despite what the painting showed, a torture tree had taken root. The tamarind stood in the grounds of a school and, just above it, the hill levelled out and became a football field. We climbed up through some boulders and on to the pitch. It only just fitted the space, its touchlines falling away down steep ramparts of rock. As we were peering over the edge, a young teacher appeared.

'This might interest you,' he said.

The middle of the pitch was scattered with broken outlines, in brick.

'Maybe an old house?' said the teacher.

'And do you find other things, you or the children?'

'No,' he said. 'But they sometimes hear voices.'

MacDonald's head would have made a respectable trophy. For weeks, he'd been laying waste to Uva, cutting down breadfruit trees and burning the rice. 'An example of severity should be shown,' he'd said. So when Keppetipola caught up with him, on 28 February 1818, there was no shortage of volunteers, ready to finish the job. It ought to have been easy. The major had with him only sixty soldiers, defending a little pimple near Paranagama.

But luck wasn't with the *dissava*. The British would prove an obstinate irritant, pouring down fire into the rice. After eight days of this, the Kandyans began drifting away and Keppetipola pulled out. This was his first mistake, enabling the British to build a permanent stronghold, with a ruthless new tenant: Mac-Donald of Fort MacDonald. Before long, it had a fine brick residence and ramparts made of rock.

Keppetipola's second mistake was to become overambitious. At the very moment he ought to have been scattering into the hills, he confronted a huge army, newly arrived from Madras. It was a rout. In the mopping-up that followed, Uva was completely destroyed. Even seventy-five years later, it was still being described as broken and stagnant. 'When one considers this rebellion,' reflected Dr Davy, sadly, 'one almost regrets that we entered Kandyan country.'

By October 1818, Keppetipola was in chains, heading back to Kandy.

All the great players in this story have left something behind: a beautiful girl, an obelisk, or a severed head.

The girl was Brownrigg's, and had come home in his luggage. After the revolt, Sir Robert had stayed in Ceylon for another four years, collecting treasures and recovering his health. Amongst his finds was a voluptuous, life-sized, golden beauty, the goddess Tara. She was already a thousand years old, and yet glowed with youth. For a while, she lived with the Brownriggs in Monmouthshire, but, when the old governor died in 1833, the first thing his widow did was bundle her off to London.

Tara had ended up at the British Museum, and, one day, I went over to see her. For many years, she'd been considered too provocative for the public gaze, but now she was out, startling the crowds. It's impossible not to have impure thoughts at the sight of all those curves, and yet Tara is also a mystery. No one knows exactly how she was cast, or how she survived (and, to the museum's director, Neil MacGregor, she's one of the hundred objects that define our world). What Brownrigg made of her is anyone's guess. But I like to think that, through Tara, he came to appreciate the complexity of her creators, and the fine line between magnificence and chaos.

The other two items – the head and the obelisk – were still up in Kandy.

I came across the obelisk in the old, Georgian cemetery behind the temple. Dank and bosky, it was a bit like the graveyard in *Wuthering Heights*, except that everyone here had met a tropical end. As I picked my way through the epitaphs, I realised how exotically people had died, crushed by elephants or under falling houses. One man, Captain James McGlashan, had survived Waterloo, only to get here and succumb to the murderous monsoon. But, even in death, they hadn't found much peace. For a long time, the cemetery had employed a madman, who threw stones at everything that passed. Luckily, it now had a lady who was very sweet and elegantly robed, although – she told me – she still had to deal with the landslides and the wild boar.

Somehow, D'Oyly's obelisk had endured all of this, and now looked demure and aloof. He'd never mixed much with the other Europeans, and perhaps he'd regretted what he'd probably begun.

In 1821, three years before he died, he was made a baronet, but it made no difference. He gave most of his money away to the local orphans and lived off plantains. According to his old school friends, he'd become 'a Cingalese hermit . . . a native in his habits of life.' For a while, his brothers had tried to talk him into coming home. According to Henry Brownrigg, they'd even arranged an appealing line-up of suitable brides.

'And wasn't that enough to tempt him?'

Henry paused for a moment, as if thinking what to say.

'No. Probably not the marrying sort.'

The severed head, of course, was Keppetipola's. He'd lost it here on the bank of the lake, and it was now buried under the pavement. But between its removal and its final interment, the head had been on one last, spirited journey, almost halfway round the world.

First, it went to Colombo. Keppetipola's execution had been attended by an old friend, Dr Marshall, who'd asked the swordsman if he could keep the head. The doctor then sailed home for Britain, taking with him the *dissava*'s noddle. When Marshall was appointed 'Surgeon to the Forces' in Scotland, the skull went with him, and ended up with the Phrenological Society, in Edinburgh. There, it was studied for its rebellious qualities until – eventually – phrenology itself withered away, and Keppetipola moved on to the Anatomy Museum. He remained there until Ceylon's independence, when a call went out for his return. Once again, the bean was on the move, heading back to Colombo. It would re-enter the old kingdom on the back of a gun carriage, preceded by adoring crowds.

For now, this journey is at an end, under a large block of stone. But there are still those who argue that this head is too good for a hole. In December 2011, the issue was debated in the Colombo parliament. Keppetipola, it was argued, should rise up again and be amongst his people. But it never happened, and so the head remains where it fell, or just below.

Such reverence no longer surprises me. Looking back, I now realise that nowhere else do Sri Lankans experience veneration quite like old Kandy. It's a good place to have been a king, or to have lost one's head in a noble cause. Kandyans forget nothing, forgive a lot and are fulsome in their homage. Even now, said my friend at the Kandy Club, the great families jealously hoarde their royal relics: the fly whisks and daggers and pearly doublets. 'Not for show,' he insisted. 'These are just things people need to have.'

But, although the focus of devotion wasn't always religious, this was still at heart a monastery city. Despite the throb of traffic and the suburbs sprawling up the valleys, there was always a residual silence. The lake seemed to radiate serenity, and all eyes were constantly drawn to it and to the temples on its shore. Unsurprisingly, I often found myself immersed in little outbreaks of worship. Once, it was a busload of women, weighed down with fruit. 'They're off to see the goddess Pattini,' said Sanath, 'to pray for more babies'. At other times it was the taxis, belting out *suttas* as if powered by prayer. After a while, I began to see supplication everywhere, even in the billboards. *LITRO GAS*, ran one. *Illuminate your Life*.

My last night, I sat on the edge of the lake and watched the city whirr itself to sleep. Eveything, I decided, was more mystical here, including rush hour. The trucks were painted up like the great guardian deities, the tuk-tuks wailed and the entire lake began to spin, as if it were a wheel of brilliant white lights. Just occasionally, some ancient machine would detach itself from the rest and come ticking out of the past: a Morris Minor, perhaps, painted apple green.

I was sorry to be going, and to be leaving behind this ethereal city. Ever since arriving, I'd been charmed by Kandy, or perhaps under its spell. But earlier travellers hadn't always felt like this. J. B. Priestley (who'd called by in the seventies) declared that Kandy's 'abominable cruelties' had somehow 'poisoned the air'. Others thought it was Kandy that had driven Michael Ondaatje's father to drink, or sent Vivien Leigh over the edge. But, whether true or not, the British had never felt easy here. For them, Kandy was too spiritual, too awkward, too quiet and yet also too loud. They preferred the openness of the hills, particularly those they'd scraped of forest.

Sanath didn't protest at the thought of hill country. Inside every Kandyan there's a wild-haired, rock-thighed country bumpkin, raring to get out and pound the ancestral uplands. Sanath even became weirdly cheerful. 'You going to like it,' he said. 'It's just like England up there.'

7

Land of Hope and Tea

The wind had just swept clear the whole valley of
Nuwara Eliya. I saw, deep blue and immense, the
entire high mountain system of Ceylon piled up in
mighty walls . . .

Hermann Hesse, *Aus Indien*, 1913

In time, the jungle tide will swing once more, and
then those who care for other things than wealth will
wander back to the wet side of the monsoon line, and
while elephants browse where tea is now plucked,
antiquaries will unearth the ancient bungalows of the
British period.

John Still, *The Jungle Tide*, 1930

Sanath's vision of England was soon taking shape.

The hills swelled up in front of us, green and cool. Puffs of woolly grey cloud hung in the valleys above, and I remember copses and stone walls and little clusters of cottages. These places often had names like 'Warleigh' or 'Somerset', and there was always a country pile somewhere nearby – a 'Melfort', perhaps, or a 'Lavender House'. The higher we climbed, the more clipped and disciplined everything seemed, until, eventually, we could see nothing but gardens rising all around. Huge bouquets of red and yellow cannas were now erupting out of the verge, and sometimes – way off amongst the shrubs – a tiny stone church would appear, as if this was Sussex. The rivers, too, could behave like Avons and Stours, at least for a moment. One minute they'd be gliding dreamily through the trees, and, the next, they'd hit a lip of rock and heave themselves out of the landscape, vanishing in a wisp of vapours.

It was England all right (except for the monkeys and the banana trees): England turned on its end and drenched with colour.

I began this highland journey at the end, or perhaps a new beginning. It's now many years since British settlers left, and yet I'd somehow found one who'd only just arrived. David Swannell had been an unusual pioneer. After Oxford, he'd become a financier and, by the age of forty, he'd had his own chauffeur and a penthouse on Hyde Park. At some stage, he'd even acquired a large country house in the Kandyan hills, and had renamed it 'Ashburnham'. It would be an obvious bolt-hole when his gilded world started falling apart, in recrimination and divorce. In 2008, David Swannell had jumped out of his life, and reappeared up here.

I asked him once if he was quick thinking, or just impulsive.

'Both, I suppose. I bought it on a whim, and yet here I am, still here.'

'Perhaps you'd always wanted something like this?'

'Maybe. As a child, I dreamt I'd own a bank, an elephant and an island.'

'And have you?'

'Not the island. But I did keep an elephant up here, at least for a while . . .'

Starting again hadn't always been easy. Ashburnham was only ever superficially English. It looked like a large 1930s villa which had been plucked off the front at Torbay. Immediately surrounding the house, there were giant tulip trees ('Always a sign of the English'), but, beyond them, the mountain fell away in terraces. Way below were the hills of 'Hampshire' and 'Wiltshire', now a feathery, silver-green haze of *albizia* trees. It had taken David months to coax electricity back up the mountain, and to explore the plot he'd bought. Although mostly Arcadian – an extravagant rock garden of gigantic grasses and cotton trees – its wild outbursts could still surprise him. His dog had got the worst of this, her head blown away. 'That was the poachers,' he said. 'They make little bombs and wrap them in rice . . .'

But eventually he'd found happiness, or the calm he'd needed. He'd also added a huge castellated tower to the house, and met a beautiful girl who worked at the bank. 'Indee and I were married within a month,' he told me, and now there were children, and a scattering of tractors across the porch. David had also started taking in guests, and suddenly there was nothing left of his former life, except for the Jag, parked out in the drive.

'Let me show you the waterfalls,' he said.

It took us an hour to scramble down through the terraces. But I enjoyed the walk and David's banter, and his slightly feral thoughts. He told me that one day Britain would freeze, and that coconut oil was the key to health. He was also good at prising off the leeches and finding his way through the rocks. In the last five years, he said, he'd discovered at least three enormous cascades.

'Do you think you'll stay?' I asked. 'Is this as good as it gets?'

'Yes,' he said. 'Yes, it is. Except when the wild boar eat my banana trees.'

Outsiders setting up home in hill country have always found it like this. Hearing the tales of its latest settler reminded me of those of one of its first.

Samuel Baker was an odd person to find settling down. In later life, he'd roam round Africa, discovering Lake Albert, exploring the Nile and eventually ending up as the governor general of Equatoria. But, in 1846, at the age of twenty-five, he arrived in Ceylon. He was looking for twelve months' hunting (or 'sport'), and his memoir of that time makes ticklish reading. It's extravagant in its praise of the author, and lavishly contemptuous of native life. Before long, Baker is blasting away at the elephants (a 'gigantic scale of amusement') and beating his bearers. Once, all this would've thrilled a Victorian readership, but over the years it's become painfully boorish.

But, for all his faults, Baker was truly intrepid. Although others had headed for the highlands, no one had gone quite so far, or with quite such verve. Nowadays, Baker would have his own TV show, and would be tossing back the creepy-crawlies and spearing hedgehogs. Back then, he did the equivalent, which was to try and establish a Little England somewhere absurd. It took him a year to gather what he'd need, and, in 1848, he returned to Ceylon with his brother and an extraordinary entourage. On their march into the highlands, they'd have with them three rams, a bull, a prize cow, a pack of foxhounds (most of whom would be eaten by leopards), a carriage and horses, and twelve English yokels. The latter included a blacksmith, a bailiff and a drunken coachman called Henry Perkes. It's said that Perkes looked like a bulldog and wore an eyepatch. 'Notwithstanding this disadvantage in appearance,' noted Baker, 'he was perpetually making love to the maidservants.'

Things were soon going wrong. The prize cow died on the walk, and the carriage, unable to cope with the mountain roads, had to be abandoned. Later, Perkes was sent back to fetch it, but the drink had done nothing for his driving. Here's the message he sent back up to Baker:

Honord Zur, I am sorry to hinform you that the carriage and osses has met with a haccidint and is tumbled down a precipice and it's a mussy as I didn't go too. [. . .] the hossess is got up but is very bad – the carriage lies on its back and we can't stir it no how. Mr— is very kind, and has lent us a hundred niggers, but they aint more use than cats in lifting. Please Zur come and see whats to be done.

Your humble servt, H. Perkes

Somehow, an elephant was found. Perkes had never ridden one before, but, after a slug of brandy, he climbed on its back. Then, in Baker's words, 'he tooled the elephant along', as if it were a horse. Remarkably, Perkes managed to cover seven miles like this until something burst and the tusker dropped dead. Baker didn't seem to notice this setback, or the death of the horses and most of his dogs. He and his new villagers just kept plodding on into the hills (and, later, our paths would cross again). Even more peculiar, he didn't seem to notice that, all around him, the countryside was – once again – in a state of advanced revolt.

From Ashburnham, I could see a faint glow in the hills below. This was supposed to be the very centre of the island, a town called Matale. Before heading south, Sanath and I drove down there, descending through a forest of eucalyptus and pine. Under the trees, women were gathering up firewood in hessian bundles, and, whenever we stopped, we were enveloped in birdsong. I hardly noticed as Matale began appearing amongst the trees. Even as we reached its centre, I barely registered a town, it was all so green and dark. Perhaps that's why the things I remember seem so unconnected: a life-sized tyrannosaurus rex, a Hillman Minx with white-walled tyres, and statue of Baden Powell. It was almost as if we'd stumbled on the Lost World of 1958, or perhaps a bit before.

Amongst all this was an obelisk in the middle of the road. Clearly, lots of people had crashed into it, breaking off the edges. They won't easily forget the revolt of 1848, and nor have the pundits. The story is often retold and re-filmed, its heroes ever growing in stature. The revolt also finds the British at their most unlovable, with up to two hundred rebels arrested and hanged. It was a response so brutal that the British even surprised themselves, and all the main players were sacked and sent home. This, after all, wasn't 1817, and the people of Matale had a genuine grievance. The colonial administration had been taxing everything, including carts, labour, dogs and guns. When a rumour went out that women were about to be taxed according to the size of their breasts, the province rose in revolt.

It only lasted three months and was over by September 1848. At the very moment that Samuel Baker was setting out – Noah-like, into the wilds – the last rebels were being rounded up. They were found at Elkaduwa, near Ashburnham, hidden away – like the waterfalls – amongst the boulders.

There wasn't much to celebrate, with the end of the revolt, but it was at least the last. The Ceylonese would learn to become indifferent to the British – who could be tactless, insensitive and undemocratic – but they'd also enjoy an unprecedented period of change. Roads would splay out across the island so that nowhere was secret anymore or detached from the whole. Feudalism would disappear, to be replaced by factories, courts and a huge civil service. This may not always have suited the Ceylonese but at least they ran most of it themselves. There was even a new aristocracy, who gave themselves names like 'Totty' and 'Cholmondely', and who were British in their habits, but always Ceylonese at heart. Even better, there was the Pax Britannica. Ahead lay over a century of almost uninterrupted peace, beginning in 1848. That, if nothing else, had to be worth an obelisk.

These mountains still eat transport, swallowing up cars and trucks by the dozen. Every day the papers would carry stories of the airborne and the deeply impacted. Once, near Devon

Falls, we came across a huddle of auto-rickshaws on the edge of an abyss. Sanath pulled in amongst them. 'I'll find out what's going on.'

A few minutes later he was back.

'Tuk-tuk,' he said. 'Must have missed the corner.'

I noticed that some red-faced macaques, sensing curiosity, were also peering over the edge. 'How far down is it?'

'Two hundred metres, they say.'

'And it's just happened?'

Sanath shook his head. 'Maybe three days ago . . .'

'And the driver . . . ?'

'The woodcutters only just found him.'

'Not good, I imagine . . .'

'No,' said Sanath. 'The wild animals have eaten his face.'

We both fell silent.

It was Sanath who spoke first. 'Can we go down there?'

From way below came the sound of voices in the trees.

'No, Sanath, let's leave it to others.'

'OK,' he said. 'I'd just like to go, to see the body.'

Sanath never got to inspect the half-eaten man, and was unfazed by this brush with eternity. He still drove like a fighter pilot and blamed the English whenever the road wasn't there.

In a sense, he was right. A lot of these roads were English, many of them engineered by a single man: Thomas Skinner. He began building highways in 1820, at the age of sixteen. 'Ceylon,' the governor had said, 'needs firstly roads, secondly roads, and thirdly roads.' For the next forty-seven years, Skinner worked to this brief, covering the island in over three thousand miles of road. They creep along ledges, spiral up mountains, bore through rocks and wobble over forty-seven bridges. Now, each year, for hundreds of Sri Lankans, the last thing they'll ever see is one of Skinner's works of art.

'Look! Bloody idiots everywhere!' Sanath snarled, as we soared round Kandy and plunged off south. I was soon being taunted by the thought of trains. It was always at the worst moments – the ravines and the gorges – that a mountain railway appeared. In this stupendous rockery, it was like a tiny Hornby train set, the colourful carriages clinking round the curves. I envied the faces at the windows, staring out dreamily over the chasm. If Samuel Baker had only waited another twenty years, he'd have been able to join them (it was all up and running by 1867). This was a particularly soothing image: a carriage full of foxhounds and sheep. One day, I promised myself, I'd be up there with them.

But, for now, I had the hairpin bends, the switchbacks, the voids and my driver, a Kandyan Biggles.

About twenty miles south of Kandy, we came to a halt by a chimney breast, standing alone on the edge of the jungle.

We'd been driving all morning though *camellia sinensis*. It was the same topiary that I'd seen before: flat topped and a waxy dark green. But now it was everywhere, surging up the mountain walls, over the top, and into the valleys beyond. There were larger trees amongst it – dadap, *albizia* and chunky grevilleas – but the overwhelming sensation was always one of carpet. This great, bristly horizontal hedge would spread out over seven hundred square miles of hill country, and from now on, wherever I looked, it was always there. It was, of course, tea.

We stopped at the chimney because, according to tea people, this was where it all began. It was still a lonely place, inhabited only by orioles and woodshrikes, but, from up here, the rest of hill country looked small and compliant. Until 1852, no one knew what to do with this overgrown end of the Loolecondera Estate. But then a gigantic bearded Scotsman appeared, ready, it seemed, to tear out the forest. Little is known about James Taylor, except that he weighed 246 lb and that his men called him *samy-dor*, or the master god. His chimney is all that remains of his cabin, and everything else has rotted away. It was, however, an uncomplicated life without wives, neighbours or churches. For forty years, he lived and worked by this hearth, growing ever more gigantic. When he eventually died, it took twenty-four men to carry him down to Kandy.

Since then, the saplings he planted have never stopped spreading. By 1940, there were over 1,200 tea estates, containing up to four million bushes each. The leaves they produced would transform Ceylon's economy and make it the world's greatest exporter of tea. The hill country, too, was transformed. It had acquired not only a rich green covering of pile, but also two new races, and a beautiful workforce of women.

All around, the hills had erupted in work. Everywhere there was plucking, climbing, trimming, bagging, heaving and weighing. But in this landscape of verbs, it was only ever women. Collectively, they were exquisite: a mountainside speckled with colour and saris. But, close up, they could look obdurate and wary. Most worked barefoot, a knife at the hip, a basket slung from the forehead and a plug of gold through the nose. As young women, they could be statuesque, but the life soon shrank them, blackening joints and shrivelling faces. Few looked up as we passed, and the work went on, anxiously and without expression. To qualify for her day's pay, each picker had to climb the hillside, plucking around half her body weight in new shoots, or 'flush'. For this, she'd earn around three pounds.

Surprisingly, Sanath hardly seemed to notice these women. They didn't belong in his version of the highlands, and were incomprehensible, heathen and foreign. They not only sent money back to India, they worshipped thousands of gods, and their language – Tamil – sounded like bulbuls. But they weren't even like the Tamils from the north of the island. The 'Tea Tamils' – as he called them – were mostly *sudras*, a caste so low they were almost a sub-life. Nor did he care that they were amongst the most poorly paid workers in the country, and that many were virtually stateless and unable to vote.

'If they don't like it, they can always go home.'

'Home', for the Tea Tamils, was a complex idea. Although they'd been here for many generations, they'd never truly belonged. They knew that, in their ancestry, there was a sea voyage and a point of origin. For a long time, they'd referred to India as 'the coast', as if they'd just left. It didn't seem to matter that they hadn't yet arrived anywhere else. They were famously fatalistic and congenitally poor. All that mattered was getting through today, and tomorrow would take care of itself. This had made them profligate with money. *Kudden ill'arth'arl, moolay ill'arth'arl*, as they'd say (He that has no debts, has no brains).

Such stoicism had made them ripe for uprooting. It was the coffee planters who'd spotted their mobility and their weakness for wages. Until then, it had been hard to find paid labour (a concept the Kandyans still found repulsive). But, by 1840, the British were recruiting in India, and over the next ten years, over a million *qulis*, or labourers, arrived. This is not a proud moment for the planters. The Tamils were shipped over in foul conditions and then made to walk the last 150 miles from the coast. Almost a third died on the way to work, and the planters soon learnt to order twice the number they needed. 'That's why we're so strong,' a Tamil once told me, 'because we survived the voyage.'

They continued to arrive for the rest of the century. When a blight called 'Devastating Emily' wiped out the coffee, it was replaced by tea, an even greedier employer. Many estates would need up to 1,500 workers, or one per acre. By 1900, the Tea Tamils made up seven per cent of the population, and yet still this wasn't home. The Sinhalese regarded them as Indian, and – after independence – had them stripped of the vote. Between then and the sixties, huge numbers were 'repatriated', even though Ceylon was the only home they'd ever known. Strangely, their linguistic cousins, the Sri Lankan Tamils, raised little objection. Even for them, the Tea Tamils were just too foreign – and, of course, the wrong caste.

Once, near Ambewela, I broke the old rules and headed down to 'the lines'. In the heyday of tea, Europeans would never have done this. Not only were the workers' shacks considered unhealthy, it was also important to maintain a tradition of distance. This was as much for the Tamils' sake as anyone else's. Out in the fields, the white man may be the *periya dorah*, or big master, but he was also born of a pariah caste. To have him in your home was spiritually unhygienic.

Things may have changed, but it was still a novel idea, a visit.

'I've not had such a request,' said the old watchman at my guest house.

When the day arrived, he came to collect me in a clean turban and with an umbrella caught in the collar of his coat. Although it was a good mile down to the lines, village sounds were soon clattering upwards through the tea: pans, pails, fireworks, a set of crackly loudspeakers, some hoarse mantras, and a pair of clapped-out lungs. The watchman told me that these lines were 120 years old, that the people were good Hindus, and that everyone had coughs.

'And next week, we have a festival, and the young boys will hang.'

'*Hang*?'

'It's our tradition. They're suspended on hooks.'

To demonstrate, he took up a pinch of skin on his arm.

'But that must be agony . . .'

'They pray, and Lord Shiva protects them.'

The old man smiled, as if everything was clear, and on we went. Eventually, we reached the village, and the unfamiliar territory of men. It's strange that, in the old Kandyan kingdom, it was the women who'd disappeared, and now it was the men. The watchman explained that they usually worked in the tea factories, or in small work-gangs up in the hills. These gangs, he said, worked by themselves, led by their *kangani*.

'And how do they choose him?' I asked.

The watchman looked puzzled. 'Not choosing. It's a matter of caste.'

There were more men in the lines, looking after children. It was like a scene from an old daguerreotype: two rows of brick hovels, open drains, grimy infants, stepping stones through the muck and the odd inconsolable goat. But the watchman was proud of his home, and invited me in. There were three tiny rooms, although, in the dank and gloom, I couldn't see anything but smoke and an open fire. I could, however, hear tiny hooves on cement, but, as I stepped towards them, they skittered away into the darkness beyond. I imagined that this was the old man's bedroom.

'No,' he said, 'we sleep anywhere. There are nine of us here.'

It wasn't easy to take all this in. It felt as if I'd wandered into a story from which pieces were missing, and whose beginning bore no relation to its end. Tea had once made Sri Lanka rich, and had paid for motorways and drones, and yet here I was amongst those that grew it, in their obstinate Victorian slum.

Amongst the old planters' homes, there was still a sense that they'd lived charmed lives. Many of these great British mansions were now owned by the Colombo rich, all eagerly nostalgic for a past they hadn't had. Millions had been spent reinvigorating old herbaceous borders, laying out the willow pattern, mounting weapons back up the stairs and getting the Twyfords to gurgle again. The results could be ghoulishly British. These places often took guests, and to stay there was to return to the age of Enid Blyton. But the Famous Five had long since gone, and so had everyone else. Usually, I had a whole great mansion all to myself.

One of these places was called Taylor's Hill, on the edge of the Loolecondera Estate. It was a handsome house, with a long gravel drive and a cascade of lawns. I was met at the door by 'Cook' and the butler, Silvaraj. They showed me everything from the linen cupboards to the servants' hall, and then left me in a huge room with a four-poster bed. It had thick chenille curtains like my grandparents' house, metal windows, and a small brick fireplace. I unpacked, and then, all of a sudden, felt lonely and spare. Perhaps it was all these details from home. Or perhaps it was the thought of those who'd lived here before, never quite sure if they'd been blessed or forgotten.

I went down downstairs, in search of distraction. Whoever had created this Little England had forgotten the photographs, the dog baskets, the copies of *Pears'* and the piles of *Country Life*. But the sideboards were well cluttered with glassware and candlesticks, and, at five, Silvaraj produced a tray of drinks. It was funny to think of all these things loaded on to ox carts and creaking into the hills, along with the toilet bowls, grand pianos and clawfooted baths. Silvaraj wasn't old enough for the ox carts, but he remembered all the servants.

'These houses had twenty, sah. Maybe thirty!'

'What did they all *do*?'

'I don't know.' He giggled. 'Cooks, cook's assistant, kitchen boy . . .'

'And then all the maids . . . ?'

'Yes, them, and the sewing lady, and all the gardeners . . .'

'And a butler? And a driver?'

'Yes, yes – them too! And even a boy to walk the dogs!'

Silvaraj was still laughing about this as he clattered off down the hall.

I took my drink outside. The lizards were laid out across the terrace, catching the last of the warmth, and, from down in the lines, I could hear the sound of chanting. When it stopped, there was a very brief moment like Herefordshire. But then the sun went down and the sky did what it always does six degrees north of the equator, and turned a sudden black. For a while, I sat and watched as the fireflies swirled around like a runaway cosmos. Then I got up and went back in. Silvaraj had already lit all the fires and was soon settling me down amongst the tureens for a sumptuous feast of mushroom soup and cauliflower curry.

Not everyone had appreciated this lonely, overpopulated life. In 1948, one old planter, Harry Williams, tried to make sense of his time in the hills. His book, *Ceylon: Pearl of the East*, portrays the world of the planters as curiously sterile. The British were only ever boarders, he said, working their contracts until it was time to go home. They'd left almost nothing of themselves: no theatre, no opera, no ballet, no orchestra and no library of note. They hadn't even understood the island around them. Travel was difficult; there were railway tours but no hire cars, and the rickshaw touts were 'utterly corrupt'.

For the wives, life revolved around the servants or the district club. They never worked, and often no longer had their children. At the age of seven, the Little Britons were sent 'home', leaving their mothers with an unpleasant choice: to follow them and divorce, or watch them go. A few sought consolation in affairs. Spouses, noted Williams, 'were apt to stray under the stresses of the lovely surroundings'. But spare lovers were hard to find. Coupling with a Ceylonese was considered unthinkable, and across the Uva Province (an area the size of Yorkshire) there were only two hundred planters. The men had become picky, too, after years in Asia. In Leonard Woolf's case, his tastes had changed in only a matter of months. Writing to Lytton Strachey in 1905, he said that European women now disgusted him, with their 'drawling' and their 'dried-up faces'. 'My God,' he wrote, 'they give me the creeps.'

For men, sex was more abundant but equally complex. A young expatriate couldn't expect a white girl, but – if he played by the rules – he might find a local beauty. Woolf said his employers never discouraged this: 'According to the Ceylon Government, you may copulate but you must not marry or become engaged.' There were then two other important rules. First, all mistakes had to be paid for, with ruinous awards of alimony and houses. Second, a white supervisor, or *durai*, should never sleep with the company's tea-pickers. If he did, he'd be fired and repatriated, and she'd become an outcaste.

But, within these rules, anything (or most things) went. In this, the Tamils could be surprisingly generous. According to Williams, they regarded the white man's celibacy as unnatural, and fecundity as the obligation of males. It wasn't uncommon for a man to offer a *durai* his daughters as concubines. Some whites never grew out of these arrangements, and men, like the archaeologist H. C. P. Bell, were always helping themselves to the pick of the pickers. Even now, there are respectable Tamil families who claim they've got H. C. P. clambering around in their family tree.

For some, these encounters – mute and impassive – were no doubt good sport. But, for most, it was still the same loneliness, except with a girl.

Of all the houses I stayed in, the remotest was near Horton Plains.

It was so high up here that sometimes Scotland appeared. On the plateau, there were bogs and waterfalls, and a gnarly, black forest, trailing strands of mist. In places, giant ferns arched out of the undergrowth like lacy green umbrellas, dripping with cold. Then, as the forest fell back, the road petered out on a fog-rinsed savannah of patana grass. Sanath pulled over on to the moss, and, a few moments later, an enormous black nose appeared in the window. But it was the antlers that made more of an impression, and the thought that we were about to be pronged by the Monarch of the Glen. Luckily, however, Sanath's head was still in the right country, and he recognised a gentler creature: the sambur deer. 'How could people ever shoot these animals?' he snarled, and gave it a chocolate biscuit.

But, for the Victorians, this great spongy plain was far too much like home. Once they'd shot all the elephants, they treated it just like Scotland, even adding a few touches of their own: bracken, hares, trout, a hunting lodge and that most invasive of Westerners, *ulex europaeus* (otherwise known as gorse). It will take the Sri Lankans generations to de-Scottify this sedge, but at least the sambur had made a comeback. I also spotted another group of survivors, sitting around in their woolly trouser-suits. They were the bear monkeys, and I could only assume that, because they'd never appeared in the shooting logs, they weren't much good to eat. Some day, they'll be one of the few creatures to have watched this Scotland come and go.

The house was just below the plains, in Ambewela. It was still higher than anything in Britain, and if Ben Nevis had been there, I'd have been able to peer down on its summit, some 1,500 feet below. At night, we all gathered around the fireplace (except Sanath, who was now holding court in the pantry). Unsurprisingly, the house had been built by a Scotsman, and he'd understood about fires. But his Caledonian home hadn't fared well in the post-British years, and had fallen into ruin. It was eventually restored by one of my Colombo friends, Hiran Cooray, and had become a small hotel. 'It was hard,' he said, 'to find workmen prepared to work in the cold.'

The next day, the lawns looked as if they'd been bombed.

'Wild boar,' said the houseboy, Robert.

Ah, I thought, not so Scottish.

'We're always being raided by animals.'

'I hear the civet cats come for the goats.'

'Yes,' said Robert, 'and leopards have eaten all the village dogs.'

'Why's it always the dogs?'

'Tethered dogs? It's like dinner on a plate.'

A few miles short of Mount Pidurutalagala, we caught up with Samuel Baker again, or at least his carrots.

In his memoir, Baker doesn't mention Pidurutalagala. It was a big thing not to notice: the tallest mountain on the island. I'd like to say we climbed the 8,281 feet to the top, but actually we drove. The army had built a road up its flanks and were now perched on the top. It wasn't hard getting in; when the soldiers saw Sanath, they laughed and waved us through ('Old friends,' he muttered, unconvincingly). Across the summit, there was a thick grey fuzz of aerials and wire. I don't know who else was listening to its electronic chatter, but the frogs had tuned in. The whole mountain seemed to throb with amphibian ringtones.

An officer with a swagger stick appeared and showed me the view. The last three weeks were now scattered round my feet: Adam's Peak, Horton Plains, tea country, a great kingdom and the little empire within. But, off to the south, we could also make out a small hummock of tobacco-coloured soil, known as Mahagastota. It was here that Baker had built his visionary village.

Later, we drove over there, but – as so often with dreams – it hadn't survived the stark light of day. Half of Baker's land had now disappeared under a noisy sprawl of asbestos called the Republican International School, and the rest had been divided up into tiny plots like pieces of cake. Each one was so rich and golden that, to plant his seeds, the farmer had only to poke his finger into the earth.

Baker would've been pleased to see the survival of his vegetables, given that everything else had perished. I was still finding it hard to like him (especially after reading that he strangled a dying leopard with his necktie, so as not to spoil its pelt). But he had at least persisted when anyone else would have run, screaming, back to Colombo. First, his horses died, and then the rams, his twenty-six bullocks and the bailiff's wife. Meanwhile, the grubs ate all his potatoes and his barley was plundered by deer and hogs. For seven years, he stuck it out, eventually resorting to carrots and leeks. Finally, in 1855, he packed it all in.

But it wasn't all in vain. Mahagastota's weevils would give the world a great explorer, and the vegetables he'd unleashed would spread out, up the valley. Mahagastota may have failed, but the next-door village, Nuwara Eliya, would flourish on its greens and become the capital of carrots.

With its deep-rooted vegetable wealth, Nuwara Eliya was now the hub of hill country life. Out of the fogs, an enormous mock-Tudor town had appeared. It was like Windermere, but almost fifty times higher and three times the size. There were clock tow-ers, parks, pavilions, Victorian villas (with names like 'Ferncliffe' and 'Spencer Park'), war memorials, tea kiosks, several miles of iron railings, a Gothic post office, at least one Holy Trinity, a lake (of course) and perhaps the last racecourse in the land. It was said there were only fifteen racehorses left, but Nuwara Eliya didn't mind, and still liked to watch them going round and round.

The half-timbering seemed to cover everything, even the cor-rugated iron. I don't know what you call this style (neo-pavilion-ism, perhaps? Or mock-tropic?), but the wealthy loved it. They were always flying up from Colombo and landing on the lake. For them, the mist and cold were novel, and so was the idea of a last little bit of England still in their midst, magically preserved in isolation's aspic. On a good *poya* day, they'd fill up not only all the villas, but also several turreted hotels, including the Glen-dower, the Windsor and the splendidly lugubrious Grand.

Surprisingly, even Sanath seemed happy.

'I'm going to come and live here,' he announced.

'And what will you do?'

'Collect rent and watch girls.'

'So you'll be looking for some property?'

'Exactly,' he said. 'Like an apartment or something.'

And, with that, he stalked off and didn't reappear for the next two days.

Left to myself, I soon got into the Nuwara Eliya way. The shops kept English hours and sold everything from butter cake to gold braid, but mostly cake. At around noon, the mounted police came trotting through town in their polo shirts, as if they were off to play a few chukkas. Huge Tamil families would then take their picnics down to Victoria Park, the children all dressed up in cardigans and socks. People kept telling me how English everything was, and I suppose it was in a way – except for the bare-chested priests, the dancers dressed as horses, the beggars with their drums and the wild boar grubbing up the golf course.

Once, an old man stopped me to tell me about his son.

'He died in London. Had a brain tumour.'

'I'm so sorry,' I said, 'That's terrible . . .'

'But isn't it funny, too? Born in Little England, died in the Big One.'

Some afternoons, I went down to the lake. The Wahabis loved it here, and their black-robed women would arrive in huge numbers, hire all the pedaloes and then set out over the water. Once, I was sitting under some cedar trees, next to a young couple having a picnic. For them, it was obviously a special occasion – at least until a carcass landed in their rice. It turned out to be the indigestible parts of a rat, dropped by the crows. The couple recovered well from this intrusion, but its suddenness brought us together.

'The lake's like a stage,' I suggested. 'You can't look anywhere else.'

'They were going to drain it once, and put the silt on the carrots.'

'*Aiyo!* Not that story, Sivan!' said the girl. 'He's *visiting* . . .'

But Sivan ignored her. 'The army objected . . .'

'Oh,' I said. 'Worried about pollution?'

'No, they didn't want us to see all the bodies.'

The ghosts of an earlier era still met in Nuwara Eliya, up at the Hill Club.

It was all exactly as they'd liked it: a wide swoop of lawns, a baronial clubhouse (neo-Tudor, of course, but with a touch of Argyle), fires blazing in every room, an elephant's foot for wet umbrellas, two snooker tables, and various cuts of wildlife hanging off the walls – pigs, bald leopards and a long, thin rasher of python. There was also a library, called 'The Monsoon Room', full of crumbling magazines and, every night, a hot-water bottle appeared in my bed. The old rules, too, had survived: No Dogs, No Cooking in the Rooms and No Women in the Bar. At some point, I was discreetly advised that I'd need a jacket for my stay. As I hadn't come with any planter-wear, one was produced from a huge wardrobe of Harris tweed.

Club life continued as if all the old Britons still called by. There was even a dinner laid on for them every evening. The tables would be set with linen and silver plate, and a small army of waiters – dressed in braid and white drill – would hover amongst them. It was always good planter food: Norwegian salmon, perhaps, with roast potatoes, followed by Victoria sponge. When I'd finished, my coffee would be laid out under a portrait of the

Queen, aged about twenty. Although I was the only obvious guest, the waiters would still hurry around, clattering the cutlery and gathering plates. Perhaps the planters really were out there, and I just couldn't see them.

At night, I'd hear dancing in my sleep. Sometimes, the sound was real, drifting up from beyond the trees. But mostly, it was simply the echo of the day.

Life in 'Little England' would often break out in ritual. One day, three large chariots were dragged through the town. They were towering constructions, pieces of multistorey furniture, strewn with garlands and light bulbs, and inhabited by priests and huge wooden horses with bulging eyes. It's said that, once, women would have thrown themselves under the wheels as an act of devotion. Things were calmer now but no less intense. As each *teyru* rumbled past, all work stopped, and even the nurses would pour on to the street with offerings of fruit. Almost everyone here seemed somehow involved. Tea Tamils, unlike Sri Lankan Tamils (a quarter of whom were Christian), were almost universally Hindu. To be a non-believer up here was to be an outcaste, unable to marry or feast or live in the lines.

Another day, I followed a procession out to the *kovil* of Sita Amman. In some ways, it all looked familiar, like one of the temples in London. There was the same focus on Shiva, the god of war, the same dense clusters of lesser gods, the same outbreak of colour and the same phalluses and *yoni* to remind us all of our reproductive duty. But there was also a long pavement of smouldering charcoal and some musicians, who seemed to fill the air with both anxiety and ecstasy. As the crowd groaned with excitement, the old woman next to me began flailing the air with her arms and her hair. The firewalkers, dressed only in sarongs, were pushed to the front and, as the crowd roared and wailed, they set out, one by one, along the coals. It was their dance that would revisit me at night, with their feet in the embers. But, at the end, they always walked away, no doubt reaffirming – amongst thousands of worshippers – the awesome power of magic.

These days we probably worry less about what we don't understand, especially as we realise how much there is to comprehend. But the planters had struggled with all this, and the faith of those who'd filled their lives. To diarists like Harry Williams, the worship of Shiva was particularly difficult. How could a 'destroyer' be an architect of human existence? And how could he demand abstinence when he appeared to have lived his life in 'a drunken stupor'? And was Vishnu any better? Hadn't he also lived a life of debauchery, respecting neither his sisters nor his mother, and taking sixteen thousand wives? Williams was also puzzled by the revered imagery of genitalia. It seemed so unremarkable to the Tamils, and yet – as he put it – 'they shrink from the vulgarity of the human body'.

The mystery was never resolved. Although the British would become fond of the Tea Tamils, they were always strangers. It seems odd now, to have lived like this for over a century; going to bed, listening to the dances and understanding nothing.

One evening, I had dinner with Christopher Worthington, the last of the planters. We met over at the golf club. In the last seventy years, this place had been as much his home as anywhere else. His name was everywhere, up in the varnish. He was also its most conspicuous member, a huge stooped man in a serge suit the colour of milky Earl Grey. Although he was genial – jovial, even – he could also be rigorously exacting. That evening, he called the steward over twice. 'Why isn't the mustard out?' he demanded. 'And why are your shoes so squeaky?'

Sometimes he broke out in Tamil, which made everyone gape. Across the world, there must now be only a handful of white men who can speak fluent Tamil. When he spoke it, it sounded like Churchill played backwards. Later, I teased him about this.

'You don't make it sound very Asian,' I said.

He smiled. 'Far too colonial for that.'

During the evening, this is the story that emerged:

'I first came to Ceylon in 1946 with my mother and stepfather (I was always lucky. Two of everything; two mothers, two fathers . . .). My first school was just over there, Hill House, on the other side of the lake (all gone now; just an army camp). And then I was sent back to England, and went to Heronwater and Sedbergh and Trinity, Dublin. Well, then a bit of national service. Benghazi. Euugh! But then, in 1958, I joined a London firm and got back to Ceylon, and so here I am . . .

'Yes, it's been a good life, or at least I liked it. When you start, you're known as a creeper. It's a sort of apprenticeship, and you spend six months living in the manager's bungalow. There was a hell of a lot to learn – Tamil customs and the language. We had to learn *twenty* new words a day! But, you know, we never learnt to write it, and nor can they. And I never learnt Sinhalese, either. Can hardly speak a word. But then I don't care much for the coast, only here, hill country.

'It's true, it could be lonely. At the end of those six months, we were given our own bungalow, a mud-brick place, up in "The Field". We each had a houseboy, but he went back to the lines at night. So, yes, it could get quiet. There was the district club, once

a week, and we got a bit of leave, of course. Six months at the end
of the first five years. I liked England, but was always happy to be
back . . .

'Yes, a good life, but I suppose it couldn't last. When tea was
nationalised, most people left. There'd been four hundred planters up here in 1958, but, by 1976, there were only two. I stayed
because I didn't really know anywhere else. Funny to think that I
once managed a thousand acres of tea, and now I've got fifteen.
And the visa situation's always a bit iffy. Perhaps they'll heave me
out? I may yet end up in a bedsit in Fulham . . .'

A few Britons had grown rich in Ceylon, and there was still a
scattering of stately homes across the hills. One of them was
Adisham, which was supposed to have been modelled on Leeds
Castle in Kent. It was now a Benedictine retreat, but – with a letter from a Catholic priest – I'd be allowed to come and stay.

It was an unusual version of Kent. A large troupe of monkeys
sat around the gates, and the drive ended on the lip of a deep
escarpment. Great, clammy clouds would detach themselves
from the jungle below, roll up the mountain and pour over the
garden wall, drenching everything in cold. The house didn't look
much like Leeds Castle, either, although it was a formidable pile
of turrets and granite and Gothic arches. There was also a large
studded front door and heraldry all over the drainpipes. This
identified it as the house of Sir Thomas Villiers. In 1887, he'd
arrived in Ceylon, aged eighteen, with only ten pounds to his
name. Forty years on, he'd become so wealthy, he'd needed a castle, and an army of craftsmen had arrived from India, and
building began.

Eventually, my hosts appeared – the monks. They were all

Sinhalese, dressed in white habits. They told me they lived to a rigorous cycle of prayer, but that they also made jam. 'We've kept all the old fruit trees,' said Brother Jude.

'Just like the other Adisham,' I said.

He looked a bit uncertain about this. 'That's in Scotland, no?'

Once we'd put all the Adishams back in the right place, he showed me my room. It was in an old pantry, and was so full of bunk beds we could hardly get in. I was to eat next door, in Sir Thomas' garage. It had large sliding doors and space for two limousines. 'One of them was a Daimler. Bright yellow, they say,' said Brother Jude, and then he disappeared, and I never saw him again.

'Don't trust them,' said Sanath.

I'd almost forgotten about Sanath, trailing sullenly behind. He hated the foreignness of it all: the cassocks, the statuary and the bleeding hearts. 'Be careful,' he said, maliciously. 'Always lock your door . . .'

'You think they'll steal my things?'

'Everything. I'm out of here. I'll stay in the village.'

Alone, I could now hear the house in all its detail: the sound of heavy doors closing, the ticking of an old clock, sandals on stone and the rasp of a key in a lock. For a while, I was unsure if I was welcome in the main parts of the house, but when I heard thin, reedy voices gathered in evensong, I crept up the passage into Sir Thomas' quarters. To my surprise, it was almost all exactly as he'd left it – the clocks on the mantelpiece and the irons in the grate. The dining room had its original red silk wallpaper, and the drawing room was still hung with Lady Villiers' watercolours and swagged in yellowing damask. Even the ancestral portraits had survived around the library walls – great dukes and eminent Bedfords and at least one whiskery prime minister. It was a curiously durable family seat for a couple whose only child had been killed in the trenches.

The monks never used these rooms. The armchairs in the library were covered in camel skin, and seemed almost new. But the surfaces were lifeless, and the huge glass lampshades silted with moths. Most of the books were about the Great War, and I had a sudden image of Sir Thomas whiling away his twilight years, searching the pages for the son he'd lost. Lady Villiers had already died in 1938 (she'd succumbed to the long voyage back from Europe, and was buried at sea). Sir Thomas would struggle on for another eleven years before shutting up the house and sailing home. He made his last great journey in 1959, off to the crematorium at Putney Vale. But, here, his portrait still hung in the morning room; a man great enough to rebuild the world in the wrong place, but without the luck to enjoy it.

'The eyes follow you everywhere, don't they?'

It was Brother Michael, the oldest of the monks.

'Probably just checking you're looking after it all,' I said.

'In over fifty years, we've hardly touched a thing.'

'And will Adisham still be Adisham in another fifty?'

'Yes,' said the monk, 'unless the porcupines eat all our trees.'

After Adisham, Sanath and I parted ways. I'd been plotting this for days, but I needed a railway and wheels of my own. Part of me was sorry it had come to this. I'd always hoped that, during our weeks together, an understanding might develop and that we'd end up buddies. But this didn't happen. It wasn't just because he'd piss wherever he wanted, catcall the girls and steal all the forks. Sanath's anger loomed far too large, and, most of the time, not even he could find his way through it. He could love things with vehemence – like trees and woodshrikes – and then work himself into a rage over Muslims or Tamils or all things American. Between these two extremes, there was a subtler range of antipathies, none of which made sense. He loathed the 'English' roads, of course, but there was also contempt for lorries, dogs, waiters, politicians and women who coughed. After several weeks of this, I'd had enough. Although I never came to think of Sanath as typically Sinhalese, it often troubled me that I felt I'd seen him before. Then I remembered where: the photographs of Black July. In his gleeful fury, Sanath, it seemed, was the face in the mob.

Not much had disturbed the Pax Britannica. But one thing that did was the arrival of five thousand prisoners of war, in August 1900.

The Boers had lived in the wide valley a few miles below Adisham. With its cold, dry air and grassy slopes, Diyatalawa had often been compared with the African veldt. Perhaps that's why it was chosen as a camp for the captured armies of President Kruger. Hammered together in only five weeks, it was known as 'Silvertown' because the tin sheets glinted in the sun. But, really, it was two towns: Kruger's Dorp for the Transvaalers, and Steyn's Ville for those from the Orange River Colony. Just for a moment, it was another Dutch world, captured in miniature: barracks, latrines, *winkels* (or shops), a scattering of arc lamps, and a ring of barbed wire.

Although I realised that none of this would have survived a century of rain and termites, it still intrigued me, the idea of an Afrikaans town, high in the hills. The only trouble was that it was now part of the military academy, slap in the middle of the ranges. Naively undeterred, I besieged the Ministry of Defence with letters, and then, one day, a colonel called. 'Captain Herath,' he said, 'will meet you at the station.'

Archaeologically, it was a day full of surprises. Whilst Silvertown never reappeared, nor had it entirely vanished. An Edwardian garrison town still flourished nearby. There was a soldierly church, a suburb of dark green tin, and a row of shops selling everything a cadet could ever need, from dress swords to camouflage socks. Meanwhile, Captain Herath was polished and clipped, and carried a short leather crop. Although little over twenty-five, he was already a war veteran. He also had with him a sheaf of sepia photographs, which made him a kindred spirit. We stopped first at the commandant's house, a long, creaking bungalow of corrugated iron. Here, the captain had arranged a large chocolate cake.

'This place used to be a ship,' he said.

'A *ship*?'

'Yes, the navy took it over, after the Boers. Called it HMS *Uva*.'

'Funny to think of a warship, in the mountains . . .'

'Not just one,' said Herath. 'There's a whole fleet up here.'

After excavating the cake, we drove up through the great metal hulks to the gates of the academy. Polo fields appeared, and soldiers who looked as if they'd been starched into their uniforms, and then pressed and ironed. Their assault rifles had brilliant amber stocks and grips, and, whenever they snapped to attention, they made a sound like breaking sticks. Someone – them, perhaps – had whitewashed all the kerbstones, which now coiled upwards through the pines. Near the top, the trees parted, and, out of the straw, snipers emerged, shapeless and ogre-like in their robes of shaggy camouflage.

'The ranges,' announced the captain.

Up here, his photographs starting coming to life. There was

one of a single tree, which I could now see was deep in the rippling grass, a concrete pool in which the Boers had bathed, and the little *kopjes*, or hills, where the guards, the Gloucesters and Worcesters, had set up their guns. Once, there would've been little figures in this scene, forlorn men in bits of uniform, watch chains and battered hats. Most of them were farmers, pious men who'd busied themselves in their devotions. But there'd also been Russians and Norwegians up here, a professor of mathematics, 250 children (captured with their parents), Kruger's son, an Irish-American brigade, thirty-two engineers, a conjurer, a boxing champion, an undertaker and a soldier of fortune called Captain O'Reilly. It was a motley collection of dissidents, those who'd confronted the empire.

There was a crackle of gunfire, but Herath didn't flinch.

'Here,' he said, 'I think this is where the huts stood.'

It was now an empty plot of orange soil. We walked out along the camp's old track, these days scattered with bullets. For two years, the Boers had lived up here. The things they'd made still turned up in Colombo from time to time – tobacco jars and paper knives. They'd also produced a couple of newspapers, called *Prikkelraad* (or *Barbed Wire*) and *Dum-Dum*, and some had taught themselves cricket and taken on the British. A few had even joined a road-gang, earning a rupee a day to dig their way to Bandarawela.

'Still there,' said Captain Herath. 'We call it the Boer Road.'

Beyond the plain, the forest began again. Few prisoners had tried to escape, and those that did were driven back by hunger and the leeches. Only two made it home, after jumping overboard in Colombo harbour and clambering on to a Russian ship. Their journey took them as far north as they'd ever imagined, via Aden, the Black Sea and St Petersburg, and then south through

Berlin, Amsterdam and German West Africa. Amongst Afrikaners, they'd attain mythological status, known forever as 'The Swimmers'.

I asked Herath if he knew where the dead were buried.

He nodded. 'Over there. The end of the thousand-metre range.'

We drove out to the firing point. The machine-gun fire was all around us now, but, up in the bushes, there were two stone columns. One was for the Gloucesters, who'd already lost half their number at Nicholson's Nek, and who – in Ceylon – were hit again, this time with 'enteric'. The other monument was for the Boers, who fared even worse during the epidemic of December 1900. Amongst the names, I spotted a boy of sixteen, and a man who must have thought he was Elijah himself, giving his age as 144.

Apart from this monument and the knick-knacks, the Boers had left little of themselves behind. By the end of 1902, the war was over, and they were marched back up to the station with all their monkeys and parrots and carvings, to begin the journey home. The Irish-Americans were shipped off to Boston, and the Austrians to Trieste. The rest went home to Africa. Until the last, the young Kruger had resisted all temptation to speak English, and now couldn't wait to leave. He'd jumped on the first ship he'd found and disappeared off to Zanzibar.

It was the end, too, for Silvertown. With the departure of the Boers, it would soon rust away, and within a few years had reverted to grass.

This part of my journey had also come to an end. For a few unforgettable hours, I'd ridden the railway to Badulla. It was like watching an old film of everything I'd seen, tea country ticking past at a few frames per second, the landscape retouched in improbable greens, and the lives of the Tamils, captured forever in panoramic vision. But, at Badulla, all this seemed to flap off the spool as the railway suddenly ended, along with the mountains, Little England and the tea. Beyond the town, there was only one more ridge of jungle, and then a deep drop on to the coastal plain.

Badulla was, I suppose, like anywhere else at the end of a line. There was that feeling that things had arrived, but that nothing had ever left. The Kandyans had brought their forts and temples, and the British their gingerbread gables, and it was all still there, heaped together. Even now, there were fresh flowers in the graveyard of St Marks, and hymns wafting out of the church. My hotel looked newish on the outside, but, inside, it was cluttered with history. It wasn't just gramophones and elephants' feet; the cutlery – old airline stock – had gathered here from around the world. Nothing, it seemed, had ever been thrown away. The hotel's owner, whose father had been a steward with the British army, also did a stalwart line in military sandwiches – huge objects, assembled with mustard and cheese. Then, whenever I went out, he'd go and read all my papers, just to make sure I was getting it right.

'Mr John,' he'd complain, 'you haven't said much about my hotel.'

The day before I left, Badulla had a carnival, and dragged everyone out of the past. It was supposed to be a march for the United National Party. If any party was the heir to British rule, it was the UNP. It was years since they'd held power, but they still marched around under the banner of an elephant. That day, they'd called together everyone they could from across the old kingdom: trumpeters, tea-pickers, conjurers, drunks, some dancing dwarfs, a few Kandyan acrobats, a man dressed as a skeleton and a full-sized aeroplane made out of cardboard. I noticed that, wherever they went, they left a trail of broken shoes. They'd also managed to co-opt a dozen English girls into their ranks. I recognised them from my hotel – volunteers at an elephant sanctuary. One of them had a tattoo across her navel, which the man next to me studied with interest.

'Prostitutes,' he concluded.

'Right,' said his friend, 'that UNP guy must be jumping them all . . .'

'And what about these people?' I asked.

Ahead of us were five grizzled, half-naked axemen.

'Veddas. Live in the forest.'

'Out east,' added the other. 'It's a bit bloody crazy down there.'

8

The Wild East

In these inhospitable forests, the most wild and arid
on the island, where food is scarce and only attained
with great hardship, the Vedda is king.

R. L. Spittel, *Wild Ceylon*, 1924

What lay ahead wasn't worrying, but it did feel unknown. Of all the island's regions, the south-east always seemed the most mysterious and the most remote. The ancient chronicles hardly mention it, and, on early maps, it's just a blank, dappled with scrub. It would be defined by what it didn't have – in particular, rain, reservoirs and rivers. Victorian map-makers left huge chunks of it empty, or marked 'Unknown mountainous region'. Where names did appear, they looked hurried and inept, like 'Westminster Abbey' or 'Capello de Frade', the Friar's Hood. Even in the 1920s, visitors like R. L. Spittel tended to think of themselves as explorers, uncertain what they'd find.

The region still felt unvisited. If the island were a clock face, between three o'clock and six, there was almost nowhere to land a ship. Meanwhile, inland, there were fewer roads than anywhere else, and only one railway, veering off to the north. It seemed that anything could be out there, lurking in the bush. In 1924, it was a man-eating leopard, but more recently it's been bands of guerrillas, hiding out in caves. Then there were all the creatures of local mythology. One, called the Gawara, was said to have the head of a buffalo and a tongue so rough it could lick away flesh. Worse, perhaps, were the Nittaewo, a race of miniature cannibals, who attacked in huge numbers, filleting the locals with their long fingernails. To those planning a visit, none of this was particularly encouraging.

But the hostility had also made this land a refuge. Somewhere out there were the last of Sri Lanka's original inhabitants. They were the Veddas, the same axemen I'd seen mooching through Badulla. Out here, however, they were hunters, or, in some cases, the hunted. I tried to think how I might reach them, and then I remembered an old friend, Anurudha Bandara. He'd made contact with the Veddas, and often made trips. I asked him if there was any chance of taking me along.

'OK,' he said. 'Meet me in Mahiyangana.'

It was a long and dreamlike journey through the eastern foothills. All morning, the bus howled its way downhill, but then the highlands reappeared off to our left, in a gorgeous backdrop of purple and clouds. The forest now felt hot again, and we were back amongst villages made out of branches. In one, a dog rushed out to challenge us, before disappearing heroically beneath our wheels. Another time, we were passed by an excavator, with three Chinese labourers asleep in its bucket. The road was always trying to buck us off. Sometimes it would plunge through huge drifts of drying rice, and then, at other times, it would vanish altogether and we'd find ourselves gushing through sand, or jolting down a riverbed.

Eventually, however, the road found its rhythm. As the howling died away, I pulled out my notes and began to read.

For almost two and a half thousand years, the Veddas have been considered half-castes: royalty, but with the blood of demons and snakes. It's an insult they've never truly shrugged off, and yet it wasn't always like this. In the preceding fifteen thousand years, they'd probably had the island all to themselves, and their *waruges*, or tribes, had prospered. They may even have benefitted from the arrival of the Tamils and Sinhalese, soaking up survivors when their great cities collapsed. But the new arrivals also brought with them a dangerous idea. The Veddas, they said, were descended from the island's original demon-queen, the product of her nights with Vijaya, the Sinhalese prince. This immediately made the Veddas both awesome and vile, a royal vermin.

Little had changed in the next two thousand years. The Veddas would inhabit the margins of Sinhalese society, picking up the language but none of its habits. By 1681, Knox reported that they were living as honoured outlaws, raiding travellers and fighting their own tiny wars. At night, they'd leave meat with the blacksmith and if, by the morning, he hadn't left them arrowheads, they'd kill him. But the Veddas were also trusted. In times of invasion, they'd take care of the Kandyan queens and the royal treasure. They could also be found at all the great battles, pouring their arrows on to European heads. But none of this changed them. In 1821, Dr Davy described them as 'solitary animals . . . resembling more beasts of prey, in their habit, than men'. The same thing might have been written at any time in the previous two millennia.

As far as the British were concerned, the Veddas were thrilling. Here were people who had no idea how old they were, who had no sense of time and who'd yet to learn how to laugh and smile. They wore clothes made of bark, and carried a slice of human liver to make themselves more fierce. To the Victorians, it seemed that at last they'd linked up with Neolithic man. One writer described the Veddas' existence as an 'interlude', adding that they were 'due for extinction.' This idea, that the Veddas were somehow an accident from another age, was still popular, even today. In Colombo, at least one travel agent was offering 'Stone Age' tours.

They were lucky, perhaps, to have anything left to tour. The twentieth century had been particularly cruel. In 1911, there were 5,342 Veddas, and yet, a hundred years later, there were barely five hundred. Some had perished in the Spanish flu pandemic, but many others had simply lost their lands and vanished in the mix. In almost no time at all, the *veddarata*, or Veddas' range – which once extended to the coast – had shrunk to nothing. The worst year was 1983, when huge tracts of land were swallowed up in a hydroelectric project. At about the same time, the civil war began, and the Veddas were deprived of their guns. After perhaps eighteen thousand years of hunting, the Veddas now had nothing to do, and nowhere to go. Many of them had drifted off to Bintenne, or – as the Sinhalese called it – Mahiyangana, the town now appearing on the plains ahead.

The next few days felt like a play in which all the actors had become somehow trapped. It was as if a storyline had entered their lives and possessed them, and now all they could do was keep the show going. Anurudha had warned me about this. 'I'm going to take you to Dambana,' he said, 'a few miles from Mahiyangana, and home to about 350 families. We pay them some money, and they show us their lives. If they don't want to take part, they stay out of the way. OK, I know, it's not perfect, but it's a livelihood. The Veddas can't hunt anymore, and have no tradition of farming. It's all they have left, putting on a show.'

In this play, the sequence of events didn't seem to matter, and so we began with a curtain call. That night, a cast of Veddas turned up at our campsite, as if to say goodbye. There were six of them, looking just like the figures the Victorians had photographed: bearded, barefoot men, wearing only loincloths, and each with an axe. Lining up on the rocks, they bowed and danced, and made me a gift of leaves. Then something odd happened – perhaps it was all the lantern smoke – and I was copiously sick. There was nothing in their script about the audience vomiting and running off into the jungle, and so the Veddas just carried on bowing and dancing and presenting their leaves. By the time I got back, they'd crept off, vanishing into the dark.

'They looked tough,' I remarked to Anurudha.

'Even tougher, once. They could separate fighting bears.'

The next morning, three of the Veddas reappeared, out of the grass. They carried their axes hooked over their shoulders, and moved noiselessly, like cats. The oldest was about seventy, and the youngest had his hair tied up in a bun. But the third one was the most powerfully built, his beard so wild and silvery-black that, for a moment, I thought he was entirely covered in hair. He was also the only one to have a bow and arrow, a knife, and a name: Uru Waruge Sudubanda, or 'Sudda'. It was once thought the Veddas had little use for names, and that people just were who they were – the Fat One, perhaps, Oldie, or the Boy.

At first, they hardly seemed to notice me, and merely assumed their roles. Sudda loosed off his arrows, and the others fanned out into the trees, pursuing an imaginary pig, which they then killed in a frenzy of shrieks and gurgles. Later, an interpreter appeared – rat-faced and malevolent with drink – and we all set off, deeper into the forest. After a mile or so, the Veddas suddenly stopped and listened. I couldn't hear anything, but they all padded off through the leaf mould until they came to an old tree. There, the boy listened again, and then, with his axe, he reached up and severed a huge lobe of honeycomb. With their beards now full of bees, they offered me a dollop and were surprised that I liked it. Did I like the other things they ate, like iguanas and monkeys? They told me hornbills had been popular, and the little swiftlets that went *chee-chee-chee* when you put them on the fire.

'And what about porcupines?' I tried.

The Veddas all looked at each other in horror.

'*Eeugh*,' they said. 'They're for the dogs.'

Things changed after the honey, and our day began all over again. Everyone presented their knuckles in welcome, and we clasped each other's forearms. Sudda even reintroduced himself, with a cluster of stories that never quite finished. He said he made charms out of elephants' teeth, and that many of the women had gone away to be housemaids, and that it was now dangerous to hunt, and that some of his friends had been shot, and that chewing betel had given him cancer, and that – beneath the beard – half his jaw had gone. Perhaps, he suggested, I'd like a monkey-skin drum? Or maybe he could make me a bow and some arrows?

I tried to explain that Vedda bows were too big for the plane.

'OK,' he said. 'And now it's time to see the king.'

It was a grim thought, a king. Who would I find at the heart of this performance? A figure of fun, a pearly king? Or perhaps some half-crazy Asian Lear, busily presiding over his own demise?

But Uru Waruge Wanniya was neither of these things. He lived in a small, thatched house, where he made baskets and bottled honey. He was a 'king' in the sense that he was the son of the greatest Vedda, Tissahamy. Like his father, he'd also become a champion of aboriginal rights, and across the wall there were photographs of him shaking important hands and meeting the generals. These pictures were the only furnishings he had, apart from a mat and a chopping block. Nor was he apparelled in velvet and ermine. Although his beard was tidier and his eyes were rimmed with fatigue, he was dressed just like the hunters.

I was offered a seat on a low mud wall.

'I understand you've been to Geneva,' I said.

This was translated first into Sinhalese and then *Veddi Basava*, and the king nodded. 'I was away for a month,' he said, 'and spoke at the United Nations. They'd never heard of the Wanniyala-Aetto (or "Forest People") before, but things got better after that. My father had said that, if we were moved into communities, we'd become beggars, but we're still here. Some changes are good, and some not. We're not sure about the schools, but we don't like the shirts and the shorts.'

'And what about the tourists?' I asked.

'They're all right, as long as they don't try and change us.'

We'd been talking an hour, and the king now looked even more exhausted.

I got up to go. 'Just one thing. How did you like Geneva?'

'I know how lucky I am,' he said, 'not to have that noise.'

On my last day, we had several visitors to our camp.

The first were two snakes, who came slithering in amongst the tables. One was a rat snake and the other a krait. Sudda had already given me something to ward off serpents: a *cacuna* seed, shaped like a python's head. Despite its magic, I still jumped. But Anurudha smiled and carried on writing. 'One who fears snakes, sees them,' he said.

The next visitor was more welcome: Mr Gunawardene, the teacher. He was half-Sinhalese, wore a shirt and carried an umbrella. Under his arm, he had with him some books he'd written. These were probably the first stories ever published in *Veddi Basava*, and when Mr Gunawardene read one to me, it sounded like the forest coming to life. He said it was a beautiful language, but that it lacked the words to describe our times. Shoes – always hated objects – were merely 'containers', and aeroplanes had become *uda thanen mangachchana dhandu kachcha* or 'above-going machines'. But the improvisations could be endearing too. A motorbike was a *hootu hootu*, and the English language was referred to as 'birds shouting' because that's how it sounds.

The last visitor was Sudda himself. I found him a short distance from the camp, crouched in the grass. As I approached, he held something up for me. It was a bow he'd made, just the right size to go in a plane.

I finally left the mountains behind at Monoragala. There, I changed buses, for one even louder and browner. It was like a wandering factory, belching dust and peppery smoke. At some stage, a young monk got on – a boy of no more than fifteen – and everyone around me shrank from their seat to allow him to sit. His face was so drained of expression, he didn't seem to notice when the landscape of Africa appeared, or at least one of its savannahs. When I saw a speck out in the straw, I was able to watch it for ages until – just for a moment – it became an elephant and calf, and then it was gone again, shrivelling away in the windows behind.

For some reason, which I now can't remember – or justify – I made for Arugam Bay. Perhaps I'd thought that the east coast should begin with a blank, and 'A-Bay' was certainly that. It had once shown promise as a little Acapulco, with its colossal ridges of surf. But then came the tsunami, rolling everything away. There were still a few plinths along the beach which had once been hotels. Further on, around the headland, the air fizzed and crackled with salt, and angry spectres spun up out of the sand. Beyond this, there was nothing but the long, hollow groan of the sea.

Only the hardy had returned. They were mostly surfers – big, well-bouffed boys with pigskin tans. I was surprised how much noise they travelled with: phones, screens, heroics and guitars. It was disorientating, being amongst people so busily recreating somewhere else. My guest house – a collection of shacks under the casuarinas – went along with this, and, that night, I was over-whelmed by techno and Swedish. There were also a lot of Israelis around, so many – it was said – that the village now sold kosher food. I did, however, spot one couple almost as small and pale as me. They were Polish and admitted that all this sound made them feel safe. Sri Lanka, they said, could be a confusing place for East Europeans. Whenever they'd seen that big, sad smile, they'd immediately assumed they were about to be robbed.

I couldn't face a blast of breakfast, and so I checked out. But, before leaving Arugam Bay, I went to visit some Muslims, who were friends of friends. They were brothers, one a driver and the other – who I'll call Dr H – an academic. I felt strangely restored, sitting with them, drinking coffee.

The village, they said, had often been the victim of its visitors. The first surfers – mostly Westerners – had arrived in the sixties, using the forest as a toilet and then cleaning themselves with two-rupee notes. At least they were better than those who arrived in the eighties. Amongst them were both men and women. Although they didn't wear uniforms, they collected dues from the farmers. People challenged them, but didn't usually survive.

These visitors wore capsules of cyanide and carried knives. They also had a way of making themselves understood. 'One of these,' said Dr H, 'was to burn a plastic bag, and then drip the burning plastic in your ear.'

It was the Tamil Tigers, defining the outer limits of their domain.

The idea that the Tamils own part of this island is relatively new.

For centuries, they and the Sinhalese have lived amongst each other, without definable borders. Even in the far south, Tamil artefacts have been found, dating from the second century BC. Their language is all over the landscape, too, and it may even have been them who introduced the reservoirs. But Tamils weren't just everywhere; it's now thought they'd formed an integral part of Sinhalese life. Their genes are strikingly similar, and so are their homes, their clothes and their rules on kinship, caste and cousin marriage. Even in matters of religion, it's surprising what they've shared. Works of art like Tara – a Hindu goddess adopted by Buddhists – demonstrate that, in the seventh century, at least, there was a lively dialogue between the faiths.

Tamils, in fact, have popped up everywhere in this island's story. They dealt with the Chinese in Galle, in 1410; they provided the Kandyans with new princes and queens; their kings fostered Buddhism above their own faith; there's even evidence that, in 1100, it was Tamil soldiers guarding the Tooth. True, the Tamils were supplemented by invaders and tended to dominate the north (where, in the thirteenth century, a tiny kingdom formed, called Jaffnapatam), but elsewhere they merged in, amongst the Sinhalese.

This worked well until democracy appeared. Medieval kings and colonial powers had only ever needed a general consensus, and so everyone was loosely consulted. But, by the twentieth century, it was only the majority that mattered. In 1931, Ceylon attained universal suffrage, ensuring that – from now on – the Tamils were a minority and could only ever have what the Sinhalese wanted. This coincided with the move towards independence, burgeoning nationalism and – amongst Buddhists – a growing sense that this island was theirs.

It was still a long time before Tamils demanded a homeland of their own. Their *vellalas* – the English-schooled elite – still believed that everything could be sorted out in a gentlemanly fashion. But independence, in 1948, only made them more vulnerable, and the next thirty years were far from genteel. Sinhala became the official language in 1956, and, in due course, the Tamils were losing their jobs and their university places. During the sixties, a hard core in Jaffna began demanding independence, but it wasn't until 1976 that the main Tamil party adopted the idea.

On a map, the separatists' claim looked like a crab's pincers clamped around the island. Beginning just below Arugam Bay, their nation-to-be would extend all the way up the east coast, across the top (taking in the Jaffna Peninsula) and down the west coast, almost as far as Negombo. It would be known as 'Tamil Eelam', and would absorb almost half the island's coastline and a third of its land mass. Given that Tamils made up only twelve per cent of the population, it was always an ambitious claim.

But, if the extremists had got their way, they'd have had Eelam all to themselves, expelling every last Sinhalese. In their ideology, the Tamils were the original inhabitants of the island, the heirs of a great civilisation, with its roots in Mohenjo-Daro and Harappa. Their forebears had discovered America, and Jaffna was once a

South-East Asian Athens. In some versions, there'd even been a Jaffna Tamil at the birth of Christ, as one of the Magi. As for the Sinhalese, they were upstarts. Their chronicle, the *Mahavamsa*, was pure fantasy, and they'd not come from north India, or anywhere else. They were simply Tamils who'd adopted a separate identity on becoming Buddhists. If the Sinhalese couldn't understand this, then only a war would make them see sense.

'And what about the Muslims?' I asked Dr H.

'We didn't want to become a minority within a minority.'

'So you were caught in the middle . . . ?'

'Yes, like a *yak bera* drum, beaten at both ends.'

After a Muslim start, my day grew more and more Tamil as I headed north.

To begin with, I could see only minarets, out in the brush. Along the shore, most of the villages had been washed away, but some had been rebuilt. In one, it seemed that surrealists had been at work, and everyone was living in concrete teapots. I could see goats amongst them, and tottering figures wrapped in black. Aboard the bus, everyone watched in silence. Behind me, there was a bristly old army sergeant with his teenage wife. They were Sinhalese, heading home on leave, and were pleased to see me. The sergeant told me he hated it here because it was all too foreign. This didn't surprise me. On the east coast, only one in five people are Sinhalese, the rest being equally divided between Muslims and Tamils.

Further on, the sea began to seep inland, and temples appeared. There were canoes on these lagoons, and, from time to time, a thin halo of mesh would rise up out of the boats, hover for a moment, and then fall lightly on to the water. Often, the prawns would be sold at the roadside, their tiny silvery bodies still shivering with life. Liquor stores, too, had appeared, and Methodist churches. But that was as much as we ever saw of life. The villages were now barricaded places, each house surrounded with a band of tin or woven cadjan. Sitting a few feet above the ground, these weren't so much obstacles as screens. Whilst the Sinhalese had been happy to be seen and admired, the Tamils, it seemed, preferred to vanish within themselves.

Forty years earlier, tiny spurts of flame had begun to appear in this great wet triptych. It was a little light brigandage at first, but then, on 27 January 1987, an enormous war burst into life.

A few miles short of Batticaloa, I got off the bus and took a three-wheeler inland.

The driver was curious as to why I wanted to drive in amongst the lagoons, but didn't have the English to probe. Instead, he took the causeways at speed, soaring this way and that through the complex of water. After twenty minutes, the road ran out and a small, squat ferry appeared. The soldier guarding it carried an outsized assault rifle, his long, tapered thumbnail lying over the trigger. Everything would be guarded from now on, even this great lopsided raft of rust. It was only just seaworthy, and struggled to the far bank, its tiny outboard churning the water as if it were concrete. On the other side, the land was even flatter and emptier, but out on the horizon there was a thin brocade of palms.

'Kokkadichcholai,' announced the driver.

There, amongst the trees, was our destination, another secretive village. I could see pantiled roofs above the cadjan, but there was no one around. A few miles beyond, however, we came across an old man, wheeling his bicycle along the bund. 'Yes.' He nodded. 'This is the Serendip Prawn Farm, right here where we're standing.'

I asked if he'd been here in January 1987, and wrote out the date.

He nodded. 'Yes, and a lot of people died.'

'What happened?' I asked. 'Was it the Tigers?'

He shook his head, and, with his hands, filled the sky with knobbly blades.

'*Helikāptar*,' he said.

To begin with, the Tamils had shown little appetite for bloodshed. A guerrilla band, the Tamil New Tigers, was formed in 1972, but was widely despised. When, three years later, it put a few bullets through the mayor of Jaffna, most Tamils were appalled. There wasn't even a rush to arms in 1977, when three hundred Tamils were killed in riots, or in 1981, when the police set fire to Jaffna Library (then the world's greatest collection of Tamil books).

That's not to say there was no resistance. Organisations began to spring up everywhere, and soon Tamil society was a forest of initials. The main ones were EROS, TELO, PLOTE and EPRLF, but there was also the Three Stars, the Revolutionary Warriors, the Liberation Cobras and the Tamil Eelam Blood Movement, not to mention another twenty acronyms, including IFTA, TEEF, RELO, TESS, TELC, TERO, TERPLA and TPSO. But, in this battle of letters, there was one group that emerged stronger and crueller than all the others. It was the newly renamed Liberation Tigers of Tamil Eelam, or LTTE.

Everything changed, of course, with Black July, in 1983. With thousands dead in Colombo, it seemed obvious that a Sinhalese government either couldn't or wouldn't protect its Tamils. The same government then banned all talk of separatism and sent even the moderates into exile. At this point, many Tamils turned to the Tigers, and so the drift to arms began. Although their numbers would never be great – twenty thousand at most – by 1987, the LTTE had 4,700 guerrillas ready for action. As a Tamil priest once told me, 'It was all about balance, and protecting ourselves from the Sinhalese mob.'

Support had come from a surprising quarter. India had never wanted to excite the idea of independence, having sixty million Tamils of its own. But here was a chance to humiliate Colombo. The Sri Lankans had become far too close to India's old enemies, China and Pakistan, and now needed to appreciate their neighbour. Between 1983 and 1986, the Indians shipped vast quantities of arms to the Tigers, opened thirty-two training camps and trained some fifteen thousand cadres. They even trained the suicide bomber, Dhanu, who'd one day return and blow up the Indian president. Such was the dangerous game that Delhi had played.

To begin with, the Tigers made insurgency look easy. They could choose when and where to fight, and the Sri Lankan army – or SLA – couldn't be everywhere at once. The army was also hopelessly prepared for the struggle to come. Until 1983, it had been largely ceremonial, and was kept deliberately small to stop it launching coups. In the next three years, it would grow from eleven thousand to fifty-six thousand, but it was never enough. As my friend, the army surgeon, put it: 'Back then, the army had no plan. The initiative was always with the Tigers, and we could only react. We'd recapture territory and then, a few days later, we'd be driven back, and it would start all over again. A terrible waste of life! Morale, too, was poor, and so was the equipment. There was no protection against mines, and many were blinded. Eventually, we got anti-blast vehicles from South Africa – called Buffaloes – but then the Tigers just used bigger charges . . .'

It soon became a real war, without any rules. For a while, the army took a righteous line, but – out east – no one was looking. It might've been different if the enemy had observed the niceties of fighting, but they hadn't. Simple, semi-literate soldiers would struggle with this and the sight of their comrades, melted into their seats or their faces blown away. In the madness this spawned, the only way to fight atrocity was with rage of their own. When a rumour went out that the enemy had friends at the Serendip Prawn Farm, it seemed the perfect place to stage a revenge. What happened out on the bunds would ensure that the war was always bigger after this; that there'd be more volunteers, more atrocities, more rage, and another twenty-two years of fighting.

It happened much as the old man had told me. The raiders swooped in and killed eighty-seven people. In some accounts, the prawn farmers had their eyes gouged out before they were shot. The dead were then heaped up on tyres and burnt. Afterwards, the army would claim that it hadn't been them that carried out the slaughter, but it was always the helicopter that gave them away.

It was late when I arrived in Batticaloa, and I had to creep through the city in the dark. In places, the lighting had failed altogether, and I found myself trudging through soft, unfamiliar shapes. Was it ever possible, I wondered, to enjoy a city that disappeared so thoroughly at night? Although I'd discover that, by day, 'Batti' could be startlingly pretty – a city of islands on the lagoon – by night, the doubts always returned. I never felt like this about any

other Sri Lankan city, but this ambiguity would soon taint everything. Even now, I'm not quite sure whether Batticaloa was truly
horrifying or just a little strange.

The hotel I was looking for was in the Tamil quarter, on the
waterfront. To get to it, I had to edge down a long alleyway of
drunks. No one stirred as I stumbled through the bottles. One of
the bodies was dressed only in shorts. Every part of him was
unconscious except his mouth, which was still giving lessons or
shouting out orders. Beyond him, the alley opened into a courtyard and there was the little cement hotel. It's said that these
surroundings had protected the Subaraj Hotel from bombs and
from the gunmen who'd swum over the lagoon. During almost
three decades of civil war in Batticaloa, this was the only hotel to
have remained open throughout.

The staff were asleep on mattresses in the lobby. The youngest
of these boys got up to find me a piece of soap and a room. He
said his parents had once sold liquor and breakfasts, but not anymore. According to the register, there'd only been twenty-two
guests in the last two months. 'Take any room you want,' said the
boy, and so I chose one next to the lobby. In the morning, I discovered that the windows had been painted over, and so – unlike
the rest of Batticaloa – it never got the days, just the long, unfath-
omable nights.

Although I remained the hotel's only guest, every day there
was a visit from a Spaniard called Consuela. Tall and flowingly
robed, she rode everywhere by bicycle. Once, she'd been part of a
consultancy, advising on tourism and how to survive the peace.
But the NGO had long since gone, leaving only half-finished jobs
and Consuela. As far as I could tell, she lived on nothing and all
alone. She said it was hard to mix in Tamil circles when women
seldom ventured out. What's more, in Batti it was often thought

that whites were an untouchable caste, and that all their women had AIDS. A proper woman should be betrothed in childhood, should wear her hair tied back in a ponytail, should never be seen in less than a sari and should fête her husband with sons. Until boys appeared, she'd be considered 'barren' (and there'd be a special place in hell for the husband).

'It sounds as if you've given yourself quite a task,' I said.

Consuela smiled. 'Hotels painted violet . . . mismatched sheets . . .'

'Rooms without windows?'

'Yes, that as well. And then there's alcohol.'

'What, too restricted?'

'No, too much. People think it's the government, trying to kill them off.'

The city was always different in the light, and could be disconcertingly quaint. Out on the lagoon, there were little outriggers suspended in the glitter. People had often described this as an Asian Venice, but, however silly this sounded, Batticaloa was, in some ways, better. It had coconuts, kingfishers, a pretty fort and a world-famous choir of singing fish (or were they molluscs? No one seemed quite sure). Bread was sold from bicycles, and, for breakfast, I had strawberry ice cream at the Bombay Sweet House. There was also an esplanade and a natty little teahouse, built for the coronation of George V. Even the place names – Moor Street, Lady Manning Road and Love Lane – sounded happy and united.

But the ambiguity was always there. Wherever I went, I was never quite sure if I was being welcomed or despised. People could be co-operative but wary. Waiters had a special cold smile, and, in the fort, an old policeman with a rifle insisted on taking me around. Was he helping me, or watching me? The children, too, were different here, and would study me without any expression at all. After a while, I wasn't even sure about the quaintness. Whenever I thought the waterfront couldn't get prettier, the amputees would appear. These were always the hardest cases, the widows and the beggars without hands and feet, or with faces blown away. Nowhere else had suffered like this. Batticaloa had provided more guerrillas than any other city, and had suffered the highest losses. Some twenty-seven thousand women had been widowed, and – even now – there were eight thousand people whose fate was simply unknown.

No one would understand the ambivalence of Batticaloa quite like the Indians.

To great cheering, they'd arrived here with an army in July 1987. It had been a vicious six months since the prawn-farm massacre. In June, the Tigers had stopped a bus full of monks, just south of the city, and slaughtered them all like sheep. Meanwhile, the army had tried to reclaim rebel-held land up north, and were bogged down in Jaffna. A new weapon had appeared: the suicide bomb. The first one, in a truck, had killed 120 soldiers in a single click. It had also sent out a bleak message of despair and commitment. When India began parachuting food into Tiger territory, Colombo paused. Seven weeks later, the two countries signed an accord, and on 30 July 1987, a new army appeared: the Indian Peacekeeping Force.

What followed was the weirdest part of this war. To begin with, the Indians were seen as liberators in places like Batti – Hindus come to rescue Hindus. It was like a shopping trip at first, as the jawans (or Indian troops) bought up things they couldn't find back home: whisky, foreign electronics and imported cigarettes. But, by October 1987, the Indians had fallen out with the LTTE, and so a three-way war began. This would be India's own little Vietnam, although they couldn't see it at the time. For the next three years, the world's fourth largest army would slog it out with the Tamil Tigers, whilst Colombo's army was confined to barracks.

The Indians were horrified to find that nothing was quite as it had seemed. Their first casualties were their commandos in Jaffna, captured and necklaced, or hung up on meat hooks. At that point, the peacekeepers tried to capture the city, an operation for which they'd allowed only two days. Instead, it went on for months and, with no maps and little intelligence, the Indians never knew where they were. Their response was to pour in more men, until eventually they had 100,000 troops in the country, at a cost of $3 million a day. Often, they outnumbered the Tigers by seventy to one, and yet they controlled nothing but the roads. The Tigers held everything else, and could vanish like vapours. They'd also learnt how to knock out a T-72, and how to rewire a house. It might look normal from the outside, but turn on the lights and it would all explode.

As the war got madder and madder, the Indians began to forget why they were there. With no enemy in sight, they shelled everything. *Your safety is our priority*, ran their leaflets, but no one believed it. In Jaffna, over 1,400 civilians died in the shelling. Elsewhere, the jawans let the shopping go to their heads and pilfered whatever they could. In Batti, people have never forgotten this, nor how, at the roadblocks, they were relieved of everything from cigarettes to watches. One man told me he'd seen the Indians bundling goats into their armoured cars, and gorging on cooking oil and bunches of bananas. But it wasn't just things, they'd also helped themselves to the women. My friend, the surgeon, Dr Goonetilleke, said it was often left to doctors to pick up the pieces. 'The jawans were animals, mad for sex . . .'

Amongst the Tamils, he said, the effect was murderous.

'Either the victims killed themselves, or their husbands killed them.'

This insanity did eventually end, but with a particularly Byzantine twist. In April 1989, Colombo went behind India's back and did a secret deal with the Tigers. They agreed to work together to rid themselves of the peacekeepers, so that – inevitably – they could get on with fighting each other. Under the deal, the government would not only pay its enemy but also arm it. Ten trucks of grenades, T-56 rifles and mortars were sent off to the Tigers, all of which were bound to reappear when the civil war restarted. The LTTE was also to have its wounded smuggled out through an Indian blockade by the Sri Lankan navy. Amongst those on the boats was Ravi, or, as he then was, Commander Weerapperuma. 'It was crazy,' he told me. 'We were helping the enemy in order to defeat the peacekeeper.'

All this was too surreal for Delhi, and within a year it had pulled its troops out. Its first attempt to police the region had ended in elaborate confusion, with thousands dead and a bill for over $1.25 billion. Meanwhile, with the jawans gone, peace returned to Batticaloa, or at least a state of ambivalence.

One day, I went looking for a man from New Orleans who'd spent much of his life patching up the peace. Harry Miller's name crops up many times in the troubled story of the east. At the various peace talks, he'd often represented those too fearful to appear on their own behalf. He'd also started an index of those who'd disappeared, and founded the 'Peace Committee' in order to find them. But this, I realised, was not what he'd had planned for his life. Arriving in Ceylon in 1948, he was one of five American priests sent out by the Jesuits to teach. This they'd done for the rest of their working lives, introducing basketball (amongst other things) to Batticaloa. Now, however, only Father Miller remained. Three of the others had gone home, whilst Father Hebert had been abducted by guerrillas and never seen again.

I began by walking over to the city's little Vatican, a few streets of baroque and booming prayer. The centrepiece was a long, sky-blue cathedral, with its own population of monkeys. During a lull in the prayers, I stepped inside. Some crows were roosting in the plasterwork, and the clatter of their wings seemed to fill the building. The cathedral had often struggled to survive. In the last sixty years, it'd suffered floods, cyclones, riots and the general disaffection of war. At least one priest had been murdered, and, on Christmas Day 2005, more gunmen burst through the door. That time, they'd killed a Mr Joseph Rajasingham, whose neph-ews now ran my hotel, the Subaraj.

'We don't know who did it,' they'd told me, 'or why.'

Across the road was another great survivor, St Michael's Col-lege. Like the cathedral, it was a huge, foreign structure of arches and plinths, but with an outbreak of saplings up in the plaster. Inside, it was dark and noisy. Around the cloisters, there were rows of open-sided classrooms, each a spirited rabble of forty boys. Eventually, I found the principal's office. 'Yes,' she said, 'Father Miller's still here.' And she found me a boy to take me upstairs. It was a long climb up a series of old staircases, fixed to the walls. By the time we got to the attic, the whitewash was peel-ing away and the floorboards were velvety with dust. The boy pointed at a door, and left.

'Come in,' came a faint voice.

For a moment, I could make out nothing but the tree roots, dangling from the ceiling. No wonder the boy had fled. To any child possessing a passing familiarity with *Harry Potter*, it was all too much: the roots, the mouldy telephones, the shipwreck furniture, the washing lines and the heaps of colourless books. Even Father Miller, now emerging from an alcove, had something about him of the Hogwartian professor. He was fantastically old and genial, and wore glasses so thick his eyes seemed to swim out and meet me. Only his outfit was unwizardly – a khaki T-shirt and shorts.

After introductions, he waved me into a rattan chair.

'I'm pleased to find you,' I said. 'I thought you might've gone home.'

Miller smiled. 'Home? I tried to return to the US once in 1970, but I didn't recognise anything and so I came back here. Then I tried again, in 2009, just after the war. Well, for a while, I lived in a Jesuit home, but I no longer knew what to say to an American congregation, so again I returned. Meanwhile, they'd sold all my things, and so this is all I have left. But it's what I know, and I guess it's home. Sure, I'm eighty-eight and the door's closing, but, for now, I can still crawl downstairs to the Peace Committee, or to eat a daily meal.'

'So, thirty years, and you're still in the thick of it?'

'I suppose so. The war never went away. We even had a few bullets come through here. And we used to get a lot of people, seeking sanctuary. We couldn't keep them, of course, but we always made sure they went safely on their way.'

'Tell me about the people who've disappeared.'

The old priest paused, as if unsure where to begin. 'We don't really know how many are missing. Eight thousand is just the number we registered. But everyone lost someone, and the trauma's *unimaginable*. Not just for families but also for the city. People don't know how to put the past behind them, or how to trust their neighbours. Of course, some of the missing went abroad, or ran away and joined the Tigers. Or maybe they joined the army? But most were abducted. In one five-year period, we lost more people here than they ever did in Nicaragua and El Salvador.'

'And who was abducting all these people?'

'Who knows?' said Miller. 'Could've been anybody.'

'The Tigers?'

'Yes, them, but also rival groups, Muslims and the army.'

'And is there any hope of finding anyone again?'

There was a pause. Way off, I could hear the roar of the classes.

'You have to have hope,' said Miller. 'It's all we have left.'

Of all the abductions, the worst and most ambitious began just outside, in the sky-blue cathedral. Ever since the departure of the Indians in March 1990, the Tigers had been planning their next spectacle. Although there was supposed to be a ceasefire, they'd been quietly digging bunkers and stockpiling guns. By June, they were ready, and had suddenly appeared in the middle of Batti. Although there were only 250 of them, they managed to rob the city of forty-five million rupees and to round up its police force. Some of the officers were brought here, and encaged in baroque.

What happened next is so callous that people would seldom ever mention it. Perhaps everyone who remembers it feels the shame of that day – the shame of a province surrendered and the pointlessness that followed. One day, I'd meet the man who ordered this atrocity, and even he'd declaim it as if it were just a dream. I'll come back to him later, but for now it's enough to know what happened. It's not complicated. The policemen in the cathedral were removed from their sky-blue captivity and trucked out to the forest. There, they were joined by other officers from around the province, all bound hand and foot. No one can say exactly how things happened, but one thing's clear: to kill seven hundred men, shooting them one by one through the head, must take time and dedication, and not a lot of thought.

During these travels, I often met people who'd known the Tigers and perhaps even understood them. Some were Tamils, living in London. Amongst them were journalists and fundraisers and, occasionally, the odd foot soldier – now dazed, incomprehensible and probably illegal. Others I met in Sri Lanka, although I've always promised that I wouldn't say where, or who they were. Three, however, stand out. One was a priest ('Father Z'), another a doctor, and the third a more complex character I'll refer to as 'Thevar'.

There was once a time when I'd thought that, with their help, I'd find my way through the Tiger psyche. It was easy at first. Everyone described an ascetic and self-denying life. Recruits, or 'cadres', swore an oath of loyalty and carried a cyanide capsule as a token of commitment. Alcohol and smoking were prohibited, and all contact with family was severed. According to the doctor, women had to serve five years before they could marry, and men eight. Sex was considered a distraction and was generally discouraged. Adultery was always punished (and one of the London fundraisers admitted that his little affair had got him expelled). But Father Z insisted that it was never a matter of religion. 'The LTTE was a secular organisation,' he said, 'designed to include all Tamils, Catholic and Hindu.'

But Thevar disagreed, painting a more complicated picture. In the last years of the LTTE, he'd been a propagandist, writing blogs and working the web. 'We always had a spiritual dimension. We weren't like the other groups. The EPRLF were just Marxists, and PLOTE betrayed us and worked with the Indians—'

'And so you had them all killed?'

'We had to make ourselves strong.'

No one seemed to regret the death of other Tamils. Moderates and rivals were always wiped out, along with Tamil civil servants and policemen. Over 160 Tamil MPs were assassinated, as well as the leaders of the main Tamil party. It's sometimes said that, throughout the war, more Tamils were killed by the Tigers than by the army. It's certainly true that, during the eighties, the Tigers eradicated the competition, killing over 1,700 militants and absorbing all the rest.

'We had a simple message,' said Thevar. 'Fight with us, or die.'

'And what about the suicide bombs? And the killing of innocents?'

'In Hinduism, you may need to kill. It depends what's achieved.'

'And suicide?'

'We believe in *viduthalai*, or liberation. The word also refers to a liberation of the soul, or death. Our present existence is nothing. The soul, imprisoned by life, is set free.'

I must've looked puzzled.

'We're all on a journey, John, to a higher world, and freedom.'

I've often thought about what Thevar said, and about his multi-storey view of life. Had the Tigers seen beauty as they ascended through the layers? And what had become of the places where life was transferred? Had they acquired a beauty too? One day, in Batti, I got a chance to see how all this had worked. I'd read that, on 3 August 1990, a month after disposing of the police, a party of Tigers had set off for the suburbs, to Kattankudy. They'd already ordered all the Muslims out of town, and now they were off to restructure some lives. Nearly a quarter of a century later, I hired a trishaw and took off after them, curious to know what'd become of their work.

A few miles on, we were becalmed by crowds and bolts of cloth. The women were only outlines here, in their black niqabs, and the traffic had slowed to a stroll. I paid off the driver and picked my way through the unfamiliar merchandise – skullcaps, carpets and waistcoats – past the Hizbullah Hall and down towards the mosque. Kattankudy was still home to forty thousand Muslims, the largest concentration on the island. There had been more once, before the events of that day.

Eventually, I found what I was after: an empty-looking cement building, painted a powdery mauve. Across the front were the words *Meera Grand Jummah Mosque*, and, beneath them, an entrance closed off with a retractable steel grille. I walked round the side, kicked off my shoes and stepped inside.

I wasn't prepared for the sight before me. I knew the gunmen had come in through the grille, but I hadn't expected to find time standing still. The long, columned hall was exactly as it had been at 8:25 that morning, after fifteen minutes of firing. All around me, there were bullet holes. They splayed outwards over the walls, across the pillars, up the minbar steps, through daises, podia, lecterns and the imam's chair. Hundreds, perhaps thousands of divots had been blasted from the plaster. In the red concrete floor there were even bigger holes where the grenades had landed. Only the dead were missing: 103 worshippers, or – as a marble tablet described them – the *shuhudas*, or martyrs.

'But why this?' I asked. 'Why's it never been repaired?'

'It's a monument,' said the imam tersely.

I wondered what Thevar would have made of it. There wasn't

much beauty here. Nor was there any hint of resolution. Every day, this atrocity would happen all over again, relived in pockmarks and divots. Here was a reminder of the ferocity of pride, the ugliness of life and the fact that the perpetrators could still be here, living all around.

Before leaving Batticaloa, I went out to the new front lines. In some ways, they were everywhere, the city slashed into sections by religion and race. I never had to go far to find antipathy. The boys at my hotel said that no one trusted the Muslims. Others said that they were stockpiling weapons. Meanwhile, the Muslims said much the same, except the other way round. They were sure the Tamils were more violent than ever, especially with women. It always surprised me, the things people said, as if I wasn't there.

But, to get to the heart of this sweet, ruptured city, I'd need help. Fortunately, one of my Colombo friends, Mohammed Abidally, had given me a name: the Reverend Terrence. 'He's head of the local Methodists,' said Mohammed, 'and a very brave man.'

It took me a while to track the minister down, but, one afternoon, he appeared at my hotel. He wasn't like any other Tamil I'd ever met; stocky, dog-collared, open-faced and direct. At first, I sensed jollity, but I soon realised that the Reverend Terrence – unlike others – never said more than he needed to. If he ever thought he was being overheard, he didn't say anything at all. 'This is a very suspicious community. A lot of people have disappeared. You'll see. I've got my motorbike here. You OK on the back? There are a couple of places I want to show you.'

Half an hour later, we were on a long avenue of bright red dirt. It was like riding down a drain, the walls on each side rising above us, hammered out of tin. The minister slowed down and pulled over. 'This is one the fault lines that runs through the city. Tamils on one side of the street, Muslims the other. And look, no gates between them. They never come together. I can get people to shake hands, but that's about it.'

'And the children?' I asked. 'Are they any better?'

'A bit, but the kids here went a bit wild in the war.'

'Sounds as though it'll take years to sort itself out?'

'A generation; maybe more. Let me show you something else.'

We rode on until the road ran out.

'This is where we're building our church,' said Terrence.

Around us, all the houses were burnt out, with grass up to the eaves.

'But there's nobody here,' I said, surprised.

'People are frightened of it. We want to bring hope.'

Both of us were now staring out, through the rubble and weeds.

'What was it, Terrence? Why are they frightened?'

It was almost dusk now, and the distant lagoon glowed a candle yellow.

'Because, they say, this is where the bodies are buried.'

On my last day, news came through that the army had reopened an old mountain hideout. Everyone knew Thoppigala, or Baron's Cap. It always featured in the propaganda, and looked like a tombstone, rising out of the plain. There was even a picture of it, with its own little halo of choppers and jets, on the one-thousand-rupee note. But, although it was a familiar shape, no one – except soldiers – had been out there for almost twenty years. The track leading to it, however, began only just beyond the city, and I realised I'd pass the turning as I headed north. All I'd need was a rickshaw to cover the last twenty miles of scrub.

When Consuela the Spaniard appeared, I asked her if she knew one.

'Yes,' she said, 'and I want to come too.'

We made a conspicuous trio, once on the move. Consuela never missed a bargain, and so the three-wheeler was soon piled with fruit. It was odd to find her suddenly exuberant. I'd had a feeling that she was running away from something, and that, whatever it was, loneliness was better. Now, packed in amongst the papayas and citrus, she seemed happy again, a carnival queen. 'Sri Lankans love processions,' she roared over the engine, 'and that's why I love them!' Meanwhile, our driver, who was called Aloysius, was bug-eyed and pale, and spoke with a yelp like a little dog. Consuela warned me he'd never learnt to distinguish between affection and business, and so was always falling in love with his clients. After our long trip to Thoppigala, he'd call me every day for weeks. 'Just checking,' he'd yap, 'you never forget me.'

Beyond the city, army camps appeared, and more ruins.

'Never safe,' shouted Aloysius over his shoulder, 'living near army!'

'You'd get your house burnt down,' explained Consuela.

There was less destruction along the track to Thoppigala, but also less of everything else. The land around us was exquisitely raw and open; the road ahead was red, the horizon toothed in blue and the forest now merely islands out in the grass, blurred with heat. For a long time, we saw no one but woodcutters, the logs piled up in columns on their bikes. But then two girls stepped out of the bush, and we stopped to let them giggle. They'd never seen so much fruit or so many white people, and added ten lemons of their own. Another time, we stopped by a pond full of

Over seventy per cent of Sri Lankans are Buddhists and there's much talk of a 'chosen land'. Monks have a special status and even their own political party. Meanwhile, nowhere has as many holy days, whilst films like *The Da Vinci Code* are banned and kissing teenagers have to hide away under umbrellas.

In the country, it's not uncommon to come across a 'greasy pole' competition (*left*), or a man washing his elephant as if it's the family saloon car (*below*). Higher up, in Hill Country, there are the 'Indian Tamils', like this tea-picker (*above*). Although they've lived here for over a century, they're still considered unworthy and foreign. Working in all her finery and gold, the average picker earns a mere three pounds a day.

Whilst Sri Lanka often seems like paradise, it bears the scars of recent decades. The Boxing Day Tsunami of 2004 swept away 35,000 lives and whole villages, many yet to be rebuilt (*above*). Almost as destructive were the Tamil Tigers (*left*), who, between 1987 and 2009, launched over 300 suicide attacks, and overran a quarter of the country.

Modelled on Cuban revolutionaries, the JVP (*above*) twice rose in revolt, in 1971 and 1987. Altogether, up to 60,000 people were shot, burnt, or nailed up in trees. Few of the killers have ever been found; there's no memorial, and the subject is seldom mentioned.

Travelling south-east, the roads empty. On early maps, this corner of the island was just a blank, dappled with scrub. It's still defined by what it doesn't have – in particular, cities, reservoirs and rivers.

On the Jaffna Peninsular, these great mansions are now mostly abandoned. The men who built them were often born of the lowest caste, the fishermen, and made their fortunes shipping cloth. After Indian independence and the introduction of tariffs, many survived by smuggling; first, soap and motorbikes and then guns.

Across the north-east, there are still traces of a rogue state created by the Tigers in 2002. At its heart was Velupillai Prabhakaran (*left*), a separatist with god-like status. Under his austere rule, the LTTE collected taxes, built vast bunkers and established an ingenious armoury for attacking the south, like this tiny submarine (*below*).

In Britain, there are over 110,000 displaced Tamils and the separatists often march through London in support of 'The Boys'. During the war the LTTE were energetic fundraisers; by 2009, Britain's Tamils were donating £250,000 a month.

The war finally ended in May 2009, here on the beaches of Mullaitivu. This ship, *Farah III*, had been captured by the Tigers and would be used as a last stronghold. But, facing an army of 160,000, the LTTE was utterly obliterated. Even those who were captured have seldom been seen.

இனித் தமிழினம் குனியாது
எமை எதிர்த்திடப் பகை
துணியாது

With the Tigers in Mullaitivu were 130,000 refugees. They'd been subjected to the full fury of war and even now the wreckage is everywhere (*left*), including 10,000 bicycles and 25,000 burnt-out motorbikes. For all their heroic propaganda (*right*), the Tigers, by the end, were recruiting children and shooting anyone trying to escape.

Victory would leave the Sinhalese dangerously grateful to their president, Mahinda Rajapaksa (*left*), now feted as the 'Heroic Overlord Warrior of Lanka'. Monuments have appeared everywhere, grotesquely triumphant. As to the 27,745 soldiers that perished, they're often commemorated with bus shelters, painted in military colours and hung with portraits of the dead (*right*).

Not everyone would share the Rajapaksas' vision of a triumphant Lanka. Deprived of their land or livelihood, thousands have tried to leave. Some even paid people-smugglers to take them to Australia. This is one the boats that never made it and was chased ashore by the navy, near Trincomalee.

With peace restored, ordinary Sri Lankans face an intriguing future. It's hard to know what they'll make of it. For many visitors, like the writer Leonard Woolf, the mysteries of Sri Lanka have proved not unpleasantly overwhelming. 'I'm partially drunk,' he wrote, 'with the complete unreality of it all, and a very little whisky. I feel as if I were playing the buffoon in a vast comic opera . . .'

buffaloes, listening for a moment to the soothing huff and slosh of a hundred bathing beasts.

There were few reminders of the struggles that had once raged backwards and forwards through here. One of the villages had been rebuilt with American money. But there were still others, smashed and white, and scattered like seashells. War had left its flora, too, in the sprigs of steel and the coils of rusty briar. Some of these things were over twenty years old. After the massacres of 1990, this countryside had blazed. By day, the soldiers roamed around, burning villages they suspected of revolt. But, as darkness fell, they'd retire to their fortified camps, and the rebels would emerge.

From here onwards, Tamil Eelam had begun to take shape. To begin with, it hadn't felt like a breakaway state, just a smouldering dystopia, Sinhalese by day and Tamil by night. But further north, the LTTE had captured vast areas of forest, and, in July 1990, it took control of the city of Jaffna. The army made countless attempts to dislodge them, but the Tiger estate continued to grow. By 1994, government forces had only a foothold on the Jaffna peninsula, and down here – three hundred kilometres to the south – they quietly withdrew. The Tigers clambered up Thoppigala and, for the next thirteen years, it was their flag that flew from the summit.

'Look!' shrieked Aloysius. 'There it is!'

There was no mistaking the great tombstone outline, filled in with forest. Thoppigala rises almost 1,500 feet from the bush, its natural ramparts falling away in great flanks of black and orange rock. Around the base was a scattering of little army camps, together with a memorial the soldiers had built to themselves. We were met by an excitable major and a crowd of silent, teak-faced bombardiers.

'Why are they all taking our picture?' I asked.

The major chuckled. 'You're the first foreigners we've seen.'

We may even have been the first outsiders up Thoppigala in two decades. A company of soldiers was ordered to show us the way, up through the boulders. One of them had with him a wild rabbit, which he cradled like a baby. It was a steep climb, and, at one point, the clouds burst and we all had to take cover amongst the rocks. During the Tigers' time, this place had been thought of as Sri Lanka's Tora Bora, a complex of caves and bunkers with names like 'Beirut'. But all trace of them was now overwhelmed with words. Military graffiti covered everything, and, in particular, a single refrain: *COMMANDO*. In the end, it had taken the army almost three months to winkle the Tigers from this piece of rock.

Steel ladders led up the last few cliffs, and then we were on the top. It was hard to imagine it as the Tamil Tiger's Shangri-La, 'Kudumbimalai'. All that remained of their citadel was a tiny *kovil*, now spattered in names. Inside, there was still a whiskery Hindu shrine and some radio equipment. Had the battle for Thoppigala been as magnificent as schoolchildren think? Perhaps, but one thing's sure: the LTTE had given themselves an astonishing perspective. It's difficult to think of a view more commanding than this: the grasslands below, the forest with its orange filigree of tracks and roads, then the pale glow of rice and a long thin smudge of sea.

For much of the nineties, the Tigers sat up here, watching this coast turn rebel red. Although they lost Jaffna in 1995, elsewhere, huge areas of bush fell under their influence. They could now wipe out whole army camps, massacre soldiers by the thousand, and bring their bombs right to the heart of Colombo and Kandy. By the end of the decade, they controlled almost a quarter of the island, and the government was in headlong retreat.

Back on the red road, Aloysius suddenly stopped and squealed. 'See this? It's Tharavai! But look, nothing left!'

We all got out and peered into the grass. He was right; there was nothing out there but a sinewy cow and a small army post, in a nest of logs. When he'd calmed down, Aloysius explained. 'Everyone knows Tharavai. It's where the Tigers buried their dead. I heard it was a very big place, with graves and flowers and paths and everything. But now . . . it's all gone!'

I didn't, at that stage, appreciate the scale of Tharavai. But some months later, I spotted the cemetery in an old satellite picture. It had obviously been the Arlington of the Tiger world. They'd always taken dying seriously. My contact, Thevar, had told me that, originally, the dead were burnt in the Hindu tradition. 'But later, we built these great cemeteries. You know, to honour our heroes, and inspire others.'

Now, looking out across Tharavai, I could see only tussocks.

'The army,' said Aloysius, 'they put their bulldozer on it.'

'They said the graves were empty,' said Consuela, 'merely for show.'

Maybe they're right? Few people think so. The Tamils believe there's still a little army lying here, and that the dead have died all over again. That's war, I suppose. The victor gets to rewrite his enemy's story, to belittle his motives, to daub his temples, and – if the mood suits – to sweep away his graves.

All the way to Trincomalee, a monkey rode on the roof. The bus conductor told me the stowaway often travelled with them, and that, in the afternoons, he'd ride the four hours back. What was it, I wondered, that the monkey liked about that road? Perhaps it was the fishing boats pulled up, like longships, on the beach. Or perhaps it was the fishermen themselves, and the way their nets fell on the water in a hoop of dimpled glass. Or perhaps it was the pine trees that whispered their way off up the shore. Consuela once told me that, although they'd been planted to protect the coast, they were now seen as dark and sexy – places of immorality – and were due for destruction.

Or perhaps it was the feeling of renewal. The road had a fresh black top, and there were new houses along the shore. Although most of them were for outsiders and Sinhalese settlers, at least something was going up instead of coming down. One day, the building work may become too much (the government was already talking about another three hundred hotels along these empty beaches). But, for now, it was just enough to encourage a sense of life returning. In every other way, this was still a thrilling, unspoilt wilderness of broken lagoons, thumb-like mountains, swamps, rag-headed palms and *kumbara*, or empty paddy, with the occasional peacock strutting out the bush.

Just before Trinco, we crossed the Mahaveli Ganga, now bowling along like a magnificent soup. Thick rafts of vegetation were caught up in its lumpy currents, as if they were islands, off for a swim. Since Adam's Peak, the river had travelled over two hundred miles, circling Kandy and draining a fifth of the island. Once, it had protected Kandy from Europeans, and then, later, it had come to the rescue of Trinco. By 2000, it was only water keeping the Tigers out of the city. They could raid it and lob their shells over the bay, but they could never truly claim it as their own. There was always this great, holy river in their way.

But even the Mahaveli might not have saved Trinco, but for 9/11. By that time, over a million Sri Lankans were refugees, Jaffna was desperate, Colombo was burning and the Tigers were everywhere. Although they'd never have won this war, they might easily have spun it out forever. But the events in Manhattan changed all that. Suddenly, the world lost its appetite for freedom fighters and, country by country, the Tigers found themselves banned. They had no option but to sue for peace, and, in February 2002, a deal was signed.

After nineteen years of savage civil war, an ominous calm descended on the island. But, although roads reopened and Jaffna breathed, people knew it wasn't the end. Whilst, for now, things were quiet, they had no idea what lay ahead, and all they could do was watch and wait. A bit like the monkey on the roof.

9

Trinco, Trinco, Little Star

Few things surpass the tropical beauty of this harbour.

Samuel Baker, *Eight Years in Ceylon*, 1855

The most valuable colonial possession on the globe.

William Pitt the Younger, 1802

It's not often I want to be a seagull, and yet Trinco brought out my inner bird.

Instead of clattering along in a smoky bus, I'd have soared through this great watery labyrinth of coves and islets and jungle-tufted headlands. From up there, everything would've been either canopy green or cobalt blue, and I'd have begun out at Foul Point and worked my way in, through seven scalloped bays. They'd have been huge at first – Shell, Koddiyar and Tambalagam – but soon there'd be bays within bays, and, inside them, more harbours and inlets. Amongst them, it would've been like flying through the workings of the inner ear, the ocean so remote and quiet I'd have forgotten it was there. But then I'd have seen tiny tankers and forts and a sparkle of streets. I'd have followed this human glitter until it turned into a thick green promontory, stretching round across the mouth of the maze. Even with my feeble, avian brain I'd have recognised this as an arm, holding off the sea.

But how much more I'd have understood is hard to say. Outsiders have often struggled with Trincomalee, and what it is. Raven-Hart called it a 'starfish ramified', and even the great historian, Tennent, became a little purple with his comparisons to Carthage. To geographers, it's our planet's fifth-largest natural harbour, but that means little to anyone else. I prefer the assessment of Horatio Nelson, aged seventeen. Sailing through here in 1775, he declared that this was 'the finest harbour in the world'. How can he have known that? (Unless, of course, he'd had a seagull moment.)

Visitors were still a novel concept in Trinco's old town. Most people assumed I was up to something, although they couldn't work out what. Some thought I was a missionary, especially when they saw my notebook, which was biblical and black ('You with Jesus?' they'd ask). Others thought my interests were more carnal, and, that first afternoon, one of the hotel boys came skulking at my door, with a furtive murmur of massage. He looked genuinely surprised to be sent away, as if the world was not as he'd supposed. Even the traffic police were unsure what to make of me, and I'd barely made it to the end of the street before I was stopped. But they were intrigued by the idea I was lost, and insisted on swapping email addresses and buying me a map.

It was easy to get lost in Trinco. Although the seafront was breezy enough, the rest of the town was like a much bigger city that had been squeezed and distorted. At its heart, it was a compacted mass of lanes, dead ends, people, ideas, colour and great displays of gold. I once found myself in a cyber café the size of a bathroom, and almost as steamy. I was surprised, too, by the things that were sold in English. I could shop at 'YOUR LIKE RETAIL', or cram myself into 'The Cream House' or 'Cool Spot', and yet never be understood. English words would be piled up all around – in crates of *Lemon Cake* and *Farley's Rusks* – but no one knew what they meant. I tried a bit of Tamil once ('*Nan England. Eper dee sugum*?' or 'I'm English. How are you?') but it only made people laugh. It was obviously a language of great subtlety and, with its 247 characters and thirty-two different words for 'moun-tain', it clearly wasn't an idiom for foreigners to dabble in.

The Tamils hoped that, one day, this would be their Hong Kong, and yet – for now – Trinco remained obstinately private. It wasn't just the language and the tangle of streets. A few blocks out of the centre, the walls went up, together with fences of cad-jan. People often talked about the 'Cadjan Curtain', that invisible wall between the Tamil world and everyone else. Girls here only ever married within their community, and land was never sold to outsiders. Life had to be defended against everything beyond. Trinco's Tamils didn't even have much in common with the Tamils of India, and, if they'd ever got together, it would've been like a meeting of the English and the Angles.

But none of this worried Trinco. There was always an air of festivity out on the streets, as if some great show was about to begin. The men looked plump and well laundered, whilst the women would parade in saris, their hair parted in the centre and scraped back in a long glossy ponytail. Often, I'd spot a herd of deer amongst the crowds, wandering along as if they too had something to celebrate. Sometimes, I followed the flow, and we'd end up at the temple or in a game of cricket. But, mostly, people just wandered, happy to be out. This, I suppose, is what any city looks like after almost twenty years of siege. Whilst Batticaloa had fought itself from within, here the fight had come from out-side. With the Tigers ranged all around, the government had holed up at the far end of the promontory, in the old British base. As Thevar the blogger once told me, 'Not much came and went, during the war.'

Which explains why, even now, a visitor like me was faintly exotic.

* * *

In such a private city, I had to find friends where I could. Once, the traffic policemen came to tea, but they were Sinhalese and didn't know the city ('Too hot,' they'd say. 'Too far. We want to go back to Kandy.'). In theory, some navy contacts were going to get in touch, but, whilst I waited, my life emptied of people. Without human anchorage, the days started drifting into the nights, and I'd go to bed at dusk and get up at four. I grew to love Trinco during those hours, whilst the city was still twitchy and cool. I'd take long walks along the beach, and then come back just as the night's sleep was lifting away under an insistent skirl of cornets and bells.

After a few days of this, I was grateful for company, even Mr Stephen's. He'd heard I was looking for a guide, and so turned up one morning at my hotel. There, he was considered too hideous to be allowed inside, so I was ushered out into the street. I could see what had frightened the kitchen boys. Mr Stephen had skin like an old tyre, and, at some stage, half his face had been melted and scraped away. Where his cheek should have been, there was now just a mottled hollow and the lower eyelid, which had dribbled down from above. I pretended not to notice any of this, which puzzled Mr Stephen. The wrecked structures of his face tried to rearrange themselves as a smile, but all that emerged was a leer.

'You wonder what happened, ah?'

'No,' I lied, grateful the question was out.

'Guess.'

'Something to do with the war?'

'No!' said Mr Stephen, and laughed, 'A bear! *Really*, a sloth bear! I was out shooting. Nineteen seventy-five, it was. I killed the first bear but didn't notice the other one, behind me. And – *kadavule!* – she tears off my face. I was out cold three days! And in hospital six months! I got bites all over my arms and legs, but they go for your eyes.'

Hadn't my farmer friend, Mahathun, said something about bears and eyes?

'The eye doctor . . .' I murmured.

'So, you *know*!' squealed Mr Stephen, clapping his mangled hands around mine. That was the moment I became his liveli-hood, at least for the next few days. Although Mr Stephen said he had a job as a watchman, it was soon obvious that, in truth, he survived on stories and English and claims for expenses. I didn't mind; his charges were never more than a drinker needs, and the tales he told were always good, if slightly macabre. I didn't even mind that we never really went anywhere, but just drove around in tuk-tuks, clocking up commission.

Around the bottom of the Swami Rock, there was still a fort. It's thought that its walls were built from the ruins of a great temple – perhaps a 'Hall of a Thousand Columns' – which the Portuguese had rolled off the Rock. But holy stones don't make good ramparts. Perhaps that's why these ones had never kept anyone out. Eight times they'd changed hands, six of them under fire. If ever warfare was made to look like musical chairs, it was here. Since 1624, the fort's been Portuguese, Kandyan, French (twice), and then British or Dutch (three times each). Only in Napoleonic times did the music finally stop, leaving the British in the seat. They renamed the place Fort Frederick and put a new plaque over the gate: *Dieu et mon Droit*.

Inside, an unruly tropical garden thrived, along with a little of Georgian England. Although it was still an army camp, no one seemed to mind me wandering around. Overhead, a canopy of banyan trees had spread out like a great green roof, but, in the darkness, I could make out all the old lunettes and traverses, bastions, batteries and some mossy green barracks. There were cannon lolling in the grass, and plenty of bells to bring soldiers running. Even the old officers' mess had survived amongst the boulders and stands of bamboo. It now had a coat of fresh white paint, and looked almost new.

This little, half-choked mansion had never changed the course of history, but it had once given it a nudge. In late 1800, one Colonel Wellesley had called by, and stayed a couple of months. At the time, he was suffering a terrible case of 'malabar itch', for which the fort's remedy was a concoction of sulphur and lard. To no one's great surprise, this failed to shift the itch, and so the colonel missed out on his next campaign, an expedition to Egypt. But, as luck would have it, the ship on which he was due to sail, the *Susannah*, never made it up the Red Sea, and sank with all hands. I like to imagine that, but for Trinco's 'cure', Britain would never have had her Duke of Wellington, and that the rest of the century would've looked a lot more French.

Mr Stephen always had something of the Georgian about him, especially out on tour. Wherever we went, we seemed to end up in an earlier version of England, weirdly mutated by its years in the sun. There was still a School Lane, a Powder Island and a Dead Man's Cove. But Mr Stephen also saw his city as Hogarth and Rowlandson had seen theirs: a place of drinking dens and catatonic stupors; a town of fun and bawdiness and recreational chaos. People would drink their way through great elections, and then appear in flocks at any public disaster. The little riots, he said, weren't even reported anymore. Last week, a jubilant mob had appeared at the hotel where he worked, and where all the waiters were Sinhalese. For almost an hour, the two sides slogged it out with coconuts and chairs.

'Anyone hurt?' I asked.

'No, just a couple of broken heads, that's all.'

Often on these rides, great chunks of the Georgian era appeared before us. Aside from the fort, there was a large, white, neo-classical mansion on the esplanade. Although it described itself as a museum, we'd barely reached the steps before we were shooed away by guards with guns. Another time, we squeezed through a hole in the old cemetery wall and took a walk amongst the Georgians themselves. If their great, crumbling tombs were anything to go by, they'd lived carefree lives, and had died splendid deaths: falling off forts, getting 'lost in the jungle', and being blown up by their own guns. I had hoped to find Jane Austen's brother, Charles, amongst them. He'd carried on fighting until 1852, when Burma finally got the better of him at the age of seventy-three. For some reason, his tomb was here, but, it seemed, the weeds had long since claimed him as their own.

'Ghosts,' said Mr Stephen. 'We have to go.'

A small crowd had gathered on the cemetery wall. I half wondered if they didn't think we were the ghosts, me being so white and Mr Stephen so molten and black. We scrambled out through the hole and back to our rickshaw. Soon we were under way, and – as always – our day ended at a huge gatehouse, perhaps the chunkiest of all. From it, a dense thicket of posts and razor wire spread out across the promontory, decorated in places with old cannons and propellers plucked from ships. Although the area beyond was known as the dockyard, all I could see were two great ridges covered in jungle. For a while, I thought this was as a close as I'd ever get to the old British base. But then, on my third night, I got a call from the regional commander.

'You're lucky,' he said. 'I'm an old friend of Ravi's.'

His men would be round the next day to pick me up.

It was now over seventy years since the sky roared and these great ridges had shuddered in shock. The forest that morning had seized up with sound, and the air became unbreathable, like earth. A great aero fleet had appeared over the ocean: ninety-one bombers and thirty-eight fighters. On the move, this great mechanical swarm filled almost fifteen square miles of sky. It was the Japanese, bringing World War Two to Trincomalee.

In some ways, the promontory is still the place it was that day. My little escort – an officer and two ratings – drove me first up to the ridges, Ostenberg and Elephant. It was quiet up here, monkeys trickling through the treetops and the forest floor littered with half-eaten fruit. At the top of these ridges, the undergrowth cleared and great bunkers appeared. It was like a giant concrete tea-service with its huge cups and saucers buried in the cliffs. Inside, these gun batteries were exactly as they should have been, except mouldier and paintless and powdered with rust. Their six-inch guns still nosed out over the ocean, and a tiny ammunition lift could still be hand-cranked – groaning and squealing – up from the bowels of the ridge. There were even traces of the men who'd lived here in the strings of rotten webbing and the crockery marked 'RN Ceylon'. Everything was ready, it seemed, for a great battle that had never actually happened, or not as everyone had hoped.

All this fascinated the officer with me. Lieutenant Commander Thilata wore a row of medals, and had prickly hair and a neat little paunch. 'Funny, ah?' he said. 'They'd expected trouble from the sea but not from above.'

Down in the docks, an ordinary day appeared, out of the forties. We drove in along Vernon Road, through Shoebury, Oxford Circus and Waterloo Junction. All around us, sailors snapped to attention, roaring 'Morning, Sir!' before marching off lickety-split. An old language was everywhere, Navalese. *WELDING W/S*, said the signs. *JUNIOR SAILORS' MESS*. A tall, skinny officer in cobalt blue and cavalry boots was holding a parade, his sword drawn, slashing at the heat. Huge clumps of marigolds erupted from the kerbs and half a dozen gunboats nuzzled at the quay. Only pink faces and Portsmouth banter were missing from this scene. In every other respect, it was 9 April 1942.

Eventually, we got to the commandant's office to find him sitting behind a bank of phones, answering them three at once. It was a while before the ringing stopped and a thick, heavy hand reached out towards me. Commander Kumara already knew what I was after, and he was intrigued by the great fleet that had once lain offshore: five aircraft carriers, four battleships, two heavy cruisers, eleven destroyers and thirty-seven submarines. It was this fleet that had returned from Hawaii, where it had plundered Pearl Harbour.

'Show him everything, Mr Thilata,' he said, 'especially the tunnels.'

That was all he managed before the ringing began again and we were driven off by bells. 'The tunnels,' explained Thilata, 'are where we keep the ammunition.'

It was only a short walk away, through the weapons section. Everyone here wore bright white overalls, as if they were cooks. But it was more a garden than a kitchen. We passed glittering heaps of cartridges, a bouquet of rockets, a huge clump of machine guns like some wild metallic bush, and a large Victorian warehouse, empty except for a single ominous pallet. Then a miniature railway track appeared, leading away through some wrought-iron gates. Here, we were met by the weapons officer, who took us deep inside the mountain. I remember thinking how cool it was, amongst the missiles and boxes of bombs. We never reached the end of the whitewash, but came to a halt at the junction between tunnels twenty-eight and twenty-nine.

'This is where everyone hid,' said Thilata, 'when the Japanese appeared.'

It was no secret that a great fleet was on its way. Trincomalee could only brace itself against the storm to come.

It had been a frantic five months since Hawaii. In February 1942, the Japanese had mauled the British and Dutch navies in the Java Sea, and were now turning their attention west. It wasn't hard to work out their plan. They'd hunt down the Indian Ocean Fleet, destroy it in one, and then move in on India. In this grand scheme, the British would suffer their own Pearl Harbour, right here in Trincomalee. Faced with such a threat, London had responded as best it could. India was emptied of planes, and everything sent to Ceylon. Then the Indian Ocean Fleet was spirited away to the Maldives and hidden in an atoll. By the time the Japanese got to Trincomalee, there'd be nothing left to bomb except a few auxiliaries and the *Sagaing*, an old steamer with a cargo of ammunition and whisky.

None of this prevented a furious attack. That morning, just after breakfast, 129 aeroplanes poured out of the sky. Most of the pilots were veterans of Pearl Harbour, including the commander, Mitsuo Fuchida. Four days earlier, they'd made a similar attack on Colombo, causing almost half the city to flee. They'd bring the same fury to Trinco, dropping down from eight thousand feet almost into the port. For forty minutes they pounded it, setting the docks ablaze and shredding the bungalows on Vernon Road. The local air squadron was no match for this onslaught, its stately fighters being picked off like pigeons. One of them wasn't found for another eighteen months, when it was discovered buried nose-deep in the jungle.

By the time they left, the Japanese had lost only eleven planes, and would describe the day as a 'spectacle of fireworks'. Out in the bay, the last ships burned. Amongst them was the *Sagaing*, now helplessly spouting whisky and bullets.

'But it didn't sink,' said Thilata. 'Come, I'll show you.'

With that, we drove round to the waterfront, and, of course, he was right. There was the *Sagaing*, or at least its outline. With almost nothing left above the waterline, it looked like an enormous blueprint, swollen with rust. We jumped down and edged out along one of the crusty bulkheads. Peering down through the water, I could just make out the molten pipework and the contorted decks below. Its survival and disfigurement were compelling, the maritime equivalent of Mr Stephen.

I'd often asked my mutilated friend if he knew any survivors of the raid. The question always seemed to cause a little panic. I could see that Mr Stephen was torn between opportunity and honesty, but, in the end, his instincts won, and he found me an 'uncle'. He'd need the fee up front, of course, but when the uncle failed to appear, he brought me a letter instead. It began, *In the time of the Honourable Vincent Churchill* . . . and ended with the Japanese sinking everything, including the *Queen Mary*.

'I think I need to meet the witnesses,' I said.

'You don't believe me, no?'

'Well . . .'

'This tongue has taken communion. Pluck it out, if it should lie!'

Fortunately, further mutilation wasn't necessary because, the following morning, he came up with a name. Mr Alphonso was half-African and lived in a shack on a patch of wasteland above the town. Instead of asking us in, he climbed into the back of our rickshaw, the cysts on his great bare belly wobbling with pleasure. At first, his tale sounded plausible enough: a boy of sixteen, working in the docks, the planes arriving in rows of six and the sailors hiding in the tunnel. But then Mr Alphonso seemed to sense that his story lacked magic. The casualties suddenly started mounting in their thousands, and a bank blew up, showering everyone in money.

I didn't stop him. It seemed wrong to insist on history. Trinco's raid had passed into mythology, swamped by so many years of more insistent violence. As dusk fell, and British shells started falling on the town, I unrolled a few notes and let Mr Alphonso clamber free.

The departure of the great aero fleet wasn't quite the end of the Japanese raid. One of the bombers had headed inland, through the great maze, to China Bay. I asked Thilata if he'd take me over there to see what had happened. 'Sure,' he said, 'it's the Tank Park we'll need.'

Leaving the base was more cumbersome than I'd imagined. Not only did we need more ratings, but they needed guns. Then there were the cameras. As well as their T-56s, the sailors brought their iPhones and photographed everything as if they were out on a day trip. This was, however, the only spontaneity they ever showed, and the rest of time they were watchful and grim. It was also disconcerting to discover that, beyond the gates, the stares had changed – no longer quizzical, but blank. The navy still weren't liberators here, just more knights amongst a population of pawns.

We trucked round the coves until we reached China Bay. There, a huge strip of asphalt appeared, slicing off into the haze and edged with its own savannah. Once, this had been one of the greatest airfields in the world, discharging planes all over Asia. Just above it, up in the jungle, was all the fuel necessary to keep an empire on the move. It was a hill covered in giant oil tanks, the 'Tank Park'. From afar, they looked like some strange extra-terrestrial experiment; 101 enormous orange pills – each the size of an office block – rising up out of the trees. But, closer up, the orangeness was rust, and the park was abandoned. When they saw all the guns and uniforms, the guards at the gate merely waved us inside.

We stopped first at Tank 74, climbing the long steel staircase that curled round its belly. Halfway up, I peered in through a giant valve. Inside, I could sense a space the size of several ball-rooms, groaning and flexing in the heat. I could also hear boots on the plates above as the sailors hurried around, taking their pictures. When this colossus was riveted together in the 1920s, it had serviced the biggest navy in the world. Had we been here then, sitting on the top, the coves all around would have been bristling with ships, every day a Spithead Review. But now they'd all gone, and we could enjoy the nothingness again, and the jungle, way below.

It was Thilata who broke the spell. 'OK, we need to find ninety-one.'

On we went, through the huge steel suburbs. The road curled

its way upwards amongst the bowsers, each with a number and its own little clearing. The lone Japanese bomber had also been looking for a tank, although it didn't matter which. The plane was already trailing smoke, and the crew – Shinegori, Tukyagoto and Sutomu – had clearly decided to perish in style. Fixing their sights on Tank 91, they'd thrown the plane into a dive and left the rest to prayer.

The tank was still there, like some enormous pavlova that's melted and collapsed. Great, fat folds of iron had rolled to the ground, releasing over fifteen thousand tons of oil. It's said to have burnt for a week, leaving nothing but this mush of girders and plate, and turning the earth all around into brittle black glass. Most of the sailors had never seen this before, and now stared at it in horror. Months later, I still have a chunk of vitrified forest sitting on my desk, a reminder of the curious passions of humankind.

The Japanese never returned to Trinco, at least not in force. But it did trouble them, the paucity of kills: two cruisers, a corvette and twenty-three merchant ships. They'd have liked at least an aircraft carrier, and then they spotted one a hundred miles off Foul Point. It was HMS *Hermes*, hurrying south. The captain knew he'd been seen, and swerved to the west, heading for land. The *Hermes* had almost made it to Batticaloa, and was only five miles offshore when aero fleet struck.

There are few people now who remember the moment the planes caught up. But I came across one once: a man called Prince Casinader. In later life, he'd become a headmaster and Batti's MP. But in April 1942, he was a schoolboy of sixteen, and, when he'd heard the Zeros, he'd run 'helter-skelter' for the fort. 'From up on the ramparts,' he told me, 'we could see the planes, darting in and out.'

'I hear there were seventy-five, in all?'

'Yes, like *bees*! They'd hover in clusters, then come round again . . .'

Mr Casinader would describe a withering assault. What he'd seen was the Japanese at their most relentless. First, they'd harried the *Hermes* from the relative safety of nine thousand feet, and then – in all the noise and confusion – they'd sent in the low-level bombers. As one survivor put it, there was 'a constant stream, so that as one stick of bombs exploded, the next was already in the air from the following plane.' The old aircraft carrier could only take so much of this. First, the bombs splintered the lifeboats and peeled off the plate, and then they were opening up the superstructure and letting the sea pour in. Within half an hour, it was all over, and the *Hermes*, now spewing great black thunderclouds of smoke, slid beneath the waves. With her went the captain, nineteen officers and almost three hundred crew.

'Some survived,' said Mr Casinader. 'A few even swam ashore. But then, on the third day, we started finding corpses on the beach. We always gathered them up and gave them a proper funeral, and everyone attended. But the bodies were in a sorry state by then, badly decomposed. I remember two in particular, Mr Vatcher and Thomas Lewis . . . Funny, isn't it? You never forget these things.'

For a while, I assumed I'd got as close to the *Hermes* as I ever would, and that there was nothing more to find. In England, I tracked down the last of the survivors, Richard Groom, only to discover that I'd missed him by months, and that he'd died in October 2012. His daughter told me that the details of that day

349

had only ever emerged in the final years. Until then, he'd kept it all to himself: the bombs, the burns, the sloping decks and the hours spent floating around in oil. Perhaps it was right that I'd never found him, and that we'd never gone there again.

After that, I tried to think no more about it, but then one day I met a diver in Trinco. Felician Fernando was an oddly professorial figure to find in such a watery career. He wore half-moon glasses and lived out in Nilaveli, behind a panel of computers. I always thought that, in his light, unperturbed features, there was more than a hint of Portuguese, and perhaps that's where he'd got it, his understanding of the sea. Few could dive as deep as Felician, and I soon discovered that, during his underwater travels, he'd come across the *Hermes*. One day, I went to his shop to see the pictures he'd taken.

'Were you the first to find it?' I asked.

'No, the fishermen knew about in the sixties, then it was lost again in the civil war. We rediscovered it in 2001, with three boats, dragging anchors. It's in a difficult place, fifty metres down. You've got to know what you're doing down there. And the currents are very strong, and visibility's poor. People never realise how dangerous it is, and one or two have died. But that protects it, I suppose, keeps the looters away . . .'

Deep blue images were now appearing on screen.

'I never see it all at once, just a few metres at a time.'

The pictures looked like snapshots of the night, except with bearded guns and great flashes of coral. I could see racks of shells, bearded in weed, and the decks, splattered with pink and torn up like rags.

'You can't believe the destruction,' said Felician. 'The ship took forty direct hits, and there's a lot of it all smashed up. I often think about the men inside, and I never touch anything or take anything away. On the seventieth anniversary, we took a wreath down, and I tried to imagine those last few minutes. I found a wing once, from a Japanese plane, so I suppose they managed to shoot a few down. But that's not much comfort, is it, to all those who died?'

A few of those who'd perished were buried just up the road.

The War Cemetery was still a strange concept to the Sinhalese, who preferred to take their dead back home. Its long rows of epitaphs also spoke of an exotic navy. Amongst the dead there were Muslims, Burmese, Africans, Irishmen, Bengali stokers, boys of seventeen and laundrymen from China. I even found Mr Vatcher, the Newfoundlander who Prince Casinader had originally buried in Batti.

Had they lived, all these people could have been proud of the role they'd played, if not exactly jubilant. As Churchill said, in Ceylon the Japanese had made contact with bone. This would've been the biggest defeat in British naval history but for the fact that the fleet was nowhere to be seen. It was a close escape. Churchill also claimed that, in attacking Ceylon, the Japanese had squandered valuable resources, and perhaps he was right. Two months later, the great Imperial carrier fleet was wiped out at Midway, with the loss of four aircraft carriers in less than twenty-four hours. Of the pilots who'd attacked Trinco, only their leader, Mitsuo Fuchida, survived. In later life, he was baptised a Christian, and his children became American citizens.

During my last days in Trinco, there were a few reminders of the uncertainties ahead.

I'd left the old town, and moved out to one of the beaches,

further north. By then, I'd almost forgotten that Trinco was a haven, and that, beyond the city, a no-man's-land began. For decades, these hinterlands had been contested and had grown ownerless and wild. Most of the great beach hotels of the seventies now had jungles of their own, pushing up through the roof. But one of the survivors – I'll call it the Sand House – was managed by an old friend from London. The last time I'd seen Deb, she'd been breathlessly happy and about to marry a young Sinhalese. 'We'll be running the family hotel,' she'd told me, and that was her future: a succession of sunsets, and a life on the beach.

But beaches have a strange way of not working out.

Deb now looked frazzled and desperate. 'I hate it here. He treats me like shit.'

It was hard to imagine that things at the Sand House had ever been happy. I only stayed two nights, in a windowless room with a mysterious staircase that ended in the ceiling. Outside, there was an empty concrete pond. Everything here felt like an afterthought, added on with more cement. The hotel had only survived the war on prostitution, and as a billet for Indian troops. Even now, the family seldom washed the sheets, and never allowed Sri Lankans to stay. 'Foreigners don't expect anything,' said Deb, 'and never complain.'

At night, there were raves on the beach, and soldiers were hired to keep the fishermen away. There were always more waifs round the edge than there were dancers in the middle. I never stayed long, and the only other person I talked to was Rod, a circus artist from Kent. He sometimes gave displays of juggling, and then, the next morning, he'd give all his tips to the cleaner. She was a widow with three children, he said, living on two pounds a day.

Meanwhile, Deb's new groom sat at the bar, watching the

guests. Sunil was sleekly handsome in his way, although his gaze was predatory and lifeless. 'I don't matter anymore. I'm just a bloody servant out here,' snarled Deb. 'And now he's screwing all the tourists! And these Euros couldn't care less what he's like. All they want is some local to fuck their stupid brains out. And they call it a holiday romance! But they don't know what he's really like . . . What am I supposed to do? The family don't help. They just think I'm a whore. Everything's so messed up. This place is so fucked. What am I meant to do?'

If Deb had ever tried to run for it, she'd not have been alone. Along the east coast, I'd often heard tales of people-trafficking. The Australian government had even put up posters along the road: *DO NOT COME TO AUSTRALIA*. But still the trade went on. 'A one-way ticket,' said Deb, 'costs about five thousand quid . . .'

On the beach, just down from the hotel, was a shipwreck, embedded in the sand. For a while, I thought it was a fishing boat, but then, one morning, Mr Stephen turned up to say good-bye. 'No,' he said, 'that's a traffickers' boat.'

'Looks like they didn't get far.'

'They were just rogues. Float around for a while and then get chased ashore by the navy. You seen the patrols? No one can just *leave* anymore. And so the navy give chase, and these guys tell the passengers that it's the Australian navy and that they've already arrived! So everyone runs up and hides in the forest, but they're still in Sri Lanka! And they've not gone anywhere at all! But that's hard, ah? Lost a million bucks, maybe everything they own.'

'Why not go to India?'

'Because they'll only end up in the camps.'

'And why so desperate to leave?'

Deep in Mr Stephen's face, there was an uncomfortable shifting of scars.

'Where you going next?'

'Up the coast,' I said, 'into the Vanni.'

'OK, then you'll understand.'

10

Multi-barrel Love Enforcer

The Vanniyas . . . do not wear gold jewellery for fear of it being stolen.

C. S. Navaratnam, *Vanni & the Vanniyas*, 1960

There has never been any real conflict between the Sinhalese and Tamils . . . there are no historic antagonisms to be overcome, but there is a firm foundation on which a spirit of national service can be built up.

Advice to British servicemen, 1942

I took the bus north. The forest ahead had long been the home of a vicious people. Some think the Vanniyas were survivors of the reservoir cities. Others say they were the remnants of a great Tamil army from India. Perhaps they were both. But whoever they were, they'd made this jungle their own, living bandit lives and resisting all outsiders. It's said they could walk superhuman distances, and that – whenever anyone died – they'd burn down his home. But mostly they fought. Even as late as 1803, they were creeping up on settlements and killing those they could.

Their lands still looked unruly and tangled. I was now deep inside the vast hedge that sprawls across the north. There were no great cities in here, just garrisons packed with people, and the bus often stumbled and slithered on the broken road. Although I could see water in amongst the scrub, it was never where it should have been. Mostly, the paddy looked cracked and empty, but then, suddenly, we'd find ourselves skirting a lake of sunken trees. Even stranger were the great rivers that came thrashing past, looking panicky and lost. This was never tempting land, and, around Ceylon, it would always be synonymous with brutality and want. Although the Vanniyas were spirited farmers, they never had much to sell, except ivory and skins. Their huge empty world – covering a tenth of the island – would become known as 'the Vanni'.

I still hoped to find Vanniyas in the faces all around. Sometimes I thought I saw them, out in the thorn: women chipping away at the earth, or up to their necks in mud. People here still thought nothing of distance or time. I often spotted little figures in places where even the buildings had failed. I'd given up writing 'bullet-riddled' in my diary, but the sight of humans still warranted a note. Occasionally, the bus stopped and a few of these dried-up souls would climb aristocratically aboard. Now everyone was interested, although no one understood them. The Vanniyas, it's said, have their own Esperanto, a mixture of Tamil and Vedda, with a touch of the forest.

For several hours, the landscape barely changed. It was hard to imagine men still fighting over this. But the separatists had always imagined that the Vanni was Tamil, and, in 2002, it became their fantasy republic. After the long, pointless battles of the nineties, the Sinhalese withdrew and a little Tigerland appeared. It would have its own laws, its own customs, its own taxes, and a leader who called himself the *Sooriyathevan*, or Sun God, and who allowed no voice except his own.

Vavuniya still felt like a frontier town, on the edge of the unknown. Everyone here seemed to be on the move, or stocking up for whatever lay ahead. There were never enough buildings for all these people, and so city life continued under the trees. Here, beneath the maras, hair was cut, phones mended, shoes cobbled, cattle fed and fortunes told, as if this were some great gathering about to move off. In the middle of it all, there was an old church and an enclave of courts and civil servants, but they'd long since been smothered in camps: army camps, transit camps, eleven refugee camps and – around the lake – camps of polythene and sticks. Sometimes it seemed as if the entire population had arrived here in panic, or was now rushing out to fill the gaps.

I'd never known a town so fidgety and mobile. Many of the shops now had wheels, and would come bleating through the streets, announcing cakes and ice cream with a fanfare of trumpets. Occasionally, I'd see an old Vanniya amongst them, with her stumps of wizened corn. Time seemed to be moving too quickly for most people. On the food stalls, the diners swigged from the water jugs and rushed about piling their curry on to slabs of bread. Meanwhile, in the religious shops, Ganesh was stacked up with Korans, Buddhas and wounded saints, as if no one was certain where their future lay. Even the monkeys seemed disorientated, and – unsure whether Vavuniya was still the jungle or had become a city – they'd nested in the cables.

This sensation of restlessness wasn't helped by my hotel, which felt like a ship. It was called the Nelly Star and had decks instead of floors, each railed off in chrome and slathered in nautical colours. Downstairs, a huge television throbbed away as if it were the engine, and at the back was a dark, smoky hold where the drunks would gather. At night, this room was lit by a large fridge, which glowed like some heavenly portal. Perhaps, if you drank enough White Label, more doors would appear and, just for a moment, you'd be back home.

Almost everyone I met was a refugee, or wished they were somewhere else. Vavuniya, I realised, was almost entirely a creation of the war. At the outset, only thirty thousand people had lived here, and at times it had almost emptied. Now, however, it was almost ten times its original size, swollen by those pouring out of the Vanni. For months, I'd been looking for a leader amongst them, and then I made contact with Rohini Singham. Once in town, I asked him round to my waterless ship.

'Singham', as he was known, was grizzled and drawn, but had a sense of humour as dry as the scrub. Few Sri Lankans have his reputation for resolve and humanity. It's said that, thanks to his organisation, SEED, over three thousand families had rediscovered the meaning of 'home'. That afternoon, we sat under the giant screen, fending off blasts of Bollywood and ordering plates of chips. This is what he told me – the refugee's tale:

'I left Jaffna in the early eighties, when the killing began. In those days, it was easy to enter Germany, via East Berlin. I was only eighteen and I'd never been on an aeroplane before, and I wasn't even sure how to get out of the airport. But somehow I got to West Berlin, and there I was jailed. It took them forty days to find a Tamil interpreter, and I'd spend the next ten years seeking asylum. In the meantime, I became a German citizen and lived in Berlin, organising immigrants, that sort of thing . . . Then the Wall came down and there were suddenly more neo-Nazis around, and all these racially-motivated murders – thirteen people either burnt alive or thrown to their deaths . . . And so I had to decide: where was I going to die? As a black in Europe? Or as a Tamil in Sri Lanka?

'I returned here in the nineties, at the height of the fighting. Now I was a refugee again, but in my own country. And it was hard to adapt. I'd learnt so many European habits – like punctuality . . . I got very ill in the camps, with malaria and liver damage, but I absorbed the tragedy and cried every night. In one camp, there were forty thousand refugees, and many of them had been uprooted twenty or thirty times. That's when I started SEED, beginning with ten families and ten thousand Deutschmarks. People said I was mad, and, sure enough, within a few weeks we were displaced by the fighting, but somehow we persisted . . .

'It's still a struggle. Many of these IDPs have been on the move for years, and a lot of the young ones have known nothing but violence. Learning is easy. It's the unlearning that's so hard.'

Even the Sinhalese were often bewildered by the turns life had taken. These days they made up only ten per cent of the town, and I'd almost forgotten that mercurial temper. But then, one morning, I was climbing up through the decks when I was stopped by another guest. Although he was wearing only a towel and carrying a bar of soap, I had an awkward feeling I was in for a speech. It began disarmingly enough. He told me he was here visiting his estates, that I should never drink cold water and that hoppers should only be eaten with the fingers. But then a flash of anger appeared.

'You know why we're in this fucking mess?'

'Go on,' I said, intrigued by his uninvited fury.

'The Americans. The *fucking* Americans! They should get their dirty hands off this country! God will punish them, no? And the British. They *robbed* this country. We were a great nation until they arrived, and they're still robbing us. When the Queen Mother died, I watched the funeral and I thought, Who's paying for all this? Not the British people. The fucking Commonwealth! And you know who started this shitty war? India! They wanted us to be like a province. And as for the bullshit United Nations, they just kept it all going! *Chee!* Human rights? Don't make me fucking sick! We're not savages. Do you think we look like bloody bastards? That's all we ever hear about – human fucking rights.

You know who fed us through this war? Saddam Hussein! And the Chinese! They were our only friends . . .'

I didn't listen to it all. This was partly because I was distracted by a finger-like cyst growing out of his shoulder which was now wagging with rage. Is this what anger eventually does, I wondered, popping out all over your body? But then, suddenly, it was finished. The irate landlord tightened the towel around his waist, shot me a manic grin, declared that he'd die for the Rajapaksas and stalked off in search of his shower.

From here, a long, thin battlefield streaked away, over the horizon. The A9 was still the only road to Jaffna, and, over the centuries, it had seen a steady traffic of ox carts, elephants and great armies heading off to war. But, in recent years, it had often been the battleground itself. During the nineties, Colombo's forces could regularly be seen rolling north in a magnificent procession, and then – a few weeks later – tumbling south in full retreat. Mined, strafed, booby-trapped and ambushed, the A9 was, for a long time, one of the bloodiest roads in the world.

I'd always known I'd need a driver for the journey ahead. It was a grim prospect, the thought of another Sanath, or word-mangling Prinithy Hewage. But, this time, I had more luck, and the travel agent sent me a man called Kutty. Not only did he speak beautiful antique English, he was also a Colombo Tamil and had spent most of his life just blending in. Although I always liked Kutty, even now, I can hardly picture him. I remember stubble, curly hair, sandals and strange, lopsided toes, but that's all. Kutty never offered opinions or comments, and doesn't even appear in any of my recordings or photographs. It seems he'd mastered the art of melting away.

'I went to Jaffna once,' he told me, but, if this was ever a story, it never emerged.

We stopped first an Omanthai, a little railway halt a few miles north. It was now a hard-baked place of tarpaulins and logs, and not much moved in the midday sun. But, back in 2002, this was where Sri Lanka had come to an end. Between here and the Jaffna Peninsula, there'd been nothing but Tiger territory, or Tamil Eelam. This fierce breakaway state had absorbed not only the Vanni, but nearly a fifth of the island. Although Colombo still registered its births and deaths, and paid for its health, the Tigers ran the rest. Here, on the government side, anyone leaving had to show their passport and give up their car.

Up ahead, there was still a military checkpoint. I was used to checkpoints by now (some even had sponsors, and were painted up in the livery of Dulux or Munchee Biscuits). But this one was different – an enormous canopy straddling the road. Inside, the army was still making every departure seem momentous. First, we were interviewed ('Papo sovisit? Fast time?'), and then our forms were passed along a row of camouflaged clerks, where they were signed, counter-signed, thrashed through old typewriters and then bundled up and stamped. I don't know what all this was supposed to convey, except perhaps that what lay ahead was dangerously foreign.

To begin with, the Tigers' world didn't seem different. It was the same dry zone, the same expanse of brittle savannah, the same spicy red dust, the same shrivelled cattle and the same thirsty trees. Sometimes bushfires would appear, crackling through the undergrowth and then spinning off into nothing. For a while, we stopped and watched as a great coil of brahminy kites – fifteen in all – rose up out of the scrub. I remember thinking how reassuring this was; nature forming its secret patterns once again, even here by the murderous A9.

But if this highway had ever had memories, they'd now been energetically erased. A decade earlier, travellers had written of bunkers in the verge and Tiger flags on every pole. Everything had been painted in green tiger-stripes, even the vehicles used by their police. Time, too, had felt different then; the clocks had gone forward half an hour, and out on the road there'd been a new speed limit, slowing life down to a sombre forty. There was nothing the guerrillas hadn't controlled or measured or covered in slogans. They'd even had their own customs post, taxing anyone entering Eeelam, and then taxing them again if ever they left.

All this had gone now: grubbed up, burnt and bulldozed backwards into the woods.

It was also here that outsiders saw their first Tigers, or 'cadres'. These were unsettling encounters. This revolt was supposed to be one of the most vicious in the world, and yet here were the rebels, merely children. A friend of mine, a London Tamil, told me they were barely thirteen, the girls pawing through her books. The writer, William Dalrymple, had been left with a similar impression; for all their tiger-striped fatigues, these were just kids with guns. He'd also seen them watching *Rambo* and *Predator*, and had assumed that this was their training, and that somehow their lives had turned into movies. 'It was as if the Tigers actually enjoyed killing,' he wrote, 'as if to them it was a hobby, or even an art form'. This was an intriguing thought – a guerrilla army, Hollywood trained – but, unsurprisingly perhaps, there was always more to it than that.

Those who'd known the Tigers better would remember their commitment – and the cyanide capsules. Over the years, my naval friend, Ravi, had come across many cadres, and always insisted that they were 'good people', and yet, he said, they'd only ever feared failure and never death. They'd also been brutally re-educated, exhaustively trained and then dispersed in untraceable units. Often, they looked as if they'd been in the jungle for years, and would re-emerge with almost no hint of the person they'd been, except a rosary, perhaps, or the *Rambo* decal. Most got used to the hardship, having never known anything different. Once, a group of Tigers were flown to Thailand for talks. They were art-less negotiators, and were best remembered for their struggles with the safety belts, and for the huge volumes of ice cream they'd ordered up to their rooms.

Back in battle, however, the Tigers were relentless and nimble. They never wore helmets, and always fought in rubber slippers. Even on the attack, they were stripped to the basics: water bottle, a few tins of tuna, a Kit-Kat, an RPG and three hundred rounds. 'That's how you fight in jungle,' said Ravi. 'We had a lot to learn . . .'

Although the guerrillas called themselves *Potiyal*, or the Boys, many were women. They'd swapped saris for battle fatigues, and wore their hair short and tightly braided. Sworn to chastity, these girls often gave themselves names like the 'Freedom Birds'. Inevitably, in an age of Bond movies, the foreign press had found them thrilling: a regiment of Amazons, in tight-fitting drill. Their finest moment had been in Jaffna, fighting the Indians. In four minutes, they'd destroyed six T-72 tanks and a column of armoured cars, and had then held their positions for the next three days. But had these women ever truly found equality, or just the right to die like everyone else? It was still women cooking

365

the rice and dhal. Often, too, it was Freedom Birds doing the rebellion's housework: packing, cleaning, mending, minding, or – out here on the frontier – rummaging through books.

Up ahead, an enormous army had gathered in the old Tiger capital. To the Vanniyas, Kilinochchi was still the 'Village of the Parrots', although it had been years since their little town vanished, along with its squawk. Nowadays, everything was nested down in razor wire, or covered in great concrete camps. Through it all ran a long gleaming avenue of showrooms and banks, but behind the façades, the garrisons crowded in. A friend in Colombo had put me in touch with one of the commanders here. When we found his gates, we were escorted in and up through the camp. It was like a vast green truck-stop, or a castle on wheels. The brigadier lived on the far side of all this hardware, in a little bungalow on the shores of a tank.

'Pretty, ah?' he said. 'I love it here. Even brought my horse.'

I soon discovered that Nihal Amarasekara was always like this, happily unfazed. To begin with, he struck me as a sort of Sinhalese John Bull: well padded, affable and brisk. But as the day wore on, a more subtle character emerged. Although he knew that the world about him lay broken and empty, he had an engineer's instinct for fixing it up. Over tea, he told me about the mines he'd removed and the bridges rebuilt. But his latest project was to restore ordinariness to people's lives, and repair the mundane. Later, he took me on a tour of his marigolds, assembled in gigantic grey troughs throughout the town. But his real joy was Harmony Park, built in the grounds of an old plastics factory. Once, the LTTE had assembled landmines here, but now there were sappers, planting a garden. The brigadier had even added a few touches of his own, including an old steamroller and a bright red London bus.

'It's something, no?' He smiled. 'People just need to trust us.'

But despite its marigolds and its double-decker, Kilinochchi still felt obstinately martial. Soldiers were everywhere, and yet, behind all their armour and sandbags, they were also remote. The sheer acreage of men and machines was strangely over-whelming, like some great invasion that had never passed on. A few decades ago, the entire Sri Lankan army would barely have filled this high street, and now here was a little part of it, spilling out into the scrub beyond.

Despite the peace treaty of 2002, everyone knew that a great war still lay ahead. For the next five years, the Scandinavians tried to keep the two sides apart. They even sent a little army of Norse-men to monitor the ceasefire. But the firing never truly ceased, and it became merely a war of denial. This brought with it a new resolve amongst the Sinhalese. As my friend, the journalist, put, 'I used to campaign against this war but then I realised that this island wasn't big enough for two undefeated armies.'

During the lull, the Sinhalese army grew. There was no need for conscription; poverty and a sense of destiny were usually enough to fill its boots. By 2007, Sri Lanka was the most militar-ised society in South Asia, and, since the start of the war, its army had grown by a factor of thirty. It also had new teeth, thanks to a curious medley of friends: Israel, Iran, Pakistan and China. Even Britain, which had been so squeamish about the fighting, wasn't averse to shipping over some pistols and a few armoured cars.

But there was one weapon more telling than all the others: the MBRL. The multi-barrel rocket launcher is an odd machine to find in a war of unification. In a single volley, it can release forty screaming missiles. Unguided, inaccurate and undiscriminating, these will fragment over a huge area, killing everyone within. If this war had ever been about hearts and minds, it wasn't any longer. It was now about territory, and love – if there was to be any – would be rigorously enforced.

The Tigers had also been busy during the peace.

I could still find traces of them around Kilinochchi. Apart from the landmine factory, there was the ugly, concrete town hall, where their government had met. I could almost imagine them still in there, a shabby politburo of intellectuals, fishermen and teachers. It was here too that they'd held their only press conference, in April 2002, inviting over two hundred journalists, and then subjecting them to ten hours of screening. For a while, a little helipad had appeared in the playground nearby, and visiting VIPs were treated to displays of mortar fire and then served tea on the best bone china. Even the napkins had been smuggled in through the blockade. According to the BBC's Frances Harrison, no one knew what to say on these occasions – not that the Tigers minded. Like any rebels, they were enjoying the attention and sense of control.

Beneath the glossy, new façades, there were still a few shreds of their old town. On one of the new showrooms, the hoardings were flapping free, and beneath them I could see an older shop, all nibbled away like some ancient cake. This was never Pompeii, but – just for a while – it had behaved like a city. There'd been rebel restaurants, rebel shops, and a radio station called 'Voice of the Tigers'. There'd also been a guerrilla bank: the Bank of Tamil Eelam (which was still paying out, even at the end, under a hail of shells). Then there were the bureaucrats, and all the machinery for gathering tax. For many Tamils – like my journalist friend – the sight of this paperwork was heartening. 'If you live in interesting times,' she wrote, 'predictable, daily life is the stuff of dreams.'

But life was never as dull as people had hoped. A priest sympathetic to the LTTE once tried to persuade me that Eelam had been like Singapore, with everyone having whatever they wanted. But few agreed. At best, people said, it was like Eritrea: authoritarian, closed, fearful and threadbare. There was no economy to speak of, no phones, no cars and little electricity. Colombo had even prevented batteries from getting through, fearing they'd be used in bombs. Women now had to peddle their produce by the road, and soon there were more landmines than people. Children would grow up knowing the difference between incoming and outgoing fire, but never having seen a train or computer. By becoming a capital city, Kilinochchi hadn't become richer or safer, merely a larger target.

The great landmark of those days, a concrete tower, now lay on its side. It had once contained water, and stood ten storeys high. As it fell, the steel rods running through its base had snapped like little roots, and now it lolled in the sand, hollow and dead, like some vast, intergalactic tree. Inside, its ladders now ran along the floor, and I once climbed in, just to ponder its up-ended views. When, eventually, old Kilinochchi had failed, it got the Vesuvius it never deserved. They say that, as the explosions finally rumbled away, a primitive, pre-industrial silence had settled on the ruins.

Meanwhile, out to the west, the LTTE had dug itself in. Across the tip of this egg-shaped island, their little nation-in-waiting had almost vanished. My driver, Kutty, and I spent nearly two days rushing around from hole to hole, trying to work out where they'd all gone.

It seemed everyone had vanished underground. Take, for example, 'Soosi', the minister of boats. On the surface, he'd kept a few fruit trees and a little villa. But, step inside his wardrobe, and – Narnia-like – a different world appeared: a complex of cement and tunnels, extending deep beneath the surface. 'Soosi' wasn't even his real name. They'd all had subterranean titles, usually borrowed from movies or the news. 'Disco' was popular, but, amongst the arch-troglodytes, there was also a 'Regan', a 'Castro', a 'Gandhi' and a 'Captain Miller'.

At the wardrobe door, a Sinhalese officer kept guard.

'Did they always live like this?' I asked. 'Underground?'

'Always, sah. Those buggers never stopped digging.'

It took us a while to find the leader's lair. The jungle now appeared in tufts, and there was rice again, smoothing out the land. But the war had never quite gone away; there were still the ruins and the occasional field of burnt-out machines. Then we got to Visuamadu and the trees closed in around us in a maze of shadows and wire and bright orange tracks. Somewhere in here, we found what we were after: a small, thatched, clay-brick farm-house. It sat in the middle of a long, dark garden, where nothing grew except enormous clumps of military junk. As redoubts go, it was hardly Berchtesgaden, although it had been home to a mas-termind of sorts. Velupillai Prabhakaran had inspired almost all of this: the creation of Eelam, the Boys and the tiger-striped suits. So, it was little surprise to discover that, deep beneath his farm-house, there sprawled a stately warren of concrete chambers, and as the door was open, we wandered in.

* * *

Prabhakaran's life will always seem fragmentary and enigmatic, but – descending though his house – some of the pieces began to make sense.

The rooms on the surface were startlingly bland. The army was still trying to label his home 'luxurious', but there were no gold taps or fountains or collections of shoes. All I could find was a wooden bed and an old television, and everything else was painted peach. Prabhakaran had never made much of pleasure or possessions. This could easily have been the home of his father, who'd been a civil servant near Jaffna. It had been an unremarkable upbringing, although it's often said that the young Velupillai was a strange child – shy, lonely and grimly ascetic. There were always slingshots around, little home-made bombs and violence gleaned from comics. To his followers, he'd be a scourge and a redeemer, but to everyone else he was a cranky introvert, weaned on Clint Eastwood and copies of *Soldier of Fortune*.

The guns never left him. In his portraits, he looked doughy and middle aged, and yet he was always in tiger stripes and holsters, and – round the back of the farmhouse – there was still a little pistol range. Once, when none of the soldiers were looking, I ran my fingers over the bullet holes and tried to imagine the rage. Prabhakaran first killed a man in 1975, at the age twenty-one – not some fiery Sinhalese, but a fellow Tamil, the elected mayor of Jaffna. No one knows where the anger came from – some say he'd witnessed an uncle boiled alive – but, whatever it was, the rage never left him, but grew cold and precise. It was his idea to provide everyone with cyanide. 'I will never be caught alive,' he promised.

Amongst the portraits around the walls, there were two other faces. One was his wife, Mathivathani, who wore a sari in king-fisher blue, and who looked improbably delicate against her thick-limbed husband with his brutal life. Prabhakaran had little time for human affection, and no patience for the frailty of others, but Mathivathani, it seemed, had been the exception. The other face was that of their son, Balachandran, aged twelve. Although he wore a gown and mortar board, his expression was detached and precious, and he already had the jowly features of his father. One of his toys, a plastic pedal-car, was still outside, parked on the steps.

Deeper down, the concrete smelt new. In that first cellar, there was air conditioning, a towel rail and an old campaign-bed. This was Prabhakaran's combat-bedroom, finished in 2004. By then, he was fifty, and had been running the Tigers for over thirty years. During that time, he'd become dangerously divine. Starting out as *Thambi*, or Little Brother, he was a plucky bandit at first, tormenting authority. He and his band would raid and maim and wipe out the meek, and then he'd disappear for months, disguised as a priest or a peanut-seller. But whenever he re-emerged, he was always bigger than ever, and, in time, his band was no longer a gang, but a militia, twenty thousand strong. His life on the run had, however, taken its toll. By the time he'd burrowed down under Visuamadu, only the legends still thrived: Prabhakaran was the *Sooriyathevan*, he had a one-million-rupee reward on his head, he was the reincarnation of a Chola king, and he kept a pet leopard. In reality, however, he was sleepless, diabetic and overweight. Amongst his dusty effects, I noticed, there was a centrifuge and an enormous white fridge for all his drugs.

A dank staircase led down to more chambers below. The detail was much the same: blast doors, bookshelves and little tiger-striped tablecloths. Perhaps, in all this, there was some clue as to where it would all go wrong. Whilst the Sri Lankan army was on the move, the Sun God was acquiring an armchair and settling in.

Further west, a great bastion – the Gormenghast of the Tiger world – had vanished into the leaf litter. Although it extends four storeys under the forest, the complex at Puthukkudiyirruppu was never discovered during the war. Even now, it was swathed in jungle and razor wire, and deminers were still picking through the topsoil. One day, the termites will have eaten away the modest houses on the surface and it will all collapse inwards down its concrete shafts, but, for the moment, it was still a last resort, and, in its own little way, the House of Groan.

As usual, the army were now in charge, and we were met by a major.

'My men have torches; they'll show you around.'

As with Prabhakaran's house, it didn't look much on the surface. There were kitchens, a running track and a stack of old shells. We were also shown the morgue, and a last surviving work of Tiger art: an iron grille, decorated with candles and Kalashnikovs. But inside, and deep below the houses, there were more imposing structures: cavernous stairwells, an underground car park, blast-proof conference halls, an armoured map-room and huge iron doors, now all buckled and chewed like strips of jerky.

'They were booby-trapped . . .' said the soldiers.

'We lost four men down here.'

Not much of the Tigers had survived, except their apple-green paint. The air tasted of bats, their acid stink curdling the darkness even deep inside. As we clattered from chamber to chamber, our torch beams picked out a soldierly banter scrawled on the walls. But everything else had gone – the furniture plundered, wires pulled out and all the maps torn down.

I gazed upwards at the empty battens where the charts had been. Once, this was the nerve centre of one of the most powerful secret armies in the world. Its forces had included a hit-and-run squad (the 'Pistol Gang'), eleven divisions of soldiers, a navy ('Sea Tigers'), an airforce, gunners, commandos ('Black Tigers') and its own Gestapo, known as TOSIS. The Tigers had even run a merchant navy, the 'Sea Pigeons', with more than twenty ships to bring all their hardware home. Even during the great truce of 2002 to 2006, it was pouring in. It's said that, during the lull, the Tigers not only built this underground fortress, they also took delivery of another fifteen artillery pieces, together with four hundred thousand mines, ten thousand assault rifles and nearly one hundred tons of explosive. Never before had insurgents or 'terrorists' shipped such vast quantities of weapons.

We filed out, upwards, into the sunlight. It was odd to think of the great castle, spreading out beneath our feet. In this island of forts, it will seem exotic for a while, but will soon be forgotten. One day, people will wonder what it was for, and then, perhaps, they'll fight its battles all over again. Perhaps, too, this strange castle will have its own Titus Groan, surviving heroically amongst 'fists of knuckled masonry'. But, for now, it's just a ruin: dark, infested and upside down.

Apart from their caves, all that remained of the Tigers were their contraptions. The army seemed to love these gadgets, and was always heaping them together. At Prabhakaran's house there'd been a pile of tractors, each wearing armour, and a Pajero, mounted with a cannon. Beyond Puthukkudiyirripu, there was a whole field of these devices: home-made howitzers, impromptu gunboats and do-it-yourself torpedoes (with a seat for the driver).

There were even a few locally produced submarines, which looked like the spaceships that Victorians had dreamed of. They had fish fins, windows, two-stroke engines and enormous propellers. One of these madcap machines even had adapted controls to allow amputees back into the war.

The army called this collection of freaks 'The War Museum', and yet its only exhibits were here to be mocked. Here were the things that made the Tigers looked pitiful and desperate. But hadn't they kept the army at bay for almost three decades? And what about all the shipments, and the artillery they'd captured, and their MBRLs? A ferocious little army, it seemed, was being assiduously forgotten. Even its improvisation had been belittled. The Tigers were formidable designers and, in their laboratories, they were always perfecting weapons, machining parts and cooking up new explosives. Great minds would apply themselves to thinking up some of the cruellest devices man's ever known, including a first – and unsurpassed – suicide vest.

But one of their most ambitious contraptions was still there, lolling in the dunes at Wellamulliwaikkal. It was another submarine, although, this time, ninety feet long. With its great steel ribs, it looked like a whale in the making. I was once told that submarine-building presents particular challenges for naval architects (and that, if the pressure is imperfectly distributed, the whole thing implodes), and yet here was this great machine confidently rising out of the sand. The Tigers had even built it a dry dock, lined with steel-plate plundered from a shipwreck. None of this suggested pitiful to me, but, rather, ingenious and brutal.

Of the guerrillas themselves, only a swimming pool survived. I was amazed how thoroughly they'd disappeared. For years, they'd made this landscape their own – covering it in barricades and murals and jungle camps – and now they'd vanished again, just like the early days. Once more, their tiny republic existed only at night, or in the imagination of a few.

It was a cruel memorial, a swimming pool. All those cadres – once famed for their fervour and camouflage – were now remembered by this: a figment of suburbia, bland and tiled and a cheery sky-blue. There were even racing lanes, and a high board for divers. What were they thinking of? The Terrorist Olympics? Why build all this, when, through much of Tigerland, they could barely muster electric light? Only the dimensions were unusual, being almost ten metres deep. 'I'm told,' said Kutty, 'that they used to train their frogmen here.' But mostly this wasn't a place of war, just somewhere to float around, serene and surreal. There was even a picture of Prabhakaran here, bobbing along in his rubber ring.

Perhaps, too, the pool was a reminder of how childlike the Tigers had become. In the upper echelons, there were always idealists, like Thevar the blogger, and ever since the beginning they'd been joined by the dispossessed, the fishermen and farmers. But this meat grinder of a war was never sated, and soon the LTTE were conscripting anyone they could. At one point, it's said, there were no barbers left in Tamil Eelam. No one was much surprised, then, when they came for the children too. An American report identified cadres as young as thirteen, trotting into battle. Even during the truce another 4,347 children were recruited, a third of them under fifteen. The worst time was after the tsunami, when the LTTE lost some two thousand souls, all of whom had to be replaced.

I tried to imagine the new recruits, paddling around in one last burst of childhood. Their changing rooms were still there, painted the same delicate apple-green, and now punched with angry holes. To have been a teenager here during the truce would've been an ugly fate, and outsiders talked of a 'vortex of sacrifice', of children herded up in trailers and of parents beaten for resisting. But it would be even worse later, when the fighting restarted. The LTTE demanded a son or daughter from each family, and a third of all schoolchildren were taken away. For many, there'd be no happy endings, and they'd be returned to their parents wrapped in a flag. By the end, children were the most precious commodity in Tamil Eelam, and – as it all disappeared underground – they too vanished, hidden away in culverts and sewers.

A group of soldiers were sitting in the apple-green shade.

One of them spoke English. 'You seen the bullet holes?'

'Yes,' I said. 'The Battle of the Swimming Pool?'

'Exactly. They gave up nothing without a fight.'

Tiger rule was seldom forgiving.

Before leaving the Vanni, we stopped at their old prison, near Thottiadi. Derelict now, it had never been an indulgent structure: two rows of pink concrete cells in a sandy clearing. All around us were stands of weeping casuarinas, which seemed to whisper and conspire. Inside, the cells were like kennels, or concrete boxes for the storing of life. Not only were there heavy iron grilles across the doors, but each of the prisoners, I noticed, had been shackled to the floor.

In some ways, the people who'd languished here were lucky. The Tigers took few prisoners and, usually, they preferred to kill their enemies, even the wounded. Their capacity for casual slaughter never ceased to surprise the world. After the capture of Pooneryn in 1993, and Mullaitivu three years later, Sinhalese soldiers were despatched by the hundred. Only those of political value were kept alive. But it wasn't really life they were given, merely a more protracted form of death. No one survived here at Thottiadi. As the war drew to a close, the inmates were all taken out into the casuarinas, and butchered on the sand.

Even with their own people, the Tigers could be horribly terse. By the end of the eighties, they'd already wiped out most of their rivals. Even after that, critics often found themselves being beaten senseless, or blasted to bits. As a UN report once noted, Prabhakaran had no truck with dissenters or moderates, and would have them labelled traitors and suitably killed. Amongst those who died were his deputy, Mahattaya, and almost an entire society of intellectuals, the University Teachers for Human Rights. 'There will be only one party,' declared Prabhakaran, and, like some dark subterranean Kublai Khan, he grew ever more corpulent and absolute.

But Thevar once told me he'd adored him, as had everyone.

'It was spiritual. Life is nothing, and he showed what we must do.'

So, there it was again, that strange love, rigidly enforced.

The Tigers' world would always feel frustratingly obscure, but at least I had a rough idea who'd paid for it all. It was people like my neighbours, in Tooting. They were part of a vast Tamil diaspora, spread across four continents and including 50,000 in Switzerland, 200,000 in Canada and 100,000 in Indian camps. Not much united them, except a sense of horror and their Tamil pride. Many of the exiles detested Prabhakaran's tyranny and his variant of Marxism, and yet, somehow, together, they'd provided his income.

Of course, they weren't the only source of Tiger funds. Not

only did the LTTE own a shipping line, it also ran gas stations, studios, shops and charities. Then there was crime, which had always been a healthy earner. The Montreal Police claimed that the Tamils ran their heroin trade, and the Swiss said the same thing. Meanwhile, in London, the great wheeze was skimming credit cards, particularly in Tooting. But all this was small beer. Still the greatest source of money was the diaspora, and, altogether, it had donated around $250 million a year, or ninety per cent of the Tigers' budget.

In the area where I live, the giving had worked like this: First, the LTTE's agents had done a tour of Tamil homes. Most people told me they'd been happy to give, and saw no problem in supporting 'the Boys'. Each family was expected to pay £200 a year, and each business £2,000. As the war went on, the amounts increased, and, by 2009, Britain's Tamils were donating a healthy £250,000 a month. This money then went out via the *undiyal*, a shadowy network of brokers and bankers and high-street jewellers. Every time I went to Tooting, I'd pass one of these places, now innocently selling great ropes of gold.

Not everyone had paid up immediately. Sometimes, I was told, the LTTE had been forced to apply a little pressure. The United Nations once accused the Tigers of 'mafia-style tactics' amongst the diaspora, but, in Tooting, the coercion was never very florid. Most people still had family in Jaffna or the Vanni, and it was usually enough to remind them that, out there, it was the Tigers in charge.

I once asked a shopkeeper if anyone had ever gone to the police.

'You serious? Once you go the cops, you're a traitor.'

Tooting's Tamils often behaved as if the war was still going on. It wasn't just the shrines in the temples, or the portraits of

Prabhakaran hanging in the shops. Sometimes, they'd all set off to a rally in the West End, and, once, I followed. It was a magnificent black-clad occasion, the Tamils easily filling Piccadilly with their red Tiger flags. Although, since 2001, it's been illegal to wave this big-pawed, bullet-spangled banner, the police were in no mood to intervene. The crowd groaned with anger, and a grim coalition of priests and communists spat out their speeches. Occasionally, the masses would part, disgorging a veteran, still in his Tiger fatigues. Then the crowd would swirl round, and he'd disappear again before anyone noticed how many laws had just been broken.

Nobody wanted to talk much, except a woman who gave me her flag.

'We must never break the rules,' she said. 'We're here as refugees.'

But the rules hadn't always been observed. During the war, there'd been threats and burglaries, and the moderates' radio station had somehow been wrecked. But, of all these spats, the strangest was in Wembley, where the Tigers seized a temple. In court, the trustees told the judge that they'd been visiting Sri Lanka when, suddenly, they were abducted by the LTTE. Held for six weeks in the Vanni ('a mafia state'), they said they'd been forced to sign over the Wembley deeds. The judge believed them, and, in April 2005, ordered the Tigers out. The leader of the Tiger faction was called Nagendram Seevaratnam, and, as I read the judgment, I suddenly realised I knew him. We'd often had tea together in the local temple, where he was known as its 'spiritual leader'.

The following weekend, I was on the bus, heading back to Tooting.

* * *

Mr Seevaratnam was always happy to see me, and would order his priests to bring us a tray of *iddlis* and *vadai* – or cakes and croquettes – and a pot of frothy 'milk tea'. He looked frail amongst his well-bellied, bare-chested minions, and his eyes were rimmed with great coal-dust smudges of weariness and age. Sometimes, his sinewy features would halt altogether and his words would peter out, creating the impression that, whilst he was wired into this world, he was also tuned in to somewhere else. Everyone here seemed to regard him as somehow holy, and it helped that his office was heaped with old scriptures and pots of ghee, that his robes were scholarly and yellow, and that he slept on a mat somewhere up in the roof. But holiness had only come late in life, and if Colombo's press were to be believed, it hadn't come at all. To them, Mr Seevaratnam was the 'Terror Guru', and the owner of a one-man front called Sivagoyam.

'And is that true?' I asked. 'Are you?'

But Mr Seevaratnam wouldn't be hurried, and it was several more visits before his answer emerged. Not that I minded. I enjoyed the tea and the rituals, and our curious forays through a secret life. Mr Seevaratnam would never be prompted, but would whisper his story as if it were magic, and in the order that mattered to him. It emerged like some wild journey, darting backwards and forwards across the globe. We'd begin with his best friend, beaten to death in the riots of 1977, following which the young Seevaratnam leaves the island forever. Then, suddenly, it's 1987, and he's in Barnet, working as an accountant for the council and building Sivagoyam. After that, we're filling the years in between, and Nigeria appears, and huge suitcases stuffed with cash. There's even a spell in Papua New Guinea, and he's out collecting again, amongst the Tamils. Occasionally, amidst all this, we're back in Jaffna, and there's the American college and his father's boats departing for Rangoon. Then it's the sixties, and See-varatnam's working for the railways, and he gets involved with 'the Boys', and so it all begins. At one point, he's running the International Fund and thirteen accounts. But then it ends with adultery in 1991, and Prabhakaran calls and tells him he's expelled.

'So that was it? You were out of the LTTE?'

The old man hesitated. 'Every Tamil is a Tamil Tiger.'

'And you're no exception?'

But it was no good pressing, and the question only prompted more tea. The story, however, wasn't easily suppressed, and was soon up and running again. These were big accounts, said Mr Seevaratnam, up to £800,000. 'K. P. bought the weapons, not me. You know K. P.? The procurements man. He'd ring with a message, like, "Pay three greens to the man out east," and I'd always know what he meant. I'd go down to Barclays and make out a draft to some East European, £300,000. That's how it worked.'

'It sounds easy,' I said.

It was, he agreed. He was buying AKs and rockets on Tooting High Street.

I asked about Wembley's temple, and what went on in 2004.

'They were mismanaging it. The LTTE told me to take charge.'

'You must've made a few enemies, over the years?'

Mr Seevaratnam nodded. 'You've seen our golden chariot?'

I had. It lay out in the car park, a tower of charred black stumps.

'Someone is trying to kill me.'

'Maybe you should go to the police?'

'I am protected by the goddess Mara Amman.'

Perhaps he was, but even a goddess can only do so much. A few weeks later, the temple was closed down under a court order and Sivagoyam was evicted. I only saw Mr Seevaratnam once more after that, out in Croydon. He was disappearing under a welter of writs, and had turned the colour of clay. Even his priests were suing him, he said. He didn't know who to trust anymore, or what would become of his gods. A fractured, runaway community, it seemed, was gradually falling apart.

We left the Vanni via an enormous trap. Even now, when I say its name – Elephant Pass – I think of snow and Alps and Hannibal's gorges, and yet this version had none of that. It was beautiful in its way: a sort of anti-mountain, a place so exorbitantly flat and featureless that a stranger might easily think that he could set off from here and never reach anywhere at all. It didn't even have any elephants and, even if it had, they'd never have passed, because this, of course, was an enormous trap.

At the south end of the pass, I got out of the car and took a full blast of sand and briny buckshot. I could feel my face sizzle in the wind, and there was no sound but the trucks and the hiss of the sea. The nothingness of it all was compelling – just a long spindle of gravel stretching off into the haze. For thousands of years, this narrow, salt-seared, grit-lashed causeway was the only land-link between the Jaffna Peninsula and rest of Ceylon. To the Vanni-yas, it was also the perfect place to bring wild elephants, driving them out of the forest and offering them a choice: die, swim or learn to work. Generations of broken-spirited beasts would lend the place their name.

I walked for a while, but the perspective didn't change, and the car just got smaller. There was supposed to have been a Dutch fort out here, and a railway halt, but it had all been blown away. Elephant Pass was a trap for everything, especially human beings. For all invaders, whether going north or south, this was the bottleneck where their fate was decided. During the last thirty years, it was often the crucible of the civil war, these few hundred yards of emptiness more contested than anywhere else. Three times, full-scale battles had whirled up out of the dust – 1991, 2000 and 2009 – and, for over six thousand people, this was the last thing they'd ever seen: the flatness, the burnt grass and the sea like cement.

Around me, little was left of these great struggles. The army, haunted by the defeat of April 2000 – the worst they'd ever suffered – had cleared almost everything away. All that remained was a single monster, now buckled and torn and mounted on a plinth. It was an elephant of sorts: an old bulldozer, with a thick skin of crusted steel. The Tigers had ridden it down from Jaffna in 1991, and charged it at the army. But they hadn't counted on Kandyan courage and Lance Corporal Kularatne, who'd scrambled up the skin and posted two grenades. Two days later, my friend, Dr Goonetilleke, had also clambered up the side, to find the crew still sitting in their seats. 'There was nothing to be done,' he said, 'they'd all been burnt alive.'

I wondered what this wreck said to the truckers, throttling past.

You're leaving the trap, perhaps. *Think yourself lucky.*

Or, *Welcome to Jaffna: The Capital of Things that Nearly Worked.*

11

The Jaffna Peninsula

There appears to be something in the atmosphere here
different from other parts of the island; for it is only in
the tract that lies between Point Pedro and Jaffna that
sheep have been reared with any success.

Robert Percival, *An Account
of the Island of Ceylon*, 1803

Jaffna was often seen as somewhere not quite as great as, once, it nearly was.

I'd spent hours staring into the map, pondering the peninsula's precarious splendour. If Sri Lanka can be compared to an egg, the Jaffna Peninsula looks like the head of some scraggy ancient bird, trying to hatch out of the top. Above it hangs the great backside of India, mercifully inert and yet ominously close. For a long time, the Indians didn't know what to make of this freak at their rear, and, in their mythology, it was dismissed as the 'Sand Heap', or *Manatiddal*.

But between the two ran old shipping lanes and, in their heyday, everyone passed this way, especially the Arabs. During the thirteenth century, they wrote of 'meadows of gold' and Jabeh, a curious island king. By 1272, the channel was stiff with ships, and – according to John of Montecorvino – every year, some sixty were wrecked. All this attention ought to have made the peninsula rich, which it did for a while, until the next invasion.

Nowadays, the map's covered in conquest, and the names of new arrivals. They're all there, from the Pandyans and Cholas, down to the Dutch. Under each new regime, this great slab of coral – about the size of the Isle of Man – became almost great. For a while, Jaffnapatam was a kingdom of it own, and even today it still has a monarch (although he now lives in Holland and works in a bank).

Maps, however, never express obstruction well, smoothing off the hills and filling out the bogs. It was easy to forget Jaffna's segregation, and to overlook the great obstacles between here and the Sinhalese south. It wasn't just the badlands, there was also the great hedge, the sandflats, Elephant Pass and now a new barrier: a belt of mines almost a kilometre deep.

Minefields have their own ghastly, bad-tempered beauty.

For a while after Elephant Pass there was nothing but dust and trucks and stubby white ruins polka'd with dots. But then great clumps of greenery began welling up in front, and we knew we'd reached the FDL, or Forward Defence Line. The grass grew taller here, and, with it, a luxuriant spread of giant shrubs, like wild figs. Scattered amongst them were tiny red signs the size of a postcard and with that gurning skull. *DANGER MINES*, they read, or *DO NOT LEAVE THE ROAD*.

There was a pause in the trucks, so I asked Kutty to stop.

'But, sah, it's not allowed—'

'Just for a second. Turn off the engine . . .'

Kutty did as I asked, and – in those brief moments – we sat listening to the sounds all around: Jaffna before humankind. There was birdsong and silence and a hot, crackly breeze, known as the *solakam* (it blows in from India, explained Kutty, along with the Cholas). But mostly it was the hum of insects we heard, and the sound of land emptied of people. No doubt the men who'd laid these mines had also found a beauty in all of this; their devices, like sentries sewn into the soil – a harvest of fire, whenever it was needed. During the civil war, both sides were reapers, and, between them, they'd planted over one and a half million mines. This little crop was not only a kilometre deep, it stretched eleven kilometres across the isthmus.

But it was always ruthless, this primordial beauty. Nothing was spared, and almost three quarters of those maimed had nothing to do with the war. Worse, the carnage has continued long after the fighting's ceased. Often the mines were laid out in prairies – like this one – but sometimes they just appeared wherever there was water or shade. Some were plotted on maps, but others were lost, only to reappear again when the landscape coughed, sending up a fountain of limbs.

My friend, Dr Goonetilleke, once told me he'd been patching up survivors for almost thirty years. 'These things cause devastating injuries,' he said, 'even the little ones, the Jony mines. The explosion drives dirt, clothing, plastic and bacteria deep into the tissue, and destroys vessels well above the main injury. You know, it didn't matter whether they were soldiers or terrorists, it was always heartbreaking. They'd *plead* with me to save their leg. Most of these kids were only farmers.'

Suddenly, there was another sound: the blast of a whistle. A huge figure was stumbling out of the shrubs, dressed in perspex and armour, and waving his arms. It wasn't a proud moment; I realised we'd stopped during a moment of demining. Mouthing my apologies, I shrank into the seat, and Kutty started the engine and we crawled away.

These were HALO's men, plotting their way in through the mines. I recognised their uniforms having visited their yard, back in Kilinochchi. It had been a strange meeting, amongst so much neutered ordnance. I'd particularly asked to see a Jony mine, and the technician, Stan, had taken one down off the shelf.

It was no more than a wooden box, about the size of a cigarette packet and fitted with a battery. Dr Goonetilleke used to say it cost $3 to make one of these things, $1,000 to remove it, and $10,000 to patch up each victim.

I'd asked Stan how many of these HALO had found.

He was a veteran of questions and mines. 'One hundred and fifty-three thousand APs, and five hundred and sixty-two anti-tank.'

'That's a lot of legs, and quite a few lives . . .'

He'd nodded. 'We've got one thousand one hundred people out there, looking for mines.'

'Do you think you'll find them all?'

In front of us was a satellite picture of the Vanni, pimpled in red. It was often said that the war had left over fifteen thousand hectares of 'contaminated' land. Over the years, at least a dozen demining groups had set to work, probing the land, metre by metre. HALO was now the largest group, and – since 2002 – they'd cleared a Herculean 710 hectares, or 7.1 million square metres. But this, of course, meant there was still work to do, picking up in the prairies and pacifying the shade.

'Yes, we'll finish,' said Stan. 'This isn't a job you can leave half done.'

Beyond the minefields, the mood changed, and the landscape was suddenly brimming with life. It was as if we'd crossed a portal and ended up in an Asian Brueghel. Around us, the world had flattened out, and was enthusiastically peopled with doers and hewers. There was now colour too: great, green sweeps of glowing rice, strips of ginger, and brilliant fringes of brinjals and chillies. I even spotted churches nosing up out of the work, and beamy women, clothed to the ankle and deft with the scythe.

But this was no ordinary Belgium. There were neither clouds nor shadows, and all the water was missing. Across the entire peninsula, there are no natural ponds or bogs, and not a single river flows. Everything here centres on wells, sunk deep in the coral. For three quarters of the year, there isn't even any rain, and everyone just has to watch as the fields turn to stone. Then, in October, the monsoon comes, and the Jaffna Tamils do what they've done every year, and after every war: they go out, picking up the pieces and starting all over again. Eventually, their great flat world begins to flourish again, and everyone is fleetingly rich. It's Flanders all right, but built on a biscuit.

Further north, we began to find ourselves amongst the mansions. They were sporadic at first, but always hopelessly grand. Most had been abandoned, and stood, chipped and battered, like the villages all around. My favourite was Mandri Manai, or the Minister's House, built sometime in the fifteenth century. It was clearly the work of men who'd sailed the world, and looked like an enormous stack of souvenirs. There were cupolas, Greek columns, Gothic arches, and then, through it all, ran a stupendous Arabian doorway in the shape of a keyhole. These days, the only occupants were a pack of very formal dogs, who rose slowly to their feet and stood around as if they were the servants.

Another of these places, Margosa, had become a hotel, and that's where I stayed. It was like a Roman villa and had once housed a vast family of merchants, living round the pool. It was quieter now, and exquisitely orange. At moments, I could even imagine myself in the twenty-first century, but then there'd be a *power cuttee*, and we'd all be re-immersed, deep in the past. At night, I had dinner with a Tamil surgeon and his Irish boyfriend. The surgeon was here looking for the estates his family had fled. But it hadn't been easy, and he was surprised at the doors that had shut in his face.

'I suppose they think we're here to claim it all back.'

'And would you?'

His partner shrugged. 'Most of these places don't even have roofs . . .'

'Or they've got soldiers living in the kitchen . . .'

'And who knows who owns what anymore?'

There were even more mansions at the end of the peninsula. Velvettithurai (or Cotton Harbour) may have stunk of salted fish, but it had a long parade of miniature palaces. These great tottering piles of plaster, wrought iron, Calicut pantiles and teak were now turning green and crumbling away. The men who'd built them were often born of the lowest and filthiest caste – the *karaiyars*, or fishermen – but, over the years, they'd made their fortunes shipping cloth. All went well until Indian independence and the introduction of tariffs. Eventually, half the population of 'VVT' would flee to Tooting and become my neighbours, but in the meantime they'd survived on smuggling – first soap and motorbikes, and then the guns.

'Can I help you?'

A woman's face had appeared amongst a frieze of peacocks.

Kutty explained that we were visitors, and she invited us in. Our feet made a crunching sound as we edged through the hall. The house was built in the Chettinar style, said the woman, and the teak came from Burma. Her aunt had long since gone abroad, and she was the only one left. It was no longer safe to live in the house, and so she slept in a shelter under the mango tree.

'And now,' she said, 'you'll want to know where the Leader lived?'

Of all VVT's great outlaws, only the Tigers' chief had never had a mansion. Prabhakaran was born in one of the backstreets, and, that afternoon, the lonely niece agreed to show us where he'd lived. It wasn't far. There were a cluster of bungalows, each painted peppermint green. The one in the middle – the Prabhakarans' – was missing, and all that remained was an oblong of rubble. It was often said that *Thambi* had hated the merchants, and perhaps this is where his war began. But it was the army who'd destroyed his birthplace, grinding it up with a mechanical digger.

I had a sudden urge to own a peppermint nugget, and popped one in my pocket. The niece was watching.

'That's what the soldiers do,' she said. 'They treat him like a prophet.'

Along the shore, a great lunch was in progress for over five thousand people.

Temples had always been the first places to recover whenever the fighting stopped. The Portuguese had been assiduous levellers of *kovils* and *gopurams*, only to find that more temples sprang up whenever they left. Now, once again, these great red-striped halls were heaving themselves out of the rice, each with their mountain of painted gods. I'd heard that, after the artillery duels of the last ten years, Neguleswaran had been little more than a pillar of gravel, but now, said Kutty, it was being restored. One morning, we decided to pay it a visit, and joined a huge procession that was slowly winding its way through the north. I was surprised by the things that joined us on this pilgrimage, including ambulances and ice cream vans, and a man with a dancing monkey.

Eventually, the temple appeared, rising up out of its own remains. A few of the older shrines had survived, tangled in knobbly roots, but amongst them there was now a tower of scaffolding, and the pilgrims surged inside. For a billion Hindus, this is one the holiest places on Earth, and the men peeled off their shirts and sank to their knees. These were the first crowds I'd seen for days, and I enjoyed stitting there, watching the worshippers, trying to sort out who was who. There was once a time when even an outsider could have known them all by caste. Travellers like Robert Percival, in 1803, would have seen not 'Jaffna Tamils' but a rich concoction of races and rogues: *Mokkouas, Mopleys, Malabars, Belalas* ('extremely litigious and quarrelsome'), *Lubbahs, Panias, Pariahs* ('the most despicable'), *Nallaus* ('the blackest') and then all those *Chiviars, Choliars* and *Chittys*. But, I realised, he'd have beeen lost in today's society: cheap jeans and democracy had made an Everyman of all.

On the other side of the temple, we wriggled through to the pilgrims' quarters. One of the pandits here had taught a few of my Tooting friends and, to my surprise, I managed to find him. He was dressed in orange robes and a large cheap watch, and was surrounded by cooks and pappadams and almost a ton of steaming rice. Although Mr Thirumuragan spoke little English, he insisted that every pilgrim should have his lunch. Immediately, a space was cleared amongst the bodies and laid with a spoon and banana leaf. Had the original Feeding of the Five Thousand looked like this? Perhaps, except with a few little fishes instead of a tanker of curry.

* * *

Kutty drove home via the backroads. Even out here, there were pilgrims scrambling through the brush. This land was now too holy for churches, and perhaps the mixing of faiths was never wise. 'Christians here are outcaste,' said one of the pilgrims at lunch. 'No marrying, no festivals, nothing!' It had been even worse, it seemed, in 1948. According to *Ceylon: Pearl of the East*, a heretic could only rejoin society after drinking large quantities of cows' urine, and after a thoughtful course of hot embers and branding.

'And what now?' I asked Kutty. 'What happens?'

'Not that!' he squealed, but he wouldn't be drawn.

A few miles on, we came across a car as glossy and black as the day it was made, in 1956. Next to it stood a holy man, dressed only in loincloth and ash, and we stopped to talk. He and Kutty spoke for a moment, and then the old man took my arm and led me round his car. All the time, he was muttering his only English, 'Austin ay-fiftee,' and I began to wonder if it was the only thing he'd ever owned. I mentioned this to Kutty as we drove away.

'Maybe. He's very low caste. Does the job no one else will touch.'

'And what's that?'

'He cleans up the dead.'

During those few days amongst the mansions, I was left with an odd impression of Jaffna society, more a mosaic than the full panorama.

People described a closed and secluded world. Only the plasterwork was rich in peacocks and out on display. In VVT, the lonely niece had said that women own everything here, and that it's passed around in dowries. The house would never be sold, she told me, and she'd rather have a ruin that an outsider next door. It was the same at Margosa, where nearly all the windows faced inwards. 'Men never visited each other at home,' I was told. 'And if you had something to say, you met in the temple.' The surgeon, too, was rediscovering his cloistered past. 'We're like the Scots,' he said. 'Thrifty and careful. A woman's life revolves around her husband, and a man's around his work.' He also told me he'd never been to the coast before. 'We were *Vellalar* caste, and it was too horrible, the idea of running into fishermen and wreckers. And so we never went, ever.'

One morning, the surgeon showed me a story in the local paper. A married woman was being blackmailed by her former lover, who'd threatened to go to her husband. The odd thing about this tale was that, at the time of the romance, the woman had been a teenager, and hadn't even known her future spouse. I must have looked surprised, but the surgeon said that a good Tamil has no past and little interaction with the world around. 'It's a matter of faith,' he told me. 'This life is a prison or a trap. We must make no connection with it, if we are ever to escape.'

There was a lot here to understand. For some reason, I decided that I'd appreciate Jaffna better if I began right out on the edge, and worked my way back in. I also realised I'd need a guide, and so, after a flurry of emails, I was found the perfect person: a novelist called Mr Santhan. He was perfect because he saw everything with the eye of an outsider, and the understanding of a local. 'We're different to the Sinhalese,' he once told me. 'They live a life they can't afford, and we live a life we can't enjoy.'

I immediately liked Mr Santhan, and had the strange feeling I'd known him all my life. This was partly because he and his wife were like the old couple in a children's book. They lived in a tiny green bungalow, and had a very ancient Ford Prefect in cus-tard yellow. Although I never got beyond the porch, inside I could see a scene from *Robinson Crusoe*, with all the furniture lashed together from driftwood and scrap. After a life in English litera-ture, Mr Santhan might have enjoyed this allusion, although he'd always hoped for Barchester Towers. 'I was born in the wrong age,' he'd say, half joking. 'And I'm always trying to escape, in old books and old cars.'

We drove for miles, looking for somewhere to begin our jour-ney. Out west, the villages fell away, and we found ourselves in a great, dry forest of palmyra palms, like a field of fortified mops. As we drove, I asked Mr Santhan about the present and the life into which he'd been so reluctantly inserted. He told me that everyone had left, that he now had more family in England than Jaffna, that he'd survived three wars, but that he'd never felt the need to leave. He was also surprisingly forgiving, and referred to the carnage as 'the Aggravation'. 'I don't blame anyone anymore,' he said. 'It just started and no one knew how to stop it.'

Ahead, a little university had appeared amongst the palms.

'Jaffna College,' said Mr Santhan. 'This is where I taught.'

We hadn't meant to stop here, but somehow found ourselves wandering in through the chapel doors. Up the far end were a cluster of plaques to the great Americans of Yaddukoddai: Sand-ers, Meigs and Daniel Poor. Back in 1814, Americans wouldn't have been welcome within the empire, but no one seemed to mind them settling here. The college they'd founded would be the Harvard of Ceylon, cultivating imitators all over Jaffna. 'We had cameras and printers here long before Colombo,' said Mr Santhan. But the greatest gift of the Americans was the facility for English, and soon Jaffna's Tamils were setting out all over the empire, as civil servants. Only in Colombo was this resented, sparking the anger of the fifties and the riots of 1977. 'And that's when I came home,' said Mr Santhan, 'back here, where it all began . . .'

Outside, Kutty was waiting with the map. 'OK, where next?'

'There,' I said, with my finger on Delft.

It was a tiny island, almost off the page.

All around us lay the remains of a miniature Irish empire: a mansion in ruins, some sixty wells and a sandy canal. Even the dry-stone walls were said to be an Irish idea, sprawling over the island.

Strictly speaking, it was an empire within an empire, although its creator had paid little regard to British niceties. Appointed superintendant in 1811, Lieutenant Nolan had run Delft like his own little raj. He was said to have 'skin as white as milk', and had soon discovered that people would do whatever he asked. He was supposed to have been growing flax, but, instead, he built stables and tamed the wild horses. For thirteen years, he'd lived like this, building, judging, breaking, and making love to the local girls. Even today, many Delftians, they say, smile with Irish eyes.

As to how Nolan's one-man empire survived so long, the answer has to be sand. Officialdom is still hundreds of miles away, through grit and thorn, and – until the railway was built, in 1905 – it took three days just to get to Jaffna. From there, an even sandier journey begins, out to the islands. Whilst coral may hold it all together, this is an archipelago of dunes. There are no streams or contours, and, amongst the thirteen islands, the sea is seldom more than a few feet deep. It's been perfect for coconuts, migrating birds and would-be sultans, like Edward Nolan.

* * *

The islands had often intrigued me, although there was little encouragement to visit. I'd never met anyone who'd been there, and most people thought they'd never reopened after the war. As for the *theevaar* (or islanders), they were usually described as either wily entrepreneurs or fabulously hick. It wasn't much to go on. Meanwhile, there were no guidebooks, and the only hotels seemed to be run by the navy. For weeks, I thought about this, and the islands seemed impossibly remote, like some watery Xanadu. Not even Kutty knew how to reach them, and so Mr Santhan sat in the front to show us the way.

The sea, however, proved less of an obstacle than I'd imagined. Causeways began appearing, threading their way out to the rim. Mr Santham said they linked all the big islands, and that one was almost three miles long. I enjoyed these roads, and the odd sensation of driving over the ocean. It's probably the nearest I'll ever get to being a cormorant, taking in the shallows at a height of five feet. Below us, the lagoon was busy with fishermen up to their waists. They looked like farmers reaping the sea.

Ahead, a beautiful world took shape, or rather lost its shape. For a while, everything was reduced to long strips of blue and sand and great silvery washes of salt. Only the brawniest opportunists lived here, the fish eagles and brahminy kites. But then, eventually, we'd be back amongst flora again: briny bushes, oleander and those tousled mop-heads, the palmyras. Occasionally, farms would appear, merely tufts of brilliant green under this vast pearly-grey oyster shell of sky. From one end to the other, life on Kayts was lived around the well.

Once, we stopped at a toddy shack, out in the weeds.

'Fermented coconut sap,' said Mr Santham. 'You should try some.'

Inside, the fishermen were friendly, but had urgent drinking to do.

'Just a little,' I said, and out came a pint in an old plastic bottle.

'What's it like?' urged Kutty.

'Not bad,' I lied, 'for 12p . . .'

Actually, it was like rotting cabbage, or fermented socks.

Mr Santham smiled. 'These men live on it. I suppose it blunts the edges . . .'

It was a while before we found settlements. In the islands' history, few outsiders have known what to do with them. Early Arab traders had called by, leaving only baobab trees and studded front doors. Marco Polo may also have stopped over, and so had the reservoir kings. At some point, I clambered up on to one of their giant plinths, built like a launch pad for medieval rockets. Then there were the Portuguese, still visible in a few holy ruins. Beginning in 1560, it had taken them over sixty years to bring the peninsula under control. At one point, they'd turned up at Nallur to find twelve severed heads. It was the raja's ministers, who'd unwisely suggested the idea of surrender.

Up ahead, more mansions appeared. These were far wilder and wackier than anything before: huge Indo-Saracenic fantasies, decorated with lions and piglets and fancy columns. It would be the same on Karaitivu. Over the centuries, the islanders had prospered, building ships, working abroad, or trading with India, thirty miles to the north. This time, it wasn't cloth they'd traded but elephants, and all this – the villas and the giant quays – belonged to a golden (or pachydermatous) age. Now, however, almost all of it was derelict. The *kulauay*, or fencing, which had once been planted out of saplings, had long since gone feral, bursting outwards in little forests.

'The war,' said Mr Santham, sadly.

'What, even out here?'

'Yes, I'm afraid so. It was everywhere.'

There wasn't much sign of the merchants returning, but we did find a few. Later that day, we joined a funeral party, where we drank pink milkshakes and made offerings to Shiva. Many of the mourners had been living in Malaysia, and this was their first time back in thirty years. Some said they wanted to stay ('We've kept everything,' they reminded me. 'Tamils never sell land.'). In their plan for the islands, there was no place for anyone else: hotels, outsiders or government. I could see the struggle that lay ahead.

Eventually, we ran out of causeways, and found ourselves on Punkudutivu. At the end of the road was a crowd, and a litter of lumpy old boats. Some of the passengers were pilgrims, heading for Nainativu, where Buddha had preached on his second great tour. The rest of us were packed into an ancient ferry (180 passengers, seats for 100) and sent spluttering out to sea. It was a long, hot hour – the water now loppy and dark – but the reward for it all was Delft.

Delft was different from all the other islands, and even the war seemed to have passed it by. About half the size of Jersey, it was still home to almost six thousand islanders, five thousand cows and a herd of a hundred wild horses. It seemed that nothing had ever changed, and even the Portuguese had known it as the *Ilha da Vacas*, or the Isle of Cows. Mr Santham said that, in the rains, everyone rushed about, teasing onions out of the sand. But, that afternoon, there was no rush at all, and life had a dreamy antique feel: no cars, no plastic, just a crumbly, yellowing patchwork of *seemals*, or paddocks, pocked with sinkholes where the coral had collapsed.

Mr Santham hired us a tuk-tuk, and off we went through the lanes.

'I love this place,' he said. 'I wish it was me who'd thought it up.'

Everyone had left a bit of themselves behind. We were shown a giant's footprint, four feet long, and a baobab tree as big as a house and almost as hollow. Then there were the tiny Zanzibari doors, built so small it was like entering a cupboard. Meanwhile, the Portuguese had left not only a fort – like an enormous, half-eaten cake – but also the magnificently fiery horses. (How had that happened, I wondered, did they just *forget* them?) Then there was the Irish empire, and the stables that Nolan had built, big enough for a hundred broken beasts. In 1819, he was finally tried for abuse of power, and – on the islanders' evidence – gloriously acquitted. But he didn't stay, preferring to cash in his pension and return to Ireland. He died twenty years later, at about the time the stables folded.

Before leaving, we went to watch the horses – free again – grazing the crisp red grass at the end of the island. Despite their foreign genes, I like to think they had about them something of the spirit of this archipelago: grand, disowned and obstinately wild.

This wasn't my last island foray. A few days later, Kutty drove me back to Karaitivu, where I'd booked a room on Hammenheil, a resort for the chronically ghoulish.

Hammenheil still looked like a warship moored out in the channel. By night it was spotlit, and rode the horizon in a red-hot glow. But, by day, it was dark and lumpy, a squat little fortress built on the sea. The Portuguese had known it as the Fortaleza Real, and had vowed to defend it 'till the last drop of blood'. But they hadn't reckoned on the Dutch, who'd appeared in the estuary in August 1658. When a cannonball smashed the fort's cistern, the struggle for Jaffna became a battle of thirst. With his vision failing and his tongue turning black, the commandant had forgotten his vows and surrendered the post. Before they knew it, the peninsula was Dutch.

The fort was still run by the navy, and a couple of ratings took me across.

'Our first American guest!' they said.

'Oh. But I'm from London.'

They shrugged. 'First English too!'

I was also the only guest, a chatelain just for the night. But the fort was smaller in close-up, more like a courtyard rising out of the waves. There were only two buildings, set high in the walls, and down below were the casements, all vaulted and damp. The Dutch had worked hard to perfect their new fort, sinking thousands of tons of coralstone into the sandbank. They would always enjoy this archipelago, and were determined to keep it. Perhaps it reminded them of their own salty islands, and their lives on the tide? In time, they'd even given the islands homely names – Rotterdam, Leyden, Amsterdam and Haarlem – although, these days, only one survives, and that's Delft.

Meanwhile, the fort had become a hotel, although the navy weren't natural hosts. There was nothing to eat, and only a fridge of Mexican beer. At one point, the sailors reappeared in outrageous outfits – braided turquoise and plastic shakos – as if we were under Ruritanian attack. They were obviously struggling in their latest role. Only six years earlier, the navy had been running this place as a secret prison, and there were still rows of concrete beds down in the casements. For a whole generation of dissidents, this was the place to come and contemplate oblivion, although – if I looked carefully – I could still find their names, scratched in the plaster.

Naturally, I didn't sleep well amongst such history. It wasn't just the wind, whining at the window. I found myself dreaming about thirst and walls and the men laid out below, on their ominous cold slabs. At times, the air conditioning joined in, adding a gruesome rattle to this crypt of ideas. Then, just before dawn, all its lights blinked into life, and the room was suddenly full of eyes: defaulters, dissenters, Tigers, Maoists and the parched Portuguese.

Mr Santham laughed when I told him about my haunted night.

'They'd never let Tamils stay there. We're far too *suspect*.'

'Can I write that down?'

'Write what you like! I always do . . .'

This was true, although Mr Santham was instinctively generous. In his novel, *The Whirlwind*, his characters never look for blame, only escape. The story is set in 1987, a bad time for Jaffna City. For six months, it's been under Tiger control, and then, that July, the Indian Peacekeeping Force arrives. Its soldiers, the jawans, are big, faceless men, readily brutalised by the warring city. In their search for 'terrorists', they pound it with artillery and raid the hospital. Finding no one, they kill the patients and the doctors, seventy in all. The novel's characters, however, regard these outrages not with fury but disbelief, as if their world has developed some inexplicable fault. Mr Santham once told me that this was how he remembered it, and I realised that he'd created not a cast of characters, but a city of Santhams.

Another time, we were driving into the city from the north, when we came across a plinth. It was built after the peacekeepers departed in 1990, and was supposed to be their monument. But the statue had long since vanished, and the plinth was still being daubed and pelted. For many in the city, it had been a rude shock, this first encounter with their giant neighbour. 'We used to call this place Little India,' said Mr Santham, 'but not anymore.'

The city may not be Indian anymore, but it's still a mini Calcutta or Bombay lite.

There's the same exhilaration, that madcap defiance. A vast fort – the strongest in Asia – blocks off the sea, and yet from behind it emerges a great durbar of architectural dandies: pavilions, spires, domed kiosks with Bangala roofs, gopurams, minarets, Mughal cupolas and a Victorian clock tower with an onion top. In the middle is the library, like an enormous, turbaned head, whilst all around the streets are flushed with colour. The main drag, *Parangi Theru* (or Foreigner Street) is buttercup yellow, and the Hotel Rolex a throbbing, citric green. Other streets are named after Stanley and Victoria, although nobody knows who they are. Ice-cream parlours rise up out of the wasteland, and there's a bazaar that blazes all night. It's like any other market, except that everything's Indian: the saris, the movies and the rolls of silk. But then, further on, the city seems suddenly empty, the darkness velvety and close. It never lasts long, and soon the bicycles reappear, or a torrent of raucous rickshaws. *DON'T FOLLOW ME*, say the stickers. *Find true Love.*

Then, every morning, the old precincts are purified with smouldering husks of coconut, and the new day begins in a sweet karmic haze. Those who don't yet have stalls will work on the kerb, like the cobblers and typists. One man sells only planks of salted swordfish, and the liquor shop looks like a jail. But, of all these traders, easily the grandest is the door-handle man. He's making huge contraptions, of Mughal intent. It always struck me as such a poetic way to rebuild a city, beginning with the doors.

Only the cars, it seems, have survived unscratched. But these aren't new cars from old moulds, like India's 'Ambassadors'. Much of Jaffna's traffic seems to have been on the road ever since the fifties: Hillmans, Austin Cambridges and Somersets, and those prim little spinsters, the Morris Oxford and Minor. Out on the Palali Road, there's a whole orchard full of these antiques, all being lovingly polished back to life. It's often said that Jaffna Tamils love them because they remind them of an earlier age, when they were almost independent. But, true or not, there'd been little choice, and, for nearly thirty years, these were the only cars. 'And almost all of them,' said Mr Santham, 'were converted to kerosene or cooking oil. I still have to start the Prefect with a drop of thinners.'

Only a hint of the Raj remained, out in Chundikul. It was also the Catholic area of the city, a little suburb of cloisters and Gothic. But amongst the seminaries, we soon found what we were after: a large burnt-out building like a row of teeth. Despite the destruction, we were still able to climb inside and wander through the rooms. Mr Santham said that the British had built this as their *kachcheri*, or administration, and these were their offices and courts. Once, the walls were covered in *chunam*, or lime enamel, and the adjoining residence had been so huge it had required two sets of everything, including the loungers and couches.

Next to the court, we came to a thick, studded door, embedded in dust.

'The police cells,' announced Mr Santham.

The writer Leonard Woolf would've remembered the studs and the gargantuan hinges. He'd worked here for almost two years, beginning in 1905. Although never an inspiring official, Woolf has left us with a deliciously savage portrait of his fellow

Europeans. The magistrate he described as a 'bloody unwashed board school bugger . . . who doesn't know one end of a woman from another.' By contrast, Jimmy Bowes, the police superintendent, was always out wenching, and could be vile in his cups (no one was spared, particularly the prisoners. 'You stinking son of a black buggered bitch,' he'd say). As for the white women, Woolf thought they were all 'whores, hags or missionaries or all three'. But what's even more surprising is that, altogether, there were only twenty Europeans, and that Jaffna largely ran itself. As to the courts, wrote Woolf, they were mostly preoccupied with sodomy, trying endless lists of 'extraordinarily beautiful men'.

In more recent times, Jaffna has once again tried to run itself, and the *kachcheri* became a camp for the Tamil Tigers. But the impertinence cost it dear, and – in the battles that followed – it lost not only its roof, but also its gravitas, all the enamel, and several tons of Victorian sofas.

Everyone, it seemed, was busy trying to forget the past.

There were no memorials to the dead, but we never had to go far to find their homes, and the rubble. Around the centre, there was hardly a building that hadn't been nibbled. But it was worse out on Hospital Road. There, great chunks had been bitten from the street, and all the old villas now lay battered and empty. It was the same on Main Street, where the only prominent business was a funeral parlour. *ESON'S*, said the sign, *DAY AND NIGHT SERVICE*.

The railway, too, had gone, leaving only the terminus out in the weeds. On the old platform, I could see a woman hanging up her washing, and behind her the ticket hall, now open to the sky. Once, express trains left here and snaked off to Colombo in less than eight hours, but in the last ten years there'd been no trains, and just a snake of gravel. It's said that the rails were the first to go – turned into bunkers – but then came the cooks and the houseboys, and hacked up the sleepers.

I never got used to this crumbled havoc. As a child, I'd seen old bombsites in Liverpool, but they weren't like this, so painted and fresh. Some houses still had gardens, or curtains in the window, where everything else had been sheared away. If the owners had survived, they'd probably fled the city. During almost thirty years of war, Jaffna had changed hands three times, ending up with only eighty-four thousand souls, a fall of nearly a third. 'And those who've left,' said Mr Santhan, 'may never return. And nor will they sell, so we could end up looking like this for many years.'

But there had been some reconstruction. The Indian government was busy building suburbs, each a little toytown of bright orange bricks. But, of all the resurrections, the most phoenix-like was that of the library. It had risen from its ashes like a new Taj Mahal, except smaller and heavier and a startling white. Books, too, had reappeared, and a librarian once showed me a medical text, written in thirteenth-century Sanskrit. 'Tamils revere books,' he said, 'and this place was once our greatest library, with thousands of ancient scripts.' But then came the riots of the early eighties, and some Sinhalese thugs with gasoline and matches. For days the books burned – ninety-seven thousand, in all – and it would be years before the library reopened. Meanwhile, it became a focus of anger, and in 1990 trenches appeared amidst the soot and the shelves. An old battle was about to restart: the siege of the fort.

Amongst those who'd dug their way in through the library, was Thevar, the Tigers' blogger. He told me he was only a schoolboy at the time, but the war had seemed a thrilling distraction. 'It was a liberation struggle,' he said, 'we were all excited.' In March of that year, the last of the Indian troops had left, and, three months later, the ceasefire ended. Suddenly, there were Tigers all over Jaffna, and the army responded with whatever it could – usually 'shit bombs', or barrels of excrement dropped from planes. Artillery was so rare that, whenever it fired, a siren sounded. 'There wasn't much weaponry back then,' said Thevar, but still four thousand died.

Eventually, the last of the army were trapped in the fort, and so began the three-month siege. On this side, whole streets were levelled to create clear fields of fire. Then the library was fortified, and the children began extending their trenches out into the rubble. The fort was only two hundred metres away, filling the horizon. Neither side, however, had the strength to deliver a knockout blow. Across the city, the power failed and food prices rose by a factor of ten. But, in this little Stalingrad, everyone at least had the chance to become a hero. One day, one of the schoolboys strapped an enormous bomb to his back. Although he was only fifteen, he made good progress through the trenches, placing his ladder against the rampart. He'd almost reached the top when the bullets found him, igniting the bomb. The explosion, Thevar told me, could be heard almost twelve miles away.

'And that's a noise,' he said, 'I am still trying to forget.'

Only the Dutch understand perspective and how, given enough of it, the spirit is crushed. Or, at least, that's how it felt, standing there, in front of the fort. It wasn't easy to take it all in: the sky full of stone and parallel lines; a great pentagon of defences, sheer, colossal, and technically perfect; twenty-two hectares of ravelins and glacises, and ramparts up to ten metres thick. These walls were so blank and featureless that, at first, I couldn't find my way in. Wandering over the wasteland, I'd arrived at the moat, a wide band of glassy-green, zigzagging off into the distance. Only by scrambling along the bank had I come to the outer bastions, and a tunnel. It was cool in here, and the walls were like seabed or a frieze of coral. But, at the far end, there was more discouragement: a vast corridor of water and vanishing points. This would've been a testing vista for any intruder, the moment the half-hearted go home.

A narrow causeway trickled out, across the moat. It was made of sand and rubble and old ammunition boxes, and led to the door of the fort. Beyond the fancy aperture (*ANNO 1680*), there was another tunnel, its flags worn smooth by centuries of soldierly feet. As usual, this hadn't been the first fort on the site, and an earlier version had been wrestled off the Portuguese. That siege – like the one in 1990 – had lasted three months, and again had seen some unusual missiles; not 'shit bombs' this time, but tombstones, broken up and lobbed over the walls.

From the tunnel, I stepped out into the sunlight and gasped. The fort's interior had vanished. All that remained were fragments and a thick, grey bed of grit. It was like some strange, unearthly cat-tray, its dimensions exploding outwards and filled with a dune of litter. All the things I'd read about had gone: the old British tennis club, the Queen's House and the *Groote Kerk* of 1730. I suppose there was still history here, but it had to be sifted on hands and knees. Although I found a few lumps of church, everything else had been smashed and powdered, leaving only chips of clay and flecks of Delft. It was the same up on the battlements, which were now disappearing under a fresh lick of concrete. One bastion, however, had yet to be restored, and there was still a story, scattered in the sand. First, I found the bullet casings, all crusty and green, and then – next to them – one of those tiny phials, used for morphine.

The siege of 1990 had eventually ended, but not before turning grotesquely medieval. Whilst there may have been helicopter gunships at the start, they were soon driven off in a squall of missiles. That left the army with almost nothing: two hundred men, a few weapons and little food. Parcels were dropped by plane, but they always seemed to land in the sea, or amongst the Tigers. Soon, the besieged were eating unripe pawpaws and the little fish from the moat. All day the mortars rained down, ripping up the buildings and tearing through the troops. First, the morphine ran out, and then everything else. Fourteen soldiers died and were buried in the grit. Only once did another chopper appear, snatching away two of the wounded. Both men had ended up as patients of Dr Goonetilleke.

'They were in sorry state,' he'd told me. 'One had lost a buttock.'

'And had he had any treatment?'

'Not much. No saline, no pain relief and no blood.'

'What about the other man?'

'The same. Except he'd been hit the chest, two weeks before.'

By the time the siege ended, it felt like an ancient battle. First, another four thousand soldiers appeared, sailing in from the islands on a flotilla of boats. But they were soon repelled. Eventually, a much smaller band paddled in and took the survivors away. That night, 26 September 1990, the Tigers' flag was hoisted over the fort, and there it remained for the next five years.

Across Sri Lanka, there were still mixed memories of the Tiger years.

Down south, it was still regarded as period of horror. People would tell me how the Tigers had drained their captives and reused their blood. Up north, however, it was a different story. Men like Thevar saw it as a time of joy, and insisted that ninety per cent of Tamils felt the same. Mr Santhan, on the other hand, seemed to remember nothing but surviving, and told me how he'd sold all his books just to keep going ('Laurie Lee, Naipaul and Hemingway, all of them gone'). But that wasn't how Jaffna's Muslims remembered those years. For them, it was an era of upheaval and unresolved tragedy. One of the first things the Tigers had done was to announce their expulsion, and forty-six thousand Muslims were given two hours to leave. Even now, many were still in camps, dispersed through the badlands or out in Mannar. 'We were *right* to expel them,' insisted Thevar. 'The army was using them as informers. They were moved for their own protection.'

But, for my old friend, Ravi Weerapperuma, it was different again. For him, the Tiger years were a time of regret and epiphany. By then, he was with the navy, serving out on the islands. He was part of a large, ramshackle force, trying to envelop the city. 'The islands were beautiful,' said Ravi, 'and I still remember a few words of Tamil, like "What's your name?" and "Where are you going?" In those days, we burnt down houses because we were frightened. Our job was also to stop people leaving Jaffna and getting out across the lagoon. I was only junior, but it haunted me, what we were doing. There was a lot of fear. We only became more confident later. But, right then, we were frightened, and that's where things go wrong.'

On the far side of the fort, workmen were reconstructing the western rampart.

A long section – thousands of tons of sand and coral stone – had been removed by the Tigers. It seemed they'd always known their days were numbered. They'd also known that the army would return and recapture the fort, and their only concern was to render it useless. This had been a job for the punishment squads. (I was once told that there was no crime under the LTTE. 'Criminals were either put to work, or strung up in the street.') It must have been a pharaonic work of deconstruction, and now the city's labourers were once again at work, putting it back together.

In the newly disturbed dust, I found the shreds of a distinctive shirt: green and brown and tiger-striped. It had been torn in half, from the shoulder, across the back and down to the opposite hip. And what, I wondered, had become of its owner? Had he lost his shirt, or had they perished together? Or perhaps it was a woman, fighting and furious until the moment of rupture? Almost two thousand cadres had died when the army returned, although not without a fight. It took seventy thousand soldiers fifty days to cover the twelve miles from the Palali airbase to Jaffna. But, on 1 December 1995, the army were on the edge of the city, and the Tigers issued a new order, their most peculiar ever:

Abandon Jaffna. Leave only the old. Take everything else, and head for the forest.

No one would ever say much about the exodus, although almost everyone had left. Across the city, it was still a subject that had people bristling in horror and shame. But the memories were there, and every now and then they emerged, in pieces.

First, the Tigers picked the city clean. Even the hospital was harvested, and all the scanners went off to the Vanni. If the government wanted Jaffna, said Prabhakaran, then they'd find nothing left. Next, it was the turn of the people, and overnight the peninsula emptied. At one point, there were almost 600,000 people on the road, some in old cars, but most on foot. 'You can't believe it,' one man told me, 'such crowds, moving down the street. Some died by the road, and we buried them there, but others were eaten by the animals . . .' Mr Santhan hadn't seen the dead, but agreed it was an arresting sight, the city of dogs.

I only met one man who'd stayed behind: the Catholic priest I've called 'Father Z'. He and others had been concerned about the old and the sick. 'It was assumed this would all be over in days, and so people left the elderly with nothing. We gathered up ninety-seven of them, and brought them back to our place. But we never had much to give them, and as the weeks bore on, we were down to one meal a day, and sixty-six of them died.'

Over the coming months, most of the Jaffna Tamils drifted home. But many – perhaps 200,000 – stayed on, and settled in Vanni. It seemed that 'Tigerland' now had the population it needed: young, abandoned and with nothing to lose.

It was now almost twenty years since the Jaffna peninsula had rejoined the nation. But, to most people, it still didn't feel like a province, and was merely a land under occupation. 'The army's everywhere,' said Father Z. 'It's like a new invasion every day.'

These words often came back to me, whenever we were out. Around my hotel, the countryside was always covered in soldiers. They were at every junction and on guard at every substation, radio mast, pump and public building. Often, too, they were on bicycles out in the rice, or bedded down in bunkers at the edge of the road. Further out, they were harder to spot, but there was always a nest of sentries somewhere, even on the saltiest of flats.

Officially, there were only thirteen thousand of them, but it always seemed like more, perhaps because they were so ominous and foreign. 'I don't say they're bad people,' said Mr Santhan, 'but they speak to us in Sinhalese, and then don't understand us.'

For Father Z, it was exasperating. 'They just don't trust us at all.'

Even to hold a feast, he said, he needed permission.

'It's true,' agreed Thevar, 'we need permission even to piss.'

'We've no power and no voice,' said Father Z, 'we just do as we're told.'

But if this sounded like childhood-without-end, it had been worse.

'Go and see the HSZ,' people said. 'Once it was all like that: out of bounds.'

The High Security Zone began a few miles north of the hotel in a mesh of lamps and wire. We never got beyond the perimeter, but then – for years – nor had anyone else. An area almost twenty times the size of Hyde Park had been closed off, and all its inhabitants evicted. The farms had crumbled away, and so had the villages and roads. Nowadays, it was all part of the Palali Airbase, and was the last of the no-go zones. Once, there'd been fifteen of these zones, covering almost a fifth of the peninsula and displacing 130,000 people (or about the same as the population of Norwich). Spread amongst the zones, there'd been 147 army camps, and ten times the troops that there are today. After so much displacement, said Mr Santhan, he'd often wondered if Tamil culture would ever recover.

'At times, we almost felt we didn't belong.'

But now, as with the minefields, there was a morbid beauty about the old HSZs. The weeds grew bigger and wilder here, and most of the houses still lay empty. I once met someone who'd owned a mansion out here, but, by the time she got it back, it had been stripped of everything, including the sinks. When I told Mr Santhan this, he smiled. 'The government sometimes repairs things, and spends millions on brand new roads. But all people really want is just to do things themselves.'

As well as roads and razor wire, the troops had also brought a few bad habits.

Until 1995, there'd been no concept of 'the white van' in Jaffna, but, since then, people had vanished in their hundreds. According to the United Nations' experts, it was the same routine as that down south: the men in fatigues and the ride through the night; the beatings, the shocks and a mask full of petrol; then the journey back and a grave in the grass. Even when the fighting stopped, the vans didn't, and they were still out there, gathering up dissent.

One day, I met up with a student at Malayan Café.

'It's a good place to talk,' he'd said. 'There's plenty of noise.'

His name was Rapture, or at least that's what it said on his shirt. Although he was only twenty-two, he had something about him of weary old age. He said he was studying jurisprudence, and the work of Blackstone and Coke. I ordered dhal and a thick crusty pancake known as an *appam*, and it was all laid out before us on banana leaves. But Rapture didn't touch the food. Instead, he spoke very quickly for exactly fifteen minutes, and then hurried away. 'They're always watching us,' he'd said. 'All our memories are being destroyed. We cannot celebrate the lives of our dead anymore, or commemorate their death. They say we are keeping alive the principles of the LTTE. We can't even light lamps anymore, and they're always at our meetings. Every day we are defeated, over and over again.'

416

It would soon be time to leave Jaffna. For my last few days, I moved into the city, and settled down amongst the great and good.

I never saw much of the Great – except their walls and sentry boxes – but the Good were more transparent. Up near the Nallur Temple, there was a whole suburb of beneficence, laid out in enormous concrete compounds. Although their initials made them sound like the baddies – GIZ, WHO and SOS – these were the NGOs which, often enough, had kept Jaffna going. Everyone agreed that the worst time was 1995, but, even after that, Jaffna went hungry. For the next seven years, there were no road links to the south – thanks to the Vanni – and the sea was infested with frogmen and mines. It was a golden age for the GIZs and the WHOs.

I always enjoyed it up amongst the compounds. They had their own magnificent jungles, and were shady and cool. The days were measured in little rush hours – more a torrent of bicycles than anything else – or in the clank of holy bells. Then, at dusk, the light would turn grainy and orange, and the great steel gates would rumble shut, the good deeds done for the day.

My compound was different to the others, if only because it had become a hotel. Although the 'Jaffna Heritage' was still a yard with a concrete block, it had made a bold effort to 'bou-tiquify'. Everything had been polished or painted olive, a little pool had appeared and the terrace was now scattered with sculp-tures and teak. Almost everyone I met seemed to be the manager, and each morning I'd spend ages shaking my way – from hand to hand – across the lobby. But, despite all this, things were never quite perfect; my windows wouldn't shut, the room filled with fervent microfauna and – it didn't matter which curry I ordered for breakfast – I always got something American and pale. It was almost as if troubled spirits were still at work. But who could they be?

And then I remembered: the poor, beleaguered Norwegians.

The Norwegian mediators had first appeared in 1999, and would leave seven years later, despised, defeated and utterly baffled.

It had been a confusing period. To begin with, everyone seemed conciliatory, and, in 2002, the great truce was signed. But it wasn't long before the peace began to look like warfare cloaked in denial. Over the next four years, the Norwegians would count 351 treaty violations by the army and 3,830 by the LTTE. The mediators must often have wondered what they were doing here, and whether anyone wanted this war to end. Every day, they'd set out from the olive compound, shuttling between the warring parties. But the Tigers always found a good excuse for letting off a bomb. During the last year of the agreement, their targets had included a marketplace, a bus and the Norwegians themselves.

Colombo was always more willing to give peace a chance, or at least a little trickery. The vans were always out there, and so were the paramilitary gangs. The generals, too, had learned to fight as if they were guerrillas, sending out tiny units into the scrub. Lightly armed and lightly supervised, these 'atomised forces' could do what they liked, and often did. But, although this terrified the Tigers (and a good few others), it was never enough. Things changed, however, in 2005, when a new president appeared, on a warlike ticket.

As an actor, Mahinda Rajapaksa could make anything look like a movie. The Sinhalese seemed to love him, with his promise of an old-fashioned epic. But he was never as saintly as he looked, and had cast his brothers in the leading roles. Basil would run the war chest, and Gotabaya the Ministry of Defence. As a computer manager at the University of Southern California, 'Gota' might have seemed an odd choice for the role, but – back in the eighties – he'd acquired a reputation as an unforgiving colonel. Now, he brought all his geekiness to bear, expanding the army by seventy-five thousand and acquiring all the latest gizmos, including drones. He even devised an eight-point plan, a document that would've horrified Oslo. Never waver, it said, never negotiate, ignore public opinion and let the army do whatever it wants. Gota also told journalists that, if they ever favoured the rebels, they'd be chased off the island.

The Norwegians could see which way things were going, and ended up hated. The government accused them of sheltering the Tigers, and even now there were those in the army who still believed it. One such was the major I'd met at Thoppigala. He was adamant the Norwegians had been running guns. 'Look at their failures in Palestine and the Balkans,' he'd said. 'They're bullshit people.'

By 2006, the Norwegians had heard enough, and the compound closed.

I once asked Thevar why he thought they'd failed.

'They didn't understand us,' he said, 'and our local ways.'

The Tigers, too, had been suffering a bad case of 'local ways', and, in March 2004, they delivered the greatest shock of the war: half of them defected.

For many, it's the skirmishes and massacres that have shaped this conflict, but for me it's this, the great betrayal. At a stroke, six thousand cadres had abandoned the cause. Some went home, some went abroad, but many sided with the army and became yet another sinister militia. But strangest of all was the destiny of their leader, Vinayagamoorthy Muralitharan, or 'Colonel Karuna'. One moment he was the Tigers' second in command, and the next he was in Colombo, working for the Rajapaksas. Now, not only was he vice-president of their party, he was a government minister, and out every night enjoying the shindigs. 'A hillbilly,' said Father Z. 'A useless playboy figure.'

How had it happened, I wondered, this Byzantine détente? During my weeks in Colombo, I'd asked everyone I knew. 'He was paid,' said Elmo the novelist. 'Fifty million rupees.' 'The standard fee,' agreed his friends. 'No,' said others. 'He fell out with Prabhakaran.' 'Tried to take over the east.' 'He was wanted for theft.' And what about the other six thousand? Why did they defect? 'He was their leader,' said Elmo. 'This is a nation of kings.' I sought out Vasanatha, for the wise Senanayake view. 'Why not ask him yourself?' he said. 'I'll fix up a meeting.' We all met a few days later at the parliament building.

'Colonel Karuna' wasn't what I'd expected of a guerrilla leader. He was tubby and affable, wore a brown suit, a large gold ring, and was pleased to be interviewed. A tray of cakes and a silver teapot appeared, and I settled my minidisc between us. In the recording of that afternoon, I sound amateur and harmless, but the minister bubbles away about his life on the run. 'I was in LTTE twenty-four years,' he says, and we begin with his father's farm in Batti, his A levels, and the training camps in India. Then the fighting starts. 'Little, little, I became the small leader, then district level, then regional . . .'

I remind him he was running the east when all the policemen were killed.

'I didn't involve . . . I was in Jaffna at that time . . .'

'So Prabhakaran ordered it, and you didn't know?'

'LTTE was very secretive.'

We move on to more comfortable territory: the great defection.

It was about facing reality, says Colonel Karuna. To begin with, Prabhakaran was a separatist, but, after the Indian fiasco, he became a 'revenge leader' and sent an assassin after Rajiv Gandhi. After this, the Tigers were no longer considered freedom fighters but terrorists and, eventually, they were banned around the world. 'So,' says Karuna, 'I knew a hundred per cent we never win this war, but Prabhakaran didn't agree.' Later, however, the colonel was in Oslo, and saw his chance. He signed a new peace treaty on behalf of the Tigers. Prabhakaran was furious. 'He said, "You make a big mistake. You are a traitor. You sold our freedom . . ." and so that's when I broke away.'

On the tape, I can hear myself struggling with the strangeness of it all.

'And did you know,' I ask, 'that it would be the beginning of the end?'

There's a dry, joyless laugh. 'It was him made the mistake.'

'And did he come after you?'

'Five hundred died, including my brother.'

'But you always escaped?'

'Yes,' says the minister. 'Here I am, last of the LTTE.'

When I eventually left Jaffna, it was on a long, narrow outrigger, with two fishermen and a large tin of chocolate biscuits.

Kutty had never been keen on my boat idea. No one ever sailed across the lagoon anymore, and I'd need the permission of the regional commander. If I wanted to go back to Pooneryn, why not take the bus? But, to his credit, he worked at it, got the permission, and found me a captain and a sea-worthy boat. Then he left, driving off back to Colombo. It was an odd parting; I'd been with him for weeks, and yet I hardly knew him at all. 'Look out for the dugongs,' he'd said, and then he was gone.

The biscuits were an afterthought. I'd somehow imagined they'd be a useful substitute for language, but the fishermen had no great need for dialogue. They were short, jowly men with wide, flat feet and little interest in passengers. The captain lived on an Indian housing development, and we stopped first at his tiny orange house to collect a jug of petrol. Then we walked down to the lagoon, and waded out through the silky black mud. Although the boat was already a long way offshore, the captain still had to punt out to deeper water before lowering the engine. I was then seated on the prow, whilst the two fishermen huddled in the stern, covered in crumbs.

After an hour, Jaffna shrivelled into the horizon, and – just for a moment – we were in the middle of a great disc of water, minutely fringed with jungle and dunes. It was so shallow that, in places, the sandbanks – like great leviathans – broke the surface. But there were no dugongs. It's said that the capture of a 'sea pig' would once have caused great excitement amongst the Moors. Denied 'land pig' as a matter of scripture, they'd flock to the fish-market and snap up the dugong. Once sliced, it was, they'd say, almost exactly like bacon. But now dugongs were a rare sight on the lagoon, as were the Moors.

Eventually, the Vanni began to swell and gather in the haze ahead – palms at first, but then a great, pink soufflé of sand. The captain now had to slow the boat to negotiate the long, black trellises of fish traps, which were thickly cluttered in cormorants, and looked like music written on the sea. 'Where are we?' I asked the fishermen, but they merely smiled. Some way off, I could make out two figures up in the dune, picking their way through the sand. Other than that, there was nothing but the scrub and the empty shore, and, at the thought of being back in this denuded land, I felt a sudden, thrilling surge of unease.

12

The Shoes on the Shore

Mullaitivu lies in a very romantic and delightful situation.

> Robert Percival, *An Account*
> *of the Island of Ceylon*, 1803

The final stages and aftermath of the war in Sri Lanka were characterised by a wide range of violations by both the government of Sri Lanka and the LTTE of international humanitarian law and international human rights law, some even amounting to war crimes and crimes against humanity . . .

> UN report, March 2011

The Portuguese chronicler, Queyroz, leaves us with an intriguing vignette from the visit of St Francis Xavier in 1543.

The island has reached a difficult stage. Its leaders are becoming more bejewelled and absolute, and its people are learning to survive the casual violence. It is an idyllic place, but has become incomparably strange. So what will the old sage make of it? Xavier says nothing until it's time to re-embark. Then, according to Queyroz, he takes off his shoes and leaves them on the shore, 'saying that not even the dust of so wicked a land would he take with him.'

It's a powerful image, and although St Francis can hardly have understood this island in all its complexity and glory, I'd often think of his words in the days ahead.

That first morning back in the Vanni, I ate a lot of sand. The fishermen dropped me amongst the dunes on the southern shore of the lagoon. To begin with, the place seemed uninhabited, but then, beneath some hard, dark trees, whose leaves seemed to clatter together like slates, I came across a small school and a naval post. Perhaps I'd been left on an island? Then a large truck came grinding through the dunes. Good, I thought, the mainland. In fact, this was one of those peculiarly Sri Lankan landforms: a long column of sand that sets off into the sea, and then peters out twenty-five miles offshore. I was somewhere near the column's tip.

In this gritty nothingness, the sailors saw no need for uniforms, and were curious as to what I'd do next. I established that the place was called Manniththalai, but only the children spoke English. There were no buses, they said, and no more villages until Pooneryn. 'And how far's that?' I asked.

'Twenty-five kilometres,' said the oldest child.

Some walk, I thought, especially in this heat.

'Mobike,' said one of the infants, barely five, and then she ran off.

Moments later, she returned with her father and an old, sand-blasted Honda.

'Pooneryn,' she said, 'one thousand rupees.'

Her *appa* nodded, and hauled my bag on to the handlebars. Then we were off, across the drifts. In places, the bike would slide sideways through the sand, wheels squealing, bawling with rage. I could now feel the granulated Vanni on my face like tiny, hot pins, and in my eyes like gravel. Occasionally, more trucks would appear, and, just for a moment, we'd be enveloped in a suffocating nimbus of grit. But then the dunes opened out, and we found ourselves churning down a furrow, with thick white dust sparkling through the spokes. The sea was always there – a bar of incongruous iceberg-blue – and perhaps that's why this never felt like a journey with a beginning or an end, just sand. Sometimes it was coppery, and sometimes platinum, but it all tasted the same.

The sand didn't end at Pooneryn, but it did turn red. The motorcyclist dropped me at the old fort, and I climbed inside to wait for a bus. I wasn't the only person taking refuge in its shade; a large road-gang was laid out amongst the ruins, in fluorescent sleep. Around us, the little *fortaleza* felt like a carcase, all jointed and gnawed. In the last twenty years, there'd been two Battles of Pooneryn, equally inglorious. During the first, in 1993, it had become 'every man for himself', and over two hundred sailors were murdered. That was the end of the government in the Vanni, and for the next fifteen years this was rebel country, or, as I've called it, 'Tigerland'. South of Elephant Pass, almost the whole of northern Sri Lanka had fallen under LTTE rule, with their flags as red as the earth.

There were no seats on the bus, but I managed to find a space on the steps. Once under way, the redness seemed to billow upwards out of the floor, and soon everyone was brilliantly powdered in scarlet. Although it looked as if we'd all been to the same Holi festival, there was little conversation. I tried to talk to the men around me, but only one spoke English. He said his father had been a fisherman on one of the islands, until the navy had moved them inland. They were supposed to farm, but they had no idea what to do with this filthy red dust.

'And where are you going?' he asked.

'Mulankavil.'

There was a pause, and a hint of disgust. '*Why*, sir?'

I tried to sound vague, because I wasn't really sure. Mulankavil was too new for my map, and had only emerged after the war. As far as I could tell, it was just a pause in the endless red slog that had become the A32. But my friend Ravi had told me he knew the commandant there, and that he'd find me a bed. In an exchange of texts, Commander Ranathunga explained that he'd be pleased to help, but that, for security reasons, I couldn't stay on the base. Instead, he'd find me somewhere more appropriate, which turned out to be the orphanage next to the Church of St Mary.

None of this I wanted to explain to the ejected islander.

'Just visiting friends,' I said, 'and I like the Vanni.'

But this made little sense to him, and we hardly spoke again.

As for the Vanni itself, it had long since vanished in a cloud of ox-blood sand.

Those few days in Mulankavil were full of strange and unfamiliar sounds. Of course, there was always the background throb of jungle and trucks, but other noises were harder to ignore, and gave the place an abstract feel, like some great auditory mosaic made up of broken pieces.

At dawn, there was a thunder of paws, and then a barrage of rockets. My room was behind the church in a small house made of cement and corrugated iron, and it was often raided by monkeys. Whenever this happened, the girl would bang one of the big steel *thaachchis* from the kitchen, and then loose off a string of crackers. This would bring the langurs crashing back over the roof, and would set off the dogs and the frogs and everything else.

At first, I didn't see much of the priest, Father Ananthakumar, although I often heard Latin, leaking out of the church. I could hear the orphans, too – twenty-three little voices through the cadjan fence. '*Chacha Nay Bagaan Mein*,' they sang ('Old Mac-Donald had a Farm'). They'd once had a classroom in the garden, but the white ants had eaten the roof, and it was now being blown apart by falling coconuts. I never got used to this sound: the split-second whoosh and then the explosion of husk and flesh.

As the sun got hotter, the clamour subsided, and I'd wander

out into the road. Music seemed to be everywhere, booming out of the earth. But although Mulankavil made the sounds of a city, it was barely a village – more a scattering of shacks through the trees. Many of these places still wore the old uniform of a refugee: those great tarpaulins printed *UNHCR*. How many years will it be, I wondered, before Mulankavil stops feeling like a camp? The voices were always Tamil and female – a rapid, belt-fed chatter – and yet, whenever I drew near, they reduced to a murmur. Out here, it wasn't the noise I found surprising, but the aura of silence that seemed to precede me.

At dusk, there'd be different sounds. The frogs were now airborne and there was the soft thud and plop as they reconnected with terra firma. Then there was the scratching of a nib from the novitiate next door. I never saw him, and nor did I ever meet Commander Ranathunga, although every day he sent the orphans food. He'd also send me a tiffin-carrier of rice and curry, and there was always enough for all us: the priest, the novitiate, the kitchen girl and me. Each time, it was the same man who delivered it, Lieutenant Herath, and – a year on – he still sends me emails, wishing me well, and attaching pictures of his children.

On my second night, there was a new sound, way off – a long, woody rattle, followed by a series of thumps. The priest saw me listening. 'Fifty-mil cannon,' he said, 'and then some heavy guns.'

It was the army, reliving the war that had made Mulankavil.

Five years earlier, Sri Lanka's great, sleepy cataclysm of a conflict had rolled into town.

Until then, progress had been gruellingly slow. Once the truce was over, in 2006, the army had turned its attention to the east. It had taken almost a year to bring the last, loyal Tigers to heel.

Now it was the turn of the western Vanni, and in December 2007, the advance began in earnest. These days, the journey from Mannar to Mulankavil takes a couple of hours at most. Back then, it took the army almost eight months.

Part of the problem was mines, but it was also the way the army fought. Its special forces were nimble enough, but its great body of regulars would only move forward under a gale of missiles. In the previous year, the government had invested $37.6 million in Chinese artillery and ordnance, and now it laid down a storm. Everything fled before it: farmers, nuns, fishermen and elephants. Nothing was spared, and – like a carpet – the jungle would be rolled up, with everyone inside. Already, by the time the army reached Mulankavil, twenty thousand Vanniyas had been displaced, most of them running north, ahead of the barrage. 'That's why people need noise,' said the priest. 'They got used to it, during the war.'

By 13 August 2008, Mulankavil was empty, and filled up with soldiers. Most of its population had fled into the Vanni, and over the next nine months, they'd be pushed further and further east. Many would end up on the beaches on the far side of the island, where the roads ran out. Some would eventually return to Mulankavil, but they were mostly widows and orphans. Across the north, the war had created some eighty-nine thousand widows, with ninety-seven in Mulankavil alone.

'In their culture,' said the priest, 'to be raped is a matter of great shame, yet there's no one to protect them. If someone comes to their house, they can't scream, so they tend to give in. Imagine that, terrified of every man you see.'

The kitchen girl, he said, was one of the widows.

'Her husband was killed here, so now she feels she can never leave.'

Father Ananthakumar told me all this without much expression. Although he was only forty-six and only the tip of his beard was white, he sometimes spoke as if he had done enough, and seen too much. He said the war had been with him ever since school, when a boy in the playground was shot dead at his side. 'The trauma is always there,' he told me, 'deep down. I went to Australia once, to see my brother. But I couldn't stand the silence, and I began to panic and couldn't sleep. I need to be here, amongst my people and all their noise.'

By August 2008, a vast township – foul and ephemeral – had taken shape out in the forest. It may not have had walls and roofs, but it did have suburbs, of sorts. There were whole areas of buses and three-wheelers, and an enormous sprawl of carts, diggers, tractors and trucks. Crammed aboard were the Vanni's new wheeled citizens: housewives, guerrillas, teachers, herdsmen, mahouts, *kavadi* dancers, cooks, crooks, clerks, *kanganis* and children. Not only were there true Vanniyas amongst them, but also all those who'd abandoned Jaffna a decade before. As this huge ungainly mass moved east, driven on by the shelling, more people joined. By early 2009, it would have been a snarl-up visible from space. Even on the army's estimate, there were 150,000 internally displaced persons (or IDPs) out there, struggling along. The United Nations, however, put the figure at more than double that. If this great multitude had ever for a moment stood still, it would have been the second-biggest city in the country, after Colombo.

But, as before, progress was almost imperceptible. It took the army another three months to shunt its way to Pooneryn, a mere twenty-four miles up the road. There, the guns – and their huge, sad quarry – wheeled west into the Tigers' maze of earthworks and mines. All this has gone now, washed away in the rains. The army, of course, had been undeterred, and had carried on forward, in a blaze of rockets. Eventually, on 2 January 2009, this great roving mess – part battle, part slum – reached Kilinochchi, and the Tigers lost their little capital. A few days later, the entire length of the bloody A9 was back in government hands for the first time in twenty-three years.

The rebels and their wandering city were now trapped in the last quadrant of Tigerland. Once, they'd controlled almost fifteen thousand square kilometres, and now they were down to a mere two hundred. They were also short of fighters, with only a few thousand left. Everyone knew the end was near. It's thought that over three hundred artillery pieces gathered for the kill, along with 160,000 troops. Then something odd happened, and the Rajapaksas announced the first of their 'No Fire Zones'.

These would be havens, they said, free of shells.

It was now five years since that promise, but it still made me wonder: what did they look like, these No Fire Zones? In Kilinochchi, I hired a new driver, and set off east for Mullaitivu. The driver spoke little English and had never been out to the battlefields before. But it didn't matter; the United Nations had published a long and sobering report of the battle, and, at the back, was a sheaf of plans in limpid colours. With this across my knees, all I had to do was join the dots and follow the lines of fire.

To begin with, this meant driving back through the rebel heartlands, past Prabhakaran's bunker and all the Tiger junk. The countryside was just as I remembered it, serene and shattered. We passed a herd of Indian cattle grazing in the teak, and a field of burnt-out cars. Vallipunam had rallied, but there were still streets that looked like piles of broken biscuit. At first, I hadn't appreciated that this was part of NFZ1 – and nor had the refugees. To them, it felt the same as anywhere else, the air oily and black, and the sky raining trains. During the first ten days of NFZ1, its hospital was the target of some two thousand shells, or so the UN claims. The army, of course, says that not a single shell was fired.

We carried on, towards the coast, as the IDPs had done. Although the road was new, it was still fringed in ruins. One place, Puthukkudiyiruppu, looked as if it had been sucked up by giant pumps, leaving only floors and stubs and the larger concrete outlines. Even the old hospital lay fractured and open, with all its innards gone. The townspeople had paid a high price for their loyalty. This was the last town ever held by the Tigers, and they'd defend it – shop by shop – for almost two months.

Up ahead, the land flattened and turned bristly and orange. During the rains, this would flood, but, right now, it was a plain of dust, stretching almost all the way to the sea. Nothing moved out there, except the wild little flurries of dirt, and, out on the horizon, I could see not surf, as I'd expected, but a long, thin lip of built-up sand. This natural barrage is never the same on any two maps. But, on the far side, was the ocean, and, on this side, the dusty plain, which – further south – became a lagoon: the Nanthi Kadal. As for the lip itself, it was narrow, flat, dry and featureless: the perfect place to trap a rabble. On 12 February 2009, the Rajapaksas announced that it would be the new haven, or NFZ2.

The Tigers, however, weren't so easily caught, and as we drew near I could see their bunkers up in the sand. All along the edge of the lip, in both directions, the dirt had been scraped forward

435

into an enormous rampart, and then mounted with palm logs and tiny gunpits. Not even the rains had made much impression on this last great work. As the army closed in, the Tigers had got all the IDPs working up on the bund, even the women and children. It was almost as if they were digging their own grave, and that – when it was done – the last wheeled remnants of Tamil Eelam would vanish in the sand. No one was allowed to leave. The gunpits were there not just to keep the army out, but also to keep the people in. Anyone thinking of surrender was immediately shot.

As we passed through this wall at Puthumathalam, we stopped.

'Any mines here?' I asked.

The driver spoke to some soldiers, standing nearby.

'Not now. All cleared.'

I scrambled up to one of the bunkers and peered inside. The fighting hadn't left much: rust, shreds of green plastic and a damp halitotic stink. I tried to imagine the last cadres, crouched amidst the logs. There was no longer an air of invincibility amongst them. Some didn't even have uniforms, and many were now barnacled with ringworm and sores. They had few rockets left, and little artillery. There weren't even enough rebels left to man the gunpits, and every other one lay empty. They'd also learnt what it was to be hated by their protégés – the people they'd shot at in order to save. Recruiting parties now risked their lives searching the crowds for children, and at least one squad was bludgeoned to death. The anger the LTTE had so encouraged had now turned uncomfortably primordial.

The leaders, however, were never here, out on the bund. Prabhakaran was hidden away, deep amongst the IDPs. He had no plan. The most he could hope for was 'the CNN effect', that mythical international rage that brings the civilised world to the rescue. But hell didn't freeze, and nor did the rescuers come, riding their little winged pigs. Norway offered to broker a truce, but Prabhakaran refused. He was still banking on outrage, and on the short, bloody films of his tented city, shredded by shrapnel.

There were still a few silent hulks, way out on the dusty plain. It was mostly earth-moving equipment, but the machines looked like giant crustaceans that had perished in their dried-up sea. One of these great creatures was a hydraulic excavator, stolen in Jaffna and felled in the battle for the bund. In its last contorted moves, it had drawn its great rusty arm around itself, as if to ward off the blows.

The generals, however, had seldom missed a mark, and could watch in real time as their drones hovered through the chaos. But they too were being watched, and, according to the satellite pictures, soon all the big guns were trained on NFZ2. Once again, the landscape blackened and the air was sucked from the sky. The images from space depict a land that's been peppered and scorched. In places, people were simply vaporised – there one moment, and then only the smoking sand. Nothing was spared, not even the Red Cross ships, which were driven off the beach. As for the diggers, they hadn't stood a chance.

But then, on 19 April, there came a sudden lull. Here at Puthu-mathalam, the army's commandos had broken through the bund, triggering a stampede of IDPs. Hundreds died in the landmines, or under the Tigers' disciplinary fire. But there was no stopping them, and – over the next two days – 170,000 escaped across the dusty plain. The Sinhalese soldiers were genuinely horrified by the sight that befell them, and, in the pictures of that day, they're seen giving up their rations and carrying the wounded to safety.

If only the war had started like this, it might have finished decades before.

Half of the sandy barrage had now been recaptured. That left
only the southern end, 130,000 civilians, the great traffic jam,
Prabhakaran and whatever was left of his Tamil Tigers. Around
them, everything tightened, and the hail of hot metal resumed.
But then, on 8 May 2009, Gotabaya Rajapaksa announced the
last of his 'No Fire Zones'. It would be the smallest and probably
the bloodiest of all, NFZ3.

I'd always known it would be difficult, getting into NFZ3. For
much of the last five years, it had been completely sealed off.
There were mines everywhere, said the army, and it had to be
cleared. But, as usual, there was always more to it than that.
Whenever questions arose about artillery, and whether the government had used it, the issue always seemed to focus on NFZ3.
This was odd, considering that the evidence was everywhere: in
the satellite images, the witness accounts, the crushed buildings,
the empty casings and the little films made on people's phones. It
was almost as if NFZ3 held the key to all of this, and that to see
it would be to unlock the Great State Secret that wasn't really
secret at all.

Officially, there were still no big guns at the end of the war.
During those last few months, the Rajapaksa brothers had often
announced their angelic intent. Not a single drop of civilian
blood would be shed, they insisted, and all heavy weapons were
banned. Even when it was all over, they kept up this line. Not one
bullet, said the president, was fired against ordinary civilians.
His brother, Gotabaya, would go further still: 'We adopted a self-
imposed ban on air bombing, artillery and mortar fire whenever

we were confronted with battle zones which were home to civilians.' I was surprised how many Sinhalese still believed all this.
In fact, to believe otherwise had become the great heresy of the
modern age.

The government was always embellishing its version of what
happened. By 2014, the foreign minister had come up with the
idea that the Tamil Tigers must somehow have shelled themselves. The army even published a report called 'Humanitarian
Operation Factual Analysis'. 'No artillery power was used in the
NFZs', it insists, and then goes on to describe a textbook rescue.
Amongst the appendices is a remarkable inventory of all the
things captured off the Tigers, along with their value. It includes
fourteen brassiere suicide kits ($7.92 each) and eleven SAM mis-
siles ($11,000 each). Nowhere, however, is there a single mention
of the civilian casualties, either how many had died or where
they're buried. Officially, it seems, they've been forgotten.

All this, I realised, was restricting access to NFZ3. Although it
was notionally open, visitors needed permits and then, beyond
that, there was a Gordian tangle of rules and restrictions. There
was, however, a loophole; I discovered that I could bypass all of
this if a booked a little holiday direct with the army. It would be
a strange excursion (cash up front and a military escort), but at
least there was only one rule: I couldn't ask questions about the
end of the war.

After twenty-six years of fighting, the army had emerged as a
keen hotelier. It kept two small guest houses on the edge of the
Nanthi Kadal lagoon. Both were part of 'Headquarters Camp', a
huge assemblage of tin and green paint, hemmed in by teak trees.
Nothing about the camp was grand, except the gates, which were
Disneyesque in their dimensions and mounted with two

enormous Chinese guns. It was an odd motif for an army still protesting its innocence; each of these guns was capable of firing something the weight of a teenager a distance of over twenty-four miles. Meanwhile, there was little left of the village that had once stood here, just its fruit trees and wells, and the telltale outline of streets.

Neither guest house seemed to fit in. The first, down on the shore, was part pagoda, part Alpine chalet, and all slathered in varnish. Journalists love to hate this place ('Holidays in Hell'), and one report even had it full of grisly souvenirs. But it wasn't true, and 'Lagoon's Edge' was probably guilty of nothing worse than over-zealous joinery. The other place, where I stayed, was even more out of place. A large metal box, it had come with its own atmosphere: sterile, white, odourless and chilled. Like any fridge dweller, I soon lost any sense of the world beyond. At night, the regimental cooks would serve curry on white bone-china, and then we'd all sit around a tiny television as it belted out old reruns of *Friends*. After a few hours of this, it was easy to forget which continent I was on, let alone which country.

I had two guides, both veterans of the fighting. The first was a hearty, thumb-headed major, who wore a magnificent pair of chocolate-brown lace-up boots. He'd been a gunner almost twenty years, and had ended up at Thoppigala ('sorry, can't talk about that either'). At some stage, he'd also gone to Singapore, but it was not an experience he'd liked ('Two hundred and fifty rupees for one cigarette! And too many Tamils . . .'). We only went on one expedition, to Wattapala Amman, out amongst the reeds. It was the holiest Hindu temple in the Vanni, and when the major took off his boots, I suddenly realised how small he was.

'There's little difference,' he said, 'between Buddhism and Hinduism.'

'So then what's wrong with the Tamils?' I asked.

'Ungrateful buggers. Always causing trouble.'

My other chaperone was more forgiving. Lieutenant Isuru was barely thirty, dressed head to foot in camouflage and spoke an endearing textbook English ('We are worrying about your head, Mr John, especially in this heat.'). He was also a farmer's son from Matale, and, to him, war – like farming – wasn't a particularly malicious business, just something that had to be done. There weren't even good people and bad people, merely those who'd suffered together.

Our first evening, we walked down to the lagoon to watch the sunset.

'That's NFZ3,' said Isuru, 'on the opposite shore.'

Across the water, there was a long, pale purfling of palms.

'Our men were this side, and they were over there.'

It was an unsettling dusk. At first, I thought we were the only people around, but then I noticed sentries out in the grass, all armed, packed, pouched and helmeted, as if ready for battle. There were also soldiers under the pier, casting nets. They told Isuru they'd caught an eagle, and were finding it fish. Then a pack of wild dogs turned up, snapping at the hocks of a young buffalo grazing on the shore. They'd have killed it if the rest of the herd hadn't appeared, and sent the dogs, yelping and screaming, into the gloom. By then, lights were appearing in the camp and, way off down the lagoon, in Mullaitivu. But, from across the water, there was nothing. NFZ3 could be forgotten for another day, and was now in a darkness all of its own.

It took my eyes a while to adjust to the damage. That first morning began like any other on the northern gobbs: lapwings on the

shore, and the buffaloes out in the silt. Sometimes, fishermen –
now tiny charcoal figures – would appear, way out amongst the
sparkles, flickering along as if captured in celluloid. I remember
thinking how serene it all looked – or did I mean surreal? For a
long time, the only other vehicle we saw was an old Morris van,
made in Oxford almost half a century earlier, and still tinkling
along, dispensing ice creams.

But then we turned round the north-west edge of the lagoon,
and back on to the long lip of sand. There were vehicles out
here, too, but they never had windows or wheels. We passed an
ambulance out in the grass, and a couple of Austins under the
palms. There were tuk-tuks, too, clustered together amongst
buses and vans. From a distance, these looked like day trips, but
as we drew near, I saw that everything had burst, and that all the
seats had melted. I began to notice cooking pots, too, and a long
trail of rags and bottles and children's clothes. I now realised that
we'd caught up with the great, wheeled slum, and that this was its
wake – bleached and scattered – nearly five years on.

Continuing down the lip – as they had – we followed this trail
of human jetsam all the way to NFZ3. Along the road, huge
chunks of the landscape had been punched away. In places, the
undergrowth seemed almost impenetrable, a dense thicket of
acacia and spiniflex, but elsewhere the sand looked bare and
amputated, and was merely a scattering of stumps. It was the
palms that puzzled me most, either lithe and magnificent, or
sliced away at shoulder height. I remember tractor tyres, too,
ripped apart like crusts, and a small *kovil*, decorated with bomb
cases. Of the five villages that had once stood here on the spit,
little remained – although there were still a few people living in
the ruins. I even saw a tiny shop, bravely trading amongst the
wreckage.

Then, just short of Vellamullivaikkal, we came to a long crimson scarp. This, however, was no natural form, but a vast embankment of metal. Packed within its flanks were thousands of vehicles and bicycles, all grotesquely distorted and blasted out of shape. There were buses that looked as if they'd been stamped into place and then packed with tractors and scrunched-up vans. Fire had burnt off most of the paint and rubber, leaving only rust and glass. Close up, it was like some evil cake, richly compacted with cars. They say that, by the time the fighting was over, it was almost impossible to count the wrecks, scattered over the battlefield. There were ten thousand motorbikes alone, together with twenty-five thousand bicycles. Here, at this giant red heap, the Vanni's great traffic jam had finally come to an end, and NFZ3 began.

It was the last section of the spit, an area the size of Central Park.

'And how many people,' I asked, 'were here at the end?'

Lieutenant Isuru smiled apologetically. 'I can't say . . .'

'Of course,' I said, but I already knew the answers.

'Five thousand,' the president had said.

'Ten,' declared the army a few days later.

Only the rest of the world had disagreed. As far as the UN was concerned, in early 2009 there were still 130,000 precarious lives out there, on the spit.

Beyond the scarp of rust, the debris became ever more poignant.

There were still shreds of old saris knotted round the tree stumps, and cooking vessels scattered in the sand. Once, we stopped, and I got out and wandered in amongst the detail of long-forgotten lives: sandals, combs, cups, brushes – all brittle and blanched – and then the rags, and the shreds of plastic, and the books, now thick yellow crusts of pulp. A suitcase had split open, erupting tendrils of faded linen, and I also found a curious little nest of toys, just legs and wheels and a hairless pink head. But most pitiful of all were the trenches, now only a few inches deep. The sides, I noticed, had been shored up with home-made 'gunny bags' and, in all their angry colours, they looked like wounds in the sand.

During these travels I met two people who'd survived these terrible holes. One was the lonely niece in VVT, and the other was a man in London, who I know as 'Croydex'. Other survivors gave evidence to the United Nations' experts, and together they provide a description of NFZ3 that's probably as near as anything to our vision of hell.

There was little break in the shelling. Instead, the missiles poured down faster and faster into the ever-shrinking 'haven'. Now they were landing amongst the camps, the shrapnel scything through tarpaulins and people, and bringing down trees. The noise, said the niece, seemed to envelop everything, and crush it of life. 'You thought your eyeballs would burst out of your head, and even when it stopped, you didn't know if you were alive or dead.' There was nowhere to hide, except in a scrape of sand. Wedding saris worth thousands of rupees were cut up and made into gorgeous bandages or gunny bags. But even then they weren't safe as the huge shells came slamming in. Sometimes people were buried in their gunny pits, only for a new family to move in and live on top (at least for a while, until the limbs resurfaced). After a few days of this, everything began to stink of the dead or burning plastic. Only the children got used to the chaos, and would wander out of the gunny pits, there to be lopped and scorched in the squall of metal. 'I lost both my children at Mullaitivu,' said the niece, blankly. 'I miscarried one, and the other was killed on the beach . . .'

The Rajapaksas had promised food, but then sent only enough for ten thousand people. Within the micro-economy of NFZ3, a bag of rice soon cost more than a car, and, once the IDPs had eaten all their animals, they began foraging for cockles and roots. By the end, one in four of the children was suffering acute malnutrition. But the government was in no mood to feed this siege and keep the country waiting. With the departure of the Red Cross, not only had the enemy lost its last lifeline, but also the last of the witnesses had gone. Gotabaya Rajapaksa had never wanted anyone there at the end. All journalists were excluded for writing what he'd described as 'crap'. Now – unseen – he could finish the job he'd started: grinding up the last of Eeelam, starving it into submission and smoking the Tigers out.

Gordon Weiss, who acted as spokesman for the UN, offers us another reason as to why the government had become so impatient. According to his book, *The Cage*, this battlefield was still leaking soldiers, and, very soon, the total number of army deserters would reach fifty thousand. Other sources put the figure at only twenty-nine thousand, but the idea's the same: this was still a young army that could only take so much. The generals, says Weiss, had to punch their way through the crowds whilst they still could. All this has yet to be investigated, but in the meantime it provides a bleak explanation where otherwise there isn't much to go on.

If there's ever an inquiry, my guess is that it'll reveal an army of muddled intent. That may sound trite, and yet, strangely, no one believes it. In Sri Lanka, the army is regarded as either a cast of heroes or a band of thugs. But, surely it's been both? Inevitably, there'll have been heroism and humanity amongst the soldiers at Mullaitivu; in an educated, democratic and essentially humane society, you'd expect nothing else (never for a moment had I imagined that the fundamentally decent men I'd met – Ravi, Isuru, the Kilinochchi brigadier and the Yala major – were either unique or particularly unusual). But there was also, I suspect, a deep seam of malice. The army's denials have often been grotesque, and even its top brass – like General Fonseka – have occasionally come out, denouncing its crimes.

It's the impunity, however, that worries people, and the idea that here's an army that countenances evil. I always think you can see this best in the statistics for sexual violence. According to the government's own figures, not a single soldier was charged with sexual abuse between 2005 and 2010, and there was only one conviction for rape. That's odd considering that these are figures from the war zone, and that – during that time – several hundred thousand men were posted here, often young, fired up and absorbed in the violence. Perhaps the army had enveloped itself in some other-worldly aura of virtue? Or perhaps it just didn't care what the little devils did.

These days, it's not hard to spot a demon. Every soldier seems to have carried a phone, and their pictures and films are all over the web. Women don't always fare well in these shots. 'We've killed your leaders,' sings one of the YouTube soldiers, 'and now you are our slaves!' It's worse for the female cadres. They're often having their breasts and underwear inspected, and they're usually dead. One image in particular I find hard to forget. At the edge of the frame, there's a very thin soldier. 'I want to cut her titties off!' he shrieks, but in his sunken, whiskery face there isn't lust or mischief, only months of ingrained terror.

Meanwhile, across the dunes, the Tigers had been busy with atrocities of their own.

'Where were their lines?' I asked Isuru.

'Everywhere,' he said. 'That was the problem.'

It was still impossible to tell family pits from those for guns.

'But I can show you their positions out on the perimeter.'

It was only a short drive away, through the bright red lanes of Karaiyamullivaikal. A few hundred yards from the sea, we came to a halt at the last of the Tiger defences. There wasn't much left; the wind had smoothed away the berm, leaving only a wide furrow, tufted with gunny bags and scattered with rags and lumps of steel plate. Amongst the junk, I spotted a long thin cartridge, which, at some stage, must have been in a fire, and had exploded.

'One of yours?' I asked Isuru. 'Or theirs?'

'Anti-aircraft shell. Could be either. We both used them.'

By that stage, the Tigers were throwing everything into the battle, even the civilians. For months, the LTTE had been sheltering amongst them, harvesting the children. Now came the time to hurl them into one last, magnificently futile fight. Although the rebels were outnumbered thirty to one, they still had snipers to pick off the cowards. Teenagers who'd hardly held a gun before were ordered into spectacular headlong assaults, with little hope of anything except sudden death. Others were packed with explosives and sent wandering off into army lines. Everyone had a role to play, even the wounded cadres. They'd wait in a bunker for the army to come, and then they'd flip the switch and blow everyone up. This level of commitment terrified the soldiers, and, in time, there'd be plenty more like the You-Tube man – wild, sinewy and mad.

But eventually the instinct for survival triumphed, even out here on the berm. Slowly, the hopelessness of it all began to seep amongst the cadres. A few of them even began heaping up their weapons and setting them on fire (and perhaps my cartridge was part of the pyre). This, however, was not an edifying moment, and nor was the sight of Tigers peeling off their stripes and merging into the crowd. It was only a matter of diehards now, and hunting down Prabhakaran.

Amongst those peeling off their Tiger stripes was the mysterious Croydex.

I met him some months later, in London. Until then, I'd always been wary of people who'd described themselves as cadres. Suddenly, there seemed to be a surplus of heroes, particularly at the West End parades. But Croydex was different. At first he'd denied that he was anything to do with the LTTE, but he was so strange and broken that it was hard to imagine him as anything else. He was tall and skeletal, with very dark skin sucked in tight around his features. This made his eyes look huge and anxious, and yet the rest of face was peeled back in a smile. I noticed that he never liked to sit, but preferred to stalk around, his fingers working at his forearm, smoothing out the bobbled scars.

It was Mr Seevaratnam who'd introduced us, and who'd agreed to translate. But, as the man was here illegally, everything had to be secret. The first time we met was at the West Croydon temple, and – as I was never given his name – he appears in my notes as the 'Croydon Ex-combatant', or Croydex. Even that, however, betrays a secret. If it's ever known that he was one of the

Tigers, he'll never get asylum in Britain or anywhere else. To survive, said Mr Seevaratnam, it's probably best if he doesn't exist. This is the story of how his life vanished:

'I am thirty-three years old and I was born in a fishing village near VVT. My brother joined the Boys in 1991, and was killed four years later. That's when we all left Jaffna, along with everyone else. I worked in the Vanni as a fisherman for the next three years. It was dangerous because of the patrols, but we fished at night on the lagoon. After that, I joined the LTTE, and stayed with them until the Accord. I was injured a few times, but I got used to the life. Ever since I was a child, we've been moved around, so it didn't bother me. But the Accord weakened us, because everyone left. I got married and had children, and went to live in Jaffna.

'But then, in 2006, it all started again, and the Boys appealed for help. So I rejoined, and it was much harder now. Towards the end, the government kept telling people to go to the safe areas, and would then bomb them all the same. We were there to help people, and to protect them from the army. You can't imagine the things I saw.

'Eventually, we realised it was hopeless and we threw away our capsules and our uniforms and gave ourselves up. I was taken to Vavuniya with all the others. I don't know how many. Two or three lakhs? Maybe two hundred thousand. Then, at night, Colonel Karuna's people came round, identifying cadres. I had to get out, and so on the third night I escaped, and got a train to Colombo. From there, I managed to get away to France. I applied for asylum but they said I was LTTE, and so, after a long time in jail, they put me on a plane and sent me back to Colombo. There, I was arrested, and taken to the fourth floor at CID, and kept for

449

three and a half months. They asked me everything. What did I do in the LTTE? Who else did I know, and who did I see in Paris? Sometimes they used pliers, sometimes the electric things. I still have the marks up my back and on my arms. They also turned me over, and they had this bag, which they filled with petrol and put over my head. I often felt I was drowning or burning. I was sick for weeks afterwards. My father got me out. He paid a bribe of one million rupees, and I took a plane again.

'That's it. I never want to fight again. I've lost everything. I never want to see another T-56, or another war. I've had enough. I'm finished.'

Along the shore, a few of the diehards had made their stand. Their colossal iron citadel so dominates the beach that, at first, you hardly notice what a stupendous space it is. The sea here is like liquefied twilight, and, in each direction, vast sweeps of silvery-pink curl off into the distance. It's a white-hot desert with another one, blue and cold, beyond. But then, in the midst of it all, there's an immense black wreck: ten thousand tons of bulkheads and plate, and crusted cranes. Although only the length of twelve double-deckers, it seems somehow to own the horizon, and the beach empties before it. This, of course, is the improbability at work, and the concept of a vast freighter caught in mid-action as it plunges through the sand.

'The pirate ship,' announced Isuru. '*Farah III!*'

It was a long way out, but I could see that part of the plating was missing. Some of it had been laid out across the sand, and so we set off down the metal road. There was also an anchor chain zigzagging out to the wreck. It looked like the spine of some giant, desiccated snake lying twisted and dead on the beach. By now, I could hear *Farah III* moaning softly and clanking in the heat, and the sea, heaving around in her hull. Where the plating had been removed, the sand had gushed in creating a new beach that boomed and glugged in the dark.

It was a cruel fate for such a harmless old tramp. In December 2006, *Farah III* had been sailing from India to South Africa when she was hijacked by the Sea Tigers, and ran aground. Although this wasn't their first act of piracy (since 1994, they'd captured, on average, a ship a year), it was one of their most profitable. People often told me about the booty enjoyed across Tigerland, the glut of rice and cement, and the surplus of motorbikes. Once the Boys had emptied the holds, they'd started cutting up the plate and making it into submarines and armoured cars. The steel would've kept them going for decades if the army hadn't have arrived, on 14 May 2009.

Close up, I noticed that every surface was pitted in gunfire.

'There must be *thousands* of bullet holes . . .' I gasped.

Isuru shrugged. 'That's the Sea Tigers for you. Their last stand.'

It was compelling, the sight of such ferocity, preserved in steel. Many of the rounds had welded themselves into the plating, but then came larger bullets, which had punched their way through. In places, the Tigers had tried to staunch the holes with gunny bags, only to find larger missiles bursting through the hull. The tanks' shells, I decided, gave the iron the texture of rotten apples – not just reddish brown, but swollen and split. Whole sections of the bridge and the superstructure had been scooped away, and it was hard to imagine anyone surviving this. By the following day, the *Farah III* had been silent.

The long spit finally ended in dirty water, as had NFZ3 and the civil war.

By the time we got to Vadduvakallu (or Wadduwakal), there was brine on three sides: the sea to the left, the lagoon to the right, and, up ahead, a wide shallow channel that linked the two. Out there, the water was a claggy, kaolin beige, and I could see two fishermen standing motionless on their tiny rafts. They looked like statues, grounded in the sludge. Although it was shallow enough to wade across, there was also a narrow causeway, threading out through the mud. Whilst parts of it looked mottled and broken, it was still the only road heading south.

I suddenly realised that I'd seen this inlet already, thousands of miles away, and several years before. The films of 'Wadduwakall Bridge' were some of the first and most memorable to emerge from the battlefield. The Rajapaksas had released this footage because they thought it looked like a rescue. But, in my kitchen, it had looked more like a rout, with thousands of people struggling away through the muck. Down in Tooting, the Tamils had risen in fury, and had packed themselves off to Parliament Square. *STOP THE MASSACRE*, read their banners, but they were already too late. This wasn't war anymore, merely its unremitting aftermath.

I stepped out on to the causeway, picking my way between the holes. A priestly cluster of cormorants watched me from their roost, a sprig of metal out in shallows. I wondered if any of them remembered that day and the strange creatures floundering through their mud. It had, presumably, been an unforgettable time, even for birds. On 15 May 2009, the day after the siege of the *Farah III*, the LTTE had ordered its people to set fire to their weapons and flee. As the dunes exploded all around, the great slum rose up out of its holes. The next morning, the survivors were funnelled away, in their tens of thousands, through the sludge.

Meanwhile, the two great prongs of the army had met on the beach. For the first time in decades, the entire coastline of Sri Lanka was back in government hands. As for what remained of Tigerland, it was now barely two hundred yards across, and yet it was still seething with rage. Almost to the moment of its annihilation, the LTTE was ringing round, demanding sanctuary for its last thousand cadres. Not even the Tiger's head of policy, Nadesan, seemed to appreciate the carnage all around. Nor had he realised that, in Colombo, his fate had already been decided. He and his lieutenants were killed on the last day of the war, 18 May 2009, in a cleansing burst of machine-gun fire. They were carrying white flags at the time, as they emerged from their enclave. The last thing they'd heard was the sound of disbelief. It was Nadesan's wife, struggling under the bullets. 'He's trying to surrender!' she protested. 'And you're *shooting* him!'

That left only *Thambi*, or the elusive Little Brother.

'Was he there?' I asked. 'In the enclave?'

'No,' said Isuru. 'I'll show you. He was trying to escape.'

We turned round and drove along the edge of the lagoon, until we were back in the bright red dust. Just as before, the plain here looked burnt up and bristly, but it was also wider, and scattered with oil drums and coils of wire. Way off, on the far side, I could see a faint strip of mauve, edged in mustard trees and tiny specks of mangrove.

'That's where we found him,' said Isuru.

'A day no one ever forgets,' I suggested.

'Yes, I was only a few miles away, but I got the news immediately.'

'And the photos?'

'Sure. The pictures went viral.'

There were still many versions of Prabhakaran's disappearance. The photographs taken by the soldiers suggest a watery end. As Eelam's Sun God had passed through the cheering crowds, they'd all taken snapshots, making him one of the most photographed corpses on Earth. There's always mud in these pictures. Sometimes Prabhakaran's lying by it, or in it, and sometimes he's naked and it's daubed all over his body. Then he's dressed again, and appearing on television with the mud in the distance. The pictures of his twelve-year-old are equally confusing. One moment, Balachandran is lying in the dirt, dotted with holes, and then, in the next shot, he's in captivity, nibbling biscuits. Only Prabhakaran's head never changes, with the cranium blown away. In the army version of events, he's killed whilst trying to flee, and, in the firefight that follows, so are his family and all his men. Amongst the loot, the soldiers say they pick up twelve million rupees, a can of petrol and some diabetic pills. The petrol's there to burn Prabhakaran in case he's killed, but events happen so quickly, it's never used.

'All lies,' Thevar the blogger had told me. 'That's not what happened.'

In his version, Prabhakaran killed himself.

'Put the gun in his mouth, and *bang*! My friend was *there*.'

'But why did he do that?'

Thevar scowled. 'Our cause could only continue if he was dead.'

In Tooting, there'd be more versions, and, in some, he hadn't died at all.

'He escaped in an ambulance,' I'd be told.

'He was disguised as a Muslim woman.'

'They had a submarine waiting.'

'He's still alive,' insisted Mr Seevaratnam. 'I pray for him every day.'

Before leaving the battlefield, I took one last walk through the dunes. We'd stopped near Vellamullivaikkal, where the final hours of the war were fought. This time, I left Isuru in the car and waded out through the sand in the direction of the sea. The only things that grew here were either whiplash supple or covered in spines, and the grass was wispy and pale. It was like an outbreak of alopecia, spreading out as far as the eye could see. But there was also the same thin carpet of litter, and, at some stage, several large, shallow holes had appeared, each with huge tyre tracks leading back to the road. Someone, it seemed, had been quarrying in amongst the gunny bags and corrugated iron. Even at the time, this struck me as odd, so I took some pictures and hurried on.

I made slow progress, picking my way through the plastic and rust. What will archaeologists make of all this, I wondered, hundreds of years from now? What will they think of this war? That it was fought with spoons and polythene bags? Or that it was fought over nothing, just a cataclysmic scuffle in the sand?

And what will they make of the bodies (if ever they find them)? Will they be broken and scattered, or lined up lovingly, as if shot by their own? If the Rajapaksas were to be believed, it will be an orderly grave: just the 'terrorists' and the few civilians they'd managed to shoot. On the army's version, it will be slightly larger, although still no bigger than a village of the dead. They'd always said that, across Mullaitivu, three thousand civilians had been killed, although they'd never revealed who they were or where they'd ended up.

That left only the Tamils and their more apocalyptic assessment of what's in the sand. Both in Jaffna and Tooting, I was often told that there were 146,000 people missing, and that most of them were out here, folded into the dunes. Over the years, the Sinhalese press had energetically fought this figure, and now the battles of the Vanni had become a battle of maths. But, without the evidence, it was all speculation. Meanwhile, the Tamil figure was still too bold for the United Nations, although its own reckoning – up to forty thousand – was almost as hard to compass. If true, it meant there was the equivalent of 3,636 football teams out here, scattered beneath my feet, or forty trains packed with commuters, or the entire population of an English town like, for example, Dover.

Or perhaps there was no one here at all, and that's what the quarries were all about? A few months after my visit, a new story broke across the world's press. In it, the Sri Lankan army was accused of digging through the evidence, and trucking it away. In Australia, the 'Public Interest Advocacy Group' claimed that huge graves had been opened up, with thousands of bodies disturbed. Even in death, it seemed, the great wheeled city of the Vanni was up and on the move.

At last, the spiky undergrowth began to thin out, and the ocean appeared. It was still only a long thin blade of blue, far out across the sifted flats. There might have been a figure out there, or perhaps just a speck of debris. But what really caught my eye was the tidemark, a rim of dark scurf now rippling away along the edge of the straw. It had seemed unremarkable at first, but, as I drew close, I realised it was rich in heels and soles, flip-flops, sandals and slippers. I was suddenly reminded of Queyroz's story, of St Francis Xavier. It was almost as if thousands of Xaviers had come this way, and this was all that was left of their rage: the shoes on the shore.

13

Green As Ever

Hail Ceylon, pearl of greenness, flower of the islands,
tower of beauty! . . . My ideas and my poetry owe
much to this island. I have known and loved its generous people.

Pablo Neruda, Colombo World Peace Council, 1957

The surface texture of life so full of ease and grace
rested atop great harshness and unpredictability . . .
what passed for equanimity was often an illusion
beneath which raged emotions deeply repressed . . .

William McGowan, *Only Man is Vile:*
The Tragedy of Sri Lanka, 1992

I had hoped to feel angry as I headed south, but of course it didn't work like that. Sri Lanka has a strange way of subverting the conscience. I sometimes wondered if there wasn't some vast emotional transponder buried deep in the island, scrambling all the signals. How else had the tourism survived, as the bloody battles raged? On the day the war ended, my sister was in Galle on a fashion shoot. She brought me back a newspaper and, in it, there's the war, of course, but all the other stuff, too, about Wimbledon, and Michael Jackson's nose, and the Kandyan lady who lost her handbag. Even as history was blowing itself to bits, life could seem mysteriously normal.

Everyone was at it, thinking things they shouldn't. I'd expected outrage amongst the Tamils, and yet all I'd found was exuberance. This was the defeat they'd always expected; they'd performed their duty, and now out of perdition would come renewal. 'The cycle ends,' said Thevar, piously. 'The cycle moves on.' Not even Father Z was interested in justice or an investigation. 'What's the point? Bad things happened on both sides. Going over it all will only transfer the hatred to a new generation.'

The Sinhalese could be equally ambivalent. Victory had left them reflective and uncertain. This always surprised me, wherever I went. I'd imagined more pride and a burst of ebullience, and yet what I'd often found was bewilderment, as if no one knew quite what to feel. The fighting had cost the country $200 billion, had lasted four times as long as the Second World War, and yet there was still so much unresolved. Whilst the Sinhalese had always had an urge to forget, this bit of history would be hard to bury. The Rajapaksas had tried to make them feel triumphant, but with little success. So old and obscure were the origins of this war that, to anyone under forty, it didn't even feel like theirs. It was merely the context in which they'd lived, an abstraction, fought out in the woods, or in the back of their mind.

I thought about all of this as I sat on the bus, heading back to Colombo. It was full of people beginning their thinking again: monks, schoolchildren, a few teenage farmers, some soldiers playing with their phones, and a wandering minstrel who sang for his lunch. I enjoyed the idea of them all starting anew, unencumbered by the certainties of war. In this great wild forcefield of thought, who knows what future they'll devise? Not me, for sure, although I had at least realised this: a murmur of rage from me, and I'd only seem more foreign than ever.

As the landscape got greener, I felt my affection restored. I still feel guilty about this, and the ease with which I began to enjoy, once again, the world all around. But it was impossible to resist the loveliness of it all: the shimmering slots of water; the ancient, knobbly woods; the great pink pebbles the size of basilicas, dropped in the rice; the circus of brilliant creatures and everywhere their ringmaster, the tireless drongo in his long black tailcoat.

In Sri Lanka, it was always thrilling, the signs of life that reappeared just when you thought nothing had survived. On that ride back through the dry zone, we passed a road-gang in flip-flops, a curd-seller, a pair of elephants carrying logs, and a bicycle race. Although the cyclists looked shrivelled and drenched, the marshalls who drove in amongst them seemed wildly exuberant, as if they themselves were about to triumph. At some point, we all breezed past a filling station with a notice over the forecourt: *NO SMORKING*. It seemed a perfect word at the time. I'd been 'smorking' for miles: riding along, empty of thought, and enjoying the cruel beauty of somebody else's world, smug in the knowledge that I was only passing through.

The other passengers did nothing to alleviate this untroubled pleasure. The men were courtly and shy, and their wives – always gorgeously robed and jewelled – seemed hardly to move. Although the air gushing in was hairdryer hot, no one appeared to notice. I felt like a beast amongst them, colourless and clumsy. They will never love this country as I have, superficially. A Tamil friend of mine in London – the journalist – would record her feelings of unbearable longing in a blog. 'Writing about Sri Lanka,' she once said, 'is bloody terrifying after a lifetime of looking at the subject sideways. If I look at it full on, it's too awful to bear . . . I'm writing this on a sea of red wine and chocolate . . . anything to distract me from my reality.'

I now realise how little I understand this. Perhaps it's always the same for outsiders. You get a tiny glimpse of 'reality' and you think it will haunt you, but then the sheer splendour of this country wells up all around, and you love it all over again.

Near Vavuniya, we passed the refugee camps, not that we saw them. Thorn and grass had closed in around us, and there was no view except the road, ahead and behind, like a pipeway through the forest. I could almost sense the other passengers emptying their minds as they stared out at the attenuating lines. But there hadn't always been so much of nothing. Once, there were twenty-one camps out here, each a vast polythene town, defined in barbed wire. Together, they'd held almost 290,000 people, including several thousand children and amputees, and some fifteen thousand wounded. The largest of these camps was called Menik Farm, and was only a short ride from Vavuniya. During my time there, I'd asked Singham if there was any chance of a visit.

'No, they'll pick you up before you're anywhere near.'

'Who? The police?'

'Yes, maybe them, or Military Intelligence.'

That was a complication I could do without, and so I settled for a virtual visit, via Google Earth. Even from beyond the outer atmosphere, Menik Farm looked agricultural, covered in human cloches. The plastic was dazzling, and I could see that it was divided into smaller and smaller allotments, like tented suburbs, each with its own ring road of mud. Back in 2009, it had become the largest refugee camp in the world.

I'd met several people who'd done their time, including Singham, Croydex and the lonely niece. They all described the same things: the stink and the dust, and the startling sense of having vanished. The worst part was arriving, said the niece, and being stripped down in front of everyone else. But, even after this, she was never safe, and there were always soldiers on hand to watch her wash. According to the UN, for some soldiers it was not enough to watch, and sex became the crude currency of survival and revenge.

Croydex, too, remembered the terror, and Colonel Karuna's men.

'The paramilitaries came round at night, wearing balaclavas.'

'And what if they'd found you?'

Croydex twitched. 'I don't know. So many cadres disappeared.'

It had taken the government nearly two years to identify those they'd wanted, and to release all the rest. But, by April 2011, the process was almost over, and the camps were down to their last eighteen thousand. They were sorry specimens. Some had been born into the Tigers, and had never known anything else. Others were vocational, and would require more vigorous retuning.

There were still some out there, the day I trundled past. No one ever saw them, and they'd never been tried. But they were there somewhere, deep in the brush: the last four thousand cadres, learning to unlove *Thambi*, and to love the Big Brothers.

Sanitised of Tigers, the rest of the A9 would often feel like Rajapaksa-land. The brothers seemed to be everywhere now, beaming out of the billboards and grinning all over the towns. It wasn't just Mahinda, the president. Basil and Gota were up there too, wreathed in adoration and scooping up the praise. I always thought they looked like otters: sleek, glossy, bewhiskered, pleased and replete. Their names were everywhere: on highways and housing projects, and on the brilliant new stupas now ballooning out of the scrub. By merging the Ministries of Defence and Development, they'd made themselves unstoppable, and now everything was built in the name of national security. The army even had its own construction outlets, and ran a few hotels. It didn't matter that all the money was borrowed, this was the beginning of the Rajapaksas' ancient world.

Back in Colombo, my friends had often found this funny.

'They've even hired archaeologists to give the Vanni a Buddhist past!'

But, out on the road, it was always Mahinda who loomed the largest. He was now a medieval character, usually the height of a house. *SHREE WICKRAMA LANKADHEESWARA!* declared the hoardings (or, Heroic Overlord Warrior of Lanka). I wondered what the Tamils and Muslims made of this and the sinister paeans that appeared at junctions. *YOU ARE THE SUN AND STARS,* read one, *AND YOU WILL BE PRESIDENT FOREVER!* This was no idle threat. Never before in Sri Lankan history had one man held so much power. Not only had Rajapaksa filled the government with family, he'd also brought all his rivals into the fold and given them jobs. Sri Lanka now had the biggest cabinet in the world, with 130 ministers, each with a stately car and a little posse of thugs.

But it wasn't all glory, our ride through Mahinda's kingdom. Along the road, there were many reminders of those who'd died. Often, it was the bus stops that had become the focus of grief. They'd be painted in air-force colours or camouflage, and inside there'd be flowers and portraits of the soldiers killed. I was always touched by the democracy of these places, and by the idea of waiting and the journey ahead. The government had never seemed to understand this, and its own memorials were always clumsy and triumphant. Every town had its golden soldier, a giant toy-like figure, making war on the roundabout. Then there were all of Gota's trophies, huge organs of concrete, swelling out the debris. 'They're so fatuous,' said Elmo the novelist, 'that they'll remind us forever of what we've wasted.'

To me, however, the most troubling memorial of all was that at Jayanthipura, on the edge of Colombo. With its victorious tracts and its ten-ton lions, it was a work of Rajapaksian splendour. On the day I'd called by, there were two Amazons on duty, flawless and wordless in their royal blue saris. They escorted me out to the

466

walls of remembrance, where the names of dead were set out in order of departure. We began in 1983, and finished five walls later with the 27,745th name. It was a sobering walk, but what really worried me was the long expanse of blank marble and the spaces left for yet more walls. What was that supposed to say? That this wasn't the end, but only the beginning?

I was glad to be back in Colombo, breathing in its disobedience.

It took me a day or so to get used to the chaos, but then I suddenly realised how much I'd missed it. Here were torrents of people again, all sweeping the rules aside. I'd forgotten how they drove as if they were the only ones out on the road; how they built whatever they felt like, and how they played their cricket wherever they wanted; how the days got more and more frenetic, until eventually the sun toppled into the sea, and how, in the darkness, everyone vanished; how the nights felt mischievous and close, and yet how – wherever there was neon – it was only a *devala* or a statue of the hapless St Sebastian, pinned out like a moth. I'd forgotten, too, Colombo's incorrigible zest, even now, in the Age of Purity. Everyone here was either in business, in hock, in flagrante or in love. What other city spends so much time punishing its lovers, with so little success? There was a hint of anarchy everywhere, even on the trains. People would fight tooth and nail to get aboard, but then, once on, they were all suddenly friends.

The Rajapaksas weren't royal here, despite all their palaces. There were no giant otters, or, if there were, they were buried in bustle. Colombo had little time for the brothers, and even the rich could be thrillingly seditious. Basil was now known as 'Mr Ten Per Cent', and there was always a bit of Gota madness in the tittle-tattle. If I looked hard enough, I could even find papers prepared to print these stories. Once, the *Sunday Leader* had run a tale about a puppy, and how Gota had diverted a flight to bring it back from Zurich. The minister hadn't been pleased to read this, and had phoned the reporter, Frederica Jansz. 'Your type of journalist,' he told her, 'are pigs who eat shit! Shit! Shit! Shit journalists!'

'I hope you can hear yourself, Mr Rajapaksa,' said Jansz.

But Gota had already lost his thread, and trailed off in a whirl of expletives.

As always, I walked everywhere. One day, I set off down Galle Road, across the green and along the waterfront, ending up at Fort. It was a beautiful day, and the city felt light and theatrical. I was excited to be back, and yet, as always, I could never quite work out why. There was a little cluster of gunboats off shore, and a pack of hairless dogs roaming the green. As I passed the Ceylinco building, I remembered the conman from my first day, and the story of the bomber embedded in the asphalt. Even in those few months, Fort had changed, growing in clamour and confidence. It was like a mini Shanghai, slowly returning to life. Fruit vendors were now filling the shade, and, on the corner of Chatham Street, there was a mounted policeman in enormous shiny boots. I'd often wondered why my friends hadn't moved back here, and nested down amongst the Art Deco. 'We can't,' they said, 'the Rajapaksas already own it.'

I ducked down Chatham into York Street, and reached the old police building. It had a terrible reputation, and was one of the few places still whiskery with weeds and the colour of the forties. I now realise that this is where Croydex was brought, to be treated with petrol. In fact, he was probably there on the very day I called by. Out of curiosity, I'd decided to venture inside, and, from the entrance, I followed a tunnel which led deep under the building and which was lined with corrugated iron. It emerged by an X-ray machine, and in a giant sock of steel mesh, a bit like a fish trap. A pair of old hooded eyes watched me from across the machine.

'What you want, sah?'

This, I realised, was as far as I'd get.

'Nothing,' I said. 'I'm in the wrong place.'

Perhaps Croydex was saying much the same upstairs, on the fourth floor.

When I met him, months later, in London, he said this: 'I hope your police don't send me home. England is a rich country. People have new cars, and sometimes they use their saris only once. English people drink alcohol and spend a lot of money on their birthdays. But I am happy to be here, although sometimes I think about the petrol, and that's when I cry.'

I spent my last few days in a state of half-departure, wanting to be home but not wanting to leave. This time, I'd avoided the big hotels and stayed in a guest house, out in Bambalapitya. Part of its appeal was its name, 'The Ottery', but there was also penury involved, and an element of pilgrimage. During the early years of the war, it had been a hang-out for writers, like William McGowan, and the photographer, Stephen Champion. Perhaps I'd hoped to absorb some of their brilliance, or even their anger. I'd met Champion once, in London. He told me that, through his pictures, he still lived with the eighties, but that Sri Lanka was as compelling as ever, and that each year he returned to the Ottery. 'It's just the same,' he'd said. 'A bit smaller, maybe, and it's lost its piano and the billiard table.'

To my surprise, even the old landlady, Mary, was still there. Now in her seventies, she was huddled into the last few rooms of her large concrete home. The rest of the house had been rented out to psychologists, and beyond lay the coast road, a railway track and a huge drench of empty, grey beach. Mary had never seen the need to prettify her world, and her only ornaments were powdered with age: a few Madonnas, an African carving and an old television, wrapped in a veil. It was said that she was a Tamil, that she'd been married to a Sinhalese, and that, together, they'd been formidably austere. Guests still weren't offered tea or breakfast, and for years everything had been banned, including kissing. As Mary told McGowan, 'People will think we have no morals.'

But now, it seemed, the rules no longer reached the upper floor. In the next room, I could hear a young Sinhalese couple, who spoke urgently and passionately, as if they shouldn't be there. I don't think they realised we shared a bathroom, or that, every time I passed their door, I could see them sprawled naked on the bed, utterly spent.

My own room was almost empty. It had yellowish walls, a bed and some enormous wooden pegs, for giant hats, perhaps, or horses' tack. Back in the late eighties, McGowan had lived up here, working on his memoir, *Only Man is Vile*. The war had left him edgy and fractious. He'd been around when the bombs went off, and he'd seen the bodies and the morgues. Back in Bambalapitya, he'd craved 'communication', and had sought solace in the prostitutes. His only friend was 'Mr Crab', a deformed beggar on the beach, who he'd carried up Adam's Peak and taken on holiday to Unawatuna. By the end, he'd despised everything: Buddhism, Sri Lankan society ('constant lying and subterfuge') and the Sinhalese themselves ('full of agreeability and menace'). His book would influence American thinking for the next twenty years.

Lying there, in my strange cell, it troubled me that I didn't feel any of these things. Perhaps I'd understood Sri Lanka even less than I'd imagined. That first night, I lay awake for hours, trying to make sense of the way I felt. The perplexity was easy enough, and so were the twinges of horror, but I also recognised affinity, wonder and regret. Was it odd to feel like that about this beautiful country? Maybe it was different for McGowan, seeing it all through the prism of war. Or maybe the faithful are right, and there are lots of different Sri Lankas, each to be found in its own little afterlife. Or perhaps it really is a labyrinth, and your perception of the whole entirely depends on where you are at the moment you get lost.

There were lots of goodbyes. I had coffee with Elmo, pizza with Ravi, and dinner with Mohammed out at the golf club. Professor Wijesinha took me to the Green Café, where, years ago, he'd whiled away a more innocent age. I also met up with the investigative journalist, who'd recovered from his fear of arrest and now looked resplendent again in his sporting whites.

Then there was Vasantha, who thought I should leave on a more majestic note, and drove me out to the ancient temples at Kelaniya. For this outing, he wore not one of his usual fancy T-shirts, but a plain white tunic and sandals. He knew all the statues and paintings, and I had a feeling that he came here often to recharge his spirit. Other politicians seemed to derive their power from the ancient world, but, for Vasantha, it was a source of duty. Although he never discussed the injustices of recent years, it wasn't hard to guess what he felt, and, in his measured manner, there was often a hint of his statuesque forebears, pondering solutions. I was, however, always thrilled how assured he seemed, as if somehow he'd heard that it would all be all right. 'We're a new generation,' he told me, 'and things will be different.'

I also went back to Gangarama, for one last moment with the temple's elephant. Science tells us that these magnificent beasts have no particular insight, no greater understanding of the world all around. But it never looks that way. That afternoon, the elephant was lying on its back being scrubbed by its mahout. That's a remarkable posture for a creature born wild, and as I peered into that tiny eye, I couldn't help feeling that there was something it knew.

My last morning, I wandered down to Galle Face Green, to find that it had almost vanished under a bubbling, dark-green mass of troops. Ocean spray curled over the columns like smoke, and from time to time the formations parted and great blocks of khaki and olive came marching through, all thickly hedgehogged in rifles and flags. Amongst them were tanks, rocket launchers, half a mile of field guns and a couple of acres of navy blue. It was supposed to be a rehearsal for the next magnificent parade, but no one was watching. Colombo had clearly wearied of soldiers and victories. That meant I had the whole spectacle to myself, and, naturally enough, it felt like a send-off.

No one seemed to mind me ambling in, through the ranks. Here were the Sri Lankans as I'd never seen them before: the women slung with guns; the amputees, wheeling past, row after row; cyclists in leopard-spot pyjamas, and all the top brass in their Victorian best. Then there were the special forces men, with their matching beards, and the tank commanders, in immaculate silk cravats. One of them even clambered down off his gargantuan machine and addressed me in flawless Etonian English. Meanwhile, in the middle of all this was a mini-submarine, riding along on a float, like some enormous holy fish. I have an uneasy feeling that, in my dotage, this is all I'll remember of these travels, and that the end of the war will seem like some crazy burlesque, with finishing touches by Damien Hirst.

But at least, that day, it was only me looking out of place. The soldiers had never seen anyone so white and unwarlike, and they often called out as I flip-flopped past. The questions were always the same: 'How many children you got?' 'Can I have your address?' Some infantrymen even hauled me up into their armoured car, and there we sat, swapping pictures in the hot, oily fug. They were excited and talked about Matara, Matale, Kurunegala, their villages, the fishing boats, the mountains and their farms. We never had the language to finish their stories, but I think I got the sense of what they were saying. Like my journey, an era had ended and now it was time for us all to go home.

Afterword

A few months after my return, Colombo hosted the Common-wealth Heads of Government Meeting. Schools were closed, streets were repaved and all the strays were rounded up. One local newspaper called it the 'Emperor's Picnic', but it was never the pageant the Rajapaksas had hoped for. Only twenty-three 'Heads' turned up and, during the conference, the hotels remained eerily quiet. By the end, a night in a five-star hotel was down to fifty-five dollars.

The Rajapaksas were finally ousted in January 2015. When the president saw the way the votes were going, he asked the army to stage a coup. To everyone's surprise, the generals refused.

Much to Sunethra Bandaranaike's regret, her sister has remained in politics. Former president Chandrika Kumaratunga was instrumental in the defeat of the Rajapaksas, putting together a coalition of defectors, ex-ministers, Tamils and Muslims.

The outgoing minister of defence, Gotabaya Rajapaksa, now stands publicly accused of the murder of Lasantha Wickrema-tunga, editor of the *Sunday Leader*. He and his brother, Basil, have also been remanded on allegations of corruption.

Without the Rajapaksas, Hambantota's airport finally emptied of planes. Although built at a cost of $210 million, its monthly revenue was down to $125, or slightly less than that of a corner shop.

Under the new president, my friend Vasantha Senanayake was promoted to Deputy Minister of Sport and Tourism.

My other great friend, Commander Ravi Weerapperuma, continues to demonstrate his love for his country, and now works in marine conservation.

In Jaffna, Aiyathurai Santham continues to write. His second novel in English, *Rails Run Parallel*, published in March 2015, was shortlisted for the country's Gratiaen Award.

The Tamil Tigers are said to be out there still, amongst the diaspora. A new leader, however, has yet to emerge.

For Nagendram Seevaratnam, now seventy-eight, the struggle for an independent state of Tamil Eelam continues. At his temple in Croydon, he begins every day with prayers for 'The Leader', Velupillai Prabhakaran, who, he insists, is still alive.

'Croydex' was unsuccessful in his application for political asylum, on the grounds that he'd been a combatant. He now lives – illegally – in Paris, where he faces an uncertain future.

Further Reading

The people and places of Sri Lanka have been energetically documented. As well as countless internet sources and my own materials (seven journals, four thousand five hundred photographs and twenty hours of recordings), there were hundreds of books and papers to be considered. In the selection below, I've included only those which I found particularly useful or enjoyable.

General Reading
Sri Lanka has one of the oldest written histories in the world. Compacting it into a single tome is a solemn task, but there are several great works. Currently, the most respected is that of K. M. De Silva, *A History of Sri Lanka* (OUP, 1981, Oxford). Somewhat older, but equally magisterial, is E. F. C. Ludowyk's *The Modern History of Ceylon* (Praeger, 1966, New York). The last century or so also finds itself splendidly – and sometimes horrifically – illustrated in Victor Ivan's *Paradise in Tears* (Sahajeevana Centre for Coexistence, 2008, Colombo).

As for guidebooks, I relied on three. The fullest and most useful was *The Rough Guide to Sri Lanka* (Rough Guides, 2012, London). However, for exquisite illustrations, there's nothing quite like *Sri Lanka* (Insight Guides, 2006, London). Also helpful was Royston Ellis' *Sri Lanka* (Bradt, 2011, Chalfont St Peter). However, as a resident of the island, Ellis has to tread carefully. That said, this is a charming and well researched volume.

For general reference, there was C. A. Gunawardena's indispensable *Encyclopedia of Sri Lanka* (New Dawn, 2006, Delhi). Although a little out of date now, it's still the place to look up anything Sri Lankan, from Adam's

Peak to Zahira College. Even more enjoyable – and delightfully readable – is Michael Meyler's *A Dictionary of Sri Lankan English* (Michael Meyler, 2007, Colombo). It's the only dictionary I've ever read from cover to cover.

When it comes to negotiating the complexities of Sri Lankan society, there are several helpful guides. The best is *Culture Shock! A Survival Guide to Customs and Etiquette: Sri Lanka* (Marshall Cavendish, 2009, New York) by Robert Barlas and Nanda Wanasundera. Also useful, if more superficial, is Emma Boyle's *Sri Lanka: the Essential Guide to Customs and Culture* (Kuperad, 2009, London). For those needing an introduction to caste and Sinhala, there is J. B. Disanayaka's *Understanding the Sinhalese* (Godage Poth Mendura, 1998, Colombo). This book is also full of vital information, such as how to feed a Sinhalese baby and how to bury your dead (thumbs tied together, apparently, and toes).

Travellers' Tales
There are plenty of outsiders who've tried to portray this island. My favourite modern work is that of Tim Mackintosh-Smith, who came in here in pursuit of Ibn Battutah and whose own adventures are brilliantly described in *Landfalls: On the Edge of Islam from Zanzibar to Alhambra* (John Murray, 2010, London). However, there is also Jan Morris' memorable essay, 'Ceylon', included within *A Writer's World* (Faber, 2003, London). Other visitors who've left enjoyable jottings include Paul Bowles, Hermann Hesse, D. H. Lawrence, Pablo Neruda and William Dalrymple. The latter made a flying visit during a lull in the civil war, and his impressions appear in *The Age of Kali* (Flamingo, 1999, London).

More difficult is the work of Major Roland Raven-Hart. After fifteen years spent travelling the island, he knew it as well as any other writer. Although his writing can be jumbled and chatty, there's no doubting its scholarship, and – in matters archaeological – *Ceylon History in Stone* (Lake House, 1964, Colombo) is an impressive work. More troubling was his interest in boys, who appear, largely naked, throughout the pictures. Nowadays, a book like this would land you in jail.

The Island in Fiction
Strangely, for a country where English is a minority language, there's a strong tradition of Anglophone novels. Michael Ondaatje leads the way,

with works like *Anil's Ghost* (Bloomsbury, 2000, London), an exquisite and sinister tale, set during a JVP revolt. Ondaatje, however, is no longer resident in Sri Lanka, and, amongst local authors, two books have stood out in recent years. Shehan Karunatilaka's *Chinaman* (Vintage, 2012, London) is a lugubriously witty take on Colombo life, although, in truth, you have to like cricket to really get it. More inclusive is Romesh Gunesekara's *Reef* (Granta, 1994, London), a curious tale of love and cooking. There's always something delicious on the page, and something indefinable, smoldering away in the subtext.

The blurring of cultures – Oriental and Western – is a popular theme amongst contemporary novelists. Ashok Ferrey makes light of it in his satires, *The Good Little Ceylonese Girl* (2006, Colombo) and *The Professional* (Random House India, 2013, Noida). But for Rajiva Wijesinha, it's a more serious business, and in *The Moonemalle Inheritance* (Orient, 2013, Colombo) and *Servants* (McCallum, 1995, Colombo), a society emerges that's never quite Oxbridge, but never quite Asian either. Earthier, perhaps, are the novels of Carl Muller, like *The Jam Fruit Tree* (Penguin, 1993, Delhi). This time, the focus is on the island's old Burgher families, now rough, hard drinking and working class.

Recently, the war has begun to feature in native fiction. During my travels, I met Ayathurai Santhan, and I describe his novel, *The Whirlwind* (Pathippagam, 2010, Chennai). But the biggest hit of the last few years has been Nihal De Silva's *The Road from Elephant Pass* (Vijitha Yapa, 2003, Colombo). Much of it is set in the wilds of Wilpattu, where – ironically – the author was killed by a landmine.

Colombo

I only came across one guidebook: the quirky and happily unreliable *Colombo 7° Guide* (Sri Serendipity, 2011, Galle). The more beautiful elements of the city are best left to David Robson's sumptuously illustrated biography, *Geoffrey Bawa: The Complete Works* (Thames & Hudson, 2002, London). Meanwhile, the seedy side of life is portrayed by Carl Muller in his dark novel, *Colombo* (Penguin India, 1995, Colombo).

My understanding of the Bandaranaikes, their circle and their haunts, was greatly enhanced by James Manor's biography, *The Expedient Utopian: Bandaranaike and Ceylon* (Cambridge University Press, 1989,

Cambridge). Although the political story is dense and impenetrable, an intriguing portrait emerges of the great families, their institutions and their hold on Colombo. S. W. R. D.'s own words can be found in *Speeches and Writings: S. W. R. D. Bandaranaike* (Department of Broadcasting, 1963, Colombo).

Anuradhapura and the Reservoir Kings

In addition to the general histories above, there were a number of specialist works I found particularly helpful. Professor Senake Bandaranayake has written widely on Anuradhapura and Sigiriya, but the book that stands out is his beautifully illustrated volume, *The Rock and Wall Paintings of Sri Lanka* (Lake House, 1986, Colombo). As to the reservoirs themselves, the best and most recent study is P. B. Dharmasena's 'Evolution of the Hydraulic Societies in the Ancient Anuradhapura Kingdom of Sri Lanka', published in *Landscapes and Societies: Selected Cases*, edited by Peter Martini and Ward Chesworth (Springer, 2011, New York). I am also enormously indebted to Dr Roland Silva for sharing with me his unpublished thesis on the evolution of an emporium at Mannar.

As to the island's earliest visitors, I particularly enjoyed two works. The first was H. A. J. Hulugalle's compact and accurate *Ceylon of the Early Travellers* (Wesley Press, 1969, Colombo). The second was Matthew Lyons' 'The Legate's Tale', recounting the fantastical journey of Giovanni dei Marignolli from 1338 to 1353, and included in Lyons' collection of stories, *Impossible Journeys* (Cadogan, 2009, London).

Flora and Fauna

These days, no one writes about the island's wildlife better than my friend, Gehan de Silva Wijeyeratne. His *Wild Sri Lanka* (John Beaufoy, 2013, Oxford) provides a comprehensive guide to what to see, and where. His pocket guides, too, are invaluable, including *Birds of Sri Lanka* (John Beaufoy, 2015, Oxford). For ornithologists, John Harrison's *A Field Guide to the Birds of Sri Lanka* (OUP, 1999, Oxford) is also regarded as indispensable.

The Portuguese and the Dutch

Aside from the general histories, there were several books which I either enjoyed or which filled me with horror. R. H. Bassett's oddly named

Romantic Ceylon (Palmer, 1929, London) contains some charming vignettes from early colonial life. By contrast, the atrocities of the Portuguese period and the Dutch conquest are magnificently recounted (and illustrated) in Philip Baldaeus' history, first published in 1672: *A Description of the Great and Most Famous Island of Ceylon* (reprinted by Asian Educational Services, 1998, Delhi). Also Dutch, but not quite so bloody, is Francois Valentijn's *Description of Ceylon*, published in 1726 (and reprinted by the Hakluyt Society in 1978).

As to what remains of those times, I could have done with more. Fortunately, however, I had Kees Zandvliet's *The Dutch Encounter with Asia, 1600–1950* (B. V. Waanders Uitgeverji, 2002, Zwolle), published to mark the 400th anniversary of the VOC. I was also indebted to William Nelson for his great round-up of ramparts, *The Dutch Forts of Sri Lanka* (Canongate, 1984, Edinburgh). Last but not least, there was Riccardo Orizio's delightful study of the last Dutch descendants, which appears in *Lost White Tribes* (Secker & Warburg, 2000, London).

Kandy and the Great Road

Although the road has vanished, its story survives in numerous accounts. I've mentioned Baldaeus and Valentijn, above, but there are also two great English travellers who described it in its last few years. The first is Robert Percival with *An Account of the Island of Ceylon 1803* (reprinted by Tisara Prakasakayo, 1975, Dehiwala). The other is John Davy, who describes every aspect of Sinhalese life in mind-boggling detail, in *An Account of the Interior of Ceylon and of its Inhabitants with Travels in that Island* (reprinted by Tisara Prakasakayo, 1969, Dehiwala).

Best of all, however, is Robert Knox's memoir, *An Historical Relation of Ceylon* (Royal Society, 1681, London). His description of his Kandyan captivity still informs our understanding of the kingdom. Katherine Frank does a remarkable job, setting it all in context with *Crusoe: Daniel Defoe, Robert Knox and the Creation of a Myth* (Bodley Head, 2011, London). As for the artwork of the kingdom, there is probably still no better commentary than Ananda Coomaraswamy's *Medieval Sinhalese Art*, originally published in 1908 (reprinted by Pantheon Books, 1956, New York).

The end of the kingdom is described, thrillingly and tragically, by Geoffrey Powell in *The Kandyan Wars* (Leo Cooper, 1973, London). The intrigues and the espionage that followed are then taken up by Brendon and Yasmine Gooneratne, in *This Inscrutable Englishman: Sir John D'Oyly, Baronet, 1774-1824* (Cassell, 1999, London and New York).

Tea Country and British Ceylon

Ceylon's colonists, it seems, have always enjoyed recounting their adventures, and I often found myself overwhelmed with memoirs. But there are good ones amongst them. Although Samuel Baker may be boorish and boastful, his *Eight Years in Ceylon* (Longmans, 1884, London) provides lavish proof of the perils and terrors of Victorian settlement. Rather less exuberant is the work of Leonard Woolf. His autobiography, *Growing* (Harcourt, Brace & World, 1961, New York), and his novel, *The Village in the Jungle* (Edward Arnold, 1913, London), portray colonial life as bleak and pointless. A century on, Sir Christopher Ondaatje recreated his travels with a fascinating foray of his own, described in *Woolf in Ceylon: An Imperial Journey in the Shadow of Leonard Woolf, 1904-1911* (The Long Riders Guild, 2006).

The lives of the planters, I discovered, could be full of surprises. Ondaatje's brother, Michael, describes a chaotic, hedonistic existence in the story of his father, *Running in the Family* (W. W. Norton, 1982, New York). For others, like Harry Williams, author of *Ceylon, Pearl of the East* (Hale, 1948, London), the sex was strange, infrequent and foreign. Although he wrote fondly of his time in the hills, the local people – as he frankly admits – remained a mystery. Meanwhile, great homes like Adisham seemed to exist in complete denial of the country all around. Its story is told in *The Dream House of Sir Thomas Lister Villiers* (Monte Fano, undated, Kandy).

For my research into the Boer POW camp at Diyatalawa, I turned to a series of articles under the heading 'Boere Krygsgevangenes in Ceylon' (Journal of the Dutch Burgher Union of Ceylon, Volumes XVIII, XXXVI, XXXVII and XXXVIII). I also came across a remarkable article by William Steyn, who returned home via Aden and Russia, and whose story appeared as 'How we escaped from Ceylon' (the *Wide World Magazine*, 1903).

My understanding of Ceylon in the Second World War owes everything to Michael Tomlinson's *The Most Dangerous Moment* (Granada,

1979, St Albans). For further background material, I also had the benefit of H. G. P. Jayasekara's slightly eccentric *How Japan Bombed Tiny Ceylon* (Stamford Lake, 2013, Colombo). Equally intriguing was a small pamphlet I found, published for the benefit of visiting servicemen. Beautifully written, and entitled *Ceylon and Its People* (Ceylon Daily News, 1942, Colombo), it betrays an administration now anxious and eager to please. 'The Sinhalese and the Tamils,' say the authors, 'are the heirs of civilisations far older than any that have flourished in Europe . . .'

The Wild East: Veddas, the Vanni and the LTTE

Again, I am indebted to a fellow author for sharing with me work in draft. Swedish anthropologist Wiveca Stegeborn is probably the leading authority on the Vedda people, and her latest paper is called 'Climate Change, Nature Conservation and Indigenous Peoples: A Case Study on the Wanniyala-Aetto (Veddahs) of Sri Lanka'. Stegeborn is a courageous advocate for the Veddas, inheriting the role of R. L. Spittel, who wrote *Wild Ceylon* (The Colombo Apothecaries, 1927, Colombo), and C. G. and B. Z. Seligmann, authors of *The Veddas* (Cambridge University Press, 1911, Cambridge).

Surprisingly, there has been little written about the wild region known as the Vanni. I did, however, chance upon a fascinating little volume by C. S. Navaratnam, called *Vanni & The Vanniyas* (no publisher, 1960, Jaffna).

Sadly, the Vanni will now be known, for years to come, as merely the home of the Tamil Tigers. They too have their advocates, like Adele Balasingham, who wrote *The Will to Freedom: An Inside View of Tamil Resistance* (Fairmax Publishing, 2003, London). Elsewhere, they emerge as fanatics and terrorists, and, from this perspective, the most important studies are probably those of M. R. Narayan Swamy, namely *Tigers of Lanka: from Boys to Guerrillas* (Konark, 2002, New Delhi) and *The Tiger Vanquished* (Sage, 2010, Delhi). As for encounters with the cadres, there are fascinating descriptions to be found in the works of William Dalrymple, above, and in *Tea Time with Terrorists* (Soft Skull, 2010, New York), by Mark Meadows. Equally compelling are the photographs of Stephen Champion, whose haunting portraits of the child soldiers appear in *War Stories* (Hotshoe, 2008, London) and *Lanka 1986–1992* (Garnet, 1993, Reading).

Jaffna and the Tamil World

From my earliest encounters with Tamils in London, I've come to appreciate how shy they can sometimes seem. Much of what I learnt about my neighbours would be garnered from official documents and government inquiries. Tooting's temple, for example, fell under the spotlight in a report by the Charity Commission in August 2010. Other useful reports include 'Funding the "Final War"' (Human Rights Watch, vol. 18, New York), 'The Sri Lankan Tamil Diaspora after the LTTE' (International Crisis Group, 2010) and 'Sri Lanka Bulletin: Treatment of Returns' (UK Border Agency, 2012, London). Tamil sources, however, were few and far between. I was therefore grateful to Dhananjayan Sriskandarajah for sharing with me his well-balanced paper, co-written with Camilla Orjuela, 'The Sri Lankan Tamil Diaspora: Warmongers or peace builders?' (OUP, 2008, Oxford).

As to the Tamils in Sri Lanka itself, there was a similar dearth of accessible resources. The Tamil areas are barely identified in the guidebooks, and Jaffna still gets only the briefest mention. Baldaeus, Valentijn, Williams and Woolf provide some colourful colonial insights, but the modern Tamil world can still seem eerily obscure. Discussion of the conflict entirely dominates the literature, and it's almost as if the lives of ordinary people have vanished from print. Over the last few decades, the best descriptions of the Tamil east have often been foreign, including William McGowan's *Only Man is Vile* (Farrar, Straus and Giroux, 1992, New York).

The Sri Lankan Civil War

Needless to say, the war has generated mountains of paper. Much of it is covered in opinion, and the full facts have yet to be determined. That said, there have been some admirable attempts to analyse the causes and to chart the uneven course of events. In this, the best books are K. M. de Silva's *Sri Lanka and the Defeat of the LTTE* (Vijitha Yapa, 2012, Colombo) and *Reaping the Whirlwind* (Penguin, 1998, Delhi), Robert Johnson's *A Region in Turmoil* (Reaktion, 2005, New York) and Rohan Gunaratna's *Indian intervention in Sri Lanka: The role of India's intelligence agencies* (South Asian Network on Conflict Research, 1993). Professor Paul Moorcraft has produced a fascinating military history, *Total Destruction of the Tamil Tigers; The Rare Victory of Sri Lanka's Long War* (Pen & Sword Books, 2013, Barnsley), although, by its own admission, it's 'controversial'.

The real difficulty lies in ascertaining what happened at the very end. The jury is still out as to exactly what crimes were committed, and by whom. The principal source of evidence is still the 'Report of the Secretary-General's Panel of Experts on Accountability in Sri Lanka' (UN, March 2011). Gordon Weiss does, however, bring his own memories to bear, with his gruelling masterpiece, *The Cage* (Bodley Head, 2011, London). Likewise, Frances Harrison has brought together a number of witnesses in *Still Counting the Dead* (Portobello, 2012, London), an utterly remarkable 'account of the victory from the perspective of the defeated'. But not all her witnesses are to be believed (I lost faith in the person who talked of babies born 'with bullets already lodged in their little limbs'). The Sri Lankan army, meanwhile, denies all guilt, and has produced its own bare-faced response, 'Humanitarian Operation Factual Analysis July 2006–May 2009' (Ministry of Defence, July 2011, Colombo).

A few other memoirs have emerged from amongst those who took part. Even the LTTE have their own literary hero, 'Malaravan'. Killed in action at the age of twenty, he left behind a journal that would become a best-seller: *War Journey: Diary of a Tamil Tiger* (Penguin, 2013, Delhi). But the memoir that really caught my eye was *In the Line of Duty* (Unigraphics, 2008, Colombo), written by an army doctor. It so intrigued me that I tracked down its author, Gamini Goonetilleke, and we've been friends ever since.

Acknowledgements

This book wouldn't have been possible without the generosity, wisdom and patience of a great number of people. Things being what they are, many specifically asked to remain anonymous. My thanks go to them nonetheless. At the same time, I'd like to extend my enormous gratitude to the following:

In Colombo – Vasantha Senanayake, MP; Lieutenant Commander Ravi Weerapperuma (retired); the great cricketers Aravinda de Silva and Sidath Wettimuny; Mohammed Abidally; Sunethra Bandaranaike and her sister, ex-president Madam Chandrika Kumaratunga; Hiran Cooray, who was endlessly generous with his hospitality; Dr Gamini Goonetilleke; Vinayagamoorthy Muralitharan, MP ('Colonel Karuna'); Michele Thurairaja Mirchandani; Suresh and Mandy Ferrey; Dr and Mrs Roland Silva; Chloe de Soysa ('Auntie Chloe'); Dr Pruthiviraj Fernando, who helped me to understand the world of elephants; Chandra Ediriweera of Ceylon Tours; Thilanga Sumathipala, MP; Mohammed Mahuruf of PEACE; Mary at the 'Ottery'; Kenny Speldewinde (Tintagel's manager); Angeline Ondaatjie; Anuruddha Bandara of Eco Team (www.srilankaecotourism.com); Mark Forbes; and the indefatigable Professor Rajiva Wijesinha.

In the hill country and Kandy – Christopher Worthington, MBE ('the last planter'); Ravana Wijeyeratne; Dr Amal Randhir

493

Karunaratna; Brigadier Indunil Ranasinghe RWP (Commandant of the Sri Lanka Military Academy) and Captain HMS Herath at Diyatalawa; E. L. Senanayake of Taylor's Hill (and the butler, Silvaraj); the monks at St Benedict's Monastery of Adisham (www.adisham.org); David Swannell of Ashburnham (www.ashburnhamestate.com), Helga de Silva Blow Perera; and Mrs Suketha Manojani, who gave us tea on top of Galagedara Hill.

Around the south-west and the east coast – Kushil Gunasekera of the Foundation of Goodness in Seenigama; Deputy Minister Niyomal Perera and his wife, Chrysantha; the Reverend Terrence in Batticaloa; Father Harry Miller of St Michael's College; Sam of Samantha's Tours (Hambantota); Felician Fernando, who shared with me his experience of HMS *Hermes*; Major Sunil Perera (retired); Pietro Addis, manager of Amanwella; Harin Fernando, MP; and Lieutenant Thilata and Commander S. J. Kumara (COPO-East) at the Trincomalee Naval Dockyard.

In the Vanni, Jaffna and the north – Maulie de Saram (www.galkadawala.com); Rohini Singham of Vavuniya; Father S. Ananthakumar of St Mary's church, Mulankavil; Lieutenant Thusitha Herath and Commander Pradeep Ranathunge at Mulankavil's naval base; Colonel Saman Perera; the staff of the Jaffna Heritage hotel; K. Vaseekaran of Expo Aviation (Jaffna); General Mark and Lieutenant Isuru at Headquarters Camp, Mullaitivu; Brigadier Nihal Amarasekara in Kilinocchi; Stanislav Damjanovic of HALO; and Aiyathurai Santham.

In Switzerland – Mark Dangel and Martin Keutner for their help with introductions.

In Sweden – Wiveca Stegeborn for her help and advice in relation to the Veddas.

In England – Dr Tom Widger; Sue Marsh and the Friends of

Sri Lanka; Shevanthie Goonesekera; Gehan de Silva Wijeyeratne; Professor David Robson; William Richards; David Tatham, CMG; Guy Willoughby, formerly of HALO; Professor Ravi Tennekoon; William de Segundo; Barnaby Rogerson; Mark Ellingham; Robin Hanbury-Tenison and Sophie Grig at Survival International; Sir Christopher Ondaatje, CBE; Tracey Lawson; Dr Shihan de Silva Jayasuriya; Felix Vicat; Olivia Richli; Anthony Wynn; Jayan Perera; Brian Martin, OBE; Sheila Darzi; Rob Beckett; my sister, Philippa Hayes, and my brother, Matthew Gimlette; Alistair Mortimer; Liz Jameson; Philip Hamilton-Grierson; John Rajan Yorke; Dhananjayan Sriskandarajah; Nagendram Seevaratnam; Sridevy Sriskandarajah; Dr Anton Emmanuel; Meera Selva; Henry Brownrigg; William Richards; Stephen Champion; Widget Finn; Melissa and Jonathan Taylor; Jemma Hewlett; Rogier Westerhuis; and Sam Clark.

I am also extremely grateful to Audley Travel (www.audleytravel.com) and Experience Travel (www.experiencetravelgroup.com), who both provided highly effective and generous support for parts of these travels. Some of the episodes in this book first appeared – in a rather different form – in the *Financial Times* and the *Daily Telegraph*.

As for the writing and production of this book, I am also extremely grateful to Philip Blackwell; Yvonne Bunn for logistical support; my agent, Georgina Capel; Sonny Mehta and Diana Coglianese at Knopf; and Jon Riley and Rose Tomaszewska at Quercus. I also extend my special thanks to my parents, Dr and Mrs T. M. D. Gimlette, for all their help and encouragement, and for their invaluable suggestions on the draft manuscript.

Finally, there's my wife, Jayne, and daughter, Lucy. As usual, they've borne with great patience my long periods of absence (both in Asia and the attic). I couldn't have done any of this without Jayne, who has been a tireless source of inspiration and support. Lucy, too, has shown great understanding, and – although only ten – has allowed a little of my curiosity for Sri Lanka to become her own. To both, my gratitude therefore comes, as always, with all my love.

Index

INDEX